RETHINKING LYRIC COMMUNITIES

Cultural Inquiry

EDITED BY CHRISTOPH F. E. HOLZHEY
AND MANUELE GRAGNOLATI

The series 'Cultural Inquiry' is dedicated to exploring how diverse cultures can be brought into fruitful rather than pernicious confrontation. Taking culture in a deliberately broad sense that also includes different discourses and disciplines, it aims to open up spaces of inquiry, experimentation, and intervention. Its emphasis lies in critical reflection and in identifying and highlighting contemporary issues and concerns, even in publications with a historical orientation. Following a decidedly cross-disciplinary approach, it seeks to enact and provoke transfers among the humanities, the natural and social sciences, and the arts. The series includes a plurality of methodologies and approaches, binding them through the tension of mutual confrontation and negotiation rather than through homogenization or exclusion.

Christoph F. E. Holzhey is the Founding Director of the ICI Berlin Institute for Cultural Inquiry. Manuele Gragnolati is Professor of Italian Literature at the Sorbonne Université in Paris and Associate Director of the ICI Berlin.

RETHINKING LYRIC COMMUNITIES

EDITED BY
IRENE FANTAPPIÈ
FRANCESCO GIUSTI
LAURA SCURIATTI

ISBN (Hardcover): 978-3-96558-076-3
ISBN (Paperback): 978-3-96558-077-0
ISBN (PDF): 978-3-96558-078-7
ISBN (EPUB): 978-3-96558-079-4

Cultural Inquiry, 30
ISSN (Print): 2627-728X
ISSN (Online): 2627-731X

Bibliographical Information of the German National Library
The German National Library lists this publication in the Deutsche Nationalbibliografie (German National Bibliography); detailed bibliographic information is available online at http://dnb.d-nb.de.

Cover design: Studio Bens. Based on a paper collage by Claudia Peppel, *Being Flooded by the Outside World*, 2023, 14.7 x 21.2 cm.

In Europe, volumes are printed by Lightning Source UK Ltd., Milton Keynes, UK. See the final page for further details.

Digital editions can be viewed and downloaded freely at: https://doi.org/10.37050/ci-30.

ICI Berlin Press is an imprint of
ICI gemeinnütziges Institut für Cultural Inquiry Berlin GmbH
Christinenstr. 18/19, Haus 8
D-10119 Berlin
publishing@ici-berlin.org
www.ici-berlin.org

Contents

Rethinking Lyric Communities: Introduction
IRENE FANTAPPIÈ, FRANCESCO GIUSTI, AND LAURA
SCURIATTI 1

Lyric Address and the Problem of Community
JONATHAN CULLER 15

Millay Repairs Baudelaire
SABINE I. GÖLZ 31

Gestural Communities: Lyric and the Suspension of Action
FRANCESCO GIUSTI 71

Rabindranath Tagore's সমাজ/Samaj/Communities of Song
PETER D. MCDONALD 97

The Transnational Lyric Community of Soviet Unofficial
Music under Late Socialism
PHILIP ROSS BULLOCK 113

Mina Loy's Interrupted Communities
LAURA SCURIATTI 135

Lyric Poetry and Community Good: Kaaps and the Cape Flats
DEREK ATTRIDGE 159

Casting Dispersions: Revising Lyric Privacy in Simone White's
Of Being Dispersed
WENDY LOTTERMAN 183

'So Clear That One Can See the Breaks': Colonialism,
Materiality, and the Lyric in Jen Bervin's *The Desert*
TOBY ALTMAN 209

Lyric, Detachment, and Collectivity: On Carl Phillips's 'Hymn'
HAL COASE 235

Being a Perpetual Guest: Lyric, Community, Translation
A CONVERSATION WITH VAHNI ANTHONY EZEKIEL CAPILDEO . . 259

References 277
Notes on the Contributors 299
Index 303

Rethinking Lyric Communities
Introduction
IRENE FANTAPPIÈ, FRANCESCO GIUSTI, AND LAURA SCURIATTI

> In listening as in speaking, both meaningfulness
> and meaning are at stake. To trace the lines
> of reciprocity through which they are estab-
> lished is to map a social space, a community.
>
> Lyn Hejinian, 'Who Is Speaking?'[1]

SHAREABILITY

In 1935, W. H. Auden opened his introduction to the anthology *The Poet's Tongue* with the oft-quoted words: 'of the many definitions of poetry, the simplest is still the best: "memorable speech".'[2] From Sappho onwards, a defining feature of poetry in the Western tradition appears to be the availability of its language for repetition. This availability is particularly relevant for lyric poetry, both in the long history of the genre and in the current theoretical debate. Where the former is concerned, it suffices to think of the direct exchange of poems in a call-and-response dynamic in the Middle Ages, or the writing of sonnets

---

1   Lyn Hejinian, 'Who Is Speaking?', in *The Language of Inquiry* (Berkeley: University of California Press, 2000), pp. 30–39 (p. 38).

2   W. H. Auden, 'Introduction', in *The Poet's Tongue: An Anthology*, ed. by John Garrett and W. H. Auden (London: Bell & Sons, 1935), pp. v–xxxiv (p. v).

in a poetic code shared across Europe for centuries in transnational Petrarchism. Lyric poetry, moreover, was employed in premodern times to build or strengthen several kinds of communities: ones of poetic filiation, social positioning, political grouping, religious bonding, affective engagement, and spiritual connection. According to W. R. Johnson, among others, lyric has lost its communal dimension in Western modernity, and for Virginia Jackson, the lyricization of poetry in the nineteenth century implied its reduction to 'the genre of the person' with its identification as the utterance of an individual.[3] Yet modern and contemporary lyric poetry seems to have retained certain linguistic and rhetorical features that make it particularly shareable, as well as certain premodern modes of circulation and transmission, as is apparent, for instance, from the dissemination of poetry through social media in recent years, especially in the context of episodes of collective action and political resistance.[4]

Introducing the last chapter, titled 'Lyric and Society', of his influential 2015 book *Theory of the Lyric*, Jonathan Culler challenges Theodor W. Adorno's claim that lyric poetry, in its utopian force, offers resistance to the language of commerce and alienation, as well as Jacques Rancière's declaration that 'the poet belongs to politics as one who does not belong there, who ignores its customs and scatters its words'.[5] For Culler, the very fact that a lyric poem is meant to be repeated by different readers in a variety of contexts implies that it can be put to very different uses and enlisted in conflicting ideological projects. Whether in relation to the circulation of poetic forms across different languages and traditions globally, to the envisioning of local,

---

3   W. R. Johnson, *The Idea of Lyric: Lyric Modes in Ancient and Modern Poetry* (Berkeley: University of California Press, 1982); Virginia Jackson, *Before Modernism: Inventing American Lyric* (Princeton, NJ: Princeton University Press, 2023), and see also her previous *Dickinson's Misery: A Theory of Lyric Reading* (Princeton, NJ: Princeton University Press, 2005).

4   For a comprehensive study of the circulation and use of poetry in the European tradition from ancient Greece to the Renaissance, see Derek Attridge, *The Experience of Poetry: From Homer's Listeners to Shakespeare's Readers* (Oxford: Oxford University Press, 2019). For an analysis, within a Rancièrean framework, of the use of poetry in the famous case of the Gezi Park protests, see E. Attila Aytekin, 'A "Magic and Poetic" Moment of Dissensus: Aesthetics and Politics in the June 2013 (Gezi Park) Protests in Turkey', *Space and Culture*, 20.2 (2017), pp. 191–208.

5   Jonathan Culler, *Theory of the Lyric* (Cambridge, MA: Harvard University Press, 2015), pp. 296–97.

national, and transnational discourse communities, or to the negotiation of poetic filiations and social positions, lyric poetry has in recent years offered a favourable site for enquiry into community formation and its politics. Various theoretical approaches have cast poetry in this distinctive role, from French and French-oriented political philosophy (exemplified in the famous exchange between Maurice Blanchot and Jean-Luc Nancy begun in the 1980s) to the re-evaluations of poetry's roots in orality and performance in reader-response criticism and postcolonial and decolonial studies.[6] Opening up the discussion to include non-Western traditions, this volume explores the possible relationships between lyric, community formation, and society at large, as well as asking whether lyric poetry might contribute, if not to the reformation of society, then at least to the formation of (minority, resistant) communities. Such communities may be based on the circulation and reperformance of particular poems and poetic codes, or on the representation and enactment of specific communities and collectivities within single poems or poetic corpora.

Commenting on the way of being together in the events of May 1968, Maurice Blanchot wrote in his *Unavowable Community*:

> It was not even a question of overthrowing an old world; what mattered was to let a possibility manifest itself, the possibility — beyond any utilitarian gain — of a being-together that gave back to all the right to equality in fraternity through a freedom of speech that elated everyone. Everybody had something to say, and, at times, to write (on the walls); what exactly, mattered little. Saying it was more important than what was said. Poetry was an everyday affair. 'Spontaneous' communication, in the sense that it seemed to hold back nothing, was nothing else than communication communicating with its transparent, immediate self, in spite of the fights, the debates, the controver-

---

6   Maurice Blanchot, *The Unavowable Community*, trans. by Pierre Joris (Barrytown, NY: Station Hill Press, 1988); Jean-Luc Nancy, *The Inoperative Community*, trans. by Peter Connor and others (Minneapolis: University of Minnesota Press, 1991); Jean-Luc Nancy, *The Disavowed Community*, trans. by Philip Armstrong (New York: Fordham University Press, 2016). On the antecedents to this discussion, see Nikolaj Lübecker, *Community, Myth and Recognition in Twentieth-Century French Literature and Thought* (London: Continuum, 2009). For a critique of the loss of collective frameworks in Derrida, Lyotard, and Nancy based on literature by writers of North African immigrant origin, see Jane Hiddleston, *Reinventing Community: Identity and Difference in Late Twentieth-Century Philosophy and Literature in French* (London: Legenda, 2005).

sies, where calculating intelligence expressed itself less than a nearly pure effervescence (at any rate an effervescence without contempt, neither highbrow nor lowbrow).[7]

In this passage, Blanchot links the manifestation of the possibility of being together to the possibility of saying, and this in turn to poetry as an everyday affair. Poetry, for Blanchot, has to do with spontaneous communication, with the very possibility of communicating, beyond the use of language as a means of conveying specific messages. Community formation has been described variously, in different fields, as being based on mutual identification among individuals as members of an imaginary group; on communal systems of knowledge, values, and beliefs; on shared interpretive strategies and responses to culturally selected objects; on joint goals or interests; and on collective affects and moods.[8] However, with his idea of a spontaneous coming together, Blanchot seems to be pointing to a form of community that precedes or temporarily escapes an identity to be shared by its members, such as a knowledge system, an interpretive strategy, an interest, a position, or a practice.

Blanchot's suggestion was the basis for the two workshops that led to this volume, held at the Christ Church Research Centre (Oxford) on 23 June 2022 and at the ICI Berlin Institute for Cultural Inquiry on 5 July 2022. These two workshops aimed to bring the investigation of historical poetic communities into dialogue with theories of community and recent developments in the theory of the lyric. While discussing a variety of phenomena in modern European poetry that have been at the centre of the critical debate — the poetics of the frag-

---

7   Blanchot, *Unavowable Community*, p. 30.

8   Sara Ahmed, 'Collective Feelings; or, The Impressions Left by Others', *Theory, Culture & Society*, 21.2 (2004), pp. 25–42; Sara Ahmed, 'The Skin of the Community: Affect and Boundary Formation', in *Revolt, Affect, Collectivity: The Unstable Boundaries of Kristeva's Polis*, ed. by Tina Chanter and Ewa Plonowska Ziarek (New York: SUNY Press, 2005), pp. 95–111; Benedict Anderson, *Imagined Communities: Reflections on the Origins and Spread of Nationalism*, rev. edn (London: Verso, 2006); Roberto Esposito, *Communitas: The Origin and Destiny of Community*, trans. by Timothy Campbell (Stanford, CA: Stanford University Press, 2010). For historical overviews of feminist debates on community, see e.g. Kathryn Gleadle, 'The Imagined Communities of Women's History: Current Debates and Emerging Themes; A Rhizomatic Approach', *Women's History Review*, 22.4 (2013), pp. 524–40; *Feminism and Community*, ed. by Penny A. Weiss and Marilyn Friedman (Philadelphia, PA: Temple University Press, 1995).

ment, the obscurity or polysemy of language, Blanchot's and Nancy's unworking (*désœuvrement*) of the work, Jacques Rancière's change of aesthetic regime[9] — the workshops also explored the lyric, in its longer history and transnational features, as a particular mode of discourse that may offer alternative models of community formation. The Oxford workshop also included a conversation with the poet Vahni Anthony Capildeo; the Berlin workshop concluded with an evening event with Christian Hawkey, Daniel Tiffany, and Capildeo, who read a selection of their poems and offered their reflections on poetry, community, and translation.[10]

The volume includes six chapters by participants in the workshops (Derek Attridge, Philip Ross Bullock, Jonathan Culler, Francesco Giusti, Peter D. McDonald, and Laura Scuriatti), with the addition of four chapters by scholars who became involved in the research project at a later stage (Toby Altman, Hal Coase, Sabine I. Gölz, and Wendy Lotterman). The volume closes with a conversation between the editors and Vahni Anthony Capildeo about community formation and a communal dimension in general in their poetic practice and theoretical reflection. Bringing the investigation of historical poetics into dialogue with lyric theory and debates on community formation, this volume explores a set of fundamental questions. What is it that makes the lyric particularly shareable? How was (or is) it actually shared in its social and cultural contexts? What kind of community formation did (or does) it enable, facilitate, or envision? How are communities formed by the ways in which the texts are shared? How are these communities shaped and imagined through dialogues between poets, sometimes centuries apart from one another? And finally, can similarities in these phenomena be traced across languages, epochs, and traditions?

---

9   Jacques Rancière, *The Politics of Aesthetics: The Distribution of the Sensible*, trans. by Gabriel Rockhill (London: Continuum, 2004); Jacques Rancière, *Dissensus: On Politics and Aesthetics*, trans. by Steven Corcoran (London: Continuum, 2010); Jacques Rancière, *The Flesh of Words: The Politics of Writing*, trans. by Charlotte Mandell (Stanford, CA: Stanford University Press, 2004); Jacques Rancière, *Politics of Literature*, trans. by Julie Rose (Cambridge: Polity, 2011).

10 *Poetry, Community, Translation*, staged reading and discussion with Vahni Anthony Capildeo, Christian Hawkey, and Daniel Tiffany, moderated by Irene Fantappiè, organized by Irene Fantappiè, Francesco Giusti, and Laura Scuriatti, 5 July 2022, ICI Berlin Repository <https://doi.org/10.25620/e220705-1>.

INDEXICALITY

One of the main ways in which lyric poems make themselves repeat-able, and thus shareable in each 'now' of reading, is through their use of indexicals: from pronouns such as *I, you, this,* and *that,* to spatial and temporal adverbs such as *now* and *then, here* and *there.*[11] Through the open referentiality of indexicals, lyric poems allow for their reper-formance by different individuals in a variety of contexts. As Bonnie Costello writes in her book on the poet's use of the first-person plural *we,* 'poetic address can be considered as practice or paradigm, then, for social and ethical engagement'.[12] Looking at the ambiguous use of *you* in a range of texts from songs sung at sporting events to lyric poems from Petrarch to John Ashbery, Jonathan Culler's opening chap-ter discusses how the *you* 'can implicate the reader, as addressee of the poem, but when the reader voices the poem, can also evoke others, singular or many, as well as serving as a general pronoun',[13] and warns us against taking it as a given that the formation of lyric communities is inherently good. Indeed, through circulation in their historical context and transhistorical transmission, poems can also iterate and crystallize perspectives and values around which readers can coalesce to the ex-clusion of others.

Towards the end of his chapter, Culler introduces Sabine I. Gölz's investigation, also included in this volume, of the ways in which Baude-laire's 'L'Invitation au voyage' invites its readers to iterate and thus ratify a masculinist perspective on a feminized *you,* and how this 'mis-ogynist poetics of control' is repaired in Edna St Vincent Millay's 1936 retranslation, 'Invitation to the Voyage'. For Gölz, the two poems present not only two different poetics but also two radically divergent subject positions and ways of reading. If the textual strategies of a poem tend to close the referentiality of its indexicals by defining the

---

11   Indexicality in lyric poetry has been studied extensively, focusing on different periods, traditions, and phenomena; it also plays an important role in Culler, *Theory of the Lyric.* On its relation to diction, see Daniel Tiffany, 'Lyric Poetry and Poetics', in *Oxford Research Encyclopedia of Literature* (Oxford: Oxford University Press, 2020) <https://doi.org/10.1093/acrefore/9780190201098.013.1111>.

12   Bonnie Costello, *The Plural of Us: Poetry and Community in Auden and Others* (Prince-ton, NJ: Princeton University Press, 2017), p. 66.

13   Jonathan Culler, 'Lyric Address and the Problem of Community', in this volume, p. 28.

characteristics of its *I* and *you*, a subsequent translation or rewriting can reopen them and redefine its boundaries of inclusion and exclusion. The poetry of Mina Loy, as Laura Scuriatti's chapter illustrates, also makes use of various forms of textual instabilities — from multilingualism to shifting pronouns — to propose 'a feminist stance that refuses participation in patriarchal or oppressive forms of togetherness, aiming instead to imagine possible alternatives'.[14] Engaging with the question of shareability, Francesco Giusti proposes a notion of gesture, developed from Bertolt Brecht, Walter Benjamin, and Giorgio Agamben, that links the deictic power of language deployed by the lyric to the reperformance of cultural gestures. Poems preserve gestures as 'suspended' actions, and readers can turn those gestures into actions by performing them in their own context — or refuse to do so. These gestures available for repetition open up the potential for the formation of what Giusti dubs 'gestural communities' — a form of community that is not based on pre-established identities.

IDENTIFICATION

The association of the lyric *I* with a specific identity has been strongly contested, not only in the various forms of experimental poetry of the twentieth century but more recently in poetic practices that, while not fully rejecting the lyric as such, question the very premise of a presupposed individuation. If the seeming openness of the first person singular that appears to be a dominant characteristic of the lyric can invite readers to occupy that position, it is also true that it tends to be associated with a relatively defined identity in the tradition; this has prompted poets and critics to question both the processes of community formation associated with the form and the types of community thus produced or invoked. Virginia Jackson, for example, has recently argued that 'lyricization', as a way of reading developed in the nineteenth century, relied upon the merging of different forms of address 'into one big genre of address associated with the genre of the person rather than with the genre of the poem', and that the type of

---

14   Laura Scuriatti, 'Mina Loy's Interrupted Communities', in this volume, p. 136.

subjective expression made possible or denied by this process involved the erasure of racialized subject positions and voices.[15]

On the other hand, (Anglo-American) modernist poetics tended to reject the kinds of individuation and subjectivities associated with earlier and traditional lyric forms, and also to rethink modes of reception. This involved debates about the role of poetry and its dialogue with selected groups or a broader public — a choice which was also connected to concerns about the waning of the 'legitimacy of poetry' in post-World War I society.[16] Questions of reception also involve the kinds of institutions in the public sphere that make circulation and reception possible: particularly in the early twentieth century, little magazines, informal publications, and salons became fundamental vehicles for the circulation of poetry and for the creation of receptive audiences and communities of readers, generating widespread debates about the desired and suitable audiences for experimental modernist poetry.[17] Sociability, conviviality, and the type of conversations cultivated in salons have not only been practised by poets but also evoked in poetic texts as spaces where (utopian) literary or lyric communities were possible. In their chapters, Philip Bullock and Laura Scuriatti explore the significance of the practices of conviviality, illegal gatherings, and salons in the Soviet Union of the Khrushchev Thaw and in Anglo-American modernism respectively, pointing to the potential political impact of poetry (and music) in the public sphere.

Modernist authors who were interested in poetry's interventions in the public sphere initiated debates about the relationship between genres of modernist poetry and the different types of voices and situ-

---

15 Jackson, *Before Modernism*, pp. 3, 9–10.

16 David Ayers, 'Modernist Poetry in History', in *The Cambridge Companion to Modernist Poetry*, ed. by Alex Davis and Lee M. Jenkins (Cambridge: Cambridge University Press, 2007), pp. 11–27 (pp. 12, 23).

17 For accounts of some of the debates concerning the types of audiences envisaged for modernist poetry in the American and transatlantic context in the 1910s, see Ezra Pound and Harriet Monroe, 'The Audience', *Poetry*, 5.1 (October 1914), pp. 29–32; David Ben-Merre, '"There Must Be Great Audiences Too" — *Poetry: A Magazine of Verse*', *Modernist Journal Project*, esp. section 3 (n.d.) <https://modjourn. org/there-must-be-great-audiences-too-poetry-a-magazine-of-verse/> [accessed 9 March 2024]. Whenever they address community, these debates do so mostly indirectly, as they are centred on the role of poetry and poets in societies marked by crises, rather than on technical questions such as those concerning lyric subjects, address, or iteration.

ations of address,[18] as well as on the status of poetry with respect to history and science. According to Peter Nicholls, this led to a shift to types of poetics based on a 'partial and strategic dissociation of the poet from the poem' and a rejection of expressivism (as exemplified by T. S. Eliot's 1919 essay 'Tradition and the Individual Talent'), inaugurating a tradition in which 'partial self-effacement' and the presence of 'personae' coexist with models based on the poet's subjectivity.[19] Mina Loy's poems and her essays on poetry complicate the possibilities of these choices by playfully deploying modernist fragmentation, polyglossia, and poetic personae in order to create spaces for a non-normative feminist voice in relation to the types of communities that would make such a voice possible. As Scuriatti shows, Loy's celebration of polyglossia, her multilingual poetics, and her affirmation of a gendered perspective may partially adhere to modernist cosmopolitan aesthetics or specific early twentieth-century feminist projects, but her poems produce mobile forms of identification and affiliations to ephemeral, interrupted communities.

INDIVIDUATION

A scepticism or even radical suspicion of community, which exposes the ways in which the concept has also been made to stand for rigid, crystallized, and sometimes conservative or exclusionary approaches to commonality and shared identification, is at the heart of the poetic practices of the poets Simone White and Carl Phillips, discussed here by Wendy Lotterman and Hal Coase. Comparing White's 2016 collection *Of Being Dispersed* with George Oppen's 1968 poem 'Of Being Numerous', Lotterman's contribution investigates the rejection of a process of individuation that excludes the social life of racialized individuals and subjects, and proposes a crucial distinction between Oppen's 'numerousness' and White's 'dispersion' as two incommensurable conditions. Coase's chapter turns its attention to queer critiques of community and analyses Carl Phillips's poem 'Hymn', mobilizing the

---

18   See e.g. T. S. Eliot, 'The Three Voices of Poetry', in *The Lyric Theory Reader: A Critical Anthology*, ed. by Virginia Jackson and Yopie Prins (Baltimore, MD: Johns Hopkins University Press, 2014), pp. 192–200.

19   Peter Nicholls, 'The Poetics of Modernism', in *Modernist Poetry*, ed. by Davis and Jenkins, pp. 51–67 (p. 51).

idea of 'counterintimacies' proposed by Lauren Berlant and Michael Warner, whose 1998 essay 'Sex in Public' programmatically attempts to rethink the notion of community to account for the practices and shared experiences of gay people in the public space.[20] Berlant and Warner's substitution of 'community' and 'group' with 'world' and 'public', as Coates shows, makes it possible to avoid the 'identitarian alignment of a community',[21] and to conceive of a more mobile, open, and 'messier' coming or being together. If the notion of community seems to presuppose pre-existing identities that can come together or an identity that subsumes individual practices, the queer poetics of Phillips's lyric explores instead 'the erotics of waiting for a future collectivity'.[22]

Another form of criticism of the nineteenth-century understand-ing of the lyric and its association with a specific form of subjectivity is discussed by Toby Altman, addressing the problematic origins of the (lyric) subject as theorized by John Stuart Mill in relation to capitalism and colonial imperialism, and thus participating in critical discourses which aim at rethinking the status and social role of the lyric in history. Altman shows that Jen Bervin's 2008 artist book *The Desert* reflects on the modern subject's roots in the appropriation and exploitation of land — and therefore ultimately in property. Bervin sewed over parts of the reprinted text of John C. Van Dyke's *The Desert: Further Studies in Natural Appearances*, an account of his travels through the desert in the American West between 1898 and 1901, creating a poetic work made of certain words in Van Dyke's text that have been left unsewn. According to Altman, this process and the ensuing work disrupt the lyric by restoring the social world of its material production and com-munal labour, as well as contesting its imbrication in colonial practices of land use.

The forms and reception of lyric poetry produce communities that are textual, as well as being determined by and anchored in reading practices and marked by identification, iteration, and public perform-

---

20   Lauren Berlant and Michael Warner, 'Sex in Public', *Critical Inquiry*, 24.2 (1998), pp. 547–66.

21   Hal Coase, 'Lyric, Detachment, and Collectivity: On Carl Phillips's "Hymn"', in this volume, p. 237.

22   Ibid., pp. 256–57.

ance. The unquestioned operations behind the canonization of specific works, as well as the habits associated with specific practices of reading and reception, can produce communities that are potentially exclusionary. While, in Altman's analysis, Bervin's *The Desert* exposes the exploitative implications of the lyric subject in nineteenth-century American poetry, Gölz approaches this question from the perspective of reparative translation with a focus on the situation of address and the figure of apostrophe in love poetry. Baudelaire's poem 'L'Invitation au voyage' ('Invitation to the Voyage'), according to Gölz, creates not just an object marked as a 'feminized other' but also a pattern of iteration which implies a default alignment between the iterator and the opposite of that 'other' — a practice that, once again, would point to a kind of community that is both marked by an exclusionary notion of identity and imbricated in power and subjection. It is a pattern which erases the feminine perspective and subjectivity — a pattern which Edna St Vincent Millay's retranslation of the poem, Gölz argues, repairs through a reconfiguration of indexicals in the translated text.

TRANSLATION

If iterability is a core feature of the lyric, lyric is intrinsically intertwined with translation: the very fact that a poem is meant to be repeated by different readers in a variety of contexts triggers processes of transformation, retransformation, and 'manipulation' of the text in other languages.[23] The idea of translation itself presupposes an understanding of the text as transferable and thus sharable between different social and cultural environments. When texts are particularly sharable, as in the case of lyric poems, translation significantly contributes to the formation of communities across time and space.

How does translation shape a community? In recent decades, translation studies has strongly questioned the notion of equivalence.[24] Translation, one might therefore argue, generates communities which cannot, and do not intend to, be equivalent to the 'original' one. The circulation, transmission, and reuse of lyric

---

23   *The Manipulation of Literature: Studies in Literary Translation*, ed. by Theo Hermans (London: Routledge, 1985).

24   See e.g. Theo Hermans, *The Conference of the Tongues* (London: Routledge, 2007).

poems is unpredictable. Even if produced in particular contexts, they can be reperformed across generations, put to other uses, and bent to very different purposes, as exemplified here by Peter D. McDonald's exploration of the case of the songs composed by Rabindranath Tagore, which became the celebrated national anthems of India and Bangladesh despite his radically anti-statist vision of community. On the other hand, in their transnational circulation, verses written in Spanish by Federico García Lorca were translated into Russian and reused as lyrics for music produced in the underground or unofficial culture of the Soviet Union in the Khrushchev Thaw. Bullock explores how composers, including Sofia Gubaidulina and Alfred Schnittke, established transnational lyric communities through their engagement with avant-garde circles in Western Europe, and examines their experimentation with a cosmopolitan range of literary texts and a radical musical language.

The impossibility for a translation to be equivalent to its 'original' does not necessarily imply a loss. As David Damrosch has argued, a text can 'gain' in translation, and this 'gain' can be intended in a variety of ways.[25] For instance, translation can be reparative, as Gölz shows in her analysis of Millay's retranslation of Baudelaire. Repairing a poem also means creating the possibility of sharing it with another community — a community that has a different, and more inclusive, understanding of textual gender mechanisms.[26] A text can also gain in translation in terms of recognition (in general or within a specific community, as Bullock shows).

More generally, lyric comes to readers and poets with a significant degree of prestige that is linked to its language(s), and can be used to generate forms of exclusion and control as well as to engender cultural and social respect. The lyric — as much as it can induce readers to reproduce entrenched perspectives without questioning them — can also become a space in which minority languages and ways of speaking usually associated with lack of education can find a status more usu-

---

25   David Damrosch, *What Is World Literature?* (Princeton, NJ: Princeton University Press, 2003).

26   See Emily Apter, 'Afterword: Towards a Theory of Reparative Translation', in *The Work of World Literature*, ed. by Francesco Giusti and Benjamin Lewis Robinson (Berlin: ICI Berlin Press, 2021), pp. 209–28 <https://doi.org/10.37050/ci-19_09>.

ally associated with the great poets of a particular tradition. As Derek Attridge shows, the publication of lyric poetry in Kaaps, the language spoken by the coloured community of the Cape Flats, can be instrumental in advancing the status of the language, not only when it is read by members of the community in which it is produced, who can identify with it as a form of protest but also as a source of pride, but even more so when it is read by middle-class white Afrikaners, who may be invited 'to see themselves as part of a much larger Afrikaans-speaking population and to value the cultural productions of places such as the Cape Flats'.[27] Language issues are also crucial when it comes to the lyric expression of multiple personal and social identifications, as shown by Scuriatti's investigation of how Mina Loy's multilingual coinages, together with her use of pronouns, produce extremely complex and mobile clusters of communities.

ACKNOWLEDGEMENTS

We would like to thank the Oxford–Berlin Research Partnership and the ICI Berlin Institute for Cultural Inquiry for making the two workshops and this publication possible. Collaboration with Bard College Berlin and EXC 2020 Temporal Communities at the Freie Universität Berlin was also crucial to making the workshops so successful. Christoph F. E. Holzhey and Manuele Gragnolati showed enthusiasm for the project from the start, and we are particularly pleased that this volume is part of ICI Berlin Press's Cultural Inquiry series. Claudia Peppel was a source of tireless support and inspiration, and we have her to thank for the cover image. Louisa Elderton's support was most helpful throughout the publication process. We are extremely grateful to Alastair Matthews for his impeccable work on the manuscript. We would like to extend our thanks to all of this volume's contributors, as well as to the other speakers and participants who joined us for the workshops and the poetry event in the summer of 2022: Adele Bardazzi, Roberto Binetti, Manuele Gragnolati, Christian Hawkey, Karen Leeder, Emily McLaughlin, Jahan Ramazani, Daniel Tiffany, and Anita Traninger.

---

27 Derek Attridge, 'Lyric Poetry and Community Good: Kaaps and the Cape Flats', in this volume, p. 169.

Lyric Address and the Problem of Community

JONATHAN CULLER

The idea that lyric poems may create community is an enticing one, especially for those eager to show that poetry has social and political effects; and certainly, there are numerous cases, ancient and modern, where it is claimed that poetry has had such a function. In archaic Greece, melic or lyric verse functioned as epideictic rhetoric — a discourse of praise and blame and a source of wisdom — which, performed on various public occasions, shaped communal judgments and worked to create a Panhellenic community. Gregory Nagy writes that Pindar's victory odes, which celebrate a particular event, articulate general values and are made to be reperformed elsewhere: each 'aimed at translating its occasion into a Panhellenic event, a thing of beauty that could be replayed by and for all Hellenes for all time to come'.[1]

A rather different case is the international community generated around the Petrarchan sonnet, which, building on the new structures of feeling introduced by troubadour love poetry (love as a spiritualized devotion to an inaccessible mistress, etc.), provided a set of scenarios, tropes, and oppositions, to be played out in different languages, as

---

1   Gregory Nagy, *Pindar's Homer: The Lyric Possession of an Ancient Poet* (Baltimore, MD: Johns Hopkins University Press, 1990), p. 114.

a form of refinement and self-distinction. It succeeded in creating a broad European community of readers who worked within the distinctive oppositions and figures of this *discours amoureux* and produced their own sonnets. Petrarchism became a courtly mode adopted by a politically influential class across Europe, and its conventions offered opportunities for exercising and refining national vernaculars: a language proved itself by developing its own Petrarchan poetry.[2] The cultural influence of this imagined community was considerable, and the traces of its conception of the suffering lover and of life structured by impossible love have persisted, well beyond the vogue for displaying one's culture by writing love sonnets.[3]

When we consider these instances and others described by those contributing to this volume — for example, the communities coalescing around a localized minority practice such as Soviet underground music, or, at one extreme, the dispersed community of readers of elegies who vicariously accept the implicit invitation of these poems to participate, albeit momentarily, in the mourning they stage — what seems evident is that the notion of lyric community is scarcely simple and can cover a wide variety of situations in which poems or songs create a recognition of some sort of sharing among people who may be gathered together on a particular occasion or widely dispersed spatially and temporally. What is shared might be a particular experience or a general set of values, momentary or enduring; but how much members of these imagined communities actually know about the community

---

2   See Leonard Forster, *The Icy Fire: Five Studies in European Petrarchism* (Cambridge: Cambridge University Press, 1969); William Kennedy, *The Site of Petrarchism: Early Modern National Sentiment in Italy, France, and England* (Baltimore, MD: Johns Hopkins University Press, 2003); Daniel Javitch, *Poetry and Courtliness in Renaissance England* (Princeton, NJ: Princeton University Press, 1978). C. S. Lewis, *English Literature in the Sixteenth Century* (Oxford: Oxford University Press, 1954), writes of the Elizabethan love sonnet that a good sonnet 'was like a good public prayer: the test was whether the congregation can "join" and make it their own', binding them into a community. He calls the body of sonnet sequences 'more like an erotic liturgy than a series of erotic confidences' (p. 491).

3   The notion of imagined communities derives from Benedict Anderson's *Imagined Communities: Reflections on the Origin and Spread of Nationalism*, rev. edn (London: Verso, 1991). Although his focus is on the growth of the idea of the nation, the concept has broad application. For some discussion, see *Grounds of Comparison: Around the Work of Benedict Anderson*, ed. by Pheng Cheah and Jonathan Culler (New York: Routledge, 2003).

also varies. The readers of elegies may not think of themselves as participating in anything communal, even as they do so.

The examples I propose to consider will also be varied, as I explore the question of what role, if any, lyric address plays in the creation of communities. Previously, I've been especially interested in address to people or things that are not a plausible audience, as in apostrophic address to the wind, to birds, or to death, but here I want to think about the *you*, often unspecified, that may seem to designate the reader. If a poem addresses an indeterminate *you*, as so many do, does that help to create a community? How does that work?

The example of the creation of lyric community through the Petrarchan sonnet suggests that community-building depends upon repetition, on taking up, making your own, and repeating, either the poems themselves or variations on them. In our day, the most obvious cases of communities fostered by poetic language may be communities brought together by poems become songs. A famous case is 'You'll Never Walk Alone', from the musical *Carousel* (Richard Rogers and Oscar Hammerstein, 1945), which has become the bonding ritual of Liverpool football supporters and others, sung by thousands before every match:[4]

> When you walk through a storm
> Hold your head up high
> And don't be afraid of the dark.
>
> At the end of a storm
> There's a golden sky
> And the sweet silver song of a lark.
>
> Walk on through the wind
> Walk on through the rain
> For your dreams be tossed and blown.
>
> Walk on, walk on
> With hope in your heart
> And you'll never walk alone.

There seems to have been little research on the functioning of the second-person pronoun in songs. In singing along with 'I want to hold

---

4   E.g. sn0wfall, 'Awesome You'll Never Walk Alone Liverpool vs Chelsea 27.04.2014', YouTube, 27 April 2014 <https://www.youtube.com/watch?v=N51jWNsW3F8> [accessed 24 August 2023].

your hand', is the listener positioned as 'I', wanting to hold the hand of some *you*, or as the *you* whose hand someone wants to hold, or simply as an observer of the lyric *I*'s desire for another? (Presumably, it very much depends on the song and the disposition of the listener: probably few take 'You ain't nothing but a hound dog' as addressed to them.) An elaborate statistical study of second-person pronouns in popular songs concludes that songs with second-person pronouns are more popular (in terms of purchases) than those with third-person pronouns or no pronouns, and it links this success to a fostering of social connection — not, however, by fostering lyric communities, but by leading listeners to think about some *you* in their own lives. These researchers not only conclude that songs with second-person pronouns are more popular but also identify

> a novel psychological mechanism by which second-person pronouns engage listeners. Songs with more second-person pronouns were liked more not because 'you' words directly addressed the audience as a protagonist or conveyed normative imperatives (possibilities considered in prior research) but because 'you' invoked another person in the listener's mind. This supports suggestions that one of music's fundamental functions is to foster social connection.[5]

But in this study the choice offered to test subjects seems to have been whether listeners imagine the *you* to be someone whose hand the *singer* wants to hold, or whether listeners think of holding the hand of someone in their own lives.

'You'll Never Walk Alone' addresses a generalized *you* and urges all to 'hold your head up high', promoting what Grant Packard and Jonah Berger call 'a normative imperative'. It seems likely that listeners and singers take it not as evoking someone else in their lives but as addressed to themselves and others. And the communal singing of the final lines, 'Walk on, walk on | With hope in your heart, | And you'll never walk alone', would seem to induce the bonding experience of singing this to each other (to supporters who have suffered the adverse

---

5   Grant Packard and Jonah Berger, 'Thinking of You: How Second-Person Pronouns Shape Cultural Success', *Psychological Science*, 31.4 (2020), pp. 397–407 <https://doi.org/10.1177/0956797620902380>.

fortunes of their team), assuring one another that as fans 'you'll never walk alone'.

For me this is a strange case, because it is not a particular catchy tune, unlike, say, Neil Diamond's 'Sweet Caroline', the song of the Boston Red Sox baseball fans but also sung at many other sporting events in the United States and elsewhere. There are many examples available on YouTube.[6] Copyright considerations discourage extensive quotation (the complete text is easily found online), but shortly after the opening, the *you* (initially presumed to be Caroline) is introduced:

> Was in the spring
> And spring became the summer
> Who'd have believed *you'd* come along.

But then the song rises to a musical climax with

> Hands, touching hands
> Reaching out, touching me, touching *you,*

as singers reach out, touching, pointing, binding *me* and *you* together, involving all those singing in this community. The *New York Times* reports:

> 'Sweet Caroline' may seem like an odd anthem for sports fans. It's a love song, and the lyrics ('Good times never seemed so good!') are sentimental. But there's something about the way the bridge builds to a soaring chorus that always seems to lift spectators out of their seats.[7]

Then the chorus itself encourages a ritualistic chanting:

> Sweet Caroline — OH! OH! OH!
> Good times never seemed so good — SO GOOD! SO GOOD! SO GOOD!

After 'Sweet Caroline', everyone, even those not actually singing, gets to shout 'oh, oh, oh', in what seems an extra degree of involvement (not

---

6   E.g. freddiejg, 'Oz and Pitt Crew Singing Sweet Caroline', YouTube, 30 September 2012 <https://www.youtube.com/watch?v=bdPb8rUZYiI> [accessed 24 August 2023].

7   Jacey Fortin, 'Why Do English Soccer Fans Sing "Sweet Caroline"?', *New York Times*, 11 July 2001 <https://www.nytimes.com/2021/07/11/sports/soccer/why-england-sweet-caroline-euro-2020.html> [accessed 24 August 2023].

just singing the words of the song itself but embellishing); and then after 'Good times never seemed so good', the crowd can echo 'so good, so good, so good', which cannot but engender good fellow-feeling.

Like 'You'll Never Walk Alone', which lacks these rousing moments of chanting that promote community, 'Sweet Caroline' evokes the possibility of solitude and trouble, albeit as something surpassed:

> I've been inclined
> To believe they never would [be so good].
> But now I
> Look at the night and it don't seem so lonely
> We filled it up with only two
> And when I hurt
> Hurting runs off my shoulders
> How can I hurt when holding you?

But the reference to a singular *you* gets eclipsed in the repetition later in this second and final stanza by 'Hands, touching hands | Reaching out, touching me, touching you', both projecting and reflecting community. 'Sweet Caroline' starts with references to the past, but in performance, with the participial phrases ('touching hands | Reaching out, touching me, touching you'), the act of performing makes this a present event of bonding among *us*, despite the original reference of *you* to Caroline. In collective performance *you* may effectively come to mean *us*.

But the examples of crowds in stadiums singing or chanting seem rather a special case, with limited relevance to the solitary reading of a lyric poem. What happens there? When poems address *you*, does this work to foster lyric communities?

The simplest case might be prefatory uses, with their appeal to a community of readers who are supposed to share or might be persuaded to share not only the experience of the poem but certain attitudes. For instance, the opening poem of Baudelaire's *Les Fleurs du mal* starts with a first-person plural:

> La sottise, l'erreur, le péché, la lésine,
> Occupent nos esprits et travaillent nos corps,
> Et nous alimentons nos aimables remords,
> Comme les mendiants nourrissent leur vermine.
>
> (Folly and error, avarice and vice,
> Employ our souls and waste our bodies' force.

As mangey beggars incubate their lice,
We nourish our innocuous remorse.)[8]

Readers are invited to consider whether they are part of this universal-
izing *we*, whose forms (*we, us, our*) appear in the explicit declarations
of the first eight stanzas, such as 'C'est le Diable qui tient les fils qui
nous remuent!' (The Devil holds the strings that move us!); for if a
reader should resist inclusion in this hapless, sinful community, the
final stanza, identifying the worst of our vices, throws down a chal-
lenge, claiming that the reader does belong after all. 'In the infamous
menagerie of our vices, | There is one more ugly, more wicked, more
filthy!':

> C'est l'Ennui! L'oeil chargé d'un pleur involontaire,
> Il rêve d'échafauds en fumant son houka.
> Tu le connais, lecteur, ce monstre délicat,
> — Hypocrite lecteur, — mon semblable, — mon frère!
>
> (Boredom! He smokes his hookah, while he dreams
> Of gibbets, weeping tears he cannot smother.
> You know this dainty monster, too, it seems —
> Hypocrite reader! — You! — My twin! — My brother!)

Even a virtuous reader may not be well placed, having read the poem, to
deny the knowledge the poem offers, without at least a bit of hypocrisy.
Baudelaire's strategy is unusual in the complex structure of its claim to
induct readers into a community of addressees.

A different case is the opening sonnet of Petrarch's *Canzoniere*,
which sets the speaker apart from the audience addressed, while none-
theless seeking common ground:

> Voi ch'ascoltate in rime sparse il suono
> di quei sospiri ond'io nudriva il core
> in sul mio primo giovenil errore,
> quand'era in parte altr'uom da quel ch'i' sono,
> del vario stile in ch'io piango e ragiono
> fra le vane speranze e'l van dolore,
> ove sia chi per prova intenda amore
> spero trovar pietà, non che perdono.

---

8   Charles Baudelaire, 'Au lecteur' ('To the Reader', trans. by Roy Campbell; originally
     published in *Poems of Baudelaire* (New York: Pantheon Books, 1952)) <https://
     fleursdumal.org/poem/099> [accessed 24 August 2023].

Ma ben veggio or sì come al popol tutto
favola fui gran tempo, onde sovente
di me mesdesmo meco mi vergogno;
e del mio vannegiar vergogna è il frutto,
e 'l pentersi, e 'l conoscer chiaramente
che quanto piace al mondo è breve sogno.

(You who hear within these scattered verses
the sound of sighs on which I fed my heart,
in my first errant youthful days, when I
in part was not the man I am today;
for all the ways in which I weep and speak
between vain hopes and my vain suffering,
I hope I may find pity, not just pardon,
from those who know love through experience.
    Yet I see clearly now I have become
for a long time the talk of people all around, so that
it often makes me ashamed of myself;
and the fruit of all my vanities is shame,
and remorse, and the clear knowledge
that worldly joy is but a fleeting dream.)[9]

Indicating that he knows he has been the subject of much gossip, he
hints at the existence of two communities: one of readers who find his
complaining aberrant and another of those who, knowing the trials of
love, can pity and forgive.

But prefatory poems tend to address the reader explicitly and have
a special liminal role, both part of the collection and outside it, as pro-
logue.[10] Within poetic collections there may still be explicit attempts
to create community by addressing readers, as in Walt Whitman's
'Song of Myself':

I celebrate myself, and sing myself,
And what I shall assume you shall assume,
For every atom belonging to me as good as belongs to you.[11]

---

9   Petrarch, *The Canzoniere; or, Rerum vulgarium fragmenta*, trans. by Mark Musa (Bloom-
     ington: Indiana University Press, 1999), pp. 2–3 (poem 1; translation modified).
10   Often such work is done in a prologue in prose: Victor Hugo introduces *Les Contem-*
     plations with 'Helas! Quand je vous parle de moi, je vous parle de vous. Comment ne
     le sentez vous pas? Ah! insensé, qui crois que je ne suis pas toi!' (Alas, when I speak to
     you of myself, I speak to you of you. How can you not see this? Ah, fool, who believe
     that I am not you!; *Poésie*, 3 vols (Paris: Seuil, 1972), I, p. 634; my translation).
11   Walt Whitman, 'Song of Myself', in *Leaves of Grass: The Complete 1855 and 1891-92*
     Editions (New York: Library of America, 1992), pp. 188–247 (p. 188).

'To You' addresses readers necessarily unknown, boldly claiming intimacy:

> Whoever you are, now I place my hand upon you, that you be my poem,
> I whisper with my lips close to your ear,
> I have loved many women and men, but I love none better than you.[12]

A democratic American community of readers seems clearly the aim, but the more the poems claim to single out *you* alone, as below, the less well they seem to me to work.

> My songs cease, I abandon them,
> From behind the screen where I hid I advance personally solely to you.[13]

The more they single *you* out, the more questions they raise (what about other readers?), even if one ignores the over-the-top moments, as in:

> It is I you hold, and who holds you,
> I spring from the pages into your arms — decease calls me forth.[14]

I'm tempted to conclude that the explicit effort to create community with the reader through address is counterproductive when it involves claims that so invite scepticism.

John Ashbery echoes something like Whitman's gesture in the final poem of his collection *Your Name Here*:

> But I was totally taken with you, always have been.
> Light a candle in my wreath, I'll be yours forever and will kiss you.[15]

I think his case is particularly interesting. Critics speak of the floating *you* in many of his poems — a *you* which might be the reader or an unnamed other, or the poet himself.[16] Bonnie Costello writes:

---

12   Walt Whitman, 'To You', in *Leaves of Grass*, pp. 375–77 (p. 375).

13   Walt Whitman, 'So Long', in *Leaves of Grass*, pp. 609–12 (p. 611).

14   Ibid.

15   John Ashbery, 'Your Name Here', in *Your Name Here* (New York: Farrar Straus and Giroux, 2000), pp. 126–27 (p. 127).

16   Bonnie Costello, *The Plural of Us: Poetry and Community in Auden and Others* (Princeton, NJ: Princeton University Press, 2017), notes that among Auden's heirs, 'John Ashbery's floating pronouns, both "you", and "we", have received the most critical comment' (p. 241).

> An unidentified 'you' inhabits the pages of Ashbery's work,
> especially in the seventies, and critics have speculated variously
> on the role and nature of this ubiquitous, amorphous 'other',
> suggesting that the 'you' serves as a reimagined self, an erotic
> partner, a syntactic counterword. It serves, of course, all these
> functions; its importance lies in its ambiguity. [...] Accepting
> the fruitful ambiguity of the second person pronoun, we find
> that Ashbery's poetry is not only fictively addressed to another,
> but that at least one very concrete reification of 'you' is the
> actual reader.[17]

This seems the least that one can say: the *you* functions both within the representational space of the poem and outside it, in its relation to the reader. Ashbery himself remarks in an interview,

> What I am trying to get at is a general, all-purpose experience
> — like those stretch socks that fit all sizes. Something which a
> reader could dip into without knowing anything about me, my
> history, or sex life, or whatever. [...] I'm hoping that maybe
> someday people will see it this way, as trying to be the openest
> possible form, something in which anybody can see reflected
> his own private experiences without them having to be defined
> or set up for him.[18]

In *John Ashbery and You*, John Vincent writes, Ashbery's poetry

> offers the reader a feeling of being addressed or accompanied
> even in the most forbidding terrain. The reader may finish a
> poem with no purchase on meaning or patterns but with a
> feeling of connection to it and the poet. Critics have been
> stumped about how Ashbery can write patently difficult poetry
> [...] and generally frustrate a gentle reader's desire for sense,
> but still hold an eager audience.[19]

And he suggests that this *you* might be the answer. But this is a special sort of community — of those who are willing to go on reading Ashbery, I would say. I do feel myself part of this community, though I

---

17   Bonnie Costello, 'John Ashbery and the Idea of the Reader', *Contemporary Literature*, 23.4 (1982), pp. 493–514 (pp. 494–95).

18   A. Poulin, 'The Experience of Experience: A Conversation with John Ashbery', *Michigan Quarterly Review*, 20.3 (1981), pp. 242–55 (p. 251).

19   John Vincent, *John Ashbery and You* (Athens: University of Georgia Press, 2007), p. 145.

think in a sort of meta way: I like poems such as Ashbery's 'This Room', from *Your Name Here*, which ends 'Why do I tell you these things? | You are not even here', perhaps less because I feel addressed, though I do, than because I like to think and write about this sort of address.[20] I join a community of those who sometimes think or write about Ashbery.

Various recent books indicate a strong desire among critics for lyric communities — or at least a desire that lyrics can be said to contribute to a spirit of community. Let me just mention two: Walt Hunter's *Forms of a World: Contemporary Poetry and the Making of Globalization*, and Bonnie Costello's *The Plural of Us: Poetry and Community in Auden and Others*. Focusing on contemporary anglophone poetry that engages with problems generated by globalization, Hunter argues 'that poetry imagines powerful alternatives to the present', and that

> exhortation is one of the modes, stances, or registers of poetry
> that attempts to call forth a collective 'we', the 'we' of lives that
> in some cases lack a state at all or in other cases refuse to link
> their identities to an oppressive regime.[21]

He explores poems where 'the ecstatic, proleptic, and sometimes desperate calls to come together [...] become the wishful image of a future in which the rejection of the global present is at one with the revolutionary songs that the poem sustains'.[22] But the emphasis is always on the wishful, the hope that critiques of aspects of the global capitalist order might engender a spirit of community among those who suffer from these conditions, and he finds it hard to show how the poems he reads actually do this: we seem asked to take it on faith that the obscure poets he discusses 'call a globalized "we" into existence, though not into a direct view'.[23]

Bonnie Costello's rich and astute study, on the other hand, focuses on W. H. Auden as public poet, but one highly suspicious of the didactic gestures in which he himself often indulged, as in his cele-

---

20   John Ashbery, 'This Room', in *Your Name Here*, p. 3.

21   Walt Hunter, *Forms of a World: Contemporary Poetry and the Making of Globalization* (New York: Fordham University Press, 2019), pp. 1, 15–16.

22   Ibid., p. 18.

23   Ibid., p. 88.

brated rejection of his famous line 'We must love one another or die'.[24]
'The problem for the modern poet', Auden wrote, 'as for everyone
else to-day, is how to find or form a genuine community'.[25] Costello's
magisterial study of the complexities of attempts to write public poetry,
by Auden, Wallace Stevens, George Oppen, and other modern poets,
highlights for me the problems posed by that first-person plural pro-
noun, *we*, which so easily comes to seem presumptuous. 'Can the
poet construct a "we" that retains multiplicity within its choral force?',
Costello asks, and over a wide range of cases she explores 'how the
genre might propose or project open, reflective, splayed community,
create a sense of potential in "us" that is not predicated on consen-
sus, domination, or the mentality of the crowd'.[26] 'When the poem
dramatizes its struggle with the personal, when it becomes interactive
or self-questioning, the first person plural revitalizes civic poetry and
animates the space of the common'.[27] Poets cannot help but try to
speak of *us* and our concerns, but the obstacles are considerable, and it
may well be that the floating or undetermined *you* might often have an
advantage in the business of plausibly positing community.

So far, all the cases adduced have presumed that the creation of
communities is a good thing (the communities of European soccer fans
have occasionally proved dangerous, but generally, fan communities
offer harmless satisfactions of camaraderie); but while thinking about
how poems addressed to a *you* might foster community by bringing in
readers and reciters who feel addressed by the *you*, I received an un-
published paper by a former student, Sabine I. Gölz, of the University

---

24 W. H. Auden, 'September 1, 1939', in *The Complete Works of W. H. Auden: Poems*, ed.
    by Edward Mendelson, 2 vols (Princeton, NJ: Princeton University Press, 2022), I:
    1927–1939, pp. 375–77 (p. 377). In 1945 and 1950 editions of his poems, he omitted
    the stanza in his 1939 poem containing this line, and explained in a letter of 1957:
    'Between you and me, I loathe that poem. It is rhetorical in the worst sort of way and
    much too "pi". I tried to save it by cutting out what seemed to me the falsest verse (It
    is simply not true that *We must love one another or die*. We must love one another and
    die.) But the cut doesn't help, the whole poem has to be scrapped.' See the notes in the
    edition cited (I, p. 779).

25 W. H. Auden, introduction to *The Oxford Book of Light Verse*, in *The Complete Works of
    W. H. Auden: Prose*, ed. by Edward Mendelson (Princeton, NJ: Princeton University
    Press, 1997–2015), I: *1926–1938* (1997), pp. 430–37 (p. 436).

26 Costello, *Plural of Us*, pp. 9, 225.

27 Ibid., p. 224.

of Iowa, which offers a different take on the creation of community — an unfortunate or even nefarious community. Entitled 'Millay Repairs Baudelaire', her paper looks at Baudelaire's famous 'L'Invitation au voyage' and Edna St Vincent Millay's translation of it, which brings out the masculinist perspective into which Baudelaire's poem inducts its readers.

The poem addresses a feminine *tu*:

> Mon enfant, ma sœur,
> Songe à la douceur
> D'aller là-bas vivre ensemble
> Aimer à loisir,
> Aimer et mourir
> Au pays qui te ressemble.
>
> (My child, my sister,
> Think how sweet
> To journey there and live together!
> To love as we please,
> To love and die
> In the land that resembles you!)[28]

And it invites readers to repeat this address. It serves, Gölz writes, as 'a matrix for further iteration', so we can ask

> what does it model for us to repeat and what does it program for the culture where it circulates [...]. Any repetition of the poem will orient its iterator-apprentices within the gendered-apostrophic force field of European literature like iron filings in a magnetic field. Each repetition will renew the call for her to go 'là-bas' and assimilate yet another iterator to the role of speaker.[29]

She quotes Allen Grossman's account of such poems, where

> there is a self, and the beloved of that self, which always has a transcendental character ascribed to it, and a third — the third

---

28 Charles Baudelaire, 'L'Invitation au voyage' ('Invitation to Journey', trans. by Richard Stokes) <https://www.oxfordlieder.co.uk/song/2632> [accessed 24 August 2023]. Millay's translation, 'Invitation to the Voyage', not used here, can be found at <https://fleursdumal.org/poem/148> [accessed 24 August 2023] (originally published in *Flowers of Evil*, trans. by George Dillon and Edna St Vincent Millay (New York: Harper and Brothers, 1936)).

29 Sabine Gölz, 'Millay Repairs Baudelaire' (unpublished paper), pp. 5–7; a more recent version of the paper is included in the present volume.

being the audience, the ratifier, the witness, and the inheritor
of the drama of the loving relationship.[30]

Readers become ratifiers.

'Caught in the spotlight of apostrophic address,' Gölz writes, 'the
beloved fades from empirical existence, from person to poetic func-
tion.' Making the apostrophized feminine other fade from empirical
existence ('Mon enfant, ma sœur', identified only in relation to an im-
agined country; 'là-bas', which resembles her), 'the apparatus confines
its iterators in a bubble from which it becomes impossible to conceive
of any she as a speaker.' 'The feminized addressee thus comes to operate
as a mere hinge around which readers and iterators keep getting folded
again and again into the perspective' of utterance, that of the *not-she*.
This has real-world consequences.

I cite this as a different take on the well-known problem of Baude-
laire's misogyny, interpreting it not merely as thematic but as produc-
ing, through the structure of address, a community, shall we say, that
is induced to treat the feminized other from the perspective of the
male speaker. Compared to other Baudelaire poems, this one seems
pretty innocent, really — there is no sadism, and it evokes a desire that
may not even be sexual — but it does remind one that the fostering of
community by poetic structure might not always be a good thing.

Crucial in all these cases is the ambiguous functioning of *you*,
which can implicate the reader, as addressee of the poem, but when
the reader voices the poem, can also evoke others, singular or many,
as well as serving as a general pronoun, a more colloquial version of
one. The ease with which fans singing 'Sweet Caroline' in a stadium
pass from the *you* that invokes Caroline herself to the *you* that leads
them to point to the others around them is testimony to the flexibility
of poetic language that is central to the possibility of community-
formation. Costello writes that 'poetic address can be considered as
practice or paradigm, then, for social and ethical engagement' because
deictics and other pronouns can function on different planes, internal
to the representation or external to it, in the interaction of author
and audience. 'Poetry moves freely among discursive orientations and

---

30   Allen Grossman, *The Sighted Singer* (Baltimore, MD: Johns Hopkins University Press,
      1992), p. 13.

shifts its object of implied reference from one framework to another.'[31] A perfect example is the conclusion of Ashbery's 'This Room': 'Why do I tell you these things? | You are not even here.'

---

31   Costello, *Plural of Us*, p. 66.

Millay Repairs Baudelaire

SABINE I. GÖLZ

INTRODUCTION

Repetition

Literary and cultural spacetimes proliferate through repetitions. Every time we read, write, allude, cite, or translate, we contribute, however little, to that process. Those repetitions create patterns, favour one feature over another, amplify or mute, turn perspectives that way and not this. Massively repeated actions swarm, cluster, and give rise to profound asymmetries that grip our signifying spacetimes. We all conform to a host of habits, settle into an untold number of patterns that become 'language' and 'reality' for us. No individual reading, translation, or retranslation escapes these force fields. And yet, those processes also rely on each of us. We are the ones who, again and again, do the repeating. Of the decisions we thus make, of the subliminal signals we obey and that channel our readings into predictable traffic patterns, of all these we are overwhelmingly unaware. We ourselves are 'the unknown [...] right here in the very center of the known'.[1] To resist

---

*   I would like to express my profound gratitude to Barbara Agnese, Dina Blanc, Jonathan Culler, Rosemarie Scullion, Jan Steyn, Oleg Timofeyev, Joshua Wilner, and two anonymous reviewers for their feedback on earlier drafts of this essay.

1   Barbara Johnson, *The Wake of Deconstruction* (Oxford: Blackwell, 1994), p. 84.

this oblivion to our own agency, to the choices we constantly make, and ultimately to ourselves, we must begin to ask new questions. A choice can be recognized as such only if we can perceive the option to do otherwise. In this essay, therefore, I pair two texts in a contrastive reading: Charles Baudelaire's poem 'L'Invitation au voyage' and Edna St Vincent Millay's 1936 retranslation of that poem.[2] Baudelaire's poem can stand in as a particularly lucid metapoetic description of the gendered mechanisms by which Western literature has kept its readers docile. Millay helps us perceive these *because she breaks with them.* She finds a new vantage point and creates a divergent poetics. The systematic revisionary critique instantiated by her translation is not entirely unique, however. It has parallels in the works of many other women writers who tend to find similar solutions to a problem they all face.[3] A brief introduction and conclusion situate the essay in relation to selected positions in retranslation theory.

Antoine Berman's 'Space of Translation'

In his essay 'La Retraduction comme espace de la traduction', Antoine Berman argues that while originals are forever young, translations are intrinsically marred by impermanence. We need to retranslate because translations 'age', they are 'subject to time', and none of them is 'the one'. But, he continues, while translations are thus subject to aging and expiration, retranslations can sometimes escape that fate, overcome their 'essential incompletion', and become 'great translations'.[4] First translations are 'blind and hesitant', but they can give rise, as an 'après-coup', to

---

2   Charles Baudelaire, 'L'Invitation au voyage', in *Oeuvres complètes*, ed. by Claude Pichois, 2 vols (Paris: Gallimard, 1976), I, pp. 55–56; Charles Baudelaire, 'Invitation to the Voyage', in *Flowers of Evil*, trans. by George Dillon and Edna St Vincent Millay (New York: Harper and Brothers, 1936), pp. 74–77.

3   E.g. Karoline von Günderrode and Ingeborg Bachmann. See respectively Sabine I. Gölz, 'Günderrode Mines Novalis', in *The Spirit of Poesy*, ed. by Peter Fenves and Richard Block (Evanston, IL: Northwestern University Press, 2000), pp. 89–130; Sabine I. Gölz, 'Apostrophe's Double', *Konturen*, 10 (2019) <https://doi.org/10.5399/uo/konturen. 10.0.4509>. While the profound gendering of this apparatus of inequality incentivizes women far more frequently to break with it than male writers, there are exceptions. Heinrich von Kleist is one of those exceptions, and an extremely lucid one at that.

4   Antoine Berman, 'La Retraduction comme espace de la traduction', *Palimpsestes*, 13.4 (1990), pp. 1–7: 'aucune n'est *la* traduction', 'L'Histoire nous montre qu'il existe des traductions qui perdurent à l'égal des originaux et qui, parfois, gardent plus d'éclat que

the possibility of a 'traduction accomplie' (accomplished/completed translation).[5] To become 'great', a retranslation must enter what he calls the 'space of translation',[6] a space of 'l'accompli' (accomplishment/completion) that can, 'de temps en temps' (from time to time), be reached by retranslations.[7] Repetition over time also furnishes the 'experience' needed for translation to become 'conscious of itself'.[8] Berman's argument thus is predicated on the distinction between time — as the impermanence and transience of translation — and space — which he associates with the durability and permanence of 'originals' and 'great' translations.[9] Curiously, however, the transition from one to the other, from incompletion (time) to completion (space), is to be achieved via the reduplication of the same fundamentally incompletable process — 'from time to time' — of translation itself. The secret to the stability of both 'originals' and 'great' translations will be found in the processes of repetition themselves — and thus in our own actions.

There is, however, another pattern to Berman's list of 'great translations': his list contains exclusively names of male translators — often canonical authors in their own right. Even more intriguingly, the name 'Baudelaire' is particularly fortified by repetition: it appears twice, as both translator and translatee.[10] The predominance of male authors

---

ceux-ci. Ces traductions sont ce qu'il est convenu d'appeler des *grandes traductions*' (pp. 1–2; emphasis in original). Unless otherwise indicated, all translations are my own.

5   'Toute action humaine, pour s'accomplir, a besoin de la répétition. Et cela vaut particu-lièrement pour la traduction, en tant qu'elle est déjà originairement une opération de redoublement, de duplication. La répétitivité première du traduire est comme redou-blée dans la retraduction. C'est dans l'après-coup d'une première traduction aveugle et hésitante que surgit la possibilité d'une traduction accomplie' (ibid., pp. 4–5).

6   'Le thème de cette intervention est: la retraduction comme espace de la traduction. Par "espace", il faut entendre ici espace d'accomplissement. Dans ce domaine d'essentiel inaccomplissement qui caractérise la traduction, c'est seulement aux retraductions qu'il incombe d'atteindre — de temps en temps — l'accompli' (ibid., p. 1).

7   Ibid.

8   'Il faut tout le chemin de l'expérience pour parvenir à une traduction consciente d'elle-même' (ibid., p. 4).

9   For a lucid critique of this opposition, see Doreen Massey, 'Space-Time, "Science" and the Relationship between Physical Geography and Human Geography', *Transactions of the Institute of British Geographers*, 24.3 (1999), pp. 261–76.

10 'La Vulgate de Saint Jérôme, la Bible de Luther, l'Authorized Version sont de grandes traductions. Mais aussi le Plutarque d'Amyot, les Mille et Une Nuits de Galland, le Shakespeare de Schlegel, l'Antigone de Hölderlin, le Don Quichotte de Tieck, le Paradis perdu de Milton par Chateaubriand, le Poe de Baudelaire, le Baudelaire de Stefan George' (Berman, 'Retraduction', p. 2).

suggests an additional criterion at work in the decision whether a trans-
lation joins the pantheon of the 'greats' — one that Berman does not
mention, and may himself not be particularly conscious of. The sug-
gestion that gender may be a factor in deciding which works become
canonized is, of course, hardly news. The more interesting and more
difficult question to answer is how: *how* does gender intervene in lit-
erary iterations? Edna St Vincent Millay's translation of Baudelaire's
'L'Invitation au voyage' can serve as a case in point. Millay is an estab-
lished poet — yet she is a female one. So, how does her translation
compare to Berman's criteria of greatness? Preceded by two earlier
translations into English (both published in 1909),[11] hers is, at least
by that rather mechanical standard, a retranslation. We will see that
it also fulfils the criterion of being conscious of itself as a translation.
There is one way, however, in which Millay decisively departs from
Berman's criteria: rather than aspiring to the space of canonicity, she
systematically prioritizes time, and thus impermanence and change.

Literary traditions have developed elaborate poetic strategies to
prefigure and align our fleeting readerly actions, corralling them into
patterns. Only by making reading predictable, by scripting our read-
ing habits and thus ultimately our perceptions, can these strategies
generate the canonical stability to which writers such as Berman and
Baudelaire aspire. What Berman calls 'space', therefore, actually arises
out of and exists in time: as a constantly renewed *pattern of coordinated
repetitions*. But since those strategies are thoroughly predicated on the
gender binarism, they do not work for a woman poet such as Millay; or
rather, they work to opposite effect. For her, they produce not perman-
ence but deletion from the canon, not acknowledgement but elision.
There is a good reason, therefore, for why Millay revises Baudelaire's
strategies of control and replaces them with a different poetics that is
ungendered and non-exclusionary.

---

11   Charles Baudelaire, 'Invitation to a Journey', in *The Flowers of Evil*, trans. by Cyril
      Scott (London: Elkin Mathews, 1909) <https://www.gutenberg.org/cache/epub/
      36098/pg36098-images.html#Invitation_to_a_Journey> [accessed 4 January 2024];
      Charles Baudelaire, 'The Invitation to the Voyage', in Jack Collings Squire, *Poems and
      Baudelaire Flowers* (London: New Age Press, 1909), pp. 56–57. Squire's translation is
      reprinted in *Baudelaire in English*, ed. by Carol Clark and Robert Sykes (Harmonds-
      worth: Penguin, 1997), pp. 71–73.

Millay's poem exemplifies a break with a pattern to which we all have been habituated, and to which we all conform. Therefore, it can help us learn from — and potentially repeat — her feat.

TWO MODES OF READING

Baudelaire's poem 'L'Invitation au voyage' begins with a rhetorical figure found in scores of other poems in the Western canon: it addresses a feminized other.[12] Let us think for a moment about how we read that figure. The very gesture of address invites us to understand the text as an utterance. We will imagine someone — 'the poet', a 'lyric I', or even 'Baudelaire' — directing those words at someone else — 'child', 'sister', 'lover', 'muse', or even at the reader, at ourselves. In that case, we will treat the poem as if it were part of an interpersonal exchange between two human beings. But poetry is not speech. It is a piece of (usually written) repeatable language.[13] Poetic texts insert themselves into an existing intertextual landscape — repeating and varying existing conventions, habits. But each one of them also serves as a matrix for further repetitions — recited, learned by heart, translated, sung, and replicated in a host of other ways. These two aspects, too, are not the same. If we look at the poem in terms of how *it* repeats pre-existing patterns, we read it as an act of repetition, and thus as an event, an utterance. If, on the other hand, we ask if and how *we* will repeat such a text, then the poem is no longer an utterance, but a pattern waiting to be confirmed and amplified — or revised. Only the latter question brings our own actions into view. How, then, does a given text present itself to us as a matrix for further iteration? What does it model for us to repeat? What asymmetries does it prefigure, what does it *program* for the culture(s)

---

12   A long chapter titled 'Lyric Address' in Jonathan Culler, *Theory of the Lyric* (Cambridge, MA: Harvard University Press, 2015), pp. 186–243, gives an overview of the range of uses of this rhetorical figure throughout Western poetry.

13   All language is, of course, repeatable. In the absence of iteration, it would not be language at all. This iterability of language, and the performativity of repetition, is explored in the work of J. L. Austin, Jacques Derrida, Paul de Man, Judith Butler, and others. For a helpful overview, see Jonathan Culler, *The Literary in Theory* (Stanford, CA: Stanford University Press, 2007), pp. 137–65. Culler also discusses the ritualistic dimension in various sections of *Theory of the Lyric*: 'Lyrics are made for repetition' (p. 120).

where it circulates? And what are our options, here and now, at the brink of yet another repetition?

STANZA 1: WHERE IS 'OVER THERE'?

Baudelaire's poem consists of three twelve-line stanzas, each time followed by its mesmerizing refrain. Its three-step development, according to Henri L. Brugmans, evokes a 'faraway country' and ultimately presents it to us as a completed 'reality': 'Seule, la première strophe *invite*. La seconde, déjà, *évoque*. Et la troisième nous présente le pays lointain, comme une *réalité accomplie*' (Only the first stanza *invites*. The second already *evokes*. And the third presents the faraway land to us as a *completed reality*).[14] Baudelaire's poems each develop different aspects of his poetics, and 'L'Invitation au voyage' indeed aims to create a certain (perception of) reality. But, as I will try to show, its project may be best understood not so much as the creation of a 'faraway land' than as the creation of what Walter Benjamin would later name 'aura': 'einmalige Erscheinung einer Ferne, so nah sie sein mag' (unique appearance of a distance, as close as it/she may be).[15]

Lines 1–6: Baudelaire

The poem opens with an address to 'mon enfant, ma sœur' (my child, my sister), exhorting an addressee to consider going 'là-bas' (over there) to a land that is said to resemble her:

> Mon enfant, ma sœur,
> Songe à la douceur
> D'aller là-bas vivre ensemble!
> Aimer à loisir,
> Aimer et mourir
> Au pays qui te ressemble!

---

14   Henri L. Brugmans, '"L'Invitation au voyage" by Baudelaire', *Neophilologus*, 30.1 (1946), pp. 3–15 (p. 6; emphasis in original). Brugmans also gives a serviceable description of the poem's formal features.

15   Walter Benjamin, 'Kleine Geschichte der Photographie', in *Gesammelte Schriften*, ed. by Rolf Tiedemann and Hermann Schweppenhäuser, 7 vols (Frankfurt a.M.: Suhrkamp, 1972–91), II.1 (1977), pp. 368–85 (p. 378).

(My child, my sister,
Think of the sweetness
Of going over there to live together!
To love at leisure,
To love and to die
In the country that resembles you!)

What resemblance is that? And where is that 'là-bas' to which the addressee is asked to cross over? To answer these questions, let us take a moment to consider the relationship between speakers and addressees in a poem.

Poetic address of the kind we see in Baudelaire, it has been argued, actually has not one but two distinct addressees. One is the ostensible addressee of the apostrophe — in this case, the 'child' or 'sister'. The second group of addressees is implicit but actual: they are the readers for whose benefit the scenario of address is displayed. Jonathan Culler quotes Allen Grossman's description:

> The presence of a poem involves a complete triadic state of affairs, in which there is a self, and the beloved of that self, which always has a transcendental character ascribed to it, and a third — the third being the audience, the ratifier, the witness, and the inheritor of the drama of loving relationship to which the poem gives access.[16]

'Love poems', Culler continues, 'are the clearest instance of Grossman's model, where the beloved acquires a transcendental, nonempirical character, less a person than a poetic function, addressed for poetic purposes'.[17] Apostrophic poetry, then, has a paradoxical effect for its ostensible addressee: caught in the spotlight of address, the 'beloved' fades from empirical existence, from person to mere poetic function. How can we explain that loss of personhood and (claim to) actuality?

To answer that question, we must look beyond the text and bring those readers into view for whose benefit the 'drama of loving relationship' is displayed, and who do have an actual existence outside of

---

16   Grossman, quoted in Culler, *Theory of the Lyric*, p. 207.
17   Culler, *Theory of the Lyric*, p. 207.

the frame of the poem.[18] Those shadowy 'other' addressees are also
the ones who are doing the repeating: they may just read the poem,
they may recite it, they may interpret it. But every time someone re-
cites the poem, they also again and again re-enact it. And in every such
re-enactment, the 'sister' will be the addressee, not the speaker. Any
repetition of the poem will orient its iterator-apprentices within the
gendered apostrophic force field of European literature like iron filings
in a magnetic field. Each repetition will assimilate yet another iterator
to the role of speaker, who will again renew the call for her to go 'là-
bas'. This leads to a non-trivial realization: not only the addressees are
doubled by the triangulation that Culler and Grossman describe; the
speakers are, too! We all are those iterators. We all, merely by repeating,
have an active role in perpetuating the models we find in literature,
poetry, and in language more generally. Why, then, is our function
as iterators so difficult to bring into focus? And why has it been so
systematically neglected by literary theory?

A question that has probably exercised every single reader of
Baudelaire's poem is 'where or what is that "là-bas"?' In Indo-European
languages, directions in space such as left, right, up, down, front, back
are indicated not relative to an absolute coordinate system but relative
to the speaker. Therefore, where 'over there' is depends on where the
speaker is. If I imagine the speaker on the side of the text, 'over there'
would be the side of the reader. If I assume the speaker to be the
reader, 'over there' would be the text. There is no absolute answer to
the question of where 'là-bas' is.

Baudelaire's poem, however, does more than send the addressee
'over there' (là-bas). It also assimilates her to that other side: line
6 announces that the land to which the apostrophized 'sister' has
been asked to go *resembles* her ('Au pays qui te ressemble!'). The
desired end of Baudelaire's poem — and, we may add, of the larger
apostrophic pattern it repeats — is 'the perfect metaphorical union of

---

18   Stephen Usher, 'Apostrophe in Greek Oratory', *Rhetorica*, 28.4 (2010), pp. 351–62,
      traces the rhetorical figure of apostrophe back to ancient Greek oratory, where speakers
      arguing a case before a court would 'turn away' (*apo-strophein*) from the judges and
      with passionate rhetorical flourish address an absent third person. The actual audience
      in that scenario, the one that needed to be persuaded, was thus not that absent
      addressee but rather the judges of the court. In poetic address, the position of the
      judges is occupied by the actual listeners or readers of the poem.

its destinatrice with the *destination*'.[19] In other words: the 'other side' comes to be gendered as 'feminine'. Where 'là-bas' is no longer depends on where the speaker is: it is defined as wherever 'she' is!

This in effect reverses the usual speaker-centric functioning of how Indo-European languages code directions. No longer does the position of an actual speaker determine where the 'other side' is — especially since those actual speakers are, as iterators and ratifiers, overwhelmingly unaware of their own actions and relative location. Instead, according to the strange magnetism by which cultures and literatures twist our perspectives, the iterators will mechanically line up wherever the feminized 'other' is not. They will repeat after and merge with the perspective of the poem's 'speaker'. The feminized addressee thus comes to operate as a mere hinge around which readers and iterators keep getting folded again and again into the perspective of 'not-she', until they consider it the only possible one. Together with hers, any divergent perspective becomes unimaginable and fades from their world altogether.

And there we have the explanation for the strange fading of the apostrophized feminine other from empirical existence: by dint of that unconscious and subliminal alignment, the apparatus confines its iterators in a bubble within which any 'she' is automatically treated as a non-speaker. This has real-life consequences. Massively amplified through our cultural spacetimes, that obedient gendered alignment of ears and gazes creates a highly probable, mobile, flexible, and for all practical purposes *absolute* frame of reference that rests on the *actual* elision — mechanically reinforced and normalized by our everyday signifying business as usual — of 'her' as a person and agent.

The word *là-bas* registers that assignment of the feminine to the role as other. On the face of it, the word indeed means 'over there'. But all it takes is to remove the accent, and the word *la* (there) turns into the French feminine definitive article, *la*. *Bas* means 'down' or 'low', and the imperative *à bas ...!* means 'down with ...!' The call for her to go 'là-bas', then, is a call not just to go *across* but also to submit to an always already hierarchized order of representation whose

---

19   Barbara Johnson, 'Poetry and its Double: Two "Invitations au voyage"', in *The Critical Difference: Essays in the Contemporary Rhetoric of Reading* (Baltimore, MD: Johns Hopkins University Press, 1980), pp. 23–52 (p. 26).

stability is founded on 'her' subjugation: 'down girl' — as Kate Manne
puts it in the title of her recent book on 'the logic of misogyny'.[20] The
consequences of this are articulated in Baudelaire's next two lines: for
the 'beloved', to follow the invitation to 'live together' means not only
to 'love' (aimer), but also to 'die' (mourir). She will be turned from a
person into a blank signifier, a universal metaphor: 'A particular kind
of commodity acquires the character of *universal equivalent*, because
all other commodities make it the material in which they uniformly
express their value.'[21] For the selected commodity to function as a uni-
versal equivalent, it must *lose the ability to express its own value.*[22] That is
what Ingeborg Bachmann calls the 'murder'.[23] For its unselfconscious
enforcers, by contrast, that scheme foresees the mere lazy mechanical
repetition — 'aimer à loisir' — of the well-worn murderous pattern.
Baudelaire's poem is part and parcel of an entire literary episteme that
has trained all of us to conform to and ratify, over and over, a vicious
misogynist apparatus.

The misogyny of Western cultures has, of course, not gone un-
noticed. Our results so far therefore may not seem overly surprising. But
'she' is not the only one who suffers consequences. The poetic apparatus
modelled by Baudelaire's poem sets out to regulate *all* of our perspec-
tives. The systematic loss of readerly self-awareness it promotes affects all
of the iterators who habitually and unwittingly fold themselves into the
perspective of the 'speaker', and who therefore can no longer perceive
texts in any other way than as an utterance. They can no longer wake
up to and reclaim their difference from the apparatus of language.[24]
Baudelaire's poem meticulously shows how this comes about.

---

20   Kate Manne, *Down Girl: The Logic of Misogyny* (Oxford: Oxford University Press, 2019).

21   Marx, quoted in Johnson, 'Poetry and its Double', p. 36; emphasis in Johnson.

22   See e.g. Karl Marx, *Capital: A Critique of Political Economy*, trans. by Ben Fowkes (New
     York: Vintage Books, 1977), p. 161. Marx's work, of course, is also part of that gendered
     discursive spacetime, which is why (as is well known) in the text of *Das Kapital*,
     commodities as objects of exchange are also insistently feminized and sexualized.

23   The disappearance of the feminine narrating 'I' at the end of her novel *Malina* is
     sealed with the words: 'Es war Mord' (It was murder; Ingeborg Bachmann, *Malina*,
     in *'Todesarten'-Projekt*, ed. by Monika Albrecht and Dirk Göttsche, 4 vols (Munich:
     Piper, 1995), iii.1, p. 695).

24   I would argue that this inability to establish a stable difference from the perspective of
     the speaker, and thus of language and representation, is also what has been called de
     Man's 'obstacle'; see Alexis C. Briley, 'De Man's Obstacles', *Diacritics*, 43.3 (2015), pp.
     40–65. To show this in detail will be a separate project.

We tend to take texts for representations. But they are in fact dispositions for actions:

> Every perception is prolonged into a nascent action [...]. Thus is gradually formed an experience of an entirely different order, which accumulates within the body, a series of mechanisms wound up and ready with reactions to external stimuli ever more numerous and more varied, and answers ready prepared to an ever growing number of possible solicitations.

This memory 'no longer *represents* our past to us, it *acts* it'.[25] Henri Bergson wrote this over a century ago. Yet a systematic consideration of how language programs our actions by handing us scripts that we then live by, and what we do to each other as a result, is largely absent from scholarly discussions of language and rhetoric. The rare exceptions to this general oblivion are most likely to be found among those of us who have abundant and painful motivation to wake up to both the fundamental dysfunctionality of the representational apparatus for ourselves and the utter inability of those surrounding us to wake up to themselves and their own actions. An army of living enforcers mechanically perpetuates the apparatus of oppression. What do we do? How can we even begin to change this intolerable state of affairs? Before anything else, we need to unglue our eyes from the page and make discernible the actions by which we all ceaselessly turn those representations into our lived reality. Only then can we first understand and then rewrite that apparatus itself, one poem at a time. And that is exactly what Millay does.

Lines 1–6: Millay

Millay's translation is no mechanical repetition. It begins by rewriting the starting point and foundation of Baudelaire's poem: Millay deletes the conventional gendered apostrophe and replaces it with an invitation to 'think'. She starts by drawing attention to our own living, breathing, and embodied actuality:

---

25   Henri Bergson, *Matter and Memory*, authorized translation by Nancy Margaret Paul and W. Scott Palmer (London: Allen and Unwin; New York: Macmillan, 1911), pp. 92–93; emphasis in original.

> Think, would it not be
> Sweet to live with me
> All alone, my child, my love? —
> Sleep together, share
> All things, in that fair
> Country you remind me of?

This initial change triggers a cascade of others that reverse, one by one, all the hierarchies Baudelaire's poem relies on, systematically rewriting his entire poetic apparatus. The rhymes change. Millay replaces the lure of Baudelaire's 'sœur'/'douceur' (sister/sweetness) with a rhyme that in his poem (which systematically excludes first-person pronouns) would be unthinkable: 'be'/'me'. Baudelaire's poem suggests that we begin by going 'over there' to live *together* ('D'aller là-bas vivre ensemble!'). Millay's begins with the *singularity* of each of us: 'all alone'. Notably, however, each of these actually results in its opposite. Baudelaire's promise of togetherness leads to the feminized other being singled out and turned into a blank signifier. Millay's invitation to live 'all alone', by contrast, invites us to embrace our singular and actual existence as separate from the text — the *conditio sine qua non* for making reading a reflexive and interactive process, and for opening a critical conversation about how language programs us. Rather than luring us 'over there', she asks us to realize that we are 'here'. With the disappearance of the gendered apostrophe, the word 'love' is de-eroticized and degendered, suggesting instead nurturing support for the (always belated) actual reader — 'my child, my love'. The threat of murder and death has simply disappeared. Where Baudelaire's lines are dominated by imperatives and exclamation marks ('Songe à [...]!', 'Aimer à loisir, | Aimer et mourir [...] !'), Millay has questions and hypotheticals ('would it not be [...]?', 'Sleep together, share [...]?'). This shift in rhetoric follows directly from her strong beginning: if readers bring their thinking — their unrepresentable, self-reflexive, and embodied presence — to bear on the text, signification becomes interactive and unpredictable. Such readers no longer take orders from texts. Whether or not I can 'live with' a given poem is not a foregone conclusion but an open question.

One deceptively small change, finally, is a dash not found in Baudelaire that intervenes between lines three and four. What is that dash?

The first word after the dash is 'sleep'. To agree to 'live with' a poem is to give up some of one's conscious distance and difference — to engage what it models for us, to temporarily go from 'all alone' to 'sleep together'. By marking it with the dash, however, Millay wakes us up to this transition itself. We can thus read the small horizontal line of the dash as a figure for the reflexive textual surface, a signal that we are crossing the *line of inversion* around which text and reader trade places, taking turns in who takes the lead. The first-person pronoun 'me' appears on both sides of the dash, figuring the indexical symmetry and reversibility that allows for this exchange of places. Which *I* is speaking here? Is the text inviting me to live with it, or am I inviting the text into my life? By placing open indexicals on both sides of that line of inversion, Millay strategically enables a reflexivity and reversibility that supports both readings. The relation between 'you' and 'me', between reader and text, is figured as a reflexive event: 'that fair | Country *you remind me of?*' Her translation invites our repetition to be reflexive, mind-ful, and self-conscious.

It is no coincidence that Millay begins by foregrounding indexicals. The latter play a critical role in the interplay between texts and readers. Let us therefore take a moment to consider how they work, and why it is so crucial that we pay attention to their placement on the matrix of the text. The *Stanford Encyclopedia of Philosophy* defines them like this:

> An indexical is, roughly speaking, a linguistic expression whose reference can shift from context to context. For example, the indexical 'you' may refer to one person in one context and to another person in another context. Other paradigmatic examples of indexicals are 'I', 'here', 'today', 'yesterday', 'he', 'she', and 'that'. Two speakers who utter a single sentence that contains an indexical may say different things. For instance, when both John and Mary utter 'I am hungry', Mary says that she is hungry, whereas John says that he is hungry.[26]

Whenever I repeat an indexical in a new context — and the context *of the iteration* is always new — what it refers to changes: time, place, speaker, addressee, and so on. The word *I* (as the example given in

---

26 David Braun, 'Indexicals', in *The Stanford Encyclopedia of Philosophy*, ed. by Edward N. Zalta (Summer 2017) <https://plato.stanford.edu/archives/sum2017/entries/indexicals/> [accessed 4 November 2021].

the definition shows) stands out, since speakers use it to refer to themselves. That is unproblematic if we are just telling a friend that we are hungry and ready to have lunch. But how does this work in literary texts? If I, in repeating a poem, assume that the one who is *really* speaking is still 'the poet' — that I am 'just quoting Baudelaire' — then I efface my own role as iterator, and thus my own agency. Millay's invitation for us to *re-mind* the text envisions a different use. She reinserts indexicals such as 'me' and 'you' in a way that makes them actualizable. Rather than effacing our own agency and presence, we can use indexicals to shift the entire frame of reference performatively into our own present. We then no longer read the text as an utterance by someone else but use it reflexively to 'come to language' ourselves.[27] It is significant that Baudelaire's poem, by contrast, includes no 'here' and no 'I'. Instead, in its first six lines, the first person is only marked twice by possessive adjectives ('mon' or 'ma') — each time relative to the addressee. The iterators of this text can say 'my' and 'mine', but they cannot say 'I'. This withholding of open, reversible indexicals tightens the text's prefigurative power over the minds of readers. Together with the gendered address, the withholding of open ungendered indexicals is the second part of a two-pronged approach to aligning readers with the perspective of the 'speaker', and to having readers snap to the grid the poem provides. Indexical consciousness, self-reflexive actualization, by contrast, allows for us to recover and reassert our difference from the text, and thus to absolve ourselves from the authority of the script. That is why Baudelaire withholds open indexicals that readers could use to wake up to their own presence — and why Millay begins with them.

Lines 7–12: Baudelaire

So, let now us see how the next six lines of Baudelaire's poem use indexicals to align readers' perspectives with one place on the prefigurative map of the poem — and train them to avoid another. They unfold an

---

27   Cf. Ingeborg Bachmann, *Kritische Schriften*, ed. by Monika Albrecht and Dirk Göttsche (Munich: Piper, 2005), p. 348.

entire canopy — metaphoric skies, complete with suns, eyes, and tears — for us to repeat:

> Les soleils mouillés
> De ces ciels brouillés
> Pour mon esprit ont les charmes
> Si mystérieux
> De tes traîtres yeux,
> Brillant à travers leurs larmes.

> (The sodden suns
> Of these clouded skies
> For my spirit have the charm
> So mysterious
> Of your traitorous eyes,
> Dazzling across their tears.)

The 'suns' appear first. They are plural, as if subject to some sort of astigmatic doubling that puts reading out of focus. They are also 'mouillés' — wet or drenched — as if the fire of actuality had gone out in them. The skies ('ciels'), plural like the suns, are 'brouillés' — i.e. cloudy, overcast, but also uneven, mixed, non-homogenous, scrambled, or blurred (of vision). Precisely *as such* however — as unfocused, divided, and overcast — those suns and skies appeal to the 'esprit' that appears in the third line of this section and that is marked with the possessive adjective 'mon'. Barbara Johnson notes the perspectivity of this desire when she writes:

> The important common denominator between land and lady, between suns and eyes, is less their shared shining roundness than *a common effect produced on the 'spirit' of the beholder.* The rhetorical meeting point between the two terms (eyes and suns) is not simply that of a metaphorical resemblance but that of a metonymical third term, contiguous to both: *the speaker's desire.*[28]

That 'metonymy' of desire is not a mere rhetorical figure. Rather, the contiguity it implies is utterly concrete: it is the contiguity to the text of a long line of iterators who, one after the other, unwittingly assimilate their perspectives to that of the beholder-speaker and take it for their

---

28   Johnson, 'Poetry and its Double', pp. 26–27; my emphasis.

own. The 'charms' of those troubled skies, therefore, are not only predicated on a specific perspective, but in repetition that perspective is also mechanically handed on to the iterators. Apprenticed to the perspective of that 'esprit', they will re-enact its triangulation, and thus they, too, will learn to find the eyes of the feminized and othered 'you' both traitorous and sparkling. For all of the metaphoric blurriness of these lines, one thing is in laser-sharp focus: their exclusion of 'your eyes'.

But whose eyes are 'your' eyes? For as long as we remain within the scenario of address that opens the poem, we will read them as the eyes of the feminized addressee — of the 'child' and 'sister'. And for the apostrophized feminine other to function as a universal equivalent, the relegation of 'her' eyes to the exterior of that readerly enclosure obeys an iron logic. They must be seen rather than seeing: 'brillant' (shining, sparkling, or dazzling), closer to precious stones than to actual seeing eyes.[29] They are 'traîtres' (traitorous) by structural necessity, since the exclusion of their perspective is the very foundation of Baudelaire's signifying apparatus. For the same reason, they (and how and what they might see) must remain 'mystérieux' (mysterious) within the perceptual bubble into which the poem is herding its domesticated readers.

However, Baudelaire's prefiguration leads his readers to exclude much more than only the 'lady's' perspective. It also excludes any actual reading that is not aligned with the perspective and desire of the (imaginary) 'speaker' — including the ones that Baudelaire's iterators would otherwise discover to be their own. The indexicals in these lines are not open and reversible as they were in Millay, where we could read 'me' and 'you', speaker and addressee, text and reader, here and over there in such a way as to (have them) change places. In Baudelaire, they are possessive adjectives attached to two separate perspectives, one marked as *mine*, and one as *yours*, one both speaking and seeing,

---

29   This conversion of 'her' eyes into a shower of precious stones arguably also takes place in Poe's 'Domain of Arnheim', which has been cited as another intertextual reference for Baudelaire's poem: *The Collected Works of Edgar Allan Poe*, ed. by T. O. Mabbott, 3 vols (Cambridge, MA: Belknap Press of Harvard University Press, 1969–78), III: *Tales and Sketches* (1978), pp. 1266–85. I am grateful to Joshua Wilner for alerting me to this intertext.

the other both seen and silent, one assimilative, the other erased. The lingering effect of the apotropaic feminization of 'your eyes' anchors that polarization in the gender binarism. It is thus the scenario of address figured as a 'drama of loving relationship' *itself* that keeps iterators properly aligned with the 'speaker'. That polarization splits the crowd of iterators into two camps, dividing the 'skies' of reading into two, and causing the astigmatism of the doubled 'suns': readers end up either excluded or co-opted. If co-opted, they can no longer find themselves *as readers*. A troubled cloud cover has been spread over their eyes: they remain under the poem's prefigurative spell and can only 'see' what the poem has them see. If excluded, they can break with that spell, but their insights remain inaccessible to all assimilated readers. This divided sky, thus, programs two entirely different subject positions into which the overwhelming majority of readers sort both themselves and each other.

Baudelaire uses the word 'ciels'. This plural form is one of two possible ones for the word *ciel* (sky). While the plural *cieux* denotes the 'undivided universality of the celestial sphere' and the higher powers associated with it ('non la pluralité, mais l'universalité indivise de la sphère céleste, ou, au figuré, la Providence, le pouvoir céleste'), the form chosen by Baudelaire denotes a sky that is 'enclosed by a determinate horizon', such as the skies of a specific country, but also a painted sky, or even the headboard of a bed.[30] Baudelaire's skies are thus self-consciously representations. Realizing this should help us reclaim 'your eyes' — the ones with which we read the poem — as our own. Let us move on to Edna St Vincent Millay's version of these lines.

Lines 7–12: Millay

Millay's translation reinstated, in its first six lines, a reflexive and reversible relation between reader and text. Let us now see how she reshapes the next six lines.

---

30   Académie Française, 'Les cieux ou Les ciels', in *Dire, Ne pas dire* (11 June 2020) <https://www.academie-francaise.fr/les-cieux-ou-les-ciels> [accessed 12 February 2022]. I would like to thank my colleague Rosemarie Scullion for pointing out this fascinating detail to me.

> Charming in the dawn
> There, the half-withdrawn
> Drenched, mysterious sun appears
> In the curdled skies,
> Treacherous as your eyes
> Shining from behind their tears.

The word 'charming' opens the stanza, turning the nominalized charms ('charmes') of Baudelaire's troubled skies into an adjective, almost a verb, a process. As my reading dawns on the poem, as my mind encounters the text's prefigurative magic and casts its own spell in turn, an open-ended process is set in motion — a doubly reflexive give-and-take, 'charming in the dawn'. In Millay, only one sun appears, correcting the double vision of Baudelaire's plural 'suns' and divided skies. This reading is conscious of its own singularity. Indexicals, too, work very differently in Millay. Where Baudelaire's poem polarized readings — one to be metonymically aligned and assimilated ('my spirit'), the other to be blocked and excluded ('your eyes') — in Millay's text, an indexical has appeared that establishes distance and difference:

> Charming in the dawn
> *There*, the half-withdrawn
> Drenched, mysterious sun appears.

The metaphoric sun appears 'there'. We may read that 'sun' as a metaphor or reflection of our metonymic presence as readers, but we do not coincide with it: it appears *there* (on the readable surface), while we know ourselves to be *here* (before it but separate from it). That is why that 'sun' remains 'half-withdrawn'. Our presence *here* is implied, but it cannot be mapped. Whatever fleeting reflections, similarities, analogies, and shifting appearances our reading mind may discover on the textual surface — those effects never, in Millay's poem, coincide with *this actual reader*. They are — akin to reflections in a mirror — performative, fleeting, incomplete, predicated on and shifting with our every move. Any movement we perform will change how they appear to us. Self-reflexive reading founds itself on its irreducible distance from representation. If in Baudelaire, the charm of 'your eyes' remained mysterious because it was coded as other, in Millay that 'sun' remains mysterious because, like all representations, it is 'half-withdrawn': incomplete. Whereas Baudelaire's poem presents us with a polarized map and used the indexical 'my' to pull its iterators into one perspective, Millay's 'there' insists on its non-coincidence with whatever appears on the readable surface, and thus preserves our freedom to differ.

The first six lines were articulated by a dash — a line of inversion. Something similar occurs in the second half of the first stanza. Millay's lines 7–9 assumed the perspective of a reflexive look *down* onto a readable surface. The next three lines rotate the perspective and bring the 'curdled skies' into view. Textual surface and readerly skies change places, underscoring that a prefigurative representation can turn the tables on its readers and reappear as a 'sky' that scripts 'your eyes'. While the sun is singular and focused in Millay, the skies in which it appears are still plural, heterogeneous, even 'curdled'. The inequities, heterogeneity, and strife Baudelaire and others like him have installed in the cultural and literary 'skies' of reading still impact an effort such as Millay's. This is why, in her poem, the metaphoric 'sun' and 'your eyes' are both treacherous, untrustworthy: both may script or have been scripted. It is indispensable to *think*.

STANZA 2: WHOSE LANGUAGE?

Lines 15–26: Baudelaire

With the second stanza, we enter a 'room' — an enclosed space, decorated with oriental splendour, and suffused with fragrances and perfumes. Baudelaire begins with a list of what 'would' be contained in that room: shiny (but unspecified) furnishings, flowers, aromas.

> Des meubles luisants,
> Polis par les ans,
> Décoreraient notre chambre;
> Les plus rares fleurs
> Mêlant leurs odeurs
> Aux vagues senteurs de l'ambre,
> Les riches plafonds,
> Les miroirs profonds,
> La splendeur orientale,
> Tout y parlerait
> À l'âme en secret
> Sa douce langue natale.

(Shiny furniture
Polished by the years
Would decorate our room;
The most rare flowers
Mingling their odours
With the vague scent of amber,
The rich ceilings,
The deep mirrors,
The oriental splendour,
There, all would speak
To the soul in secret
Its sweet native language.)

The rhetoric is impersonal and constative, so much so that the belated arrival of a verb in the conditional ('décoreraient' — 'would decorate') in the stanza's third line can no longer quite outweigh the air of factuality established by that beginning. There is a sense of beguiling luxury, but also of an eerie absence of any subject, of focus. The objects are shiny, but what they reflect is ambient unfocused light. Due to its belated appearance, the only possessive adjective — '*notre* chambre' (*our* room) — seems to attach the *we* to the room, rather than claiming the room as ours. Deictic, pointing gestures are, with the exception of the 'y' in the stanza's tenth line, absent. Aromas mingle; reflectivity remains diffuse and blurred.[31] The fragrances of even the 'most rare flowers' merge with the prevailing scent of amber. Amber or incense is itself a mix of different fragrances. It can absorb additional fragrances, no matter how rare, without turning into anything different. And whose native language is being spoken there ('y'), secretly, to the soul? The French possessive adjective 'sa' takes its gender from the feminine noun 'langue'. We therefore cannot tell if that language belongs to 'everything' (tout) or to the 'soul' (âme). Much like the scent of rare flowers is absorbed into the mix of amber, a soul vis-à-vis Baudelaire's poem will be absorbed, unable to differ from the

---

31   That impersonal and constative rhetoric, together with the emphasis on aromas and fragrances, recalls Baudelaire's famous poem 'Correspondances'. Paul de Man's by now classic reading emphasizes that 'Correspondances' portrays a space that the subject cannot 'transport' itself out of. 'Correspondances' ends on a list, while stanza 2 of 'L'Invitation au voyage' begins with a list. See Paul de Man, 'Anthropomorphism and Trope in the Lyric', in *The Rhetoric of Romanticism* (New York: Columbia University Press, 1984), pp. 239–62.

poem's language. Baudelaire's poetics is assimilative: it adds us to the room, rather than allowing us to make the room ours. The language it whispers to our souls 'en secret' sets out to become our 'native' one by preventing our birth as self-aware subjects.

Lines 15–26: Millay

Rather than with a list of objects, Millay's version of stanza 2 begins with a grammatical subject in the first person plural: '*We* should have a room [...].' To render the conditional, she could have chosen 'would', but opts instead for the form that articulates the desire of this subject: 'we *should* have a room', 'tables [...] *should* reflect', and 'all *should* speak apart'.

> We should have a room
> Never out of bloom:
> Tables polished by the palm
> Of the vanished hours
> Should reflect rare flowers
> In that amber-scented calm;
> Ceilings richly wrought,
> Mirrors deep as thought,
> Walls with eastern splendor hung,
> All should speak apart
> To the homesick heart
> In its own dear native tongue.

Baudelaire's furniture, polished by the 'years' (ans), gleams with the accumulated sheen of canonical texts burnished by the (supposedly impersonal) 'test of time'.[32] In Millay, by contrast, the polishing is done by a much more corporeal 'palm', as the scale shrinks from 'years' to 'hours' — from the authority of the 'ages' to the lived moment in which the text begins to shine under the gaze of a reflexive individual reader. That those hours have 'vanished' further underscores that what makes this surface reflexive is the transitory but embodied presence of a human life. Where Baudelaire has unspecified 'furnishings' (meubles) that reflect scattered light ('luisants'), Millay has 'tables' — horizontal surfaces that 'should reflect' not just anything, but precisely the 'rare

---

32   This is the type of ratifying repetition Berman envisions.

flowers' of self-aware, critical reading. Baudelaire's mirrors are 'deep' ('Les miroirs profonds'), but they lack the one thing that would make them actual mirrors: a reflective surface. In Millay's poem, the mirrors are 'deep as thought',[33] acknowledging that what adds 'depth' to readable surfaces is our readerly thinking. Lines 24–25 answer Baudelaire's subliminal strategy of assimilation with another assertion of distance: 'All should speak *apart* | To the *homesick* heart.' In Millay, the speaking is 'apart', separate from the heart, which is why the latter is 'homesick': it longs to return, self-reflexively, from language and representation back into itself. Precisely by maintaining itself 'apart' from representation, however, an indexically conscious reading can place the resignifying sheen of reflexivity and allegory over the found text — and thus turn what speaks to that homesick heart into the latter's 'own dear native tongue'. There is no doubt that Millay's retranslation is highly conscious of itself as a translation throughout. In addition to radically rewriting the poem's poetics, therefore, with this line Millay also signs *as a translator* who brings the poem into her own 'dear native tongue': English.

Baudelaire's stanza, then, presents itself as a lavishly decorated and endlessly suggestive 'room' whose absorptive power is owed to its careful avoidance of even the slightest acknowledgement of our readerly presence. In Millay's translation, by contrast, the stanza begins with a first-person pronoun, reflections appear on surfaces, polishing occurs in experienced, human time, thought attends to the mirror of language, and the 'homesick' heart keeps itself 'apart' from language. Millay's text not only supports but calls for ('should') the very thing Baudelaire is blocking: a self-reflexive actual reading that can break with the absorptive power of prefiguration by returning into — and thus giving birth to — itself. Each of these trajectories reaches its respective logical conclusion in the third and last stanza.

---

33   Johnson, 'Poetry and its Double', p. 26, notes the absorptive power of Baudelaire's poem as a 'mirror' when she writes: 'What is proposed to the woman is a place created in her own image', and 'the lyrical voyage, then, is a voyage through the looking-glass, a voyage into the illusory "depths" [...] of a reflection'.

STANZA 3: VAGABOND HUMOURS

Lines 29–34: Baudelaire

Baudelaire's third stanza begins by telling us to 'See [...] | These vessels sleep.' What vessels are these? And what does it mean to 'see' something when we read? If we assume that the poem 'paints a picture' for us, we will conjure a vision of a harbour in the evening light, 'see' merchant ships floating on canals, carrying treasures from the end of the (colonized) world. We may even go so far as to situate that scene in a specific place: 'Clearly, the poet is inviting his beloved to a journey with him to an idealized, almost imaginary Holland.'[34] Many would place such hyperphantasia high on their list of reading pleasures. Those with more abstract inclinations, by contrast, might give those lines an allegorical, self-referential turn. Such a reader might, for instance, read the poem itself as such a 'ship': setting out from nineteenth-century Paris, it has travelled great geographical and temporal distances, to return enriched by ever-new readings. Both of those modes of reading — and many others — are, of course, eminently possible. But they have one fundamental limitation: by taking their lead from what the poem appears to 'represent', they end up obeying what it prefigures.

Baudelaire's poem from the very start engineers readerly absorption and loss of indexical consciousness. Its third stanza, however, pushes both the metapoetic and the prefigurative description of these mechanisms to dizzying new heights. It begins by explicitly encouraging the very mode of reading that will reliably collapse any readerly self-awareness: a reading that sees words as containers.

> Vois sur ces canaux
> Dormir ces vaisseaux
> Dont l'humeur est vagabonde;
> C'est pour assouvir
> Ton moindre désir
> Qu'ils viennent du bout du monde.

---

34 James S. Patty, 'Light of Holland: Some Possible Sources of Baudelaire's "L'Invitation au voyage"', *Études baudelairiennes*, 3 (1973), pp. 147–57 (p. 147). Patty also gives a useful overview of various scholars' efforts to track down both visual and literary sources that Baudelaire may have drawn on in this poem.

(See on these canals
These vessels sleep
Whose mood is itinerant;
It's to assuage
Your slightest desire
That they come from the end of the world.)

Canals ('canaux') are channels that contain and direct a flow. The word 'vaisseaux', much like its English cognate 'vessels', also connotes any enclosure capable of holding content — jars, ships, other containers, even blood vessels. 'Vessels' on 'canals', thus, are *vessels on vessels*. Baudelaire's lines model a layered repetition of the same: a reading that sees the text as a container will itself be contained. Why? Because this assumption alone — that texts represent some pre-existing content that readers merely extract or consume — obscures the fact that texts are in fact irreducibly incomplete, and that reading is not receptive but interactive and generative. It obscures the fact that we always already make decisions about reading that way and not this. Thus, if in reading Baudelaire's lines, we 'see' a bucolic harbour scene, we will be unable to realize that they also prefigure what will be the case if we follow their lead: we will all turn into sleeping vessels — it will be sleeping vessels all the way up.

How can we instead pair this text with a reading that insists on its difference from the text and thus can bring itself into play? We have seen that the first change Millay makes is to reinsert indexicals. By reflexively actualizing these, readers can establish their difference from the text and its prefigurations. So what indexicals, if any, can we find in Baudelaire's third stanza?

In the first two lines, the same indexical occurs twice:

Vois sur *ces* canaux
Dormir *ces* vaisseaux
Dont l'humeur est vagabonde.

(See on *these* canals
These vessels sleep
Whose mood is itinerant.)

Which way do these pointers point? If we read them as pointing our gaze towards a representation, at 'canals' and 'ships' in an imaginary harbour, we will obey the order to 'see ships'. If we read them reflexively, we may begin to wake up to the fact that 'these' words could also be pointing directly at us. But Baudelaire's lines still confound us: even if we are trying to wake up to the indexical 'these', the poem still holds up the diagnosis of 'sleeping vessels' to us. A reader in the process of waking up to themselves is thus flatly denied acknowledgement by the poem itself. If they nevertheless manage to hang on to some nascent indexical self-awareness, a new perception of these lines emerges: they appear as a prefigurative textual model that thumbs its nose at 'these' readers. The poem prefigures how 'these' readers obey, are contained, and remain asleep, unable to fully wake up to their own presence. The poem tells its readers that they cannot escape its spell.

How do we get our reading beyond this impasse? Millay has a complex and layered answer. But before we go there, let us briefly reconsider the notion of self-referentiality in literature. It is most widely understood as the idea that texts can 'refer to themselves', as a writing about writing. I propose that this is insufficient in several ways. It must be supplemented, first of all, with the idea that literary texts also refer to and even prefigure reading. But even more importantly, we must realize that it is actually not the text but we ourselves as readers who have the final say, at any given moment, of what we have a text refer to. And even more importantly: readers can use texts to reflect their own embodied readerly presence. The strongest way to do so is what I have called the self-reflexive actualization of indexicals. Indexicals can serve as the fulcrum around which we can turn our perception of the text from a 'container' of meanings into a shiny surface activated by and responsive to our presence and agency. Only from the vantage point of such a self-reflexive reading do the prefigurative dimensions of the text emerge and become readable. Indexicals do not represent, they do not prefigure anything. But they can function as a crucial fork in the path of our reading: we can use them to unmoor our minds from the text's prefigurative grip.

So far, Baudelaire's poem has either studiously avoided indexicals altogether or mapped them onto the 'drama of loving relationship' (Grossman), aligning all mechanical iterations with one perspective ('mon esprit') against another ('your eyes'). The third stanza takes the issue to a new metapoetic level by confronting the problem head-on. I propose that we refer the 'ces vaisseaux | Dont l'humeur est vaga-

bonde' to the very indexicals or deictics themselves whose potential
Baudelaire's poem sets out to tame. Indexicals, also called 'shifters', are
indeed words whose references shift and wander. Yet their vagabond
inclinations are activated not by the indexicals themselves but by us
as readers and iterators. Their potential to disrupt the workings of a
poetic apparatus such as Baudelaire's poem, therefore, remains under
control for precisely as long as we as readers can be convinced to make
a habit, a very, very firm habit, of considering texts as containers: 'See
these ships …' For the apparatus to tame the 'humeur vagabonde' of
indexicals, and for readers to remain moored in the harbour of the text
like so many vessels, therefore, 'these' readers — i.e. you and I — must
remain asleep.

In this last stanza, therefore, Baudelaire pairs indexicals with a
prefigurative/antinomic representation. Even if these readers are be-
ginning to wake up to themselves, they will find that the poem decrees
them as still sleeping. That is the poem's last-ditch effort to bring read-
ers back from what otherwise would be the end of its world. The verb
form 'viennent' is ambiguous. We can read it as a simple statement in
the present indicative. We can also, however, read the expression 'qu'ils
viennent' as an exhortation and expression of desire — 'let them come',
'may they come'. *Please, colonized readers, do come back from the end of
the world, and please remain asleep, oblivious to your own labour, your de-
cisions, yourselves. Please keep attributing all of the readerly surplus value
you produce to the poem, the author, the work!* In that case, 'viennent'
would be a subjunctive, and the veneer of factuality surrounding the
return of 'these vessels' would fade, revealing the desire that informs
Baudelaire's entire poem: to overcome the 'humeur vagabonde' not
just of indexicals but of your and my own thinking minds. The poem,
then, both prefigures and theorizes — right under the noses of its
readers — how their loss of readerly consciousness is (to be) achieved.
We just need to learn to read it.

Distinctly different readings of these lines are thus possible. We
can visualize these as layers, stacked one on top of the other in order
of ascending self-reflexivity and awareness — and hence of increasing
readerly emancipation from the authority we are used to conferring on
such canonical texts. We generate this ladder of metalevels as we climb
it:

1. The first layer would be a reading that is a mere inert iteration. It puts up no resistance, lets itself be scripted by the text, obediently performs a mere mechanical repetition of the same: sleeping vessels on canals. (*The poem says the vessels are sleeping. Sleeping vessels it is.*)

2. The next layer would be a reading self-aware enough to wake up to 'these' indexicals and thus to begin to perceive that prefigurative mechanism — and possibly the entrapment it constitutes for readers. (*Oh, the poem points at these. Is it pointing at me? I am awake. But wait, it says* sleep! *Whoever believes that will not wake up* ...) To this realization, different affective responses are possible:

   (a) *Irony or mockery* at seeing the credulous readerly masses fooled — unable to wake up to the fact that their predicament is explained to them right before their eyes.

   (b) *Clandestine triumph* at discovering those strategies and the power they confer. This response can lead someone to consciously deploy and thus perpetuate these strategies of control.[35]

   (c) Finally, this realization can also lead readers to react with growing resistance and ultimately an *aversion* — a turn away from absorption and into a more self-aware reading.[36]

3. Such a self-aware reader, finally, may conclude, as Millay does, that the offending poetic strategies themselves have to be rethought and then rewritten.

Lines 29–34: Millay

Millay consistently figures reading as a separate layer, interacting with but distinct from the text. This is important in principle, because only a reading that finds a way to assert its separate existence from the text can

---

35 Walter Benjamin's 'On Some Motifs in Baudelaire' is an example of this.
36 See Gölz, 'Apostrophe's Double'.

also engage the latter as an interactive matrix and apparatus, and thus make strategic decisions regarding its design. In the translation of the first half of stanza 3, these layered repetitions manifest themselves very concretely. Millay published her translation in 1936. But at some later point, right underneath her own earlier translation, she pencilled in a retranslation of the first six lines of stanza 3.[37] She thus created a little petri dish for us to watch her retranslate her own earlier translation. A closer look at the two different versions shows that they can be precisely situated on the ladder of metalevels I have just sketched.

Millay's first (published) translation of those six lines reads as follows:

> See, their voyage past,
> To their moorings fast,
> On the still canals asleep,
> These big ships; to bring
> You some trifling thing
> They have braved the furious deep.

In Baudelaire, the vessels were merely sleeping. In Millay they are stuck — moored, tied down. Their travels are over, their voyage is history. The word 'vagabond' has disappeared entirely. The next three lines are tinted by irony or even sarcasm: all that journeying, all that bombastic effort to cross and overcome the 'furious deep' (of mirrors? of thought?) has failed to deliver the promised boatloads of exotic treasure, producing instead a mere 'trifling thing'. Even the rhymes 'past'/'fast' and 'bring'/'thing' chime in and parody a repetition that fails to produce any significant difference. By latching on to the most obvious reading, those readers/ships — 'to their moorings fast' — have gone nowhere in a hurry.

In its earlier version, then, Millay's translation articulates the second of the three reactions I mapped out above: the spell of absorption has already been broken, an aversion is developing, but the translation still gets stuck in mere irony or mockery. It runs into the impasse Baudelaire scripts for his readers.

Only in the retranslation, inserted by hand below the earlier printed translation, does Millay succeed in reshaping this most highly

---

37   See Joan St Clair Crane, 'Edna St. Vincent Millay's Afterthoughts on the Translation of Baudelaire', *Studies in Bibliography*, 29 (1976), pp. 382–86.

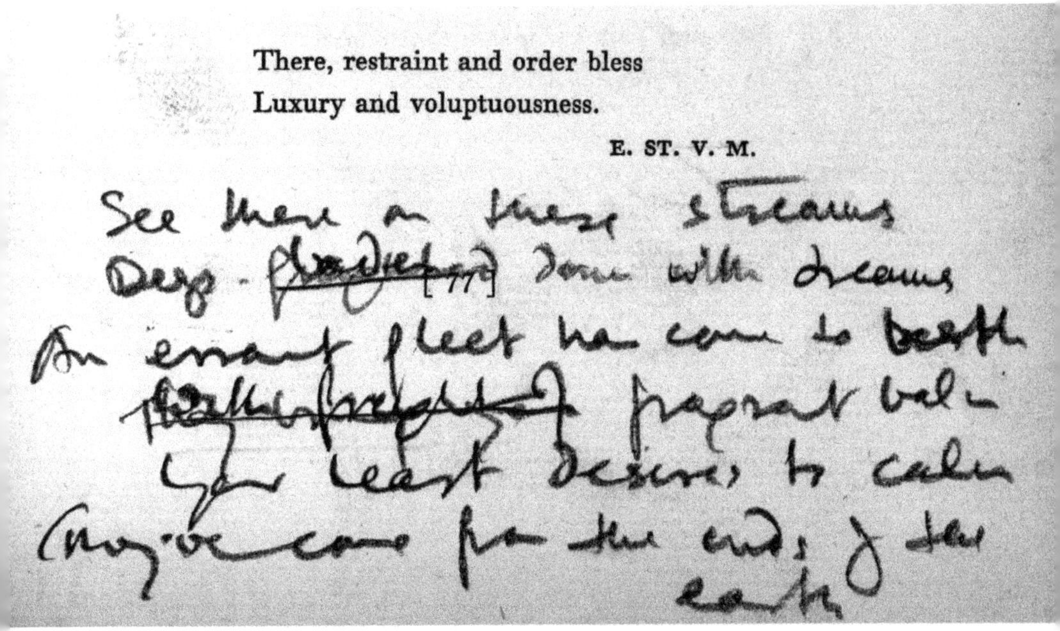

> There, restraint and order bless
> Luxury and voluptuousness.
>
> E. ST. V. M.

Figure 1. Millay's handwritten retranslation of the first six lines of stanza 3.

reflexive moment in the poem in a way that goes beyond diagnosing the problem. Only the retranslation reclaims its vagabond inclinations — and invites us to do the same (Figure 1):[38]

> See there on these streams
> Deep ~~freighted~~ laden down with dreams
> An errant fleet has come to berth
> ~~They bring you~~ With freight of fragrant balm
> Your least desires to calm
> They've come from the ends of the earth.

---

38 A small but significant formal feature registers the addition of another layer in this retranslation: only in this retranslation does the syllable count break out of the strict pattern of Baudelaire's stanzas (four pentasyllabic rhyming couplets, each followed by a seven-syllable line) by adding a syllable to all lines except for the first. The fact that reading and translation adds itself to the original is thus registered by the added syllables. Millay discusses the syllable count in her preface to Baudelaire, *Flowers of Evil*, trans. by Dillon and Millay, pp. v–xxxiv. Figures 1 and 2 are from the copy of the book in the University of Virginia Libraries, pp. 77 and 74 respectively.

The first thing Millay's line 'See *there* on *these* streams' does is reorient the indexicals to register a reflexive turn. 'See *there*' distances the text from our *here*. With that distancing, this reading unmoors itself from the representations offered in the text. It becomes fluid and uncontainable, as '*these* streams' of readerly awareness reflexively wash over the text, reopening it to change. Millay's first line no longer prefigures channels and vessels. Instead, the indexicals register the turn into reflexivity (from 'there' to 'these') and reopening of flow — 'these streams'. The word 'fleet' connotes an accumulation of many vessels rather than individual 'big ships'. It thus underscores the fact that assimilated readings tend to cluster — they can be herded into predictable places — while also hinting at their mercantile and even military functions. But the word 'fleet' also recalls the fleeting nature of what such readerly accumulations actually are made of. This mighty 'fleet' actually has nothing solid about it. It might dissipate at any moment. The adjective 'errant' similarly invokes the wandering that Baudelaire's verses aimed to neutralize, while also hinting that the readings that have 'come to berth' and given up their mobility may have made a mistake, an error. The fact that the errant fleet is 'laden down with dreams' emphasizes that assimilated readers are, ultimately, trapped by their own 'dreams' — their obedient visualizations reinforce a (lack of) imagination and self-awareness. If we read the poem aloud, however, we can hear in the word 'berth' the homophonous possibility of a new 'birth' — the moment when the homesick heart returns into itself and succeeds in converting the found language into its 'own dear native tongue'.

The two versions, Millay's printed translation and her handwritten retranslation, then, climb the ladder of increasing readerly reflexivity. Her earlier printed translation still remains, however resistantly, caught in the diagnosis of entrapment. Only her handwritten retranslation takes us to the next level and recovers its vagabond humour.

Lines 35–40: Baudelaire

Baudelaire begins the final section of the third stanza with a dash. According to French punctuation rules, this may signal that there is

a new speaker.[39] The description that follows is completely factual
and constative, as if from no perspective in particular. The setting suns
're-dress' (revêtent) fields, canals, and town — they place a layer of
'hyacinth and gold' over the landscape. And the whole world goes to
sleep:

> — Les soleils couchants
> Revêtent les champs,
> Les canaux, la ville entière,
> D'hyacinthe et d'or;
> Le monde s'endort
> Dans une chaude lumière.
>
> (— The setting suns
> Re-dress the fields,
> Canals, and the whole town
> In hyacinth and gold;
> The world falls asleep
> In a warm light.)

With those lines, Baudelaire's poem has arrived at its telos: the whole
world's going to sleep ('s'endort') is presented as a 'réalité accomplie'.[40]
'Couchants' is an adjective formed of the verb *coucher*. When it modi-
fies the word *soleil* (sun), it means to 'set' — 'the setting suns'. But there
is also a transitive version of the verb *coucher* that means 'to put to bed'.
Coucher les enfants, for example, means 'to bring the children to bed'.[41]
We can thus also read Baudelaire's 'soleils couchants' as 'suns' that put
those canals, fields, town, and finally the entire world to sleep. But
what are those suns? I would suggest that they are the various elements
— both metaphoric (prefigurations) and metonymic (indexicals) —
that serve to prefigure, align, and orient the perspectives of readers. A
new layer blankets or 're-dresses' the canals, fields, and city. That layer
is 'd'hyacinthe et d'or'. Of course, we can just read this as describing
the colours of the evening light. But Hyacinth, in Greek mythology,
is Apollo's lover and thus a figure associated with male–male desire.
'Gold' can be read as a gesture towards the function of the othered

---

39   I would like to acknowledge Marie Culpepper, who made this important point in my
     seminar on Baudelaire in the spring of 2020.
40   Brugmans, 'L'Invitation au voyage', p. 6.
41   *Couchant*, finally, can also mean 'crouching' — as a dog or lion might. The reflexive
     version *se coucher* means 'to go to sleep'.

feminine as object of exchange and universal equivalent. 'Hyacinth and gold', then, neatly sums up the two-pronged and gendered interpellative strategy of Baudelaire's text, which instals both assimilative and apotropaic traffic signs in the poetic 'fields', thus promoting the absorption of reading by polarizing the readership: the 'sister' is offered as a universal equivalent (gold) that facilitates the unselfconscious alignment with male homosocial desire.[42] With the last six lines, the poem declares its trajectory completed, its goal achieved: the whole world, everyone (*tout le monde* also means 'all people', 'everyone') has been put to sleep.

But why does Baudelaire mark off these last six lines as spoken by a new speaker? Who is that speaker? The poem's concluding lines are devoid of any indexicals, personal pronouns, or possessive adjectives. With the exception of the initial dash itself, all other traces of this new speaker are thoroughly effaced. The last six lines of the stanza are wrapped in an aperspectival, flat factuality. Who is it that could confirm that Baudelaire's strategy worked, that *tout le monde* has indeed lost consciousness, that everyone has in fact gone to sleep? Clearly, this confirmation can come neither from the poem itself nor from its implied 'speaker'. Rather, the confirmation must come from a reader or other iterator. But surely, in order to confirm that the entire world has gone to sleep, that person would have to be awake? As a matter of fact, they must not. What they have to do, rather, is accept the script the poem hands them, and repeat it somnambulantly, mechanically, unselfconsciously.

Lines 35–40: Millay

Millay, too, opens this last section of stanza three with a dash. In English, this horizontal mark does not signify a new speaker. Instead, the dash acquires significance because, in Millay's poem, it is a repetition. We recall that Millay added a dash in stanza 1 (at the end of line 3). This second dash now, together with the earlier one, creates an interior frame within the poem. The first three and last six lines are outside of

---

42   See Eve Kosofsky Sedgwick, *Between Men: English Literature and Male Homosocial Desire* (New York: Columbia University Press, 1985).

that inner frame, as transitional zones surrounding the interior framed by the two dashes. It is in these transitional zones that personal pronouns appear especially prominently ('me' and 'you' at the beginning, 'we' at the end). If the first dash, marking the entry into the inner frame, was followed by the word 'sleep', the second dash (in line 35) is immediately followed by the word 'now', which punctures Baudelaire's indexical-free, sleep-inducing sunset scenario with a wake-up call that brings us back into the present moment:

> — Now the sun goes down,
> Tinting dyke and town,
> Field, canal, all things in sight,
> Hyacinth and gold;
> All that we behold
> Slumbers in its ruddy light.

The descending 'sun' tints a 'dyke' — a barrier fortifying the canals — as well as town, field, and canal. The word also adds the feminine counterpart to the male homosocial implications of the word 'hyacinthe', restoring a gender symmetry that was missing in Baudelaire. But the final critical moment does not arrive until the last two lines of the poem, in which a first-person, actualizable, and ungendered 'we' concludes: 'All that we behold | Slumbers in its ruddy light.' Here, someone is indeed awake. Millay's last six lines present the landscape not (as in Baudelaire) from a quasi-objective non-perspective, but rather as seen by a 'we' that 'behold[s]' the text and perceives that slumber. This 'we' includes, in every iteration, *this* reader, the one who is reading or citing the poem *now*, and who hopefully has agreed to join Millay's lead and my own, as we have been thinking along with and re-minded her text. What sleeps are 'all things in sight' and 'all that we behold' — not we ourselves. We, rather, are now departing from the slumbering world of the poem, leaving it behind for other readers to re-mind it and wake up to themselves.

Barbara Johnson also comments on that dash in Baudelaire. She does not invoke its function in French punctuation — that of introducing a new speaker — but interprets it as a mark of an impersonal movement: Jacques Derrida's notion of 'spacing'. Writing, as continued *différance*, indeed cannot arrive in any specific present:

> In spite of the demonstratives ('*ces* canaux', '*ces* vaisseaux') and
> the present tenses ('ils viennent', 'le monde s'endort'), the trip's
> end-point seems curiously missing. More curiously still, this
> eclipse of the end-point is inscribed as such in the text by the
> use of a dash [...]. If the poem's language is thus organized
> around its disappearance, that disappearance turns out to be
> not an asymptotic limit external to the text — its end or origin
> — but its own necessary and inherent discontinuity, the very
> principle of its spacing, its articulation, and its rhythm.[43]

Johnson's reading of the dash as 'this eclipse of the end-point' precisely
articulates the effect of Baudelaire's poetics: readers repeat mechan-
ically, deferring to the text, and eclipsing awareness of their own
presence and actions. To any such self-effacing reading, 'spacing' will
continue to appear as the impersonal ongoing *différance* of writing in
general. But in fact, it is Johnson's reading itself that enacts this 'spacing'
by displacing and eliding another possible reading, one that could have
acknowledged *this* act of repetition in its irreducible singularity and
actuality. Johnson's text articulates this, too, with amazing precision:
'The truly unreachable utopian place, the place which is par excellence
unknowable, is not some faraway mysterious land, but the very place
where *one is*.'[44] By stopping just short of using an indexical such as *here*
or *I* to mark this place, Johnson obeys Baudelaire's prefiguration, which
systematically withholds open indexicals that would invite readers to
come to — to wake up to themselves.[45]

Baudelaire's poem works to create aura, that is, the appearance of
distance, by convincing its readers, no matter how close they may be,
to send their imaginations 'là-bas', to some faraway place. We are to
forget that we are *here*, repeating, translating, and, if need be, *rewriting*
the poem right before us. The dash is thus read in two incompatible
ways: either it marks the 'curious' and unfathomable 'eclipse' of the
very reading which itself enacts this 'spacing', over and over, by virtue
of remaining a mystery to itself; or, alternatively, it can alert us to the

---

43   Johnson, 'Poetry and its Double', pp. 39–40; emphasis in original.
44   Ibid., p. 41; emphasis in original.
45   For a related earlier argument, see Sabine I. Gölz, 'One Must Go Quickly from One
     Light into Another: Between Ingeborg Bachmann and Jacques Derrida', in *Borderwork:
     Feminist Engagements with Comparative Literature*, ed. by Margaret Higonnet (Ithaca,
     NY: Cornell University Press, 1994), pp. 207–23.

appearance of a new speaker — ourselves. The second reading is the *conditio sine qua non* for the development of a theoretical framework that could begin to describe the functioning of this metonymic shadow docket of mechanical ratifiers. For us to reclaim our own agency and to bring about change, therefore, we need to break with a central taboo of post-structuralist literary theory: we must learn to think the effects and potentialities of our own unrepresentable readerly presence. We are unrepeatable, but we do the repeating. The moored 'fleet' of normalized readers huddles in the centre of the normal distribution. But each one of us, again and again, can be the singular *one* who makes a difference.

REFRAIN

No discussion of Baudelaire's poem would be complete without attention to its refrain, which intervenes after each of the three stanzas, reassuring us again and again that there is nothing but order, beauty, luxury, and calm over there:

> Là, tout n'est qu'ordre et beauté,
> Luxe, calme et volupté.

> (There, all is but order, beauty,
> Luxury, calm, and voluptuousness.)

The refrain is of course, by definition, the clearest instance of a repeating pattern within the poem. And what it repeats is nothing but confirmation and ratification: all is in order ... There is, however, an intertextual connection that may change our perception of the refrain.

In a short article, M. Larroutis points out that there is a sentence in Honoré de Balzac's 1830 novella 'Gobseck' that reads like a subtext of the refrain of Baudelaire's 'L'Invitation au voyage': 'Tout était luxe et désordre, beauté sans harmonie' (All was luxury and disorder, beauty and disharmony).[46] Larroutis argues that Baudelaire appears to

---

46   Honoré de Balzac, 'Gobseck', in *La Comédie humaine*, ed. by Pierre-Georges Castex, 12 vols (Paris: Gallimard, 1976–81), II (1976), pp. 961–1013 (p. 972); Honoré de Balzac, 'Gobseck', trans. by Linda Asher, in *The Human Comedy: Selected Stories*, ed. by Peter Brooks (New York: New York Review Books, 2014), pp. 225–82 (p. 237). M. Larroutis, 'Une source de "L'Invitation au voyage"', *Revue d'histoire littéraire de la France*, 57.4 (1957), pp. 585–86.

respond to Balzac's line in a way that implies an opposition: *here* all is *disorder*, while *there*, all is *order*.[47] The sentence identified by Larroutis occurs in a scene, set at the moment of noon, in which Balzac's title figure, the usurer Gobseck, intrudes into the bedroom of Countess Madame de Restaud to collect a debt. That decisive scene — Gobseck's report of his entry into the countess's bedroom — is embedded in a frame narrative in which the narrator, a lawyer named Derville, repeats that report. Every time the narrator says 'I', therefore, we have in effect a double narrator — and a doubled 'I'. This alignment between the two 'I's also aligns their gazes. That fact is made explicit in another key sentence in Balzac that immediately precedes the bedroom narrative. Derville prefaces his entire repetition of Gobseck's narrative by noting that the latter passes his gaze to him: '*Là*, le vieillard me jeta son regard blanc' (*There*, the old man threw me his blank gaze).[48] That transfer of the blank gaze occurs after Gobseck's hypothetical description of how women in financial distress might try to appeal to him. Such distressed women would

> '…me prodiguer des paroles caressantes, me supplier peut-être; et moi …' Là, le vieillard me jeta son regard blanc. 'Et moi, inébranlable! reprit-il. Je suis là comme un vengeur, j'apparais comme un remords. Laissons les hypothèses. J'arrive.'
>
> ('…use that cajoling tone peculiar to an endorser of notes, murmur endearments, plead, even beg. And I' — there the old man threw me his blank gaze — 'I am unshakeable!' He continued: 'I am the Avenger, I am the embodiment of Remorse. Well, enough imaginings. I arrive at the house.')[49]

The critical passing on of the 'white' or 'blank' gaze, then, intervenes right between two occurrences of the first-person pronoun 'moi'. The first 'et moi …' is followed by an ellipsis that marks the moment when the gaze passes between the two narrators. It is eclipsed from the text because it occurs outside of it. This moment is unrepresentable. After

---

47 'L'adverbe "là", en tête du refrain, paraît impliquer une opposition. Il semble que le poète ait laissé sous-entendue une partie de sa pensée: (Ici) tout est luxe et désordre, beauté sans harmonie, à quoi répondent les deux vers' (Larroutis, 'Source', p. 586).

48 Balzac, 'Gobseck', p. 971; my translation and emphasis.

49 Ibid.; trans. by Asher, p. 235 (modified here; Asher has 'here the old man turned his pale gaze on me').

that exchange, another 'moi' returns, which only now has become 'unshakeable', impervious to the appeals of women: 'Et moi, inébranlable!' Following this critical exchange, which aligns the two narrators against those hypothetical women, a 'je' has been constituted, and the sentences move into the present tense: 'Je suis là comme un vengeur.' And this doubled, unshakeable 'I' aims to arrive in our present. Yet 'j'arrive' means 'I am *almost* there'. It stops just short of an actual arrival. The function of that 'blank gaze', then, is to inure both narrators against being moved by the words of women. The word 'là', which marks the moment of exchange and homosocial alignment, however, is now no longer 'over there', but rather marks the place in time when, again and again, that gaze is passed on to yet another apprentice and iterator. Balzac's scene thus prefigures the very intertextual apprenticeship by virtue of which a Baudelaire receives that gaze — and by which he will pass it on to his own apprentices in turn.

Millay's Retranslation of the Refrain

The refrain is the only other passage in this poem for which Millay added a pencilled retranslation. The published version rendered the refrain like this:

> There, restraint and order bless
> Luxury and voluptuousness.

To my perception, these two lines feel strained and conflicted. 'Restraint' and 'order' are in tension with the claim of 'luxury and voluptuousness', which suggest excess and abandon. Even stranger, then, that the former should 'bless' the latter. That translation seems to testify above all to Millay's still ongoing struggle with Baudelaire's poem.

In the retranslation, the traces of tension have disappeared. If anything, its affirmation that all is in order 'there' is less qualified and more definitive than in Baudelaire. Where he has a privative 'nothing but order' ('Là, tout n'est qu'ordre et beauté'), Millay's retranslation affirms straightforwardly that 'all is order'. And where Baudelaire had a more ambiguous 'calme' (which, given the troubled skies in stanza 1, may well be followed by a storm), Millay's final version achieves 'peace' (Figure 2):

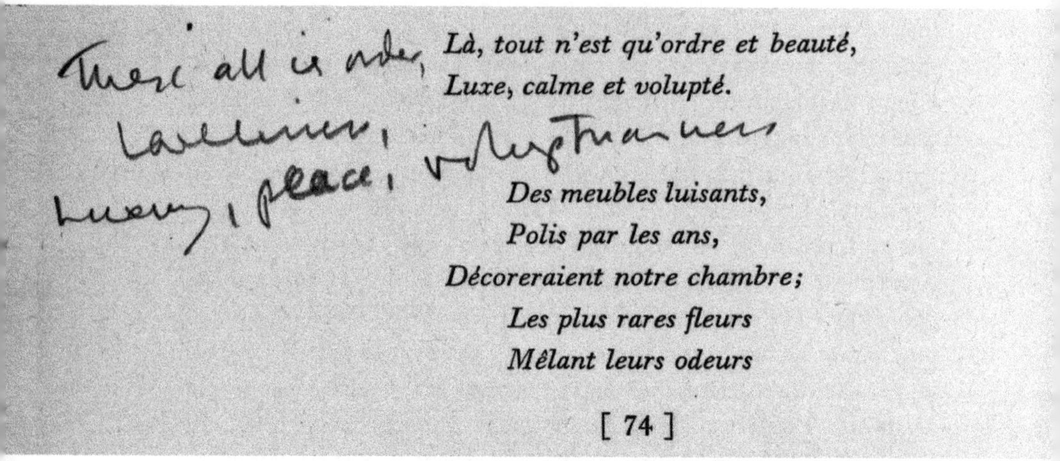

There all is order,   *Là, tout n'est qu'ordre et beauté,*
Loveliness,   *Luxe, calme et volupté.*
Luxury, peace, voluptuousness

Des meubles luisants,
Polis par les ans,
Décoreraient notre chambre;
Les plus rares fleurs
Mélant leurs odeurs

[74]

Figure 2. Millay's handwritten retranslation of the refrain.

There, all is order, loveliness,
Luxury, peace, voluptuousness.

Millay jotted down the new version of the refrain next to the French original in the bilingual edition. We can speculate that the word 'there' in the second version of the refrain confirms the final success of her own retranslation and the 'peace' that her repair of the poem grants us.

CONCLUSIONS AND OUTLOOK

Millay's retranslation systematically deconstructs the hegemonic poetics that governs Baudelaire's poem — and that has been instilled in all of us. Her poem coheres in terms of an alternative relationship to written language. This different relationship to language is what should interest us, and it is what Millay's poem can help us develop.

The Anglo-European literary and poetic canon has profoundly shaped another canon: that of our theories of literature, language, reading, and translation. Literary theories have inadvertently modelled themselves on the works they take as their object of study. As a result, they tend to conform to and function within the specific point of view that those works pass on to them. Our very conceptions of poetry or literature, of what it means to read or translate, of how texts, language, and signification work, are thus scripted by that canon and assimilated to its narrowed perspective. The foundation of that apparatus is not simply the exclusion of women. Rather, as I have tried to show, the apparatus uses feminization as a strategy to control and discourage readerly self-awareness as such. It is set up to flush such awareness — and with it the very preconditions for targeted strategic change — out of the system. The hegemony of the 'great works' will continue as long as readers and translators remain self-effacingly subservient to them. Millay's retranslation can help us discover a vantage point from which a fundamental rethinking of those theoretical models can begin. I will conclude with a brief sketch of what this might involve.

Literature and Life Transform Each Other

Henri Meschonnic is a rare translation theorist who points out that how we read and translate is critically informed by our theories of language. They make us perceive texts in certain ways — and lead us to neglect other possible perceptions. Meschonnic goes so far as to argue that in translation (but also, we may add, in reading) the theory of language that guides our actions is 'the major and even only problem': 'Without knowing it, when we think we are translating a text it is our own representation of language that we are showing, and that interposes itself between the text to be translated and the intention of the translator.'[50] The challenge of reading translations, therefore, 'consists of recognizing which representation of language is at work'. Meschonnic specifically critiques the limiting effect of a theory of language that is centred on the sign: 'if we think language is in keeping with the sign', then 'our whole attention [is] turned to meaning, since the sign knows nothing else'.[51] What we overlook as a result, he argues, are what he calls 'poetics', 'rhythm', 'voice' — and, most importantly, the ways in which language and life transform each other.

> The poem, I repeat again and again, because it must be said again, I define this as the transformation of a form of language

---

50   Henri Meschonnic, *Ethics and Politics of Translating*, trans. by Pier-Pascale Boulanger (Amsterdam: Benjamins, 2011), p. 57.

51   Ibid., p. 58.

by a form of life and the transformation of a form of life by a
form of language. Hence a poem is the maximum relationship
between language and life. But a human life.[52]

Meschonnic is helpful because he is a rare theorist who draws atten-
tion to these processes of mutual transformation, and thus offers a
starting point for a theoretical enquiry into how exactly this mutual
transformation of language and life can be understood. To such an
enquiry I hope to have contributed with this essay. As I have tried
to show, Baudelaire's poem is an apparatus that works towards having
texts script life. Millay's (re)translation revises his poetics to reopen
the inverse possibility — for our life to transform language. If the im-
portance of her achievement — and many comparable ones by other
(predominantly, though not exclusively) women writers — seems to
have gone unnoticed, this is precisely because the hegemony of that
poetics of control extends to our theories of language and literature
as well. For most existing critical approaches, her alternative poetics
remains systematically unreadable. Our critical apparatus, too, needs
to be repaired.

---

52   Ibid., p. 137.

Gestural Communities
Lyric and the Suspension of Action
FRANCESCO GIUSTI

INTRODUCTION

In recent years, a variety of parameters for defining lyric poetry and its workings have been proposed from different perspectives. Lyric is often considered as a particularly memorable, repeatable, and shareable language that makes itself available for reperformance in various contexts, sometimes with an emphasis on the transnational potential of its circulation.[1] Moving away from approaches based on the circulation of diction and form, I argue that a notion of *gesture* developed from the reflections of Bertolt Brecht, Walter Benjamin, and Giorgio Agamben is helpful in elucidating the language and discourse structures that make the re-enactment of lyric possible across time, contexts, and languages.[2] A return to the exchange between Brecht and Benjamin

---

1   Jonathan Culler, *Theory of the Lyric* (Cambridge, MA: Harvard University Press, 2015). On 'poetic kitsch', see Daniel Tiffany, *My Silver Planet: A Secret History of Poetry and Kitsch* (Baltimore, MD: Johns Hopkins University Press, 2014). On transnational circulation, see Jahan Ramazani, *A Transnational Poetics* (Chicago, IL: University of Chicago Press, 2009); Jahan Ramazani, *Poetry in a Global Age* (Chicago, IL: University of Chicago Press, 2020).

2   Francesco Giusti, 'Transcontextual Gestures: A Lyric Approach to the World of Literature', in *The Work of World Literature*, ed. by Francesco Giusti and Benjamin Lewis Robinson (Berlin: ICI Berlin Press, 2021), pp. 75–103.

in the 1930s is crucial for restoring the historicity of gestures and the political nature of their re-enactment, which are partially obscured in Agamben's reconsideration of the concept. The notion of gesture has been widely discussed in theatre, dance, and performance studies, but this article begins by tracing the specific connections of gesture with lyric poetry in Brecht's and Benjamin's writings in order to refine the notion and offer it as a critical tool.[3]

Certain lyric gestures, recurrent through the centuries, come to mind: exhortation, prayer, praise, and lament, among others. All of them, moreover, are predicated on and made possible by deixis: the linguistic gesture of *pointing to* something external to the utterance or text. Indeed, scholars have argued that, in lyric poetry, readers are invited to assume the position of the speaking 'I', or sometimes of the addressed 'you', in each 'here' and 'now' of reading.[4] As Jonathan Culler maintains, the dissemination of lyric is based on the re-enactment of its language by individuals in different contexts, with diverse meanings and to a variety of ends. Lyric poetry therefore emerges as closely intertwined with community formation and its politics, from the choral lyric of Ancient Greece to the exchange of sonnets in the Middle Ages, to the dissemination of poems through social media in recent years. Here, an exploration of how both linguistic gestures and cultural gestures work in lyric poetry will lead to the development of an idea of *gestural community* based not on pre-existing identities, as is often the case in explanations of community formation, but rather on the shareability and repeatability of gestures.

---

3   See *Migrations of Gesture*, ed. by Carrie Noland and Sally Ann Ness (Minneapolis: University of Minnesota Press, 2008); Carrie Noland, *Agency and Embodiment: Performing Gestures/Producing Culture* (Cambridge, MA: Harvard University Press, 2009). See also Vadim Keylin, *Participatory Sound Art: Technologies, Aesthetics, Politics* (Singapore: Palgrave Macmillan Singapore, 2023), pp. 115–35.

4   Culler, *Theory of the Lyric*, p. 187. Tied to actual subjects, the idea can also be found in Helen Vendler, *Poems, Poets, Poetry: An Introduction and Anthology* (Boston, MA: Bedford/St. Martin's, 1997), pp. xl–xli.

WHAT IS A GESTURE?

To clarify the notion of gesture, it is helpful to go back to Brecht's words as reported by Benjamin in his *Notes from Svendborg, Summer 1934*. Conversing about Benjamin's essay 'The Author as Producer' with its author, Brecht brings poetry into the discussion to 'improve' Benjamin's 'criticism of proletarian writers of the Becher type'. Brecht does this by comparing Johannes R. Becher's poem 'Ich sage ganz offen' (1933) with, on the one hand, a didactic poem he himself had written for the actress Carola Neher and, on the other hand, with 'Le Bateau ivre' (1871) by Arthur Rimbaud. Reporting Brecht's words, Benjamin writes:

> 'I have taught Carola Neher a variety of things', he explained. 'She has not only learned to act, but, for example, she has learned how to wash herself. Up to then, she had washed so as not to be dirty. That was completely beside the point. I taught her how to wash her face. She acquired such skill in this that I wanted to make a film of her doing it. But nothing came of it because I was not making a picture at the time, and she did not want to be filmed by anyone else. That didactic poem was a model. Every learner was expected to take the place of his "self". When Becher says "I", he regards himself (since he's president of the Union of the Proletarian Revolutionary Writers of Germany) as exemplary. The only thing is that no one wants to emulate him. They simply conclude that he's pleased with himself.'[5]

In order to teach Neher how to wash her face in the sense of performing a gesture, not just a goal-oriented action whose purpose is 'not to be dirty', Brecht writes a didactic poem that could work as a model for the actress. A basic definition of gesture is provided here: *gesture* is what is left of an *action* when it is freed from the purpose usually attached to it in ordinary social life. Gesture, moreover, seems to have an interart and intermedial character: Brecht writes a didactic lyric poem to teach the actress how to turn a private action into a theatrical gesture, and the

---

5   Walter Benjamin, 'Notes from Svendborg, Summer 1934', trans. by Rodney Living-stone, in *Selected Writings*, 4 vols (Cambridge, MA: Harvard University Press, 1996–2003), II, part 2: *1931–1934*, ed. by Michael W. Jennings, Howard Eiland, and Gary Smith (2005), pp. 783–91 (pp. 783–84).

actress reaches such a level of perfection in performing it that it can be filmed. This gesture can be embodied in a poem, such that the poem itself becomes a model for people who want to perform the gesture in their own contexts. Brecht adds something more, however: in order to work as a model, the poem should not present an exemplary individual to be emulated by the reader, as in the case of Becher's poem; instead, it has to make room for every 'learner' so that each learner can 'take the place of his "self"'.

The following comparison with Rimbaud's 'Le Bateau ivre' presents a different, but related, problem:

> On the other hand, Brecht compared Becher's poem with Rim-baud's. In the latter, he maintained that Marx and Lenin — if they had read it — would have detected the great historical movement of which it is an expression. They would have realized very clearly that it describes not just the eccentric stroll of an individual but the flight, the vagabondage, of a human being who can no longer bear to be confined within the limits of a class which — with the Crimean War and the Mexican adventure — has started to open up exotic parts of the globe to its own commercial interests. It was completely impossible to import into the model of the proletarian fighter the gesture of the footloose vagabond who leaves his own concerns to chance and turns his back on society.[6]

What Rimbaud's famous poem offers readers and future poets is not just 'the eccentric stroll of an individual' but the gesture of 'the flight, the vagabondage'. What the poem is about, according to Brecht, is not just the transcription of the experience of a particular individual (which, one might assume, might be irrelevant to others) but a gesture that was shareable in a certain epoch and representative of that epoch. Lyric poems, or at least good lyric poems, for Brecht, seem to have a singular capacity to isolate a gesture by freeing it from the meaning and purpose the corresponding action would have in its social context, to give that gesture an exemplary value by detaching it from the author or subject as a particular individual, and to offer it to present and future readers. Yet Rimbaud's case also allows Brecht to comment upon the historical and political viability of gestures. The

---

6   Ibid., p. 784.

flight Rimbaud describes was practicable for the French poet and other members of his class in their sociohistorical situation — where such a gesture reflected the position of a human being in the production process of the time — but would be 'impossible to import' into the model of the proletarian fighter'. Gestures, as embodied in poems, are historically situated. Rimbaud's poem presents readers with a gesture that was valid in its context, but according to Brecht, it is impracticable in the current circumstances. In 1934, the poetic gesture of flight has lost its historical viability to the extent that it cannot be considered as functional for the human being to whose definition Brecht intends his work to contribute. Although they cannot be erased but are preserved in their potency and transmitted to future generations by the poetic tradition, gestures can be challenged and even rejected by those subsequent readers. Therefore, choosing to re-enact or not to re-enact a certain gesture in one's own context is a political decision.

Let us return to the poem Brecht gives as an example in his conversation with Benjamin and use it to explore how history intervenes by altering the conditions of possibility of gesture. The dynamic can be observed in its evolution in the three poems Brecht composed for Carola Neher: the two versions of 'Rat an die Schauspielerin C. N.' (probably 1930 and 1956) and 'Das Waschen' (1937). In this triad, Joyce Crick traces a progressive change related to poetic authority and the relationship between poetry and action: from the intimate situation in which the poet displays his authority observable in the 1930 text; to a return to the instructions given years earlier, in a moment of powerlessness in the face of forces acting in the world outside the poem; to a retreat in the 1956 text, which can only repropose the gesture of 1930 with substantial modifications.[7]

According to Crick's reconstruction, the first version of 'Rat an die Schauspielerin C. N.', to which Brecht refers in the conversation with Benjamin, was written around 1930 'following the height of Brecht's short-lived success in the Berlin theatre, particularly as the dramatist of *Die Dreigroschenoper*', a success shared by the actress.[8] The six-line

---

7   Joyce Crick, 'Power and Powerlessness: Brecht's Poems to Carola Neher', *German Life and Letters*, 53.3 (2000), pp. 314–24.

8   Ibid., p. 317.

poem opens with the imperative 'Erfrische dich, Freundin' (Refresh yourself, my friend) and, from what seems to be a position of authority, goes on to give its addressee instructions on how to perform the act of washing her face both for herself and in an exemplary manner.[9] The theatrical context is clearly evoked, and the addressee of the instructions is associated with her role as an actress: while washing her face, she should read the difficult lines of her part from a page hanging on the wall. The actress, however, is not identified as a particular individual being elevated as a model to be imitated. Her initials appear in the title, but, as Crick observes, 'the poem is thus poised between the personal-referential of the title and the exemplary of the last line'.[10] This didactic poem (Lehrgedicht)[11] aims to teach the actress, whom it addresses with 'Freundin', thereby establishing a relationship of relative intimacy, how to turn a private action into a theatrical gesture. Washing one's face is presented as a gesture to be performed before going onstage — the actress, after all, has to rehearse her part — but there must also be theatricality offstage. Such an everyday gesture is autonomized in its isolation from a more complex action, thus assuming value in itself and not as part of a goal-oriented sequence with a contextual meaning; it is also subjected to estrangement by being positioned on a threshold of indistinction between real life and theatrical performance, which the reference to the lines highlights.[12] The poem gives the actress directions on how to wash her face in such a way that, as Brecht notes in his conversation with Benjamin, it could be filmed. The gesture that the actress performs for herself thus takes on exemplary value, and, to achieve this condition, as Brecht explains in the same conversation, the action must be detached from its immediate purpose, be removed from the circumstantial needs of the person called Carola Neher ('not to be dirty'), in order to become a gesture that finds its purpose and pleasure

---

9   Bertolt Brecht, Werke: Große kommentierte Berliner und Frankfurter Ausgabe, ed. by Werner Hecht and others, 30 vols (Berlin: Aufbau Verlag; Frankfurt a.M.: Suhrkamp, 1988–97), xiv: Gedichte 4 (1993), p. 361; my translation.

10   Crick, 'Power and Powerlessness', p. 317.

11   See Klaus Schuhmann, Der Lyriker Bertolt Brecht 1913–1933 (Munich: dtv, 1971), pp. 330–42.

12   On gesture and estrangement in Brecht and Benjamin, see Fredric Jameson, Brecht and Method (London: Verso, 1999); Samuel Weber, Benjamin's -abilities (Cambridge, MA: Harvard University Press, 2008), pp. 85–114.

in its own performance. Only in this way can it become historically shareable. When Brecht reread 'Rat an die Schauspielerin C. N.' in the conversation in Svendborg, 'history intruded upon the poem'.[13] As Crick explains, after Hitler's rise to power, both were in exile — the poet in Denmark and the actress in Moscow — and the poem is reread in terms of didactic function, and the comparison with the model offered by Becher is situated in the context of the directives on social realism promulgated at the first Congress of Soviet Writers in 1934.

In the 1937 poem 'Das Waschen', history intrudes again and the verses of 1930 return as a memory in a context which, despite the few years separating them, is radically changed. Neher is imprisoned, and 'the authoritative poet's voice of the "Lehrgedicht" gives way to an "Ich" without a role'.[14] The poems is structured around the gap between the past, 'Als ich dir vor Jahren zeigte | Wie du dich waschen solltest in der Frühe' (When I showed you years ago | how you should wash in the morning), and the present, 'Jetzt, höre ich, du sollst im Gefängnis sein' (Now, I hear, you must be in prison).[15] The self-quotation exhibits all the precariousness of both gestures — that of face-washing as well as the exhortation enacted in the poem — in the new context. The intrusion of history moulds the poem: if 'years ago' it was possible to show the actress how to wash her face in the morning, 'now' communication has been interrupted. The letters the 'I' wrote for her have gone unanswered, and the friends he asked about her remained silent. The 'I', unable to do anything for her, can only wonder whether there might be other good and exemplary gestures that the woman is performing for herself now:

[...] Wie
Mag dein Morgen sein? Wirst du noch etwas tun für dich?
Hoffnungsvoll und verantwortlich
Mit guten Bewegungen, vorbildlichen?

---

13   Crick, 'Power and Powerlessness', p. 318.
14   Ibid., p. 321.
15   Brecht, *Werke*, xiv, p. 360; my translation.

([...] How
Will your tomorrow be? Will you still do something for yourself?
Hopeful and responsible
With good gestures, exemplary?)[16]

As Crick observes, in this situation of helplessness, the poem evokes
the memory of more human circumstances and the poetic gesture
changes: it is no longer direct exhortation and teaching, but the send-
ing of a message to a distant addressee.[17] Preserving the memory of
gestures, their historical circumstances, and their political value is a
crucial function of poetry.

According to Crick, it was when revisiting the 1930 poem for
publication in the first volume of his verse published in Germany after
his return from exile, the selection *Bertolt Brechts Gedichte und Lieder*,
edited by Peter Suhrkamp (1956), that Brecht composed the variant
of 'Rat an die Schauspielerin C. N.' that would be published for the
first time in the edition of his *Gedichte* edited by Elisabeth Hauptmann
in 1961.[18] In the 1956 variant, 'Freundin' becomes 'Schwester', which
is 'the name Brecht habitually gave his former lovers'.[19] The gesture
of washing one's face remains, along with the objects it requires (the
copper bowl, the bits of ice, the rough towel), but the addressee is no
longer identified as an actress: the exhortation to read the lines of her
part is replaced by a more generic one to glance at a loved book. Theatre
has now disappeared, and the gesture is more private than professional:
the Brechtian association of beauty and usefulness is retained, but from
a perspective of resignation. The gesture seems to have an effect only on
the daily life of the woman, not on a wider public, and the poem ends
with the words 'So beginne | Einen schönen und nützlichen Tag' ('May
you thus begin | A beautiful and useful day').[20] The twenty-six years
that separate the first 'Rat an die Schauspielerin C. N.' from its 1956
version show how the gesture of washing one's face can be cited in the
later poem, detached from its initial historical context, and repurposed

---

16   Ibid.; my translation.
17   Crick, 'Power and Powerlessness', pp. 322–23.
18   Bertolt Brecht, *Gedichte*, ed. by Elisabeth Hauptmann, 10 vols (Frankfurt a.M.:
     Suhrkamp, 1960–76; Berlin: Aufbau Verlag, 1961–78), III: *1930–1933* (1961), p. 159;
     my translation.
19   Crick, 'Power and Powerlessness', p. 323.
20   Brecht, *Gedichte*, III, p. 159; my translation.

in the new context. Gesture, indeed, needs to be *quotable*, and, as Benjamin affirms, 'quoting a text entails interrupting its context'.[21] As Samuel Weber explains, gesture gives form because, while interrupting an 'ongoing sequence', it

> fixes it by enclosing it in a relatively determined space, one with a discernible 'beginning' and 'end'. But at the same time, the closure brought about by gesture remains caught up in that from which it has partially extricated itself: in the 'living flux' of a certain temporality.[22]

Benjamin ascribes a dialectical dimension to the tension embodied in gesture, and, Weber comments, 'the "fixation" it establishes through its interruption of an intentional, goal-directed movement toward meaning and totality remains singularly ex-tended, defined by and as the tension of separation and suspension'.[23]

This notion of gesture bears similarities with Giorgio Agamben's idea of gesture, in which 'nothing is being produced or acted, but rather something is being endured and supported'.[24] Gesture, once again, is not a means to an end. The exploration of its conception in Brecht and Benjamin, however, should have clarified an aspect that is not always clear in Agamben, namely that gestures are not ahistorical and that those transmitted by poems from the past — even one's own poems, as in Brecht's case — need to be recognized and evaluated in the light of the conditions of the present in order to assess their viability in the new context. It is precisely insofar as gesture is both historically situated and transhistorically, or transcontextually,[25] transferable that it is useful for considering the dialectic between historicity and transhistoricity that characterizes a lyric poem as language that happens as an event in each 'now' of reading, as Culler argues.[26]

---

21   Walter Benjamin, 'What Is Epic Theatre? (II)', trans. by Harry Zohn, in *Selected Writings, IV: 1938–1940*, ed. by Howard Eiland and Michael W. Jennings (2003), pp. 302–09 (p. 305).

22   Weber, *Benjamin's -abilities*, p. 100.

23   Ibid., p. 103.

24   Giorgio Agamben, 'Notes on Gesture', in *Means without End: Notes on Politics*, trans. by Vincenzo Binetti and Cesare Casarino (Minneapolis: University of Minnesota Press, 2000), pp. 49–61 (p. 56).

25   Giusti, 'Transcontextual Gestures'.

26   Culler, *Theory of the Lyric*, pp. 283–95.

THE SUSPENSION OF ACTION

Lyric poetry has quite a significant presence in contemporary philoso-
phy, especially in the context of reflections on community formation.
Yet, unlike other philosophers, Agamben does not seem to be particu-
larly concerned with the polysemy and supposed opacity of language
in modern poetry when it comes to thought on community. He more
often turns his attention to medieval poetry (Dante Alighieri, Guido
Cavalcanti, and the troubadours) and to the poets of his own time,
such as Giorgio Caproni, who at the peak of his grief for the death of
his mother retrieves the medieval form of the Cavalcantian *ballata* to
voice his mourning in poetry.[27] Opposing psychological readings of
the cycle Caproni devoted to his mother, 'Versi livornesi', published
in *Il seme del piangere* (1959), Agamben writes in a piece significantly
titled 'Expropriated Manner':

> One cannot, however, grasp the poetic task that is fulfilled
> here as long as one considers this poetry in the context of
> the psychological and biographical question of the incestuous
> sublimation of the mother–son relationship — which is to say,
> as long as one does not recognize the anthropological change
> that takes place in these verses. For here there are neither
> figures of memory nor even *amor de lonh*. Rather, love, in a kind
> of temporal (and hence not merely spatial, as in the Dolce Stil
> Novo poets) shamanism, encounters *for the first time* its love
> object in another time.[28]

Caproni performs what Agamben calls an 'anthropological gesture',
which entails some sort of expropriation and somehow contributes to
the endless 'anthropogenesis' of the human. Poetry both makes this
expropriation or disappropriation possible and exposes it.

---

27 Francesco Giusti, 'Mourning Over her Image: The Re-enactment of Lyric Gestures in
   Giorgio Caproni's "Versi livornesi"', in *A Gaping Wound: Mourning in Italian Poetry*, ed.
   by Adele Bardazzi, Francesco Giusti, and Emanuela Tandello (Cambridge: Legenda,
   2022), pp. 47–70.

28 Giorgio Agamben, 'Expropriated Manner', in *The End of the Poem: Studies in Poetics*,
   trans. by Daniel Heller-Roazen (Stanford, CA: Stanford University Press, 1999), pp.
   87–101 (pp. 94–95; emphasis in original).

Agamben detects two different ontologies in the Western philosophical tradition: the ontology of the indicative, or apophantic assertion, which governs philosophy and science, and the ontology of the imperative, or non-apophantic speech, which governs religion, law, and magic.[29] According to the Aristotelian distinction in *De interpretatione* (17a 1–7) to which Agamben refers, non-apophantic speech is speech that cannot be said to be true or false, because it does not manifest the being or not being of something in this world. Command, prayer, and exhortation, which are so widespread in lyric poetry, belong to this type of speech. As Jahan Ramazani remarks,

> as speech acts directed to an other, yet an other more veiled than a human interlocutor, poetry and prayer function simultaneously as acts of address, albeit partly suspended (hence address modulating into apostrophe), and as forms of meta-address, or images of voicing, because of the decontextualization of address from normal lines of human communication.[30]

In her influential essay 'Apostrophe, Animation, and Abortion', Barbara Johnson mobilizes an understanding of apostrophe that emphasizes its powers of animation: 'The fact that apostrophe allows one to animate the inanimate, the dead, or the absent implies that whenever a being is apostrophized, it is thereby automatically animated, anthropomorphized, "person-ified".'[31] Discussing the final rhetorical question in Shelley's 'Ode to the West Wind', however, she acknowledges the suspension of the animating power ascribed to apostrophe:

---

29 Giorgio Agamben, 'What Is a Command?', in *Creation and Anarchy: The Work of Art and the Religion of Capitalism*, trans. by Adam Kotsko (Stanford, CA: Stanford University Press, 2019), pp. 51–65.

30 Jahan Ramazani, *Poetry and its Others: News, Prayer, Song, and the Dialogue of Genres* (Chicago, IL: University of Chicago Press, 2014), pp. 128–29.

31 Barbara Johnson, 'Apostrophe, Animation, and Abortion', *Diacritics*, 16.1 (1986), pp. 28–47 (p. 34). Following Culler and de Man, Johnson's essay begins with the association of apostrophe and lyric voice; cf. Jonathan Culler, 'Apostrophe', in *The Pursuit of Signs: Semiotics, Literature, Deconstruction*, 2nd edn (London: Routledge, 2001), pp. 149–71; Paul de Man, 'Lyrical Voice in Contemporary Theory', in *Lyric Poetry: Beyond New Criticism*, ed. by Chaviva Hošek and Patricia Parker (Ithaca, NY: Cornell University Press, 1985), pp. 55–72. See also Culler, *Theory of the Lyric*, pp. 211–43; William Waters, *Poetry's Touch: On Lyric Address* (Ithaca, NY: Cornell University Press, 2003).

Yet because this clincher is expressed in the form of a rhetorical question, it expresses natural certainty by means of a linguistic device that mimics no natural structure and has no stable one-to-one correspondence with a meaning. The rhetorical question, in a sense, leaves the poem in a state of suspended animation. But that, according to the poem, is the state of maximum potential.[32]

Ramazani's definition of apostrophe as a 'partly suspended' act of address is related to the state of 'suspended animation' in which, according to Johnson, Shelley's poem is left. More than animating the inanimate by an act of address, lyric poetry can suspend that act and leave it in its potential. Discussing Johnson's work on apostrophe and free indirect discourse, Lauren Berlant writes:

In her poetics of indirection, each of these two rhetorical modes is shaped by the ways a writing subjectivity conjures other ones so that, in a performance of fantasmatic intersubjectivity, the writer gains superhuman observational authority, enabling a performance of being that is made possible by the proximity of the object.[33]

Yet Berlant links 'this aesthetic process' to 'the optimism of attachment':

Apostrophe is thus an indirect, unstable, physically impossible but phenomenologically vitalizing movement of rhetorical animation that permits subjects to suspend themselves in the optimism of a potential occupation of the same psychic space of others, the objects of desire who make you possible (by having some promising qualities, but also by not being there).[34]

If apostrophe is vitalizing, for Berlant, it is not because it enacts the power of poetry to animate the inanimate but rather because it 'permits subjects to suspend themselves', a suspension that is optimistic because it in turn leaves subjects in a potential intersubjectivity. Referring to the work of Tim Dean and Leo Bersani, Berlant adds: 'Like Johnson's work on projection, their focus is on the optimism of attachment, and

32   Johnson, 'Apostrophe, Animation, and Abortion', pp. 31–32.
33   Lauren Berlant, *Cruel Optimism* (Durham, NC: Duke University Press, 2011), p. 25.
34   Ibid., p. 26.

is often itself optimistic about the negations and extensions of personhood that forms of suspended intersubjectivity demand from the lover/reader.'[35] Animation and attribution of personhood are actions that apostrophe can potentially perform, but in the poem, apostrophe is suspended in a gesture. Within the poem, apostrophe can only *gesture toward* its addressee.

When Virginia Jackson discusses Johnson's and Berlant's approaches to apostrophe, the crucial effects of this suspension appear to be lost. She does so against the backdrop of Culler's and Paul de Man's equation of apostrophe with lyric, or more precisely, with what, according to her, is the 'lyricized idea of poetry' that Culler and de Man have endorsed. In this context, Jackson asks a key question: 'what happens when the rhetorical questions that apostrophe poses are literalized?' — that is to say, when they are read as 'lyric' in her sense of replacing 'the genre of the poem with the genre of the person', thus constructing the 'lyricized poetics of universal personal representation'.[36] The question, however, is relevant only insofar as the apostrophe is literalized, in other words, if the poem is 'lyricized' by reading it as the expression of a personal voice representative of a gendered and racialized identity, or, one might say, when the poem is performed and thus actualized in a particular context. Jackson points out that 'by creating an illusion of intersubjectivity (what Tucker calls "the intersubjective confirmation of the self"), apostrophic address facilitates the metapragmatic subsumption of a variety of poetic speech genres into a lyricized genre identified with and by the two-in-one apostrophic speaker'.[37] Yet, according to her understanding of 'lyricization', this is only true if the 'illusion of intersubjectivity' is taken for real, or, more precisely, for the illusion of a person. If taken in its suspension, apostrophe only offers a gesture to which readers are exposed. According to Brecht's observations on Rimbaud, turning that gesture into an action, giving a particular context to the poem and an identity to the speaker, is a political choice.

35   Ibid., p. 27.

36   Virginia Jackson, *Before Modernism: Inventing American Lyric* (Princeton, NJ: Princeton University Press, 2023), pp. 66–71, 20.

37   Ibid., p. 71. The reference is to Herbert Tucker, 'Dramatic Monologue and the Overhearing of Lyric', in *Lyric Poetry*, ed. by Hošek and Parker, pp. 226–46.

ZANZOTTO SUSPENDS PETRARCH

Sonnet 11 of Andrea Zanzotto's sequence 'Ipersonetto', published in
Il Galateo in Bosco (1978), opens with a quotation from Petrarch that
addresses the suspension of apostrophe and deixis that the fourteenth-
century poem affords.[38] Petrarch's sonnet, number 273 in his *Rerum
vulgarium fragmenta*, reads:

> Che fai? che pensi? che pur dietro guardi
> nel tempo, che tornar non pote omai?
> Anima sconsolata, che pur vai
> giugnendo legne al foco ove tu ardi?
>
> Le soavi parole e i dolci sguardi
> ch'ad un ad un descritti et depinti ài,
> son levati de terra; et è, ben sai,
> qui ricercarli intempestivo et tardi.
>
> Deh non rinovellar quel che n'ancide
> non seguir più penser vago, fallace,
> ma saldo et certo, ch'a buon fin ne guide.
>
> Cerchiamo 'l ciel, se qui nulla ne piace:
> ché mal per noi quella beltà si vide,
> se viva et morta ne devea tôr pace.
>
> (What do you do? What do you think? Why do you keep looking
> back at that time that cannot return?
> Disconsolate soul, why do you keep adding
> wood to the fire in which you burn?
>
> The gentle words and the sweet glances,
> which you have described and painted one by one,
> have been raised from the Earth; and you know well
> it's too late and untimely to search for them here.
>
> Ah, do not renew what kills us,
> don't follow the errant, fallacious thought,
> but the steady and certain one that leads us to the good end.
>
> Let's look for the heavens, if we like nothing here:
> because we saw that beauty for our misfortune,
> if, dead or alive, it had to take our peace away.)[39]

---

38   On Petrarch's presence in Zanzotto's poetry, see John P. Welle, '*Il Galateo in bosco*
     and the Petrarchism of Andrea Zanzotto', *Italica*, 62.1 (1985), pp. 41–53; Nicola
     Gardini, 'Zanzotto petrarchista barbaro: saggio sull'"Ipersonetto"', *Studi Novecenteschi*,
     19.43/44 (1992), pp. 223–34; Raffaele Manica, 'Petrarca e Zanzotto', in *Qualcosa del
     passato: Saggi di lettura del Ventesimo Secolo* (Rome: Gaffi, 2008), pp. 383–98.

39   Francesco Petrarca, *Canzoniere*, ed. by Marco Santagata (Milan: Mondadori, 1996), p.
     1113; my translation.

The sonnet opens with a series of questions addressed to a 'you' that the apostrophe in line 3 reveals to be the speaker's disconsolate soul, which keeps looking back at the past when its beloved Laura was alive. It is too late now to look for her pleasing words and sweet looks, and remembrance only rekindles the pain. The soul is therefore exhorted to desist from following such a fallacious thought and to replace it with a more stable and certain thought that will lead to a good end. If nothing can please the speaker and the soul on Earth, they should look for it in heaven. Seeing the beauty of Laura was harmful for them because, dead or alive, she has deprived them of peace. Lines 5 and 6 add a crucial piece of information: it is the addressed soul that has painstakingly described and portrayed the pleasing words and sweet looks of the beloved. The moral exhortation to find a more stable object of desire is thus combined with an implicit poetic exhortation to the poet-soul to give up its elegiac effort to find its object of desire on earth: Laura is no longer here.

Beginning with a direct quotation, Zanzotto's reading emphasizes the open referentiality of Petrarch's sonnet, turning it toward language itself:

> Che fai? Che pensi? Ed a chi mai chi parla?
> Chi e che cerececè d'augèl distinguo,
> con che stillii di rivi il vacuo impinguo
> del paese che intorno a me s'intarla?
>
> A chi porgo, a quale ago per riattarla
> quella logica ai cui fili m'estinguo,
> a che e per chi di nota in nota illinguo
> questo che non fu canto, eloquio, ciarla?
>
> Che pensi tu, che mai non fosti, mai
> né pur in segno, in sogno di fantasma,
> sogno di segno, mah di mah, che fai?
>
> Voci d'augei, di rii, di selve, intensi
> moti del niente che sé a niente plasma,
> pensier di non pensier, pensa: che pensi?

('What do you do? What do you think? And to whom is who speaking?
Who and what bird's *cerececè* do I discern,
with what dripping of streams do I fatten
the vacuity of the wood-wormed country around me?

To whom, to what needle do I give to refashion
that logic in whose threads I die out,
to what and for whom do I make language,
note by note, of this that was not song, eloquence, chatter?

What do you think, you who never were, ever
not even in a sign, in a dream of a ghost,
dream of a sign, who knows of who knows, what do you do?

Voices of birds, of streams, of woods, intense
motion of nothing that moulds itself into nothing,
thought of a non-thought, think: what do you think?)[40]

Whereas lines 3–4 in Petrarch's sonnet identify the addressee as the externalized soul, here the first line proceeds to question the identity and the very possibility of identifying not only the addressee ('a chi') but also the speaker ('chi'). Who are those words addressed to? By whom? Deixis emerges as an intralinguistic phenomenon in the twentieth-century poem: pronouns refer to previous occurrences within the text rather than to any identifiable person or entity outside it.[41] In Petrarch, the speaker and the addressee, as well as the pleasing words and sweet looks of the beloved, point to entities outside of the single sonnet and find some degree of identity only within the macrostructure of the *canzoniere*. Zanzotto suspends Petrarch's act of address by making the linguistic nature of this gesture manifest, thus emphasizing the illusory nature of lyric intersubjectivity in Petrarch's sonnet.

Zanzotto's sonnet, moreover, reuses Petrarch's language ('augèl', 'rivi') to disclose its intrapoetic, non-referential nature. Those words/sounds ('stillii di rivi') are used to fill and flesh out the emptiness of the surrounding country, just as they are used to fill the emptiness of a language that does not refer to anything outside itself.[42] In lines 12–13, the voices of natural elements (birds, streams, woods), which characterize the soundscape of Petrarch's poetry and correspond to the surging emotions of the troubled soul, are equated

---

40   Andrea Zanzotto, *Tutte le poesie*, ed. by Stefano Dal Bianco (Milan: Mondadori, 2011), p. 570; my translation.

41   For a commentary on the sonnet, see Andrea Zanzotto, *Ipersonetto: Guida alla lettura*, ed. by Luigi Tassoni (Rome: Carocci, 2021), pp. 110–17. See also Luigi Tassoni, *Caosmos: La poesia di Andrea Zanzotto* (Rome: Carocci, 2002), pp. 67–85, 107–26; Niva Lorenzini, *Dire il silenzio: La poesia di Andrea Zanzotto* (Rome: Carocci, 2014), pp. 13–29.

42   See Welle, 'Il Galateo in bosco', pp. 47–48.

with the surging 'motion' of a nothing that models itself on nothing: both the soul and the landscape have no reality. It is this 'pensier di non pensier' that thinks: 'Che pensi?' As the first tercet makes clear, the 'you' has never been, neither as a sign nor as a dream. This lyric 'you' has a fantasmatic nature: if a sign represents or refers to an entity, however abstract or concrete, here 'you' is only the dream of a sign, an interjection expressing the uncertainty of an uncertainty ('mah di mah'). Therefore, in the second quatrain, the sonnet asks to whom that logic is being handed out, for what or for whom this poem is being put into language note by note. While reusing the form and diction of his illustrious predecessor as a poetic code inherited from the lyric tradition, Zanzotto reveals the purely potential nature of the gesture that Petrarch's sonnet performs: the exhortation to the soul is not actualized within the poem, just as the speaking 'I' and the addressed 'you' do not find a stable referent.

Zanzotto's sonnet raises questions of deixis, diction, form, and gesture. As a form, the sonnet is the same in Petrarch's fourteenth century as it is in Zanzotto's twentieth century.[43] However, as Benjamin observes in his 'Commentary on Poems by Brecht', it is significant that gestures received from the lyric tradition are negotiated, critiqued, or rejected in the most emblematic lyric form.[44] Zanzotto's reuse of the sonnet, made canonical in the Western tradition by Petrarch himself, contributes to the articulation of the dialectics of nature and culture, reality and poetic code, or, in Zanzotto's words, *bosco* (woods) and *galateo* (etiquette). As Stefano Dal Bianco writes, poetry finds itself

> in a position of double 'connivance': on the one hand, it turns parasitically to the woods [the real] as its only source of sustenance and hope for an authentic life; on the other hand, it cannot but recognize itself in the rationalizing demands (for better or for worse) of the *Galateo* [the norm] as a memory stratified in the literary code.[45]

---

43 On the sonnet in the Italian poetic tradition, see Raffaella Scarpa, *Forme del sonetto: La tradizione italiana e il Novecento* (Rome: Carocci, 2012); Fabio Magro and Arnaldo Soldani, *Il sonetto italiano: Dalle origini a oggi* (Rome: Carocci, 2017).

44 Walter Benjamin, 'Commentary on Poems by Brecht', trans. by Edmund Jephcott, in *Selected Writings*, IV, pp. 215–50 (pp. 237–38).

45 Andrea Zanzotto, *Le poesie e prose scelte*, ed. by Stefano Dal Bianco and Gian Mario Villalta (Milan: Mondadori, 1999), p. 1575, quoted in Magro and Soldani, *Il sonetto*

And Fabio Magro and Arnaldo Soldani conclude: 'This is why [...] "Ipersonetto" is essentially — to extend Zanzotto's metaphor — a sort of house in the woods, built "by the book" (or the code) but made of the scattered materials collected in the woods themselves.'[46] In other words, Zanzotto delves into that dialectic at the core of the lyric tradition which the notion of gesture can help to pinpoint. The reuse of an inherited form and the emphasis on words that refer more to Petrarch's diction than to any external reality contribute to questioning the open referentiality that turns the moral exhortation enacted in Petrarch's poem into a gesture. If Petrarch's exhortation was historically situated as representative of the individual's moral tension between the transience of earthly desires and the stability of the spiritual good, Zanzotto's sonnet retrospectively exposes the nature of that exhortation as a repeatable and shareable gesture as it is presented and offered to readers by Petrarchan poetry. Gesture operates at a level between form, which, as Daniel Tiffany remarks, cannot be forged, and diction, 'which possesses specific personal and social characteristics' and can be faked.[47] Gesture makes it possible to identify what, in a poem, is both historically situated and transhistorically shareable.

Agamben seems to identify his notion of command with John L. Austin's performative.[48] This identification, however, is not self-evident: to say 'I swear' is not the same thing as to say 'Swear!' In the first case, the enunciation realizes the enunciated: in saying 'I swear', the oath happens and has consequences in the world in which it happens.[49] In the second case, the enunciation does not realize anything

---

italiano, p. 214; my translation. See also Andrea Cortellessa, *Andrea Zanzotto: Il canto della terra* (Bari: Laterza, 2021), pp. 235–40.

46   Magro and Soldani, *Il sonetto italiano*, p. 214; my translation.

47   Daniel Tiffany, 'Lyric Poetry and Poetics', in *Oxford Research Encyclopedia of Literature* (Oxford University Press, 2020) <https://doi.org/10.1093/acrefore/9780190201098.013.1111>.

48   Agamben, 'What Is a Command?', p. 60; John L. Austin, *How to Do Things with Words* (Cambridge, MA: Harvard University Press, 1975). For a reading of *deixis* and *paradeigma* in opposition to performativity in Agamben, see Justin Clemens, 'The Role of the Shifter and the Problem of Reference in Giorgio Agamben', in *The Work of Giorgio Agamben: Law, Literature, Life*, ed. by Justin Clemens, Nicholas Heron, and Alex Murray (Edinburgh: Edinburgh University Press, 2008), pp. 43–65.

49   See also Giorgio Agamben, *The Kingdom and the Glory*, trans. by Lorenzo Chiesa with Matteo Mandarini, in *The Omnibus Homo Sacer* (Stanford, CA: Stanford University Press, 2017), pp. 361–641 (pp. 535–36).

but itself. There is no way of knowing from the utterance itself whether the command will be heard, obeyed, and executed. The imperative can only ask for a response from the external world; it establishes a relation between language and world that is held in suspension in its potentiality. Petrarch's case is emblematic: the gesture of exhortation, which is never fulfilled within the poem, enacts the moral dilemma and irresolution that characterize Petrarch's 'I'. The sonnet does not offer readers a model to be imitated, but rather a gesture that embodies such dilemma and a language that articulates it. More than to Austin's performative, exhortation belongs to Culler's category of performance and finds a central rhetorical device in apostrophe.[50] This suspended relationship, which presupposes an external world and whose performance can be repeated in attempts to bring the world forth, seems to underlie lyric discourse. In other words, a lyric use of language may entail, and rest on, a suspension of the usual relationship between speaker and addressee, between words and world. To suspend the immediate referentiality of language means to make of language not merely a place of negativity — the word will never be the thing — but a place of potentiality — the word can be many things. This is why the lyric can function, as Culler remarks, as a memorable language available for repetition in different contexts and as a potential vehicle for a variety of meanings.[51]

If we stick to Austin's notion of performativity, Agamben's ontology of command, or of the Greek *esti*, what *could be*, resembles an ontology of possible (fictional) worlds. This is not what I would call *suspended ontology*, which is an ontology of the potential, not of the possible. Lyric can contain fictional elements, but the way in which a lyric utterance is framed is not inherently fictional. In reading a poem, we do not know whether the world will ever respond to being summoned, and not even whether there is a world that could respond. Abstracting poems from the residue of circumstantial functionality that exhortation still carries, lyric gestures are based on the basic linguistic gesture of deixis. Indeed, exhortation, like prayer and praise, deploys the deictic power of language. Its main effect is what might,

---

50   Culler, *Theory of the Lyric*, pp. 125–31.
51   Ibid., pp. 336–48.

with Hans Ulrich Gumbrecht, be called the 'production of presence'.[52] If the main effect of lyric deixis is to produce presence, the presence of the utterance itself, then this utterance is not performative in Austin's sense but rather a performance in Culler's sense.

Agamben's critique of teleology is not based on temporality; it rather addresses the traditional potency/act scheme. For him, indeed, the act of creation (*poiesis*) resists full actualization, its complete passage from potency to act, and the work of art retains some potentiality in its actuality.[53] In Agamben's account, the act of creation is the one performed by the human creator; I want to focus here on the act of creation performed by language itself in a poem and argue that the lyric as a mode of discourse is the use of language that most exposes the limits of actualization. In its performance, the lyric brings to the fore the very limits of performativity, of the capability of language to bring forth what it speaks about and refers to. Lyric language never attains a stable referent and never fully accomplishes an action in this world — not in the sense of a fault, a lack of potentiality, but rather as a *potentiality-not-to*, as Agamben would say. Lyric language gestures toward its referent but never exhausts its reference by producing its own world. It retains some potentiality in each of its actualizations. In this way, on the one hand, it needs a larger world in which to happen in each of its performances (the act-events of reading, as Derek Attridge dubs them);[54] on the other, it allows for its own re-enactment in different situations. Neither pointing to a stable referent (a real object in our world) nor creating its own fictional world (with fictional objects), the lyric poem evokes a world only to suspend it on the verge of actualization.

---

52   Hans Ulrich Gumbrecht, *Production of Presence: What Meaning Cannot Convey* (Stanford, CA: Stanford University Press, 2004).

53   Giorgio Agamben, 'What Is the Act of Creation?', in *Creation and Anarchy*, pp. 14–28.

54   Derek Attridge uses 'act-event' to refer to the reader's encounter with a text when the text is put to work as literature, highlighting the fact that it is both active and passive, in *The Singularity of Literature* (London: Routledge, 2004), p. 26 and n. 16; *The Work of Literature* (Oxford: Oxford University Press, 2015), pp. 59–60.

THE PARADIGM OF THE VOCATIVE

Conceptions of community are usually based on reciprocal identification among individuals as members of a group; communal systems of knowledge, values, and beliefs; shared interpretive strategies and responses to culturally selected objects; joint goals or interests; or collective affects and moods. What I call *gestural communities*, instead, are not based on pre-established identities, but rather on the shareability and repeatability of gestures. Members of such a community can re-enact historically available gestures as independent actors in their own contexts. Gestures are actualized in social actions when performed in a context in which they acquire a meaning and a goal. Reading Petrarch's sonnet 273, 'I' am called to inhabit the open position of the poem's speaker and address the disconsolate soul, thereby making the poem 'my own'. In doing so, however, 'I' am also re-enacting the old gesture of exhortation to relinquish earthly attachments and reorientate my desire toward higher goals. Zanzotto's sonnet calls attention to the purely linguistic and thus repeatable nature of such gestures, as well as to the open referentiality that makes such iterability possible.

This dialectical movement between individuation and disindividuation, historicity and trans-historicity, can be linked to the tension Agamben discerns between style, the appropriation of language pursued by the poet, and manner, a need for 'disappropriation' and 'non-belonging':

> They are the two poles in the tension of which the gesture of the poet lives: style is disappropriating appropriation (a sublime negligence, a forgetting oneself in the proper), manner an appropriating disappropriation (a presenting oneself or remembering oneself in the improper).[55]

This tension, in turn, is not so far from the dialectical tension between 'fixation' and 'living flux' operative in Benjamin's gesture that we encountered earlier.[56] According to Agamben, 'the poetic act appears as a bipolar gesture, which each time renders external what it must

---

55 Giorgio Agamben, *The Use of Bodies*, trans. by Adam Kotsko, in *Omnibus Homo Sacer*, 1011–1288 (pp. 1105–06).

56 Unlike Attridge (for whom, in line with Derrida, singularity coincides with individual uniqueness, or at least tends to that pole), and somewhat closer to Deleuze and

unfailingly appropriate'.[57] The lyric seems to embody, to the highest degree, that 'point at which language, having deactivated its utilitarian functions, rests in itself and contemplates its potential to say'.[58]

Mention of Brecht is nowhere to be found in Agamben's nine-volume project *Homo Sacer*. However, although undisclosed, it is evident how relevant Benjamin's reflections on Brecht's gesture are for Agamben's thinking on the topic. If the connections between the notion of gesture and the idea of lyric that I have been tracing so far are of even some relevance, then it is difficult to fully agree with the final objection that Christian Haines raises to Agamben's politics in his review of the *Homo Sacer* project, which appeared before the publication of its complete English edition in 2017. According to Haines, 'Agamben's project to re-found ontology, ethics, and politics can be described as a poetry of thought, because it not only generates a certain lyric intensity but also depends on it'. This 'lyric intensity', for Haines, does not allow for a proper thinking of community — and thus does not lead to a proper social and political dimension — because 'this is the other face of lyric intensity in Agamben's immanent method, namely, absolute subtraction. Immanence comes to be measured in relation to a horizon of complete withdrawal from relation.' Therefore, such 'lyric intensity' remains enclosed in an ascetic 'solitude' that Haines connects with 'a Romantic tradition of thinking poetry'.[59]

What is problematic, for Haines, is Agamben's 'break from relationality':

Agamben, I would describe as 'singularity' this dynamic space or unstable position in which the individual effaces their own particularity, at least partially, to access the trans-individual in language. In this sense, the open position of the lyric speaker would be a space of singularity. On singularity, see Derek Attridge, 'Singularity', in *Oxford Research Encyclopedia of Literature* (Oxford University Press, 2020) <https://doi.org/10.1093/acrefore/9780190201098.013.1092>.

57   Agamben, *Use of Bodies*, p. 1106; see also Giorgio Agamben, 'The Inappropriable', in *Creation and Anarchy*, pp. 29–50.

58   Agamben, 'What Is the Act of Creation?', in *Creation and Anarchy*, pp. 14–28 (p. 27).

59   Christian Haines, 'A Lyric Intensity of Thought: On the Potentiality and Limits of Giorgio Agamben's "Homo Sacer" Project', *Boundary2*, 29 August 2016 <https://www.boundary2.org/2016/08/christian-haines-a-lyric-intensity-of-thought-on-the-potentiality-and-limits-of-giorgio-agambens-homo-sacer-project/> [accessed 11 February 2024].

> The break with a politics of representation or recognition (the pillars of the hegemonic politics of our time: liberal democracy), as well as the break with the state of exception (the tyrannical supplement to that same liberal democracy), thus comes to be predicated upon a break from relationality as such. There is perhaps no better figure for this break from relationality than the lyric poem, at least in Agamben's formulation of that genre, in which sound finds its truth in silence, relation its truth in the solitude of the apostrophe.[60]

If there is a break with a politics of representation, this does not necessarily imply a 'break from relationality as such' in order to embrace the 'solitude of the apostrophe'. There is 'solitude' in apostrophe only as long as one adheres to a message-based paradigm of communication, in which a message goes from a sender to an attentive receiver. It is indeed true that the latter may not be found at the other end of apostrophic address in Romantic poetry. Yet, if one switches to what could be called a paradigm of inscription, or paradigm of the vocative, to use a grammatical case dear to Agamben (and Zanzotto),[61] what matters is that the utterance itself makes room for its own iterability, the potentiality for other speakers to re-enact the utterance. In this case, apostrophe is anything but solitary. Indeed, it does not seem entirely warranted to detect a Romantic conception of poetry (and even less a Romantic idea of apostrophe) as the basis of Agamben's approach to lyric poetry. After all, in the *inoperative*, as becomes clear from Haines's reconstruction, the 'deactivation of the scheme potential/act' entails 'the abandonment of the apparatus subject/object'.[62] In other words, in the suspension of action advocated by Agamben, there is no individuated subject who could embrace the alleged solitude and send an individual message into the void.

At the end of the review, after having articulated his dissatisfaction, Haines formulates his desire:

---

60   Ibid.

61   For Agamben, the vocative does not properly fit into the regular syntax of language; it even disrupts that syntax. See the first chapter, 'Vocativo', in Giorgio Agamben, *La voce umana* (Macerata: Quodlibet, 2023). *Vocativo* is also the title of a 1957 collection of poetry by Zanzotto. See also Gian Mario Villalta, *La costanza del vocativo: Lettura della 'trilogia' di Andrea Zanzotto: 'Il Galateo in Bosco', 'Fosfeni', 'Idioma'* (Milan: Guerini, 1992).

62   Agamben, 'What Is the Act of Creation?', pp. 23–24.

> I would suggest that the object of my critical desire can be summed up in a phrase: a poetics of potentiality. I write 'poetics', not 'poetry', in order to distance myself from the valorization of aesthetic experience as a source of reconciliation and redemption — the trap to which Agamben falls prey. This poetics can be understood as a means without end, or a pure mediality in which form is not pure semblance or style but constitutive of social form.[63]

However, if one recovers the historicity that lyric gestures had for Brecht and Benjamin, a 'poetics of potentiality' can be found in gestures as 'social forms' suspended in their potentiality. Haines's final proposal — 'let us socialize Agamben, let us communize his thought, let us liberate it from unworldliness and solitude by drawing on what is so powerful in it — not the esoteric but the relational, not redemption but friendship in struggle, not the saint but the comrade'[64] — is already embedded in the shareability of those gestures and what I have called the paradigm of the vocative.

Two different types of community formation could be derived from the two different uses of language explored by Agamben, apophantic and non-apophantic. Apophantic speech would tend to form a community whose members agree upon a certain truth-statement and the state of things in the world it denotes. Non-apophantic speech would tend to form a community whose members perform the same gesture, without necessarily sharing any knowledge about the world. The suspension of non-apophantic speech in its potentiality would keep open the very potentiality of a gestural community. Lyric discourse allows for the historical re-enactment, or rejection, of certain gestures while at the same time preserving them in their potentiality. This is one possible way to envisage the 'coming community' made of 'whatever singularities', which for Agamben is 'what the State cannot tolerate in any way'[65] — a community that is 'coming' not because it will be fully realized at some point in the future, but rather because it never ceases to come:

---

63   Haines, 'Intensity of Thought'.
64   Ibid.
65   Giorgio Agamben, *The Coming Community*, trans. by Michael Hardt (Minneapolis: University of Minnesota Press, 1993), pp. 85–86.

> Because if instead of continuing to search for a proper identity
> in the already improper and senseless form of individuality,
> humans were to succeed in belonging to this impropriety as
> such, in making of the proper being-thus not an identity and an
> individual property but a singularity without identity, a com-
> mon and absolutely exposed singularity — if humans could,
> that is, not be-thus in this or that particular biography, but
> be only *the* thus, their singular exteriority and their face, then
> they would for the first time enter into a community without
> presuppositions and without subjects, into a communication
> without the incommunicable.[66]

Such a community is always caught up in the process of coming, in
other words as *how it is*, not as *what it is*, as a manner, not an identity,
to use the terminology of Agamben's modal ontology.

If, as Culler maintains, the dissemination of lyric is based on the re-
enactment of its language by individuals with diverse meanings and to
a variety of ends, the notion of gesture is helpful for understanding how
lyric can be both historically situated and shareable in different con-
texts. Lyric poetry, as a repertoire of gestures (in the Brechtian sense of
actions freed from their historical contexts and contextual meanings),
becomes a vehicle for the transmission of those gestures across time
and space and an incubator from which social action (which implies
the implementation of a gesture in the social world) can emerge. This
is how Agamben's notion of language as 'pure mediality' is understood
here, as a language that has suspended its utilitarian use as a means to
an end and that shows its own potentiality of saying and can thus en-
able the formation of gestural communities. Commenting on the way
of being together in the events of May '68, Maurice Blanchot wrote in
his *La Communauté inavouable* (1983; The Unavowable Community):
'Everybody had something to say, and, at times, to write (on the walls);
what exactly, mattered little. Saying it was more important than what
was said. Poetry was an everyday affair.'[67] Poetry is more about saying
than what is being said. Poems do not bring to completion the perform-
ance of functions as instrumental objects or actions do; but they may
enable that functionality, or at least preserve it in its potentiality. As far

---

66   Ibid., p. 65; emphasis in original.
67   Maurice Blanchot, *The Unavowable Community*, trans. by Pierre Joris (Barrytown, NY:
      Station Hill Press, 1988), p. 30.

as language is concerned, Agamben remarks that 'the gesture is, in this sense, communication of a communicability'; it shows 'the being-in-language of human beings as pure mediality'; and, he adds, 'the gesture is essentially always a gesture of not being able to figure something out in language.'[68] If, as Agamben summarizes, *'the gesture is the exhibition of a mediality: [...] the process of making a means visible as such'*, the lyric could be considered the exhibition of the 'pure and endless' mediality of language.[69]

68   Agamben, 'Notes on Gesture', p. 58.
69   Ibid., p. 57; emphasis in original.

Rabindranath Tagore's
সমাজ/Samaj/Communities of Song

PETER D. MCDONALD

1

Ideally, you would not be reading this. You would hear it as a talk that would open with me playing two songs. (You can still hear them if you have a moment, on YouTube.)[1] The point of this initial listening exercise? To underscore the experiential difference between reading lyric poems and listening to songs, but also to remind you of our deep, biocultural embeddedness in language. Let us assume that, like me, you have no Bangla, the language of the songs, and that you are, consequently, able to respond simply to the melody as an almost wholly aesthetic experience, the pure sound of words devoid of meaning. Perhaps you experience only a stream of rhythmic phrases, since you may struggle to differentiate the words as such, given what the neuroscientists tell us about how quickly we lose our capacity to hear 'foreign' sounds in the early stages of language development.

---

1   Shemaroo, 'Jana Gana Mana', YouTube, 7 August 2014 <https://www.youtube.com/watch?v=HtMF973tXIY>; VocalNationalAnthems, 'Amar Shona Bangla', YouTube, 9 May 2010 <https://www.youtube.com/watch?v=zVjbVPFeo2o> [both accessed 21 March 2023].

2

For the vast populations of India and Bangladesh, 1.4 billion and 169.4 million respectively as of 2021, this kind of listening would be impossible. They would hear the words, sentences, and rhythmic lines as resonantly meaningful sounds. More than that: they would hear the familiar, rousing melody–rhythm–meaning complexes of their national anthems: 'Jana Gana Mana' (literally, 'Thou Art the Ruler of the Minds of All People') and 'Amar Sonar Bangla' (My Golden Bengal), both by the Indian polymath and Nobel Prize winner Rabindranath Tagore (1861–1941). This is especially true for Bangla speakers, although, as Tagore deliberately used a Sanskritized form of his own first language for 'Jana Gana', drawing on a lexicon Bangla shares with many other Indian languages, especially Hindi, the evocative immediacy of its meanings would be clear to most Indian citizens.

True, as the Indian writer-musician Amit Chaudhuri commented in early 2023 after releasing his own version of 'Jana Gana' to mark the seventy-fifth anniversary of India's independence, the anthemization of songs can itself become an obstacle to hearing. 'There's a tendency for pieces of music that are associated with nationalism or religion not to be looked at as an artistic artefact', he said in an interview for *The Hindu*; 'we cease to think of them as aesthetic objects'.[2] His own experimental version, which intersects without fusing with the Austrian jazz keyboardist and composer Joe Zawinul's 'In a Silent Way' (1970), is intended to reawaken this more primordial kind of listening, giving 'Jana Gana' a new life for Indian and world audiences alike.[3]

3

Anthemization has other effects too. While granting the songs an exceptional public status as official expressions of statehood, evident most obviously in the rules of decorum governing their performance,

---

2   Bhanuj Kappal, '"My Music Is Based on Convergences": Amit Chaudhuri on his New Compositions', *The Hindu*, 19 January 2023 <https://www.thehindu.com/entertainment/music/amit-chaudhuri-writer-singer-music-single-album-in-a-silent-way-jana-gana-mana-75-india-independence/article66395879.ece> [accessed 21 March 2023].

3   Amit Chaudhuri, 'In a Silent Way/Indian National Anthem', YouTube, 9 January 2023 <https://www.youtube.com/watch?v=xL6uhjEcHIQ> [accessed 21 March 2023].

the process also unmoors them from their origins, changing their meaning, even their form. This has consequences at every level, beginning with individual words. Consider only the most conspicuous word the two anthems share: বাংলা 'Bangla'/'Bengal'.

In 1905, when Tagore composed the original five-verse 'Amar Sonar Bangla', the title word referred to a multifaith, ethnolinguistic region, itself then part of the Bengal Presidency, the largest administrative subdivision of British India. The anthem version, a reworking of the first two verses, is mainly a lyric evocation of this geographical locality, figured as a beloved 'Ma' (Mother), in all its lived, sensuous reality. Here are lines 4–9 of the anthem in Syed Ali Ahsan's official English translation:

> In Spring, Oh mother mine, the fragrance from
> your mango-groves makes me wild with joy —
> Ah, what a thrill!
> In Autumn, Oh mother mine,
> in the full-blossomed paddy fields,
> I have seen spread all over — sweet smiles![4]

Only the final lines of the second verse hint at the darker history out of which the song originally arose: 'If sadness, Oh mother mine, casts a gloom on your face, | my eyes are filled with tears!' This references the anguish of Bengal's first partition under the British (1905–12), which Tagore and many others vigorously opposed. The full-length version makes this explicit in its last line, alluding directly to the boycott of foreign goods — 'a hanging rope disguised as a crown' — that underpinned the Swadeshi (literally, 'own country') campaign against partition.[5] More painful and permanent divisions would follow, as the regional Indian state of West Bengal and the Pakistani state of East Pakistan were carved out of undivided Bengal in 1947, with the latter eventually emerging as the independent nation state of Bangladesh in 1971. So, the 'Golden Bengal' evoked is inevitably different if we identify the first-person 'my' voice as a protesting Rabindranath-figure

---

4   VocalNationalAnthems, 'Amar Shona Bangla'.
5   Rabindranath Tagore, 'My Golden Bengal', trans. by Anjan Ganguly <https://www.geetabitan.com/lyrics/rs-a2/aamar-sonaar-bangla-ami-english-translation.html> [accessed 21 March 2023].

in 1905 or as a Bangladeshi collective affirming their solidarity as citizens today.

In 'Jana Gana', Bengal is one of seven regions of the subcontinent — the others are Punjab, Sindh, Gujarat, Maratha, Dravida (South India), and Odisha — described as responding to the call of the 'dispenser of India's destiny'. Again, at the time of composition — in this case 1911 — the word referred to the recently and still-partitioned region of the Bengal Presidency, which would, like Punjab, suffer another traumatic division in 1947 — by contrast, Sindh was wholly absorbed by the new state of (West) Pakistan, while all the others became part of the new federal Indian Republic. Again, too, 'Jana Gana' is only the first verse of Tagore's original five-verse song entitled 'Bharata Bhagya Bidhata' (Dispenser/God/Ruler of India's Destiny), which is, like 'Amar Sonar Bangla', haunted by a charged political moment: the elaborate Imperial/Delhi Durbar organized for George V's visit to India as the new king-emperor on 12 December 1911. The song was Tagore's affronted response to being asked to compose something for the occasion. 'That Lord of Destiny,' he later explained, 'that Reader of the Collective Mind of India, that Perennial Guide, could never be George V, George VI, or any other George.'[6] The later verses confirm this. While the second shifts from the diversity of India's regions to its many religions — 'Hindus, Buddhists, Sikhs, Jains, Parsis, Muslims, and Christians' — the next two detail the travails of its history, which includes periods of 'darkness' and 'ghastly dreams'. Yet these are all ultimately redeemed by the 'blessings' of the variously figured, notably supra-sectarian 'Eternal Charioteer', loving 'Mother', and 'King of Kings', and by the prospect of a post-imperial dawn to come: 'victory' for the 'dispenser', as the refrain has it, though a pointedly non-violent, anti-militaristic one — all we are told is that 'the morning breeze carries the breath of new life.'[7] Appropriately, the song was first performed in public at the Calcutta (now Kolkata) meeting of the Indian National Congress on 27 December 1911, two weeks after the Durbar. By then,

---

6   Quoted in Monish Chatterjee, 'Tagore and Jana Gana Mana', 31 August 2003 <https://countercurrents.org/comm-chatterjee310803.htm> [accessed 21 March 2023].

7   Rabindranath Tagore, 'The Morning Song of India' <https://en.wikisource.org/wiki/The_Morning_Song_of_India> [accessed 25 July 2023]. This is Tagore's own translation, which dates from 28 February 1919.

there was a small but significant victory to note: amid all the imperial pomp of the Durbar, George V had also rescinded the 1905 partition of Bengal.

It is not just the artistry of the songs that gets lost in anthemization, then. Abridged and cut adrift from the provocations that occasioned their composition, their polemical energies go too.

4

Tagore did not live to see the destiny dispensed to India and Bengal in 1947, so it is impossible to know what he might have made of the post-imperial order from which three independent states eventually emerged on the subcontinent. Nor can we ever know how he might have responded to the unique distinction he achieved as the official laureate of two states: 'Jana Gana Mana' was formally adopted in 1950, 'Amar Sonar Bangla' in 1972. What we can do, however, especially in an essay collection dedicated to rethinking lyric communities, is consider the ways in which the songs, in their original, unabridged, and so polemical form, refract the radical, multifaceted, and always evolving idea of community Tagore developed across his later writings, an idea that was at once political and something else — let's call it poetic for now. Having established these connections, we can then revisit 'Sonar Bangla' and 'Jana Gana' not just as state anthems but as Tagore songs.

Tagore worked through his disillusionment with the Swadeshi movement in a variety of forms. While *Gora* (1910; trans. 1924) and *Ghare Baire* (*The Home and the World*, 1916; trans. 1921) represent the most sustained novelistic articulations of his critique, he used the expository mode of his celebrated 1917 lectures on nationalism to voice his concerns in more direct political terms, presenting an alternative vision that was at once anti-colonial, anti-nationalist, and non-statist. India is inevitably central to his argument, though in two contrasting ways. On the one hand, countering the 'racial unity' he considered characteristic of 'Western Nationality', he pointed to its historic and exemplary diversity, arguing that it had 'produced something like a United States of a *social* federation, whose common name is Hinduism'

— 'social' in his lexicon meant 'voluntary', 'civic', or 'non-statist'.[8] Although derived from the Hindu tradition, this supra-sectarian, poetic-philosophical, rather than specifically theological, idea finds its lyrical avatar in the dispenser who unifies the many regions and religions of the subcontinent in 'Bharata Bhagya Bidhata'. On the other hand, with the rigid hierarchies of the caste system in mind, Tagore took issue with Hinduism's 'idolatry of dead forms in social institutions'.[9] This combination of respect for India's ancient inheritances and critique, all conducted in a spirit of secular revisionism, was characteristic of the reformist nineteenth-century Brahmo Samaj (Brahmo Society/Community) in which the Tagore family played a leading part. The idiosyncratic brand of humanism Tagore himself developed, which he later called 'the Religion of Man', owed much to this intellectual movement and the larger 'Bengal Renaissance' out of which it emerged.[10]

For Tagore, the 'idolatry of dead forms' an unreformed Hinduism fostered was dangerous because it blinded India to the fact that 'in human beings differences are not like the physical barriers of mountains, fixed forever — they are fluid with life's flow, they are changing their courses and their shapes and volume', always part of a 'world-game of infinite permutations and combinations'.[11] He feared a similar idolatry, this time focused on the national community as such, might come to dominate the anti-colonial struggle against British rule. 'Because we have failed to see the great character of India in relation to the world as a whole,' he wrote in 1921, 'we have been inclined in our thoughts and actions to follow a much diminished idea of it, an idea bred of our calculating minds, which casts no light. Nothing great ever

8   Rabindranath Tagore, 'Nationalism in India', in *Indian Philosophy in English*, ed. by Nalini Bhushan and Jay L. Garfield (New York: Oxford University Press, 2011), pp. 21–36 (pp. 23, 30; my emphasis). I have cited this collection because it provides a valuable larger context for Tagore's lecture.

9   Ibid., p. 33.

10   See Rabindranath Tagore, *The Religion of Man* (New York: Macmillan, 1931). For more on these lectures, and on Tagore generally, see Peter D. McDonald, *Artefacts of Writing: Ideas of the State and Communities of Letters from Matthew Arnold to Xu Bing* (Oxford: Oxford University Press, 2017); supplementary website: <https://artefactsofwriting. com/> [accessed 25 July 2023].

11   Tagore, 'Nationalism in India', p. 30.

comes of this kind of thinking.'[12] The 'calculating mind' tends, in Ta-gore's book, not only to be preoccupied with deciding what best serves any community's interests in some rationalistic sense, but with turning all it touches into a countable thing or reified fetish. Although he felt no one was immune from this kind of thinking — he saw evidence of it among academic literary critics, for instance — he believed political activists and state-makers were particularly prone to its allure.

As a product of the 'calculating mind', the sovereign, self-determining, Europeanized modern state could, in his view, never grasp, let alone articulate and promote, this labile, unpredictable aspect of diversity. This is why he put his faith not in the state, whether colonial or post-colonial, European or Asian — in the lectures he was famously critical of Japan's imperial ambitions — but in civil society and the very different 'ideals that strive to take form in social institutions'.[13] As an educationalist who founded an alternative school and university in Bengal, he chose to express his own ideals institutionally through centres of learning committed to creative expression and to forms of interculturality that would not only open India to the world but enable India to cast its own diverse lights abroad. Visva-Bharati, the university he set up in 1921, was dedicated, as he declared in an early mission statement, to upholding 'India's obligation to offer to others the hospitality of her best culture and India's right to accept from others their best'.[14] The name, as Krishna Dutta and Andrew Robinson explain, is 'a compound made from the Sanskrit word for universe [or world] and Bharati, a goddess in the Rig Veda associated with the Hindu goddess of learning, Saraswati' — literally, 'Universal/World Learning', in other words. Visva-Bharati was, he wrote, committed to 'the creation of new thought by new

---

12   Rabindranath Tagore, 'Satyer Ahaban' (The Call of Truth), in *Rabindra Rachanabali*, 18 vols (Kolkata: Visva-Bharati, 1991), XII, p. 585. For a different translation and interpretation, see Ashish Nandy, *Illegitimacy of Nationalism* (Delhi: Oxford University Press, 1994), p. 81. Nandy reads this as an articulation of Tagore's 'universalism', whereas I take it to be an expression of his commitment to the intercultural. I am grateful to Rosinka Chaudhuri for her retranslation of these sentences and for her comments on many other aspects of this essay.

13   Tagore, 'Nationalism in India', p. 32.

14   Krishna Dutta and Andrew Robinson, *Rabindranath Tagore* (London: Bloomsbury, 1995), p. 220.

combinations of truths' and to using the 'shock' of the 'foreign' to strengthen 'the vitality of our intellect' — here the 'our' referred to India as a diverse 'social federation' open to the world, not as a sovereign, geographically bounded nation state.[15] Rejecting both 'the colourless vagueness of cosmopolitanism' and 'the fierce self-idolatry of nation-worship', he insisted that all cultures not only exist but flourish, and, indeed, survive, interculturally.[16] Seen from the perspective of the 1920s, this was a declaration of faith in a more equitable, decolonized, and post-nationalist world to come, since, as he always recognized, his educational ideals were incompatible with the injustices of colonial rule.

As his intervention in an educational dispute in Bengal in the 1930s showed, these convictions not only shaped his critique of the state and state-led international relations — all 'machinery' in his lexi-con. They affected how he understood intercommunal relations and language. The highly charged quarrel, led by 'Bengali Muslims' com-mitted to 'Persianizing and Arabicizing' Bangla textbooks, centred on language teaching in schools.[17] 'Every language has a vital framework of its own', Tagore wrote in 'The Bengali of Maktabs and Madrasas' (1932), but 'there is no civilized language that has not absorbed some foreign vocabulary through many kinds of interaction with a variety of peoples'.[18] Why, he asked, pushing the underlying logic of the dispute one step further, did the textbook reformers not seek to 'sanctify the language of English school readers by sprinkling them with Persian or Arabic?'[19] By way of illustration, and in a gesture of mock solicitude, he

---

15   Ibid., pp. 220–22. This kind of thinking also underpinned Tagore's innovative con-ception of world literature as set out in his talk/essay 'World Literature' (1907). For contemporary accounts of this key intervention, see Peter. D. McDonald, 'See-ing through the *Concept* of World Literature', *Journal of World Literature*, 4 (2019), pp. 13–34; Rosinka Chaudhuri, '*Viśvasāhitya*: Rabindranath Tagore's Idea of World Literature', in *The Cambridge History of World Literature*, ed. by Debjani Ganguly (Cambridge: Cambridge University Press, 2021), pp. 261–78.

16   Rabindranath Tagore, 'Nationalism in the West', in *The English Writings of Rabindra-nath Tagore*, ed. by Sisir Kumar Das (Delhi: Sahitya Akademi, 1994–96), II (1994), pp. 418–22 (p. 419).

17   Rabindranath Tagore, 'The Bengali of Maktabs and Madrasas', trans. by Tista Bagchi, in *Selected Writings on Literature and Language*, ed. by Sisir Kumar Das and Sukanta Chaudhuri (New Delhi: Oxford University Press, 2001), pp. 358–60 (p. 359).

18   Ibid., p. 358.

19   Ibid., p. 359.

offered as an example his own rewritten version of the opening lines of John Keats's poem *Hyperion*. He acknowledged that the subject of the poem itself posed a problem for purists since it came from 'Greek mythology'. Yet

> if, despite that, it is not to be eschewed by the Muslim student, let us see how its beauty is enhanced when Persian is mixed in with it:

> Deep in the *saya-i-ghamagin* of a vale,
> Far sunken from the *nafas-i-hayat afza-i* morn,
> Far from the *atshin* noon and eve's one star,
> Sat *bamoo-i-safid* Saturn *Khamush* as a *Sang*.

The lines appear as follows in the original:

> Deep in the *shady sadness* of a vale
> Far sunken from the *healthy breath of* morn,
> Far from the *fiery* noon, and eve's one star,
> Sat *gray-hair'd* Saturn, *quiet* as a *stone*.[20]

The absurdity of the fake-hybridized version proved his point: 'no Maulvi Sahab [i.e. respected Muslim scholar] will attempt this sort of Islamisation of English literary style in a state of sanity', just as no one in their right mind would 'dispute linguistic rights over the sun', claiming that 'that the Hindu Bengali's *surya* is the true sun and the Muslim Bengali's sun is merely *tambu*'. Having said this, he ruled nothing out. For all his efforts to defuse tensions by trying to leaven the fraught debate with humour, he added, presciently given the horrors of partition that were just fifteen years away: 'Communal conflict has taken many different forms in different countries of the world; but the grotesque shape that it has taken in Bengal makes it hard for us to hold our heads high.'[21]

There is one final aspect of Tagore's political thinking to consider which, as Partha Chatterjee notes, centres on his use of the term '*svadés*'

---

20   *Hyperion*, I. 1–4, in John Keats, *Poetical Works*, ed. by H. W. Garrod (Oxford: Oxford University Press, 1970), p. 221 (my italics, marking the counterparts of the Persian elements in Tagore's version).

21   Ibid., p. 360.

(literally, 'one's own country').[22] Although the word echoes 'Swadeshi', it takes on a very different, even contrary, meaning in Tagore's later writings, following his growing doubts about anti-colonial nationalism. For him, the *dés* (also romanized as *desh*, as in 'Bangladesh') is neither a geopolitical territory or economic zone, nor a fate of birth. It is an achieved, creatively fashioned country of the mind, or, as Chatterjee has it, 'the product of our imagination'. This is how Tagore put it in 1921:

> The certain knowledge that I have a *dés* comes out of a quest. Those who think that the country is theirs simply because they have been born in it are creatures besotted by the external things of the world. But, since the true character of a human being lies in his or her inner nature imbued with the force of self-making (*ātmaśakti*), only that country can be one's *svadés* that is created by one's own knowledge, intelligence, love and effort.[23]

In contrast to the idea of community the constitutional machinery of the state typically produces, an artefact of the 'calculating mind' preoccupied with externalities, the *svadés* is an inward condition for Tagore, creatively brought into being by each individual and, in the case of the poet-songwriter, by each act of composition. This is an imagined community of song, in other words, which is at the same time a singular creative act 'imbued with the force of self-making'. Again, in Tagore's lexicon, 'creative' or 'creation' has a specific resonance, associated with his idea of knowledge achieved through an exploratory 'quest', in contrast to 'construction', which follows a rulebook and is linked to the 'calculating mind'.[24]

Having clarified some of Tagore's thinking and terminology, we can return to 'Sonar Bangla' and 'Jana Gana/Bharata' in their original, unabridged form as Tagore songs and as something more: expressions

---

22   Partha Chatterjee, *Lineages of Political Society: Studies in Postcolonial Democracy* (New York: Columbia University Press, 2011), p. 103. Chatterjee gives one of the richest recent accounts of Tagore's later political thinking, though he makes no reference to the poetry. For another take on the issues, which does discuss the anthems, see Poulomi Saha, 'Singing Bengal into a Nation: Tagore the Colonial Cosmopolitan?', *Journal of Modern Literature*, 36.2 (2013), pp. 1–12.

23   Trans. by Chatterjee, *Lineages*, p. 104.

24   Tagore, 'Literature', in *Selected Writings*, pp. 49–50 (p. 49).

of *svadés* in his sense, that is, as artefacts of a unique creative 'quest', reflecting, in each case, his 'own knowledge, intelligence, love and effort'.

5

With 'Amar Sonar Bangla', it is not the lyrics that offer the best point of entry but the melody, which Tagore adopted from 'Ami Kothay Pabo Tare' (Where Shall I Meet Him), a song originally composed by his local postal worker/messenger Gagan Harkara, who was also a Baul singer. This specifically Bangla and exclusively oral tradition, usually thought to date from the fifteenth century CE, not only influenced Tagore's creative practice. It shaped his self-understanding as a poet-songwriter — it would not be too much to say he saw himself as a modernist Baul.[25] Associated chiefly with itinerant 'beggars — deprived of education, honour, and wealth', this 'popular religious sect of Bengal', as he called it in 'An Indian Folk Religion' (1922), itself constituted a bridge between two transformative traditions in his account, one ancient and Eastern, the other modern and Western: Buddhism, at least in its original oral and pre-institutionalized form, and liberal democracy, at least in its ideal form.[26] For Tagore, this was the Buddhism that 'declared salvation to all men, without distinction', promising freedom from 'the thraldom of the self', and delivered 'neither in texts of Scripture, nor in symbols of deities, nor in religious practices sanctified by ages, but through the voice of a living man', the Buddha.[27] Similarly, though now like the modern 'idea of democracy', the 'simple theology' of the Baul preached 'faith in the individual', 'trust in his own possibilities', and a belief in the inherent 'dignity of man'.[28]

Eschewing all institutionalized and written forms of religion, whether of the church, temple or mosque, and all hierarchies 'imposed by the society of the learned, of the rich, or of the highborn' — including caste — the Baul also rejected otherworldly transcendentalism,

---

25   See McDonald, *Artefacts*, pp. 173–90.

26   Rabindranath Tagore, 'An Indian Folk Religion', in *Creative Unity* (London: Macmillan, 1922), pp. 67–90 (p. 83).

27   Ibid., p. 69.

28   Ibid., p. 80.

favouring an embodied freedom or self-overcoming in the here and now.[29] According to their 'mystic philosophy of the body', Tagore wrote, the deity, understood as the ultimate object of a wandering or questing desire, which could be another person or a humanistic ideal, was an immanent meaning- and value-giving experience, open to all in equal measure — 'not only that God is for each of us, but also that God is in each of us'.[30] Hence the longing voiced in Harkara's song, which Tagore cited in 'An Indian Folk Religion':

> Where shall I meet him, the Man of my Heart?
> He is lost to me and I seek him wandering from land to land.
>
> I am listless for that moonrise of beauty,
> which is to light my life,
> which I long to see in the fulness of vision, in gladness of heart.[31]

In Bangla, the *maner mānus* (Man of my Heart), a central Baul topos, is a gender-neutral figure of the beloved, the one who, as Tagore put it, 'gives expression to infinite truth in the music of life'.[32] As this suggests, Tagore's own humanistic 'Religion of Man' owed as much to the folk traditions of the Baul as it did to the intellectual project of the Brahmo Samaj. Since 2008, the Baul songs have been included on UNESCO's Representative List of the Intangible Cultural Heritage of Humanity, an accolade Tagore would no doubt have regarded as long overdue.

Heard as a modernist rewording of a Baul song, 'Amar Sonar Bangla' turns into something more than protest responding to the provocations of a charged historical moment and something other than straightforward lyric evocation of place. While the first two verses, which form the anthem, celebrate the local seasons and landscape in the guise of a generalized first person, the third reveals the voice to be a more specific, biographical individual recalling their childhood experience of visceral immersion in the 'dirt and soil' of the region. The fourth then reverts to a rural scene in the present with 'cattle grazing in the field', 'calling birds', and the harvest, before concluding with a declaration of solidarity, again centred on rural village life:

---

29   Ibid., p. 88.
30   Ibid., pp. 80, 86.
31   Ibid., p. 79.
32   Ibid.

'All your shepherds and farmers are my brothers.' Following Tagore's understanding of the Baul's 'mystic philosophy of the body', this is 'My Golden Bengal' as a maternal figure of the beloved *maner mānus* who dispenses meaning and value in the world — 'Bless me with your dust' — while fostering a local 'Unity in Diversity': Bengal as a lyrical, Baul-inspired Tagorean *svadés*, in other words, which, in the heat of the moment, served as a powerful protest against partition.

On this account, it is not difficult to see why 'Sonar Bangla' might be so amenable to anthemization. By articulating a moment of happy conjunction between Tagore's inner poetic *svadés* and the outer polit-ics of the Swadeshi movement, it has all the qualities of an anthem in the making. Much the same could be said of 'Bharata Bhagya Bidhata', which Tagore in his own translation called 'The Morning Song of India'. True, its addressee, the 'dispenser of India's destiny', does not appear to owe much to the *maner mānus* of the Baul tradition. With its eclectic references to Aruna, the charioteer of the Hindu sun god Surya, and the Christian/Muslim 'King of Kings', 'Morning Song' is more solidly in the reformist and high-cultural Hindu tradition of the Brahmo Samaj. This is true melodically as well, as it is based not on a Baul song but on variants of classical ragas, including Kedar and Alhaiya Bilawal. Yet the dispenser is also figured as a nurturing 'mother', recalling the maternal Bengal of 'Sonar Bangla', and as an immanent, unifying power, 'the ruler of the minds of all people', whose name echoes 'in the hills of the Vindhyas and Himalayas, mingles in the music of the Jamuna and Ganges and is chanted by the waves of the Indian Sea' — recall Tagore's reference to the 'music of life' in his account of the Baul tradition. Again, we might ask, is this India as a Brahmo-Baul inspired Tagorean *svadés* readily open to anthemization and so difficult to reconcile with the anti-nationalist and non-statist vision of community outlined in the 1917 lectures?

6

To address this question, we can turn to another poem from the same period, which is more explicitly indebted to the Baul tradition and more clearly in line with Tagore's own political thinking. Poem 106 of the original Bangla *Gitanjali* (Song Offerings, 1910) is, perhaps tellingly, not among those Tagore chose for the self-translated English edition of 1912–13 that made his name internationally and sealed his reputation, particularly in Europe and America, as an unworldly Eastern mystic. As the fifth verse shows, the poem is, like 'Sonar Bangla' and 'Bharata', explicit about the ongoing anti-colonial struggle and trauma of partition — it is dated 2 July 1910 — and, like 'Bharata', it looks to the promise of a post-imperial future. Here are the lines in Ketaki Kushari Dyson's 2010 translation:

> My mind, be strong to endure this affliction
> and listen to unity's call.
> Your sense of fear, embarrassment, humiliation —
> banish them, conquer them all.
> The intolerable pain will come to an end.
> Behold what a huge new life is about to be born![33]

As the mode of address indicates, this is an internal dialogue poem with the I-voice apostrophizing itself ('my mind') in a motivational spirit. It opens with 'Gently in this hallowed place | wake up, o my mind.' From the start, this place, like the locality of 'Sonar Bangla', is at once physical and affective, sacred and secular. The deictics also make it specific: the 'now' of utterance is a particular juncture in colonial history experienced from an equally particular location 'on *this* seashore of India's grand | concourse of humankind' (my emphasis).

Yet poem 106 is not just the Rabindranath I-voice speaking to itself. Having located the lyric moment in time and space, or, more accurately, at a particular point in an endlessly changing time-space continuum, the I then introduces another addressee, a version of the Baul's immanent *maner mānus*, in the second section of the first verse:

> Here I stand and stretch my arms,
> saluting God-in-Man;
> in grand rhythm, with great delight
> I praise Him as best I can.

Like the eclectic, supra-sectarian dispenser of 'Bharata', this figure, who is resolutely of the here and now, unifies the diverse 'streams of humanity' who have flowed, and are still flowing, across the subcontinent 'in

---

33   Rabindranath Tagore, *I Won't Let You Go: Selected Poems*, trans. by Ketaki Kushari Dyson (Tarset: Bloodaxe Books, 2010), p. 152.

impetuous cascades to lose themselves in the sea'. The second verse then begins to name them as the 'Aryans and non-Aryans', 'Chinese and Dravidians', as well as 'Scythians, Huns, Pathans, Mughals', and 'the West'; while the sixth and final verse adds 'Hindus and Muslims', 'Brahmins' and 'outcastes', 'Christians', and 'you, English people'. Given the colonial injustices intimated in the penultimate verse, the inclusion of 'the West' and 'the English' is pointed. Despite all the trauma, the I, now speaking for a collective 'we', accepts 'gifts' from 'that store' too, insisting 'we shall give and receive, mingle and harmonise', since 'there's no turning back | on this seashore' — again recall the Swadeshi boycott of foreign goods.

'Only that country can be one's *svadés* that is created by one's own knowledge, intelligence, love and effort', Tagore wrote in 1921. Poem 106 is among the richest poetic, indeed, metapoetic articulations of his own inner *svadés*. It is also one of the clearest lyric formulations of the intercultural vision of community he outlined in his 1917 lectures and of the educational ideals on which he founded Visva-Bharati. As such, it stands as a key companion poem to 'Amar Sonar Bangla' and 'Bharata Bhagya Bidhata'. On the one hand, a Tagorean country of the mind is, as poem 106 and 'Sonar Bangla' each insist in their own ways, always also a country of the finite body, of localized colours, languages, musical traditions, and visceral experiences, the lived reality of which exposes 'the colourless vagueness of cosmopolitanism'.[34] On the other hand, to be a citizen of this unique inner *svadés* is not just to be acutely conscious of history's many oceanic, sometimes nightmarish, cross-currents, as 'Bharata' maintains, but to be actively engaged in shaping its future as an ongoing, intercultural experiment and as a permanent guard against 'the fierce self-idolatry of nation-worship'. What we have, in other words, is a non-statist Tagorean community of song, where human differences are inevitably both autochthonous and 'fluid with life's flow', part of a 'world-game of infinite permutations and combinations'. The reason? 'A Tagore song', as Amit Chaudhuri put it in the interview about his own intercultural version of 'Jana Gana', is 'the

---

34   As Saha, 'Singing Bengal', pp. 3, 14–15, rightly points out, this means Tagore does not
      fit the Euro-American model of cosmopolitanism for which Martha Nussbaum and
      others have tried to claim him.

result of a conversation between [a] multiplicity of traditions, made possible by a world in which there are multiple journeys to take.[35]

7

By intersecting with Zawinul's 'In a Silent Way', and the Miles Davis jazz tradition with which it in turn intersected, Chaudhuri's 'Jana Gana' is a contemporary updating of and homage to Tagore's Baul-inspired journeying. Tagore had allies in his own time too. The deliberately foreignizing, interlingual *svadés* James Joyce fashioned in *Finnegans Wake* (1939) is *sui generis*, but, as I argue in *Artefacts of Writing* (2017), the resemblance to Tagore's is uncanny, especially when it comes to questions of the body, language, culture, community, colonialism, and the state. The convergences are fortuitously but promisingly prefigured in *Gora* (1910), where the eponymous HCE/Shaun-like figure, who is initially a fervent Hindu Brahmin, turns out to be adopted and of Christian-Irish origin — think also of Leopold Bloom's immigrant background and complex Jewish-Irishness in *Ulysses* (1922). The difference of course is that Joyce did not go on to become the official laureate of two states. Yet, as the expression of a uniquely Joycean *svadés*, the *Wake* stands, like Tagore's later writings, as a permanently vigilant counter to any narrowly statist idea of community — its ideal reader is (or will be) a 'Europasianised Afferyank' — and, like poem 106, as well as 'Bharata' and 'Sonar Bangla' in their unabridged form, it lives on as a powerful shadow anthem for any decolonized citizens of somewhere who are, like the Baul, also at home anywhere on 'ourth'.[36]

---

35   Kappal, 'My Music Is Based on Convergences'.
36   James Joyce, *Finnegans Wake* (London: Faber, 1975), pp. 18, 191.

The Transnational Lyric Community of Soviet Unofficial Music under Late Socialism

PHILIP ROSS BULLOCK

Despite its vast territorial expanse, much of Russia's culture and intellectual life has been sustained by the activities of small salons, societies, groups, and coteries (what in Russian are sometimes referred to as *kruzhki*, or 'little circles'). The vitality of these often informally constituted groupings can be traced, at least in part, to the pervasiveness of state censorship in both the imperial and Soviet periods, when severe limits were often placed on publication, expression, and activism. Even when such limitations have been lifted, or at least relaxed, salon spaces and informal communities have long played an important role in fostering a sense of shared creativity and common identity, regardless of the political or ideological views of their adherents. The limited development of the kind of independent social and cultural institutions that historians have seen as central to the emergence of liberalism and capitalism in Western Europe means that state power itself in Russia has often been exercised from within a relatively limited range of self-selecting bodies.[1] From the court intrigues of the Romanov chanceries

---

1   Jürgen Habermas, *The Structural Transformation of the Public Sphere*, trans. by Thomas Burger and Frederick Lawrence (Cambridge, MA: MIT Press, 1989).

to the insider politics of the Politburo, authority has been invested in and exercised by small groups of the elect, if not the elected.

Scholarship has done much to illuminate the activities and importance of salons, societies, and other informal groupings at various key moments in Russian history. A particular focus of attention has been the vitality of literary, cultural, and intellectual life during the first half of the nineteenth century, which witnessed both the emergence of Russian romanticism and political challenges to the primacy of the autocracy (most obviously in the form of the Decembrist uprising of 1825).[2] This 'Golden Age' of Russian culture has an analogue in the early twentieth century, when a sequence of dynamic artistic movements — from symbolism and Acmeism to various iterations of Futurism — unfolded in the apartments, salons, cafes, cabarets, clubs, and studios that were so central to the 'Silver Age' in both St Petersburg and Moscow.[3] Radical politics, too, often took place in such spaces, driven underground by the repressive policing on which the autocracy relied for its survival.[4] Later on, Soviet power would owe much to the utopian communities that thrived in the years immediately after the October Revolution, which were later swept away by Stalin's consolidation and centralization of power.[5]

---

2   See the still indispensable M. Aronson and S. Reiser, *Literaturnye kruzhki i salony* (Leningrad: Priboi, 1929), and *Literaturnye salony i kruzhki: Pervaya polovina XIX veka*, ed. by N. L. Brodsky (Moscow: Academia, 1930), as well as Edward J. Brown, *Stankevich and his Moscow Circle, 1830–1840* (Stanford, CA: Stanford University Press, 1966); A. D. Sukhov, *Literaturno-filosofskie kruzhki v istorii russkoi filosofii (20–50e gody XIX veka)* (Moscow: IF RAN, 2009); Daria Khitrova, *Lyric Complicity: Poetry and Readers in the Golden Age of Russian Literature* (Madison: University of Wisconsin Press, 2019).

3   D. M. Fel'dman, *Salon-predpriyatie: Pisatel'skoe ob"edinenie i kooperativnoe izdatel'stvo 'Nikinskie subbotniki' v kontekste literaturnogo protsessa 1920–1930-x godov* (Moscow: Rossiiskii gosudarstvennyi gumanitarnyi universitet, 2018); *Moskovskii Parnas: Kruzhki, salony, zhurfiksy Serebryanogo veka, 1890–1922*, ed. by T. F. Prokopova (Moscow: Interlak, 2006); Barbara Walker, *Maximilian Voloshin and the Russian Literary Circle: Culture and Survival in Revolutionary Times* (Bloomington: Indiana University Press, 2005).

4   See e.g. N. Bel'chikov, *Dostoevskii v protsesse Petrashevtsev* (Moscow: Nauka, 1971); John L. Evans, *The Petraševskij Circle, 1845–1849* (The Hague: Mouton, 1974); B. S. Itenberg, *Dvizhenie revolyutsionnogo narodnichestva: Narodnicheskie kruzhki i 'khozhdenie v narod' v 70-kh godakh XIX v.* (Moscow: Nauka, 1965).

5   Andy Willimott, *Living the Revolution: Urban Communes & Soviet Socialism, 1917–1932* (Oxford: Oxford University Press, 2017).

As Alexei Yurchak has demonstrated, late socialism was also characterized by the appearance of various quasi-independent groups and alternative societies that encouraged and sustained forms of cultural production and participation that were distinct from those promoted by official state bodies, which technically held a monopoly on such matters.[6] By way of example, Yurchak cites a literary club, an archaeological circle (*kruzhok*), a group of theoretical physicists, a Leningrad cafe frequented by poets and artists (as well as, in one account, drug addicts and black-marketeers), and a hangout for aspiring pop musicians.[7] Yet as Yurchak cautions, such bodies 'did not fit the binary categories of either support of or opposition to the state.'[8] Some of them may have been at least partially dissident, but the vast majority existed in a more ambiguous zone, somewhere between the official and the underground, giving rise to 'new temporalities, spatialities, social relations, and meanings that were not necessarily anticipated or controlled by the state, although they were made fully possible by it.'[9]

These groupings thrived on the practice of *obshchenie*, a term that might be translated as '"communication" and "conversation" but in addition involves nonverbal interaction and spending time together or being together.'[10] Yurchak goes on to define the ways in which *obshchenie* facilitates the formation of communal practices:

> The noun *obshchenie* has the same root as *obshchii* (common) and *obshchina* (commune), stressing in the process of interaction not the exchange between individuals but the communal space where everyone's personhood was dialogized to produce a common intersubjective sociality. *Obshchenie*, therefore, is both a process and a sociality that emerges in that process, and both an exchange of ideas and information as well as a space of affect and togetherness. Although *obshchenie* is an old cultural practice in Russia, during late socialism it became

---

6   Alexei Yurchak, *Everything Was Forever, Until It Was No More: The Last Soviet Generation* (Princeton, NJ: Princeton University Press, 2006).

7   Ibid., pp. 135–48. For a detailed study of a particularly important literary and intellectual group of the time, see Josephine von Zitzewitz, *Poetry and the Leningrad Religious-Philosophical Seminar 1974–1980: Music for a Deaf Age* (Cambridge: Legenda, 2016).

8   Yurchak, *Everything Was Forever*, p. 34.

9   Ibid., p. 128.

10   Ibid., p. 148.

particularly intense and ubiquitous and acquired new forms, evolving into a dominant pastime in all strata of Soviet society and in all professional, ideological, public, and personal contexts.[11]

By viewing late socialism through the prism of such social and personal interactions, it becomes possible to set aside simplistic binary oppositions between state and dissident, conformist and rebel, that were ultimately a product of Cold War thinking, and to pay attention instead to what Yurchak described as border zones 'that were simultaneously inside and outside of the system'.[12] None of this is to deny the often very extreme measures that were used to limit freedom of expression and control cultural production. Nor is it to downplay the impact of such measures on creative artists. Rather, such an approach facilitates a greater understanding of the means by which communities of artists withstood and bypassed the impact of state power, as well as opening up a consideration of the consequences of such strategies on their creative output.

Yurchak's analysis has proved particularly influential to scholarship on the unofficial music scene that flourished across the Soviet Union in the 1960s and 1970s. As Peter J. Schmelz and Kevin C. Karnes have demonstrated, cities such as Moscow, Leningrad, Kyiv, Riga, and Tallinn supported a lively network of composers and performers which operated not so much in an underground sphere of illegality and dissent but in a parallel world of informal communities and improvised structures.[13] As Peter Schmelz argues:

> Although active participants in a socially meaningful concert subculture, the unofficial composers were in no ways dissidents, or at least no more so than any other creative artists within the Soviet system. The romanticizing assumption is fueled by Western cold war myths of artistic production in the

---

11　Ibid.

12　Ibid., p. 128.

13　Peter J. Schmelz, *Such Freedom, If Only Musical: Unofficial Soviet Music during the Thaw* (Oxford: Oxford University Press, 2009); Peter J. Schmelz, *Sonic Overload: Alfred Schnittke, Valentin Silvestrov, and Polystylism in the Late USSR* (New York: Oxford University Press, 2021); Kevin C. Karnes, *Sounds Beyond: Arvo Pärt and the 1970s Soviet Underground* (Chicago: University of Chicago Press, 2021).

Soviet Union that do a disservice to all artists active at the time
by singling out certain ones as more heroic than the rest.[14]

Yurchak's account of late socialism, as well as work by Schmelz and
Karnes on unofficial musical culture, has implications for scholarly
understanding of state bodies too. The officially sponsored artistic
unions that were established in April 1932 after the dissolution of the
many so-called artistic 'factions' that had thrived in the 1920s have long
been seen as repressive vehicles for the repression of a beleaguered
cultural elite, the top-down imposition of Soviet cultural policy, and
the dissemination of socialist realism throughout the Soviet Union. Yet,
as work by Amy Nelson, Kirill Tomoff, Leah Goldman, and others has
demonstrated, even the Union of Soviet Composers was characterized
by a wide range of informal practices and offered its members various
modes of agency.[15] The technical demands required by the high-level
training offered at conservatories, as well as the difficulty of applying
the theory of socialist realism to a non-representational art form such
as music, meant that musical elites were able to operate with an often
surprising degree of autonomy, if not independence, even during the
Stalin era. State-sponsored initiatives such as the Stalin Prize offered a
further opportunity for composers to assert their authority and resolve
professional rivalries.[16]

A particularly programmatic account of the atmosphere of the
early post-Stalin era was given by the composer Edison Denisov in
a 1966 interview with the Italian journal *Il contemporaneo*, a supple-
ment to the newspaper *Rinascita*, published by the Italian Communist
Party.[17] Reacting to what he regarded as sketchy and inaccurate West-

---

14 Schmelz, *Such Freedom*, pp. 13–14.

15 Amy Nelson, *Music for the Revolution: Musicians and Power in Early Soviet Russia* (Uni-
versity Park: Pennsylvania State University Press, 2004); Kirill Tomoff, *Creative Union:
The Professional Organization of Soviet Composers, 1939–1953* (Ithaca, NY: Cornell
University Press, 2006); Leah Goldman, 'Art of Intransigence: Soviet Composers and
Art Music Censorship' (unpublished doctoral thesis, University of Chicago, 2015).

16 Marina Frolova-Walker, *Stalin's Music Prize: Soviet Culture and Politics* (London: Yale
University Press, 2016).

17 Edison Denisov, 'Le tecniche nuove non sono una moda', *Il contemporaneo/Rinascita*,
August 1966, p. 12. A partial version of the original Russian, Edison Denisov, 'Novaya
tekhnika — eto ne moda', appeared in *'Drugoe iskusstvo': Moskva 1956–1976*, ed.
by I. Alpatova and L. Talochkin, 2 vols (Moscow: Khudozhestvennaya galeriya 'Mo-
skovskaya kollektsiya', 1991), I, pp. 313–15 (repr. in *'Drugoe iskusstvo': Moskva*

ern media commentary on contemporary Soviet musical life, as well as to the conservatism of Soviet concert agencies and high-profile performers, Denisov set out to describe the ideals and aspirations of the so-called 'young composers':

> A characteristic feature of the majority of young composers in the Soviet Union is a striving to expand the linguistic framework of the musical means they employ and a refusal to limit these artificially to the tonal system alone — a system that is very rich in its possibilities, but which in many respects has exhausted itself. Most young composers nowadays made extensive use of the techniques of serial composition, as well as various types of aleatory technique, and in some cases we encounter compositions in which sonority is the guiding principle [...].
>
> In recent years, Soviet composers have begun to experiment more and more widely, expanding the framework of their musical language and applying new types of techniques that emerged in the twentieth century, and in this we can see a new commitment to resisting the fundamental risk that threatened our music in the post-war years — that of academism.[18]

Setting themselves against the conservatism and implied provincialism of the aesthetic of Soviet socialist realism, this new generation turned instead to the legacy of Arnold Schoenberg's serial technique, in which conventional tonality was replaced by a self-consciously atonal musical language and all twelve notes of the scale enjoyed equal status (similar experiments were subsequently applied to other musical parameters, such as rhythm, dynamics, and duration). For many young Soviet composers of the 1960s, the greatest creative priority of the age involved catching up and assimilating the principles of Western European musical modernism that had been suppressed under Stalin and aligning themselves with the post-war European avant-garde.

1956–1988, ed. by I. Alpatova, L. Talochkin, and N. Tamruchi (Moscow: Galart; Gosudarstvennyi tsentr sovremennogo iskusstva, 2005), pp. 68–70). A complete version is given in *Svet — dobro — vechnost': Pamyati Edisona Denisova, stat'i, vospominaniya, materialy*, ed. by Valeriya Tsenova (Moscow: Moskovskaya gosudarstvennaya konservatoriya im. P. I. Chaikovskogo, 1999), pp. 33–38; subsequent references will be to this edition (I am grateful to Peter Schmelz for providing a copy of this).

18   Denisov, 'Novaya tekhnika', p. 34; all translations are my own unless otherwise indicated.

An interest in Western modernism was not confined to the world of music. Interest in foreign literature and visual culture was equally widespread during the Thaw,[19] but as Denisov noted, official bodies were often slow to respond to this development. As a result, alternative venues sprang up to accommodate the needs of listeners and performers and facilitated the exchange of new creative ideas. Denisov gives a lively account of his experience of such venues:

> Interest in new music in the Soviet Union is very great, particularly amongst students and the technical intelligentsia. On the initiative of young scholars, many institutes often hold evenings of contemporary music. I have had occasion to give lectures about new music in Dubna [a nuclear research centre just outside Moscow], at the Kurchatov Institute of Nuclear Physics, at the Institute of Architecture, at the Moscow Union of Artists, and at various student gatherings, and judging by the attentiveness with which works by Luigi Nono, Pierre Boulez, Vittorio Fellegara, Iannis Xenakis, Luciano Berio, Kazimierz Serocki, and other contemporary composers were heard, one can get a sense of the ever growing interest in new music (these lectures were always followed by long conversations and discussions).

> So far works by young composers are rarely performed in our concert venues, even though every premiere takes place in packed halls and to excited ovations by the audience. We have had no occasion to encounter the fabled 'conservatism' of the public — quite the opposite — our public has a particularly acute feeling for innovation, and all our difficulties relate to the conservatism of certain of our fellow composers and above all to the so-called 'musical bureaucracy'.[20]

What emerges from Denisov's account is the development of a parallel set of institutions that were more responsive to musical innovation than official state bodies such as the Union of Soviet Composers. These alternative spaces, often linked to other branches of scholarship, science, and cultural life, succeeded in giving a platform to new works, whether by members of the Western European post-war avant-garde or by a younger generation of Soviet composers. The world of unofficial

---

19   Eleonory Gilburd, *To See Paris and Die: The Soviet Lives of Western Culture* (Cambridge, MA: Belknap Press of Harvard University Press, 2018).

20   Denisov, 'Novaya tekhnika', p. 37.

music in the post-Stalin period was rooted, then, in daily forms of *obshchenie* that sustained experimental practices not countenanced by the state. At the same time, the stylistic practices of the unofficial composers emerged from a form of transnational *obshchenie* with various foreign influences that helped to constitute an 'imagined community' (to use Benedict Anderson's influential notion) of creative individuals who were not bound by the state and its institutions.

It is precisely this interaction between liminal spaces within the Soviet cultural and intellectual environment and an international repertoire of modernist music that makes the unofficial music scene in the post-Stalinist Soviet Union so fascinating. Scholarship has tended to focus on the musical innovations that resulted from this encounter, particularly in the experimental works of the 1960s that borrowed atonal, serial, and aleatoric elements from the West. Yet, alongside this musical dialogue (which also saw works by younger Soviet composers taken up in leading Western centres of musical experiment, such as the Darmstadt International Summer Courses for New Music), the unofficial community of Thaw-era musicians had a literary aspect too, one that was expressed in composers' choice of poetic texts. Evidence of this can be found in the figure of Andrey Volkonsky. Born into an émigré Russian family in Geneva 1933, he settled in the Soviet Union with his parents in 1947, before returning to the West in 1973. He studied at the Moscow Conservatory in the early 1950s, although relations with his teachers and the authorities were not always straightforward. One reason for these complications was his interest in and advocacy of serial music — for Denisov, his *Suite of Mirrors* (*Syuta zerkal*, 1959) was as significant an event for members of his generation as Dmitry Shostakovich's Fifth Symphony (1937) had been for an earlier one.[21]

Gennady Aygi's description of Volkonsky makes clear just what it was that Volkonsky offered to younger artists of all types:

> Andrey Volkonsky, the composer and musician, whom I consider a genius, was, amongst all of us who were part of underground culture, a most refined figure of the highest European culture. What mattered to us was that he was the only one with connections to Europe. After the end of the war, his family

---

21   Ibid., p. 35.

returned from France to the Soviet Union, and Andrey, despite the danger, kept up his connections with foreign friends. All of Western literature reached him: Ionesco, Beckett, Kafka, and through him we got to know the *Encyclopedia of Abstract Art* [...]. Volkonsky's great prospects, his unusual sense of commitment and dedication to the cause of new art played a huge role that brought us all together and educated us [...]. He was the first to bring the music of the Middle Ages and Renaissance into our lives. Through him we got to know the most recent music of Schoenberg and Webern. In this sense he was a teacher of both artists, and poets and musicians. Without even suspecting it, thanks to his most remarkable impulsive, brilliant nature, thanks to his artistry, he was our Teacher.[22]

What emerges here is a portrait of Volkonsky as the embodiment of high modernism — Ionesco, Beckett, and Kafka in literature, Schoenberg and Webern in music, and the visual artists covered in Michel Seuphor's *Dictionnaire de la peinture abstraite* (1957). Modernism comes to represent not just a challenge to Soviet conservatism and the conventions of socialist realism but a form of transnational artistic dialogue that links composers, writers, and artists across national and linguistic borders.

Scholarship on the younger generation of Soviet composers has made much of their innovations in musical language, yet their work has a crucial verbal dimension too, and one that further illustrates their conception of a transnational form of artistic community. It is striking, for instance, that two of Volkonsky's most influential works from the 1960s were both settings of contrasting schools of lyric poetry. His *Suite of Mirrors* took nine verses by Federico García Lorca in Russian translations by Vladimir Burich and set them to music for solo voice and small instrumental ensemble. Lorca's republican politics and status as one of the exemplary victims of fascism meant that his poetry ought, at least in theory, to have been acceptable in the Soviet Union. Certainly there was plenty of discussion of Lorca's poetry — and its suitability for musical settings — in official publications at

---

22 Quoted in *'Drugoe iskusstvo': Moskva 1956–1988*, ed. by Alpatova, Talochkin, and Tamruchi, p. 50. For a slightly different translation of this interview, see Schmelz, *Such Freedom*, p. 69.

the time.[23] Yet, as Schmelz observes, Volkonsky deliberately chose 'evocative, abstract, and unclear texts' that 'directly opposed the clarity and accessibility demanded by the aesthetics of socialist realism'.[24] Accordingly, *Suite of Mirrors* 'portrayed another side to the revolutionary Lorca, one where heroic zeal gave way to exotic abstraction'.[25]

So much can be gleaned from the cycle's very opening words, which constitute a direct rejection of Soviet values, whether in their religious language or their ecstatic, almost surrealist diction:

> Khristov
> derzhit zerkalo
> v kazhdoi ruke.
> Oni umnozhayut
> ego yavlen'e,
> Proektiruya serdtse
> na chernye
> vzglyady.
> Veruyu!
>
> (Christ
> holds a mirror
> in each hand.
> They multiply
> his aspect,
> Projecting his heart
> onto black
> glances.
> I believe!)[26]

---

23   Cf. e.g. M. Vaisbord, 'Garsia Lorka — muzykant', *Sovetskaya muzyka*, 9 (1961), pp. 128–30, as well as S. Katonov's review of a more orthodoxly 'civic' cycle of Lorca's poetry (along with settings of Pablo Neruda) by Vadim Salmanov, 'Dva tsikla — dva resheniya', *Sovetskaya muzyka*, 2 (1965), pp. 10–13. Cf. too Natal'ya Shpiller's review of a performance of Kirill Molchanov's equally politically correct interpretation of Lorca's poetry in 'Vokal'nye vechera', *Sovetskaya muzyka*, 6 (1965), pp. 95–96. Volkonsky's resistance to the official Soviet myth of Lorca might also be linked to his awareness of Shostakovich's very popular *Spanish Songs*, op. 100, written in 1956 and based on melodies transcribed from a Soviet citizen of Spanish descent whose family had fled Franco's fascist regime. See Galina Kopytova, 'Shostakovich's Music for *Salute, Spain!* Discoveries and Perspectives', *Journal of War & Culture Studies*, 14.4 (2021), pp. 479–92 (pp. 490–91).

24   Schmelz, *Such Freedom*, p. 99.

25   Ibid.

26   The original Spanish reads: 'Cristo | tenía un espejo | en cada mano. | Multiplicaba | su propio espectro. | Proyectaba su corazón | en las miradas | negras. | ¡Creo!'.

Musically, too, the mirror image of Lorca's poetry led Volkonsky to explore a complex musical language full of 'symmetries, reflections, and refractions',[27] rather than the accessible and didactic forms of socialist realism. His next work offered a similarly creative response to language and identity. Superficially, the choice of the traditional folk laments of the Dagestani poet Shchaza of Kurkla, which Volkonsky studied on a number of ethnographical trips to the autonomous region, seems to be aligned with official Soviet nationalities policy. Yet, once again, the radical musical language of Laments of Shchaza (Zhaloby Shchazy, 1962) disrupted conventional cultural norms and turned state-sanctioned folk poetry into an expression of the pan-European avant-garde.[28]

Both works drew direct inspiration from at least one important European work: Pierre Boulez's Le Marteau sans maître (1953–54). Premiered in 1955, Boulez's chamber cantata set surrealist verses by René Char for solo voice and small instrumental ensemble, as well as exploring a highly intricate approach to the application of serial technique. Another work for solo voice and instrumental ensemble that clearly also influenced young Soviet composers was Schoenberg's much earlier Pierrot Lunaire (1912). Although noted as an important work of German expressionism, Pierrot Lunaire is in fact based on translations of French poetry by the Belgian symbolist Albert Giraud, and hence a significant prior example of the transnational lyric. Thus, through their choice of poetry and their use of a very particular instrumental sonority, Volkonsky's Suite of Mirrors and Laments of Shchaza establish a creative dialogue with important European precursors, and one that would have been immediately audible to the small coterie of composers and performers familiar with these new works.

Given his background and upbringing, Volkonsky's treatment of the lyric (both musical and literary) should come as little surprise (recall Aygi's description of him as 'a most refined figure of the highest European culture'). What is of equal significance is how his example soon came to be taken up by his contemporaries. Younger composers could signal their awareness of and relationship to global artistic de-

---

27 Schmelz, Such Freedom, p. 101.
28 The musical language of both cycles is discussed in detail in ibid., pp. 96–127.

velopments through their choice of literary texts, thereby fashioning an imagined transnational community of avant-garde artists, even — perhaps especially — as they were prevented from travelling abroad, whether to other countries in the Eastern bloc (particularly Poland, where the Warsaw Autumn became one of the most important festivals for contemporary music) or to Western Europe or North America.[29] Here, the work of Denisov illustrates the impact of Volkonsky on the world of unofficial music. His *Sun of the Incas* (*Solntse inkov*, 1964) builds on Volkonsky's *Suite of Mirrors* in that it takes a major twentieth-century Hispanic writer — here, the Chilean poet Gabriela Mistral — and similarly explores the sonorities of a small chamber ensemble and applies a number of serial techniques. Likewise, Denisov's folkloric *Laments* (*Plachi*, 1966) explicitly echoes not only Volkonsky's *Laments of Shchaza* (although Denisov uses a different Russian word, *plachi*, rather than *zhaloby*) but also Stravinsky's *Les Noces* (1923).[30] Such intertextuality is, of course, not exclusive to unofficial Soviet culture. Yet it is clear that not only did such acts of homage serve to fashion a powerful sense of shared identity and artistic friendship; they also created a form of creative community that extended across both time and space.

These chamber-vocal suites by Volkonsky and Denisov tested the boundaries of what was permissible in the context of the often hesitant liberalization of the Khrushchev era, and were often subject to ideological criticism and practical impediments on the part of the Union of Soviet Composers. Despite the advocacy and cunning of adventurous performers (such as the soprano Lidiya Davydova, the conductor Gennady Rozhdestvensky, or the percussionist Mark Pekarsky), such works did not always have a straightforward path to performance or publication, and despite a number of important premieres, they often

---

29   Lisa Jakelski, *Making New Music in Cold War Poland: The Warsaw Autumn Festival, 1956–1968* (Berkeley: University of California Press, 2017). As Peter Schmelz, 'Selling Schnittke: Late Soviet Censorship and the Cold War Marketplace', in *The Oxford Handbook of Music Censorship*, ed. by Patricia Hall (New York: Oxford University Press, 2015), pp. 413–52, has observed, the limitations placed on the younger generation of unofficial composers lent them a distinct cachet with Western audiences, and whilst their works were often criticized or ignored altogether at home, they received considerable exposure at leading Western festivals of avant-garde music.

30   Schmelz, *Such Freedom*, pp. 131–78.

struggled to retain their place in the repertoire, official or underground. They certainly were not heard by the vast majority of Soviet listeners, whether in live performance or state-sanctioned recording, remaining instead the preserve of relatively small communities of like-minded creative artists and their supporters.

There was, though, another instantiation of the musical lyric that emerged within the community of unofficial Soviet composers in the 1960s and 1970s, and which embodied a rather different set of musical and literary ideas. Here, it was the art-song — or, as it is known in Russian — the 'romance' (*romans*) that proved to be the ideal vehicle for a series of imaginary transnational encounters. Typically conceived for solo voice and piano accompaniment, the romance had a long history in Russian music, reaching back to the Europeanization of Russian culture in the eighteenth century and flourishing first in the age of romanticism before going on to find its most vital expression in the work of composers such as Pyotr Tchaikovsky or Sergei Rachmaninoff. Rather incongruously for a genre so closely associated with the rise of bourgeois domestic culture, it even survived the October Revolution and the rise of Stalinism.[31]

Scholarship on the Russian romance has tended to emphasize its intimate relationship with Russian lyric poetry, as well as its role in the emergence of a distinct form of Russian national consciousness.[32] As with its cousins, the German *Lied* and the French *mélodie*, the Russian romance is often seen as the bearer of a form of identity that is organically rooted in language and nation. As the nineteenth-century composer and pianist Anton Rubinstein argued, 'song is the only musical genre to have a fatherland'.[33] Yet the romance had a crucial transnational aspect too, with the work of foreign poets — whether in Russian translation or in the original language — figuring as a

31   Philip Ross Bullock, 'The Birth of the Soviet Romance from the Spirit of Russian Modernism', *Slavonic and East European Review*, 97.1 (2019), pp. 110–35; Philip Ross Bullock, 'The Pushkin Anniversary of 1937 and Russian Art Song in the Soviet Union', *Slavonica*, 13.1 (2007), pp. 39–56.

32   See e.g. the classic Soviet-era studies by Vera Vasina-Grossman, *Russkii klassicheskii romans XIX veka* (Moscow: Izdatel'stvo Akademii nauk SSSR, 1956) and *Mastera sovetskogo romansa*, 2nd edn (Moscow: Muzyka, 1980).

33   Anton Rubinstein, 'Die Componisten Rußland's', *Blätter für Musik, Theater und Kunst*, 8 June 1855, pp. 145–46 (p. 145).

significant element in its literary constitution.[34] Here, the work of two other unofficial composers — Sofia Gubaidulina and Alfred Schnittke — illustrates how a range of poetry could be used to sustain a musical community that was distinct from the official narrative provided by the state and its institutions.

As a student in her native city of Kazan, the capital of Tatarstan, Gubaidulina wrote her first songs to conventional enough texts by classical Russian poets such as Aleksandr Pushkin, Fyodor Tyutchev, and Afanasy Fet, and song figured in her early output at the Moscow Conservatory too. There, she discovered Mikhail Prishvin's prose poem *Phacelia* (*Fatseliya*), extracts of which formed the basis of a six-movement cycle for soprano and orchestra written in 1956 (it also exists in a version for voice and piano, in which form it was published in 1975). Prishvin — who died in 1954 at the age of eighty — was an important figure in the early years of the Thaw, when his lyric descriptions of nature became a model for a new kind of less explicitly ideological literature. The cycle became something of a calling card for Gubaidulina too. She included it in the dossier of compositions she submitted for her final examinations at the Moscow Conservatory in 1959, and again in her application to join the Union of Soviet Composers in 1961. It was performed and even broadcast a number of times, and praised in print in the official journal of the Union of Soviet Composers.[35]

Thereafter, her musical style became more innovative — and her linguistic choices more diverse and unconstrained by the Russian language. In *Night in Memphis* (*Noch' v Memfise*, 1968), she fashioned a cantata for mezzo-soprano, male chorus, and chamber orchestra out of Ancient Egyptian texts in Russian versions by Anna Akhmatova and Vera Potapova. A year later, she turned to a selection of Persian poets

---

34   For a collection of essays exploring these themes from a number of literary and musical traditions, see *Song beyond the Nation: Translation, Transnationalism, Performance*, ed. by Philip Ross Bullock and Laura Tunbridge (Oxford: Oxford University Press, 2021). See too Philip Ross Bullock, 'Song in a Strange Land: The Russian Musical Lyric beyond the Nation', in *Global Russian Cultures*, ed. by Kevin M. F. Platt (Madison: University of Wisconsin Press, 2019), pp. 290–311.

35   V. Borovskii, 'Otkroite vse okna!', *Sovetskaya muzyka*, 2 (1962), pp. 23–28 (p. 24). On Gubaidualina's early creative biography, see Michael Kurtz, *Sofia Gubaidulina: A Biography*, trans. by Christoph K. Lohmann, ed. by Malcolm Hamrick Brown (Bloomington: Indiana University Press, 2007), with comments on the songs on pp. 19, 40–41.

(translated into Russian by Vladimir Derzhavin), which she combined to make another cantata, *Rubaiyat*, for baritone and chamber orchestra. If Prishvin's prose poetry had signalled her sense of affinity with Russia's landscapes and its literary language, then the texts of *Night in Memphis* and *Rubaiyat* constitute more adventurous journeys of the literary and musical imagination. Drawing their inspiration from similar cantatas for voice and chamber ensemble by Volkonsky and Denisov (which themselves paid homage to Boulez and other members of the Western European avant-garde), these scores proved too challenging for Soviet cultural politics. *Night in Memphis* was not heard in Russia until 1989, and it initially fell to musicians from other socialist countries to promote it. It was first recorded and broadcast by Prague Radio in December 1970 (possibly as a symbolic protest at the suppression of the Prague Spring in 1968), and received its public premiere in May 1971 in Zagreb, Yugoslavia, where the atmosphere was decidedly more liberal than Brezhnev-era Moscow.[36] *Rubaiyat* was rather luckier — it was first heard in Moscow in December 1976.[37]

In these cantatas, Gubaidulina put clear linguistic and stylistic distance between herself and the legacy of the Russian romance tradition. Thereafter, she seems to have felt freer to return to lyric poetry, although her relationship to its national aspects now became complex and fluid. At some point in the late 1950s, Gubaidulina became aware of Aygi, whose description of the impact of Volkonsky on the underground culture of the Thaw has already been cited. A young Chuvash poet, Aygi was encouraged to write in Russian by Boris Pasternak and soon began to make a name in unofficial literary circles in Moscow, as well as abroad. Aygi's friendship with Pasternak at the time of the *Dr Zhivago* scandal in 1958 meant that his works went unpublished, other than in *samizdat* (i.e. unofficial self-publication designed for a small group of trusted initiates) and *tamizdat* (i.e. unofficial publication outside the Soviet Union). It was, rather, as a literary translator that he made his living.[38] His original poetry — which did not appear officially in print until 1987 — was much appreciated by trusted friends and col-

---

36 Kurtz, *Gubaidulina*, p. 92; Schmelz, *Such Freedom*, pp. 264–66.
37 Kurtz, *Gubaidulina*, pp. 82, 126–28.
38 For a convenient biography of Aygi's life, see Sarah Valentine, *Witness and Transformation: The Poetics of Gennady Aygi* (Brighton, MA: Academic Studies Press, 2015), pp.

leagues, and in the summer of 1972, Gubaidulina set five of his poems to music as a short cycle called *Roses* (*Rozy*), which was premiered on 1 March 1973 at the Moscow Youth Musical Club, one of the most important semi-official venues for the promotion of new music.[39]

A key aspect of the collaboration between poet and composer is the oblique way through which both of them approached the question of Russianness. Gubaidulina's interest in the work of a Chuvash poet might be seen as analogous to her own hybrid identity as a Russian composer of Tatar origin.[40] Moreover, Aygi claimed that his fragmented, pointillistic poems had been written under the influence of Webern's music, and two of the poems selected by Gubaidulina carry dedications to Volkonsky and to Char (the poet of Boulez's *Le Marteau sans maître*) respectively. *Roses* is a cycle, then, which emerges from an ongoing artistic conversation — a form of creative *obshchenie* — between the European avant-garde and the Soviet underground. Although Aygi and Gubaidulina both suffered from the impact of censorship and restraints on creative freedom that were commonplace in the Soviet Union, they nonetheless managed to create an imagined dialogue that extended beyond the russophone world and incorporated both aspects of the Soviet Union's own internal linguistic and national diversity, and elements of the shared legacy of pan-European modernism.[41]

Gubaidulina would develop this interest in song as form of cross-border encounter in a number of settings of the poetry of Francisco Tanzer, whom she met in Moscow in 1979.[42] Born in Vienna, raised in Budapest, educated in France and the United States, and later resident in Germany, Tanzer was a multilingual, cosmopolitan figure who was rather different from many of the Western visitors to the Soviet Union during the 1960s and 1970s (such as Luigi Nono, whose membership of the Italian Communist Party gave him ready access to Soviet

18–21. See, too, Peter France, 'Introduction', in Gennady Aygi, *Selected Poems, 1954–94*, ed. and trans. by Peter France (London: Angel Books, 1997), pp. 17–27.

39 Kurtz, *Sofia Gubaidulina*, pp. 98–100; Schmelz, *Such Freedom*, pp. 300–02.

40 For a thoughtful treatment of Aygi's relationship to language and nationality, see Valentine, *Witness and Transformation*, pp. 27–54.

41 On Aygi's multilingualism, see Natal'ya Azarova, 'Mnogoyazichie Aigi i yazyki-posredniki', *Russian Literature*, 79–80 (2016), pp. 29–44.

42 Kurtz, *Gubaidulina*, pp. 142–43.

cultural institutions in the post-Stalin era).[43] Gubaidulina first used one of Tanzer's texts as a spoken epilogue to her trio for flute, viola, and harp, *The Garden of Joy and Sorrow* (*Sad radosti i pechali*, 1980), and in 1983, she completed *Perception*, a thirteen-movement score for soprano, baritone, and seven string instruments which featured nine texts by Tanzer, as well as a number of quotations from the Psalms.[44]

Given Gubaidulina's interest in questions of translation, deracination, and dislocation, it is striking that she largely avoided the poetry of Marina Tsvetaeva, at least in song. Along with other Russian modernists of the early twentieth century (notably Akhmatova, Pasternak, and Osip Mandelstam), Tsvetaeva's poetry was extensively rediscovered in the post-Stalin period and soon taken up by composers.[45] The most famous figure to tackle Tsvetaeva's complex and challenging poetry was Shostakovich, who set six of her poems on themes of love, art, power, and posterity for contralto and piano in 1973.[46] Yet the preeminence of this cycle — whether with performers or in scholarship — has tended to overshadow the variety of other musicians who were drawn to her verse, such as the Leningrad composer Boris Tishchenko, whose Second Symphony (1964) for chorus and large orchestra is explicitly called *Marina*, and who followed this with a short cycle of three songs in 1970. Tsvetaeva's poetry even found its way into the variety repertoire (what is called *estrada* in Russian), as exemplified by the popular *chansonnière* Alla Pugacheva.

---

43   On Nono's impact on the world of unofficial Soviet music, see Schmelz, *Such Freedom*, pp. 45–46, 62–64.

44   Kurtz, *Gubaidulina*, pp. 152, 172–73. *The Garden of Joy and Sorrow* itself attests to Gubaidulina's markedly syncretic interests when it comes to questions of culture, national identity, and belonging. It arose as a result of her reading both of Tanzer and of Ivan Oganov's *Revelation of the Rose* (*Otkrovenie rozy*), a historical novel based on 'the turbulent life of Sayat-Nova, an Armenian lyric poet and folk singer of the eighteenth century who later became a monk'. As Gubaidulina recalled, her composition conveyed 'the impression of two poetic worlds that had coalesced within me into the unified image of an Eastern garden where everything lives in stillness and pain of Francisco Tanzer's Western poems. Thus the opposing elemental essences of East and West quite naturally became one in me' (quoted in Kurtz, *Gubaidulina*, pp. 150–51).

45   For a bibliography of musical settings of all four poets, see *Anna Akhmatova, Marina Tsvetaeva, Osip Mandel'shtam i Boris Pasternak v muzyke: Notografiya*, ed. by Boris Rozenfel'd (Stanford, CA: Department of Slavic Languages and Literatures, Stanford University, 2003), especially pp. 64–102.

46   Christopher W. Lemelin, 'To Name or Not to Name: The Question of Shostakovich's Interpretation of Tsvetaeva', *Musical Quarterly*, 93.2 (2010), pp. 234–61.

In many ways, Gubaidulina felt a profound affinity with aspects of Tsvetaeva's life and work. It was, she believed, 'a quirk of fate' that she had been born in Chistopol, not far from Elabuga, where Tsvetaeva took her own life in 1941.[47] Not only was Tsvetaeva one of the greatest Russian modernists; she was also a perpetual outsider, whether as an émigré in interwar Prague and Paris, or as one of the few émigrés to have returned to the Soviet Union. As indebted to German romanticism as she was devoted to Pushkin, she saw all poets — at least great ones — as outcasts. As she provocatively claimed in her narrative poem *The Poem of the End* (*Poema kontsa*): 'In this most Christian of worlds, | Poets are Jews!' (V sem khistianneishem iz mirov | Poety — zhidy!).[48] Yet, despite such potential affinities, Gubaidulina avoided setting her poetry as song. Instead, that task fell to her close contemporary Schnittke, who — as his name suggests — was partly of German and German-Jewish origin, and whose family lived in Austria in the 1940s. As a student at the Moscow Conservatory in the 1950s, Schnittke had composed conventional enough romances to poems by Pushkin, Lermontov, and Tyutchev.[49] Yet, in an interview, he claimed to prefer 'Rilke, Trakl, or Baudelaire' — hardly figures central to Soviet cultural politics, even during the Thaw.[50] In 1965, at a time when he was most fascinated by the possibility of the serial technique of composition, Schnittke wrote his *Three Poems of Marina Tsvetaeva* (*Tri stikhotvoreniya Mariny Tsvetaevoi*), a figure who might come closer to his interest in those poets (Tsvetaeva, along with Pasternak, partook in an intensive correspondence with Rilke in 1926).[51]

In an interview with Enzo Restagno, Gubaidulina suggested that part of Tsvetaeva's attraction for Schnittke — who was born in the

---

47　Quoted in Kurtz, *Gubaidualina*, p. 6.

48　Characteristically, Tsvetaeva prefers the offensive term *zhid* to the more neutral *evrei*. Marina Tsvetaeva, 'Poema kontsa', in *Sobranie sochinenii*, 7 vols (Moscow: Ellis Lak, 1994–95), III (1994), pp. 31–50 (p. 48).

49　For a discussion of Schnittke's vocal works, see Gavin Dixon, *The Routledge Handbook to the Music of Alfred Schnittke* (Abingdon: Routledge, 2022), pp. 90–101.

50　Alfred Schnittke, *A Schnittke Reader*, ed. by Alexander Ivashkin, trans. by John Goodliffe (Bloomington: Indiana University Press, 2002), p. 19.

51　Rainer Maria Rilke, Marina Zwetajewa, and Boris Pasternak, *Briefwechsel*, ed. by Jewgenij Pasternak, Jelena Pasternak, and Konstantin M. Asadowskij (Frankfurt a.M.: Insel Verlag, 1983).

Volga German capital of Engels — was the fact that she was 'a poet who also had two souls, a Russian one and a German one'. To this, Gubaidulina added a third component — Schnittke's Jewish origins, which, she argued, could synthesize the 'opposing elements' of his character.[52] Schnittke himself was profoundly aware of his ambiguous relationship to the boundaries imposed by language and culture. After his emigration to West Germany in 1990, he confessed to a friend:

> I understand that there is no home for me on Earth. In Russia I am either a Jew or a German. Arriving in Germany, even there I begin to feel that something separates me from Germans. Three things separate me: I come from Russia, I am a Jew who doesn't know Hebrew, I was born in a German region, but in the USSR. There [in Germany] I am a Russian composer.[53]

It is important not to overstate, exoticize, or essentialize the question of Schnittke's national identity (or, for that matter, Gubaidulina's), yet it is interesting to note how drawn both of them were to poets who resist easy categorization along national lines. Just as Gubaidulina had explored the poetry of Aygi and Tanzer (not to mention Russian translations of Ancient Egyptian and Persian texts), so too did Schnittke turn to non-Russian verses as a means of questioning the implicit nationalism of the Russian song tradition. His tangential relationship to that tradition can be seen in his decision, in 1988, to set three German-language texts by his brother Viktor, a German translator and noted figure in the Volga German community to which the Schnittke family belonged. Before that, in 1980, he had paid homage to Gubaidulina herself in his *Three Madrigals* (*Tri madrigala*), with words by the very same poet — Tanzer — to whom she was so frequently drawn. Schnittke's selection is strikingly transnational in its linguistic and musical identity. The first poem is a setting of Tanzer's original French text, 'Sur une étoile', followed by 'Entfernung' (in German) and 'Reflection' (in English). Each song reflects aspects of its respective musical culture

---

52   Enzo Restagno, 'Un'autobiografia dell'autore raccontata da Enzo Restagno', in *Gubajdulina*, ed. by Enzo Restagno (Turin: EDT, 1991), pp. 3–91 (p. 28).

53   Quoted in Schmelz, *Sonic Overload*, p. 290.

('an old French chanson', 'a Viennese alpine trait', 'the euphony of a spiritual').[54]

Driven underground by censorship, sidelined by personal rivalries, and resistant to the stylistic demands of socialist realism, Gubaidulina and Schnittke employ heterogeneous literary texts as a means of escaping the limitations placed on them by Soviet cultural politics. Both composers found ways of addressing their marginalized position within official Soviet culture by embarking on a wide-ranging series of hybrid literary and musical encounters with a range of non-Russian poets, or with Russian poets whose linguistic and cultural practices resist straightforward understanding along narrow national lines. As Schnittke himself argued: 'Cultural boundaries must not be preserved. The idea is inadmissible. I regard as grossly mistaken all those attempts that have been made to preserve them throughout many centuries and decades, especially in the last hundred and twenty or thirty years.'[55] For Gubaidulina and Schnittke, a sense of belonging to a wider community of writers and composers was an important reaction in dealing with their own uncertain place in late Soviet musical culture.

Moreover, song itself — so long associated with the intimacy of the salon and the world of chamber music — proved itself to be the ideal genre for a celebration of artistic friendship and creative collegiately, especially when the official structures of state life excluded the unofficial composers from full participation in the Soviet musical institutions.[56] To judge by commercial recordings and the scholarly literature, Schnittke and Gubaidulina are more often associated with vast and ambitious scores — three operas, nine symphonies, and a large number of concertos in the case of the former, a heterogeneous series of syncretic spiritual works for chorus and orchestra in the case

---

54   Dixon, *Handbook*, p. 94. The importance of Tanzer — whether as a poet or as a marker of shared friendship and artistic values — also extended to Denisov, who set five of his poems from the collection *Blätter* for soprano and string trio in 1978, as well as including his verses in his *Requiem* (1982).

55   Schnittke, *Reader*, pp. 19–20.

56   For a study of Valentyn Syl'vestrov's song cycle *Quiet Songs* (*Tikhie pesni*, 1974–77) that emphasizes its handling of artistic friendship and cultural intimacy, as well as its reflective relationship to Russian nationalism, see Philip Ross Bullock, 'Intimacy and Distance: Valentin Sil'vestrov's *Tikhie pesni*', *Slavonic and East European Review*, 92.3 (2014), pp. 401–29.

of the latter. Yet each composer also turned to the concision, precision, privacy, and even subjectivity of the lyric at key moments in their creative lives in order to engage in a form of dialogue — or *obshchenie*, to return to the term proposed by Yurchak at the start of this chapter — that emerged from the unofficial artistic venues they inhabited, as well as aspiring to a relationship with their European contemporaries that was no less forceful for being a largely imaginary one. The stories told here remind us that histories of literary and musical genres that exclude questions of translation and otherness tell us only part of the story. The underground was always elsewhere.

Mina Loy's Interrupted Communities

LAURA SCURIATTI

In 1927 the British poet, painter, and designer Mina Loy wrote an introductory essay on Gertrude Stein, whom she had met and befriended during her long stays in Florence (1906–16) and, at Natalie Barney's famous salons, in Paris (in the 1920s and 1930s). Barney ran two different types of salon in the French capital: one saw the participation of a number of French and Anglo-American writers and artists; the other was a circle of intellectual women who gathered as the Académie des Femmes, a (mostly) queer community of women artists, writers, and thinkers, conceived as a provocative counterpart to the Académie française, which excluded women.[1] Both Stein and Loy were part of the anglophone expatriate community in the French capital and participated in Barney's gatherings. Loy's essay, written and read aloud in French, was not her first assessment and celebration of Stein's work: in 1924, she had published a two-part essay on the American novelist

---

1   For an account of the salons and their participants, see e.g. Shari Benstock, *Women of the Left Bank* (Austin: University of Texas Press, 1986), pp. 268–308; Gloria Feman Orenstein, 'The Salon of Natalie Clifford Barney: An Interview with Berthe Cleyrergue', *Signs*, 4.3 (1979), pp. 484–96; George Wickes, 'Comment on Orenstein's "The Salon of Natalie Clifford Barney: An Interview with Berthe Cleyrergue"', *Signs*, 5.3 (1980), pp. 547–50. For an overview of the debates around the scholarship on Barney's salons, see also Chelsea Ray, 'Natalie Barney (1876–1972): Writer, Salon Hostess, and Eternal Friend; Interview with Jean Chalon', *Women in French Studies*, 30 (2022), pp. 154–69.

in the *Transatlantic Review*, prefaced by her famous dedicatory poem, 'Gertrude Stein'.[2]

For all their differences, both essays explore and celebrate the specificity of Stein's genius within the context of an Anglo-American modernism, and they do so by analysing the ways in which modernist literary experimentation and modernist genius emerge within, and are able to create, communities of like-minded readers and artists. Indeed, in 1924, Loy celebrated Stein's works precisely for their ability to engender a sort of 'imaginary community' of readers who, almost imitating the precise craftmanship of the author, undergo the process of understanding her experimental work. While Loy herself was never an official member of structured communities such as artistic movements or avant-garde groups, her poetry and essays often reflect and theorize on the processes subsuming the formation of such communities inside and outside the texts, and posit them as a fundamental element of the production and reception of modernist art and literature. This chapter explores the different types of modernist collectivities in Loy's works, arguing that the insistence on their ephemeral, precarious, and shifting temporality is the result not only of her participation in mobile, transnational expatriate communities but also of a feminist stance that refuses participation in patriarchal or oppressive forms of togetherness and community, aiming instead to imagine possible alternatives.

The first few lines of the 1927 essay on Stein, translated into English by Martin Crowley, are useful for understanding Loy's scepticism towards facile and stable notions of a collective, even within the rarefied small modernist world involved in debates on genius:

> Twenty years ago, people used to say to me, 'the days when a genius could appear suddenly, and be unappreciated, are well and truly gone'.
>
> They said we were so very civilized, so blasé in the face of any conceivable surprise, that no-one could ever again leave the critics baffled.
>
> Bizarrely, however, our culture is destined to find that any truly new thought will burst upon it like a fury. And it is to this

---

2   For information on the publication history of these essays, see Sarah Crangle, 'Notes', in *Stories and Essays of Mina Loy*, ed. by Sara Crangle (Champaign, IL: Dalkey Archive Press, 2011), pp. 297–416 (pp. 379–80).

destiny that the critics have once more succumbed in the case
of Gertrude Stein.[3]

In this essay, Loy stages from the outset a tension between individual
personas and collective entities. Alongside the collective designations
'people', 'we', and 'our culture', the singular 'me' appears as the ad-
dressee of a purported pessimism about the status of contemporary art.
The 'me' hovers between being a singular entity separate from what
'they' or 'people' say — the French original deploys the impersonal
'On disait que nous sommes à tel point cultivé',[4] which in the English
translation is rendered as 'They said we were so very civilized' — and
belonging in a collectivity of artists to which 'people' in general are
inimical. Similar constellations are typical of avant-garde stances, and
are also at the centre of Loy's poem 'Apology of Genius'. The collect-
ive pronouns, however, do not survive beyond the first few lines, and
give way to a critical engagement with the work of Stein which only
foresees the presence of a 'she' and an 'I', whereby the 'I' assumes the
detached position of a critic and observer of Stein's progress towards
international success.

Two interesting things happen in this essay. First, it starts with a
sort of indecision about the position of the singular pronoun, of the in-
dividual subject, in relation to different collectivities, and then resolves
this indecision in favour of a strong 'I'. Second, Loy claims for Stein and
her literary works a crucial role not only in the defamiliarization of the
English language but also in its deterritorialization, in the dismantling
of a monolithic notion of national identity:

> I doubt any of her writings has appeared in French, especially
> as the essential feature of her work is its untranslatability into
> even its own language. For our obliging pioneer has reduced
> the English language to a foreign language even for Anglo-
> Americans.[5]

---

3   Mina Loy, 'Gertrude Stein', in *Stories and Essays*, pp. 232–34 (p. 232). All quotations
     from Mina Loy's works are by kind permission of Roger Conover, Mina Loy's editor
     and literary executor.
4   Crangle, 'Notes', p. 380.
5   Loy, 'Gertrude Stein', pp. 234–34.

Loy here questions the identification of language with nationality or ethnicity,[6] referring not only to Stein's English as a foreign language but also extending the reach of English to a wider body of speakers beyond national borders.[7] In a move similar to that which occurs at the beginning of the essay, Loy in this passage posits and then immediately dismantles the possibility of a collective subject or audience identified by a possible shared reaction to the text. Closing the essay, Loy returns to using the general collective noun 'people' with which she started the essay, but qualifying it: 'Perhaps much of the opposition unleashed against Gertrude Stein stemmed from the fear of those people who claimed to be stunned.'[8]

The essay performs its scepticism towards collectivities of various kinds, and proposes a jolting journey of identification and disidentification, traversing politics, reading practices, and emotional reception. A similar contradictory position characterizes the 'Feminist Manifesto' (1914) and 'International Psycho-Democracy' (1918), which do not really produce 'isms' or real political parties with which to identify, but instead propose radical programmes using a language that does not really aim at any political activism but rather at what Martin Puchner has defined as a 'poetics that aspired to the condition of the manifesto.'[9] Indeed, the 'Feminist Manifesto' and 'International Psycho-Democracy' gesture towards the form of address found in political or artistic manifestos, but paradoxically, the first person plural, when it appears at all, is vague and shifting, as the texts also express a suspicion towards political and social forces based on collectivities.

In what follows, I shall explore the connection between Loy's textual strategies and the mobile clusters of communities produced by them. I examine in particular her multilingual coinages and her

---

6   In French, Loy uses the designation 'Anglo-Saxons' (Crangle, 'Notes', p. 382).

7   See Marjorie Perloff, 'English as a "Second" Language: Mina Loy's "Anglo-Mongrels and the Rose"', in *Mina Loy: Woman and Poet*, ed. by Maeera Shreiber and Keith Tuma (Orono, ME: National Poetry Foundation, 1998), pp. 131–48.

8   Loy, 'Gertrude Stein', p. 234.

9   Martin Puchner, *Poetry of the Revolution: Marx, Manifestos, and the Avant-Garde* (Princeton, NJ: Princeton University Press, 2006), p. 71. For further theorization of the political implications of the collective subject of manifestos, see also Janet Lyon, *Manifestoes: Provocations of the Modern* (Ithaca, NY: Cornell University Press, 1999), p. 12.

use of pronouns in the situation of poetic address. And I start from a paradox: on the one hand, Loy's aesthetic and social exceptionalism, eccentricity, and satirical stance have nurtured the impression that she kept a programmatic distance from any kind of communal or communitarian project, even within the world of modernist poetry. Indeed, as Roger Conover remarks, Loy's idiosyncratic and satirical poetic style had caused her relative isolation among her contemporaries and made her an exceptional figure in modernist poetry.[10] And so, to segue into Loy Alice Oswald's judgement on T. S. Eliot, Loy 'is a satirist, and a satirist is a brilliant critic, rather than a compassionate fellow traveler'.[11] On the other hand, Loy actively participated in modernist networks, groups, and sometimes institutions, including the Futurists in Italy, the surrealists in Paris, and a variety of salons and avant-garde gatherings in New York. Therefore, using more nuanced notions, as Stephen Voyce and Yasna Bozhkova have shown with the concepts of *mêlée* and constellations, will equip us better to account for the extremely complex and mobile set of connections, relationships, and groupings that Loy participated in, made possible, or invoked in her texts.[12] One of these useful notions is the concept of sociability, usually associated with the salon and with Loy's pamphlet 'International Psycho-Democracy', which was republished in 1982 together with the introductory 'Mina Loy's Tenets' (1918), where Loy, somewhat mimicking political pamphlets and foundational manifestos, speaks in a first person plural about 'our party' and 'our purpose', specifying that the party, is, after all, 'an Invitation, not a Control', and calls her readers to action by inciting them to 'make the world your salon'; indeed, as she defines the essence and purpose of 'Psycho-Democracy', she posits as one of its main goals the substitution of 'Sociability for Sociology'.[13]

---

10   Roger Conover, 'Introduction', in Mina Loy, *The Last Lunar Baedeker*, ed. by Roger Conover (Highlands, NC: Jargon Society, 1982), pp. xv–lxi (p. xxii).

11   Alice Oswald, 'The Life and Death of Poetry', University of Oxford Podcasts, 2 June 2022 <https://podcasts.ox.ac.uk/life-and-death-poetry> [accessed 8 January 2024].

12   Yasna Bozhkova, *Between Worlds: Mina Loy's Aesthetic Itineraries* (Clemson, SC: Clemson University Press, 2022), e.g. pp. 6–26; Stephen Voyce, '"Make the World your Salon": Poetry and Community at the Arensberg Apartment', *Modernism/Modernity*, 15.4 (2008), pp. 627–46.

13   Mina Loy, 'International Psycho-Democracy', in *Last Lunar Baedeker*, pp. 276–82 (pp. 276, 277).

SOCIABILITY, COMMUNITY, AND POETRY

As I have discussed elsewhere,[14] sociability emerged as concept and practice in the eighteenth century in texts by the German philosopher and theologian Friedrich Schleiermacher (1768–1834) and the works and social gatherings of the Jewish *salonnières* of the Haskala (or Jewish Enlightenment) in Berlin, especially Rahel Varnhagen (1764–1847) and Henriette Herz (1764–1847), and was then revived by Georg Simmel in his essay 'The Sociology of Sociability' ('Soziologie der Geselligkeit', 1911).[15] As Janet Lyon observes, for Simmel, *Geselligkeit* — 'sociability' or 'conviviality' — was a specific practice and set of social relations based on impersonal intimacy, equality, and free conversation liberated from instrumental ends.[16] In Simmel's theory, the communality of sociability/conviviality depended on the spontaneous, brief, and ephemeral temporality of the exchange and pleasure of conversation, ideally bypassing hierarchies and social constraints. It was compared to play and art, and was founded on purposelessness — a purposelessness that included renouncing the self and one's own individual pleasures or interests as the sole aim and goal of sociable communality, and opening up instead to reciprocity, whereby, for example, the pleasure of the individual was predicated on the pleasure of others. Sociability/conviviality was thus considered a possible vehicle for utopian forms of community. Sociability also functioned as a corrective to conservative theories of community such as those of Ferdinand Tönnies (1855–1936), who in 1887 compared what he saw as two opposite versions of collectivity, *Gemeinschaft* (community) and *Gesellschaft* (civic society): *Gemeinschaft* represented an organic

---

14   I have previously discussed the relationship between Simmel's theories and Loy's notion of community in Laura Scuriatti, 'Together, on her Own: A Survey of Mina Loy's Textual Communities', in *Groups, Coteries, Circles and Guilds: Modernist Aesthetics and the Utopian Lure of Community*, ed. by Laura Scuriatti (Oxford: Lang, 2019), pp. 71–96. For a discussion of sociability, conviviality, and modernist aesthetics, see Janet Lyon, 'Sociability in the Metropole: Modernism's Bohemian Salons', *ELH*, 76.3 (2009), pp. 687–711. See also Voyce, 'Make the World your Salon'.

15   Georg Simmel, 'The Sociology of Sociability', trans. by Everett C. Hughes, *American Journal of Sociology*, 55.3 (1949), pp. 254–61. For a discussion of sociability in the Haskala in relation to Simmel, see Ulrike Wagner, 'The Utopia of Purposelessness', in *Groups, Coteries, Circles and Guilds*, ed. by Scuriatti, pp. 17–41.

16   Lyon, 'Sociability in the Metropole', p. 688.

notion of community, rooted in what Tönnies thought were the shared natural values embodied by patriarchy, religion, and national identity, whereas *Gesellschaft* was an aggregate of people with little in common but artificially associated by instrumental aims, which were necessary to hold together heterogeneous organisms such as modern cities.[17] For Janet Lyon, sociability was *the* fundamental aspect, despite their differences, of the modernist salons, where the exercise of free conversation and rational discourse was connected to the 'ameliorative power of *Geselligkeit*'.[18]

Loy's appeal to turn the world into a salon in 'Psycho-Democracy', which, as Stephen Voyce and Yasna Bozhkova remind us, probably referred specifically to the Arensbergs' salon, seems indeed to aim at the creation of such ephemeral, mobile communities of choice, and to reject organic communities such as those theorized by Tönnies or embodied by political parties, institutional religions, or even structured avant-garde groups. And it also seems clear that for Loy, at least in the first phases of her writing life, this type of community could only be achieved through artistic practices and through the work of literature.[19]

Considering the delicate balance between single individuals and the group, the emphasis on reciprocity and renunciation which characterizes the mobile communities of sociability is also present in Roberto Esposito's theory of *communitas*. Esposito is helpful for considering Loy's work because he suggests a fundamental rethinking of the very idea of community, which, for him, should not be conceived as a 'fullness or a whole' or a 'principle of identification', or as a 'body' or a 'corporation', or be interpreted as intersubjective 'recognition' either. Community, for Esposito, is rather 'the totality of persons united not by a "property" but precisely by an obligation or a debt; not by an addition but by a subtraction'; working from the Latin etymology of *munus* (a gift that cannot not be given, a debt) and *communis*, Esposito proposes a concept of *communitas* held together and defined by a com-

---

17   See Lyon, 'Sociability in the Metropole'; Scuriatti, 'Together, on her Own'; Voyce, 'Make the World your Salon'.

18   Lyon, 'Sociability in the Metropole', p. 687.

19   This stance places Loy fully within the objectives and discourses of the historical avant-garde, as theorized by Peter Bürger in his seminal *Theory of the Avant-Garde*, trans. by Michael Shaw (Minneapolis: University of Minnesota Press, 1984).

mon debt, a bond, that is owed by individuals to others in order to participate in society: this is

> not a mode of being, much less a making of the individual subject. It isn't the subject's expansion or multiplication but its exposure to what interrupts the closing and turns it inside out: a dizziness, a syncope, a spasm in the continuity of the subject.[20]

This notion of community, characterized by a haphazard and ephemeral temporality, by interruptions and lack of closure, emerges from Loy's corpus, even when individuality seems to be the goal. And while ephemerality might be expressed by the sociability of the salon, I think that it gains its particular traction from Loy's handling of poetic form, without necessarily presupposing political indifference or insignificance. I see Loy's position also in relation to Charles Bernstein's scepticism about the identification of communities, especially literary ones: for Bernstein, 'any discussion of community would do well to start with the idea of institution rather than association'; if community is about having something in common — 'a place, an ideal, a practice, a heritage, a tradition' — it posits its own outside, and, in the modern literary world, this position is usually occupied by poetry:

> Many poets that I know experience poetry communities, say scenes, as places of their initial exclusion from publication, readings, recognition. Being inside, a part of, is often far less striking than being left out, apart. [...] To have a community is to make an imaginary inscription against what is outside the community. & outside is where some poetry will want to be.[21]

He therefore suggests that some types of poetry might be particularly keen on working against given notions of those versions of community, and might be reluctant to use collective nouns or to appeal to a defined collectivity — a position that is also visible in Loy's texts.

Turning to the relationship between poetry and conviviality, the latter appears, somewhat surprisingly, in Jonathan Culler's *Theory of*

---

20   Roberto Esposito, *Communitas: The Origin and Destiny of Community*, trans. by Timothy Campbell (Stanford, CA: Stanford University Press, 2010), pp. 2, 6, 7.

21   Charles Bernstein, 'Community and the Individual Talent', *Diacritics*, 26.3/4 (1996), pp. 176–90 (pp. 178, 177).

the Lyric: as he discusses Hegel's postulation of the centrality of the subjective in lyric poetry, Culler finds an unexpected opening towards a more relational type of subjectivity, precisely through the dimension of conviviality, in terms that echo Schleiermacher and Simmel:[22]

> [Hegel] evinces particular admiration for lyrics of Goethe which 'may be called convivial' in that a man in society 'does not communicate his self' but, putting 'his particular individuality in the background', amuses the company with his anecdotes and reflections, 'and yet, whatever he may portray, there is always vividly interwoven with it his own artistic inner life, his feelings and experiences'.[23]

This dynamic is fundamental for enabling the reception of poetry, in that the audience can recognize and have access to a very particular subjectivity without necessarily identifying it solely with one individual. In Culler's theory, poetic texts structurally rely not just on a situation of direct address but most fundamentally on indirect address. This involves the presence of a broad audience that is evoked as listeners or voyeurs and constitutes the real addressees of a poem, even if it is, in the first instance, addressed to an object or a lover. This structure, for Culler, is associated with the iterative quality of poetry, namely the possibility that, whatever the speaking voice or addressee, the poem can be potentially received, repeated, and rehearsed by a broader audience. Moving away from the solipsistic, expressive, and elitist model of lyrics from the Romantic period, Culler's theory opens up the possibility of lyric poetry creating a dynamic community of reception: community creation is made possible by the ritualistic nature of poetry and, especially, by its iterability, which is rooted not only in the situation of indirect address but also in non-narrative and formal structures relying on aurality and the materiality of language, such as rhyming, patterns of repetition, prosody. Through its reliance on aurality, poetry creates an effect of voicing — i.e. the effect of an utterance that can in theory be voiced, rather than the effect of a specific voice — which constitutes the poem's shareable quality and potentially opens up the poem to a

---

22   For a discussion of the relationship between Schleiermacher's and Simmel's theories of conviviality, see Wagner, 'Utopia of Purposelessness'.

23   Jonathan Culler, *Theory of the Lyric* (Cambridge, MA: Harvard University Press, 2015), p. 95.

community of readers or listeners who are able to participate in the poem's iterability.[24] My contention is that Loy's poetic style makes programmatic use of this possibility: in the texts that I explore, we do not have a rhetorical move where direct address masks or hides the real addressee or a general audience; rather, we have a multiplication of mutable audiences and addressees — potential communities ensuing from ephemeral processes of identification with the voices of the poem through different modalities of reading that are activated by poetic technique, form, and a focus on the materiality of language.[25]

A BALANCING ACT: READERSHIPS IN 'MODERN POETRY'

As examples I discuss the 1925 essay 'Modern Poetry', the long autobiographical poem *Anglo-Mongrels and the Rose* (1923–25), and then two poems from the sequence 'Italian Pictures' (1914). 'Modern Poetry' is Loy's only contribution to *Charm*, a New Jersey women's magazine published by the Bamberger's department store, which normally focused on lifestyle, fashion, beauty, and society but also made room for articles on art, politics, and culture, with contributions by important modernists, such as Djuna Barnes, Walter Pach, Man Ray, and Allen Tate.[26] Indeed, the tone of the essay is almost pedagogical and addresses poetry from the perspective of reception and readership, rather than from the point of view of authors. It teaches how to recognize and learn to appreciate modernist poetry in spite of its difficult form, obscurity, and radical language, explaining that these are inevitable, as they are the poet's tool for responding to and capturing the variety of the modern world. It offers a list of Loy's preferred poets and a succinct account of their main characteristics. It does not rely on technical

---

24   Ibid., p. 305.

25   For further reflections on readership in Loy's poetry in relation to reader-response theory and ethnography, see Sanja Bahun, '"Me you — you — me": Mina Loy and the Art of Ethnographic Intimacy', in *Modernist Intimacies*, ed. by Elsa Högberg (Edinburgh: Edinburgh University Press, 2023), pp. 129–43 (pp. 141–42).

26   Sophie Oliver, 'Mina Loy, Bessie Breuer, *Charm* Magazine and Fashion as Modernist Historiography', *Journal of Modern Periodical Studies*, 11.2 (2020), pp. 248–69 (p. 251). As noted by Roger Conover, 'Notes on the Text', in Mina Loy, *The Lost Lunar Baedeker*, ed. by Roger Conover (New York: Farrar, Straus & Giroux, 1996), pp. 175–218 (p. 217), Djuna Barnes signed some of her contributions as Lady Lydia Steptoe. I am indebted to Alex Goody for her extremely helpful suggestions concerning *Charm* and its readership.

terms or speak of problems of voice, dramatic form, images, or address, but rather asks the reader to imagine sounds and metre through comparisons with activities that would have been familiar to the white middle-class suburban audience which constituted the readership of the magazine[27] — 'Imagine a tennis champion who became inspired to write poetry, would not his verse be likely to embody the rhythmic transit of skimming balls? Would not his meter depend on his way of life [...]?'[28] Most importantly, though, Loy creates a version of modernist poetry that is at first glance affirmed as being deeply American, and made possible by the American 'melting-pot' and by the speed of urban life and economic exchanges that characterize it:

> So in the American poet wherever he may wander, however he may engage himself with an older culture, there has occurred no Europeanization of his fundamental advantage, the acuter shock of the New World consciousness upon life. His is still poetry that has proceeded out of America.[29]

As Sophie Oliver notes, Loy inserts the notion of the fleetingness of the modern into the stability of tradition — 'those I have spoken of are poets according to the old as well as the new reckoning; there are others who are poets only according to the new reckoning. They are headed by the doctor, Carlos Williams'[30] — and therefore presents a more complicated view of modernism, one that does not rely exclusively on rupture and breach but rather represents a fleetingness and ephemerality rooted in a dialectic view of history where past and present are intertwined in an unstoppable movement and the present tends inexorably towards becoming past.[31]

---

27 Oliver, 'Mina Loy, Bessie Breuer, Charm', p. 252, explains that the magazine was sent monthly for free to selected customers of the department store, and that, while the readership influenced the content of the magazine with its local interests, its editors, and in particular Bessie Breuer, were instrumental in expanding the scope of the articles to include avant-garde and even feminist topics and authors, as well as taking on a markedly cosmopolitan outlook, to compete with both *Vogue* or *Harper's Bazaar* and *Good Housekeeping*, combining 'localism with modernism'. This, as Oliver shows, meant that, even in terms of fashion, the magazine had to find a balance between celebrating novelties in fashion, art, and ideas, without being too radical.

28 Mina Loy, 'Modern Poetry', in *Lost Lunar Baedeker*, pp. 157–61 (p. 158).

29 Ibid., p. 159.

30 Ibid., p. 161.

31 Oliver, 'Mina Loy, Bessie Breuer, Charm', pp. 262–63.

The almost contradictory versions of modernism which Oliver sees as carefully balanced out in the essay, and the conflicting reading strategies that such an approach and such a readership implied, are matched by the types of audiences in the essay. They are defined by two radically different types of reception of poetry, based respectively on voice or on silent reading on the printed page:

> the sound of music capturing our involuntary attention is so easy to get in touch with, while the silent sound of poetry requires our voluntary attention to obliterate the cold barrier of print with the whole 'intelligence of our senses'. And many of us who have the habit of reading not alone with the eye but also with the ear, have — especially at a superficial first reading — overlooked the beauty of it.
>
> More than to read poetry we must listen to poetry. All reading is the evocation of speech; the difference in our approach, then, in reading a poem or a newspaper is that our attitude in reading a poem must be rather that of listening to and looking at a pictured song.[32]

Here Loy affirms a specific, ritualistic, iterative aspect of poetry which is determined by its roots in music, as reaffirmed elsewhere in the essay through comparison with jazz;[33] the different publics are addressees that, however, coalesce around the ability to receive and iterate poetry through the performance of language in its materiality. This is, for Loy, a fundamental feature not only of Gertrude Stein's style but also of modernist poetry. As Craig Dworkin argues, Loy is able to capture the fundamental characteristic of Stein's style, namely its ability to extract 'powerful elements below the level of the word and beyond "consciousness" to release a language working independently of human intentions and free from the psychologies of the speakers'.[34] This ability manifests itself in Loy's work in at least two ways: first of all in her parodic poetic

---

32   Loy, 'Modern Poetry', p. 157.

33   For a discussion of the significance of jazz for Loy's poetics, especially in relation to the poem 'The Widow's Jazz', see Marisa Jannuzzi, 'Mongrel Rose: The "Unerring Esperanto" of Loy's Poetry', in *Mina Loy*, ed. by Shreiber and Tuma, pp. 404–41 (pp. 434–37); Andrew Michael Roberts, 'Rhythm, Self and Jazz in Mina Loy's Poetry', in *The Salt Companion to Mina Loy*, ed. by Rachel Potter and Suzanne Hobson (Cambridge: Salt Publishing, 2010), pp. 99–128.

34   Craig Dworkin, *Radium of the Word: A Poetics of Materiality* (Chicago: University of Chicago Press, 2020), p. 68.

technique, which draws attention to itself through, to quote Elisabeth Frost, 'overdeterminacy of meaning in verse saturated with polysemy, alliteration, inflated diction, punning, bathos, and ironic rhyme — a ragbag of techniques that mimic poetic convention';[35] and second, in the defamiliarized English, Marjorie Perloff's 'English as a second language', that Loy praises in the following passage from 'Modern Poetry', with a distinctly Whitmanian tone:

> It was inevitable that the renaissance of poetry should proceed out of America, where latterly a thousand languages have been born, and each one, for purposes of communication at least, English — English enriched and variegated with the grammatical structure and voice-inflection of many races, in novel alloy with the fundamental time-is-money idiom of the United States, discovered by newspaper cartoonists.
>
> This composite language is a very living language, it grows as you speak. For the true American appears to be ashamed to say anything in the way it has been said before. Every moment he ingeniously coins new words for old ideas. [...]
>
> You may think it impossible to conjure up the relationship of expression between the high browest modern poets and an adolescent Slav who has speculated in a wholesale job-lot of mandarines and is trying to sell them in a retail market on First Avenue. But it lies simply in this: both have had to become adapted to a country where the mind has to put on its verbal clothes at terrific speed if it would speak in time; where no one will listen if you attack him twice with the same missile of argument. And, that the ear that has listened to the greatest number of sounds will have the most to choose from when it comes to self-expression, each has been liberally educated in the flexibility of phrases.[36]

Instead of hindering communication, this syncretic language fosters understanding among groups where it might not otherwise be found, creating what Matthew Hart calls 'nations of nothing but poetry'[37] — clusters created by the poems and realized in small groups of readers

---

35   Elisabeth A. Frost, *The Feminist Avant-Garde in American Poetry* (Iowa City: University of Iowa Press, 2003), p. 52, quoted in Sean Pryor, *Poetry, Modernism and an Imperfect World* (Cambridge: Cambridge University Press, 2017), p. 116.

36   Loy, 'Modern Poetry', p. 158–59.

37   Matthew Hart, *Nations of Nothing but Poetry: Modernism, Transnationalism, and Synthetic Vernacular Language* (Oxford: Oxford University Press, 2010). For a brief

which only partially intersect. In this account, poetry features as a kind of mediator and creator: its adoption of this defamiliarized language opens up possibilities of communication that are attuned to the present, creating its own communities, even if ephemeral and moveable, in the same way as the living, evolving language of the street that makes America possible. Simultaneously though, this language is a stumbling block that forces readers to become attentive to the process of reading and listening to poetry, and to the potentially fraught moments of identification with a stable community of speakers or listeners.

SHIFTING COMMUNITIES: *ANGLO-MONGRELS AND THE ROSE* AND 'ITALIAN PICTURES'

In order to explore the textual mechanisms that correspond to these programmatic statements, I will now turn, by way of example, to the first section of *Anglo-Mongrels and the Rose* and then 'Italian Pictures'.

Anglo-Mongrels and the Rose is a long autobiographical poem, an 'auto-mythology', in Roger Conover's words,[38] which appeared in fragments in various magazines and journals, and was published posthumously in its entirety in 1982. The first section of *Anglo-Mongrels* is dedicated to the character Exodus, who represents Loy's father, and introduces Exodus in what seems to be an uncertain, tentative English:

> Exodus lay under an oak tree
> bordering on Buda Pest   he had lain
> him down   to overnight   under the lofty rain
> of starlight
> having leapt from the womb
> eighteen years ago   and grown
> neglected   along the shores of the Danube
> on the Danube in the Danube
> or breaking his legs behind runaway horses
>   with a Carnival quirk
>   every Shrove Tuesday[39]

---

account of this passage in relation to contemporary notions of the American 'melting-pot', see Peter Nicholls, 'The Poetics of Modernism', in *The Cambridge Companion to Modernist Poetry*, ed. by Andrew Davis and Lee M. Jenkins (Cambridge: Cambridge University Press, 2007), pp. 51–67 (esp. pp. 55–56, p. 65 n. 22).

38   In Loy, *Last Lunar Baedeker*, p. 326.

39   Mina Loy, *Anglo-Mongrels and the Rose*, in *Last Lunar Baedeker*, pp. 109–75 (p. 111).

The wish to explain Exodus's predicament produces a sequence of verses in which syntactic and lexical correctness are partially disregarded: in 'he had lain | him down', the peculiar usage of the verb 'to lay down' could be transitive or intransitive, maybe even reflexive, although the reflexive pronoun is missing as an effect of the enjambement; the verb 'overnight' is a rare occurrence in the 1920s, according to the *OED*;[40] the location of Exodus's birth and childhood is expressed in an uncertain way with the sequence 'of the Danube | on the Danube in the Danube', which echoes either a nursery rhyme or a tentative sentence uttered by a foreigner trying out random prepositions in a language that they have not yet fully mastered. Here the poetic voice speaks in the third person singular, and its eloquence vacillates between the probable imitation or even ventriloquizing of the parlance of a foreign speaker and the refined rhetoric of a different persona, able to produce 'under the lofty rain | of starlight' and 'with a Carnival quirk | every Shrove Tuesday', as if shifting between identification with Exodus and an external perspective. These are two voices that are not mutually exclusive, but entangled and linked in a dialogic and dialectical manner, one implicating, but not subsuming, the other.[41]

The multilingual world of the Austro-Hungarian Empire in which Exodus grew up, however, is not a Utopia of communication like the American melting-pot in 'Modern Poetry', but is mired in the ideologies attached to each language:

> Imperial Austria taught the child
> the German   secret patriotism
> the Magyar tongue   the father
> stuffed him with biblical Hebrew and the
> seeds of science   exhorting him
>   to vindicate
>   his forefathers' ambitions[42]

---

40 *Oxford English Dictionary*, s.v. 'overnight' <https://www.oed.com/dictionary/overnight_v?tab=frequency> [accessed 23 February 2024].

41 Indeed, as Roberts, 'Rhythm, Self and Jazz', pp. 101–02, summarizes, Carolyn Burke sees Loy's poetry as a 'poetry of the subject, [...] taking up positions in language' rather than a 'lyric poetry of self (consistently confessional, homogeneous, integrated, seeking wholeness)'.

42 Loy, *Anglo-Mongrels and the Rose*, pp. 111–12.

Exodus's unhappy childhood and lapse into relative poverty and neg-
lect are accompanied by a parallel process of language impoverishment
and confusion:

> [...] hired
> Exodus in apprenticeship
> to such   as garrulously inarticulate[43]

This process culminates in his emigration to Great Britain,

> where the domestic Jew   in lieu
> of knouts   is lashed with tongues[44]

and where he begins to fluently speak

> [...] 'business English' [...]
> jibbering   stock exchange quotations[45]

Yet the language expressing Exodus's multilingual exile is extremely
refined, relying heavily on rhetorical figures such as paronomasia, allit-
eration, and onomatopoeia, which bring attention back to poetry and
poetic voice:

> Blinking his eyes
> at the sunrise   Exodus
> lumbar-arching   sleep-logged   turns his ear
> to the grit earth   and hears
> the boom of cardiac cataracts
>   thumping the turf
> with his young pulse[46]
>
>   Exodus   lifts his head
> over the alien crowds
> under the alien clouds[47]

This section of *Anglo-Mongrels* offers us not a mimetic version of a
single poetic voice within or outside the text, but the performance
of poetic language. In fact, the process of language assimilation and
alignment which Exodus has to go through in England is epitomized

---

43   Ibid., p. 112.
44   Ibid., p. 113.
45   Ibid., p. 115.
46   Ibid., p. 113.
47   Ibid., p. 117.

by the jettisoning of or return to two different but intertwined lyric traditions — the ancient one associated with the Hebrew Bible, and the Western lyric, ironically symbolized by the thrush's song — both of which are marked by music and aurality:

Hymns   ancient and modern
belabour   crippled cottage-grands
in parlor fronts
    A thrush
shatters its song upon the spurious shade
of a barred bird fancier's

The dumb philosophies
of the wondering Jew
fall into rhythm   with
long unlistened to   Hebrew chants[48]

As well as not fully empathizing with the predicament of Exodus, the poetic voice is able to represent it precisely because its language is poetic and not identifiable with Exodus. Indeed, the poem implies a multilingualism which goes beyond the languages that Exodus masters or is mastered by; for instance, the stanza which precedes the ones quoted above includes puns which seem to be specifically directed at Italian-speakers:

This jovian Hebrew 'all dressed up
and nowhere to go'
stands like a larch
upon the corners of incarcerate streets
deploring the anomolous [sic] legs
of Zion's sons
with the subconscious
irritant of superiority
left in an aristocracy   out of currency

paces
the cancellated desert of the metropolis
with the instinctive urge   of loneliness
to get to 'the heart of something'[49]

'Incarcerate' and 'cancellated' resonate and are both loanwords that can be read as anglicized versions of the Italian *incarcerato* and *cancellato*, meaning 'jailed' and 'cancelled' respectively. The significance

48   Ibid., pp. 116–17.
49   Ibid., p. 116.

of the chiming of the two words cannot be fully understood without considering the polysemy of the Italian *cancellato*: since 'cancellated' is a fusion of the English 'cancel' and the Italian *cancellata/cancello*, it contains both the notions of cancelling and of a gate with bars, thus reformulating the erasure of Exodus's identity as not just imprisonment but also exclusion.

Even when she describes such a paradigmatic narrative moment of formation and assimilation into English society and the English language, Loy decides to add an extra dimension to her defamiliarized English by interrupting and reshaping the imagined communities of her readers: these intersected and shifting communities are constituted within the possibilities of a poetic style which emphatically relies on the materiality of language in both its aural and written dimensions. Such a strategy recalls and problematizes the celebration of multilingualism as the foundation of American modernism that characterizes 'Modern Poetry', written in the same years. It also seems to invest poetry with a deeply pessimistic ironic charge: not only does multilingualism per se not provide the much-desired utopian space of communication; as Sean Pryor argues, poetic technique from specific traditions also becomes the object of satire through the use of its own tools. In this way, according to Pryor, *Anglo-Mongrels* is a modernist anti-poetic poem which performs poetry as a language that does not manage to fulfil its functions.[50]

Another eloquent example for this poetics is the sequence 'Italian Pictures'. I shall focus on 'The Costa San Giorgio' and 'Costa Magic', the second and third parts of the sequence respectively. The poems were written in 1914, during Loy's residence in Florence, and published in November of the same year in the short-lived avant-garde magazine *The Trend*, edited by Carl Van Vechten, Loy's agent. They were therefore written in Italy by an English expatriate and presented to an unknown and distant American audience, for whom the references to the Florentine life of a British expat were in all probability utterly alien — a feature that Tara Prescott and Linda Kinnahan see

---

50   Pryor, *Poetry*, pp. 93–97, 100–02, argues moreover that the materiality of Loy's poetry, especially in *Anglo-Mongrels*, 'The Effectual Marriage', and 'Love Songs', shows Loy's interrogation of the pleasure offered by the rhyming and chiming of poetic texts — a pleasure that may be seen as fostering complicity with the 'fallen' state of modernity.

expressed by the poems' play with tropes of closeness and distance between the speaking voices and the observed objects.[51]

'The Costa San Giorgio' establishes from the very beginning a first person plural which seems relatively self-explanatory and fixed: the English. This seems to be the perspective from which the poem unfolds. However, as Marisa Jannuzzi observes, the whole first stanza is shaped by the associations between words in the semantic field of the archaic 'frescoe' and the technique that this form of painting requires — namely the words 'blot' and 'stained' — and, I would add, also by the Italianate echoes of 'frescoe' and 'porta', which constitute a modification of the initial statement about Englishness — a statement that aligns with Loy's own perception as a polyglot speaker who thinks 'in a subconscious muddle of foreign languages', without a 'notion of what pure English is'.[52]

> We English make a tepid blot
> On the messiness
> Of the passionate Italian life-traffic
> Throbbing the street   up   steep
> Up   up   to the porta
> Culminating
> In the stained frescoe of the dragon-slayer[53]

The third stanza introduces another voice, which also speaks in the first person plural and claims to speak for a group:

> Oranges half-rotten are sold at a reduction
> Hoarsely advertised as broken heads
> BROKEN HEADS   and the barber
> Has an imitation mirror
> And Mary preserve our mistresses from seeing us as we see ourselves
> Shaving
> ICE CREAM
> Licking is larger than mouths
> Boots than feet[54]

---

51 Tara Prescott, *Poetic Salvage: Reading Mina Loy* (Lewisburg, PA: Bucknell University Press, 2016), pp. 14–19; Linda A. Kinnahan, 'Costa Magic', in *Mina Loy: Navigating the Avant-Garde*, ed. by Suzanne W. Churchill, Linda A. Kinnahan, and Susan Rosenbaum <https://mina-loy.com/split-texts/gender-power-in-the-street/> [accessed 9 January 2024].

52 Jannuzzi, 'Mongrel Rose', pp. 427 (for the quotation, from an undated letter written in the 1930s), 428 (for a discussion of the significance of the word 'frescoe').

53 Mina Loy, 'The Costa San Giorgio', in *Lost Lunar Baedeker*, pp. 10–12 (p. 10).

54 Ibid., p. 11.

This is probably the inner voice of the barber, who seems to speak collectively for the male gender. But this voice is interrupted by the ambiguous 'ICE CREAM', which may indicate the shouts of an ice-cream vendor or the performative utterance of an unidentified first-person speaker who screams they are screaming. Stanza 4 has yet another, different, first person plural:

> And warns the folded hands
> Of a consumptive
> Left outside   her chair is broken
> And she wonders how we feel
> For we walk very quickly
> The noonday cannon
> Having scattered the neighbour's pigeons[55]

Is this 'we' the English throughout the poem? Here, as in other poems that Loy wrote when she lived in Florence, the ability to speak in the first person plural depends among other things on the vacillation between the position of subject and object in a situation of spectacle: here, the Italians are observed and objectified by the English, but the latter become, in turn, a spectacle in the public square. Given the markedly gendered use of the first person plural in stanza 3, it is difficult to determine whether the 'we' in stanza 4 still refers to the English, or now to English women in particular. The possible meanings of these first person plurals are predicated on the unexpressed dialectic of binary otherness — the English and the Italian, male and female, those who look and those who are seen — but these positions seem to be at least potentially exchangeable. 'Englishness', for example, is posited as a contested category from the very start. First, the English are presented as different, but they are also implicated in, and are part of, the very place that they modify by being 'a blot'. Second, while a reader of *The Trend* might not have been able to detect any ambiguity in the beginning of the poem, the juxtaposition of the title 'The Costa San Giorgio' with 'we English' might have been received with scepticism by a British expat living in Florence, due to the fact that the Costa San Giorgio was located in the working-class district of Oltrarno. Admittedly, Gordon Craig had set up his theatre in that area,

---

55   Ibid.

and the Brownings' Casa Guidi was located nearby, but Loy herself was conscious of the fact that living in Oltrarno put her in an awkward position, that of someone who did and did not fully belong to the English community. Third, as Linda Kinnahan suggests, Loy's refusal to properly name the gate, Porta San Giorgio, and thus to make it clear to readers unfamiliar with Florence by quoting its name as a tourist guide would, points to a yet another addressee that would not need such indication — an English-speaking, but not necessarily English, resident of the city.[56] The uncertain first-person plural pronouns seem to probe and perform this condition, which demands the intersection and multiplication of a variety of audiences which, in turn, create different but related, interdependent textual communities.

'Costa Magic' is a narrative poem about an episode in Florentine life in which a sick girl named Cesira, considered 'bewitched', suffers not only from her illness but also from her father's tyranny; she is driven to the countryside in order to be diagnosed and cured of her disease — which is actually phthisis — by being brought into contact with an old tree. The deictic nature of the possessive adjective in the first line of the poem establishes a relationship of distance between the poetic voice and the object of its reflection, creating a narrative situation which immediately gives way to the voice of a first person, probably the father: his patriarchal desire to control is expressed by the deictics 'this one' and 'here'. The latter word, in its isolation, sounds like an injunction to come closer but at the same time remains suspended in the possibility of being appropriated by another speaker:

> Her father
> Indisposed to her marriage
> And a rabid man at that
> My most sympathetic daughter
> Make yourself a conception
> As large as this one
> Here
> But with yellow hair[57]

---

56 Linda A. Kinnahan, 'Mapping Florence: First Tour, Loy at Home', in *Mina Loy*, ed. by Churchill, Kinnahan, and Rosenbaum <https://mina-loy.com/chapters/italy-italian-baedeker/02-oltrarno-costa/> [accessed 9 January 2024].

57 Mina Loy, 'Costa Magic', in *Lost Lunar Baedeker*, pp. 12–14 (p. 12).

Suddenly, another 'I' emerges in the third stanza: a wife who is paying attention to both her husband and the goings-on surrounding Cesira's illness:

> While listening up   I hear my husband
> Mumbling   Mumbling
> Mumbling   at the window[58]

The 'I' quickly turns into a 'we' that seems to indicate a community of neighbours ready to help the sick girl and follow the indications of the 'wise woman' rather than those of the doctor:

> The doctor   Phthisis
> The wise woman   says to take her
> So we   following her instruction
> I and the neighbour
> Take her —
>
> The glass rattling
> The rain slipping
> I and the neighbour and her aunt
> Bunched together
> And Cesira
> Droops across the cab[59]

The discrepancy between scientific discourse and superstition which opens the stanza seems to vanish with the momentary agreement followed by collective action.[60] But immediately, the 'we' splits into 'I and the neighbour', and then becomes 'I and the neighbour and her aunt': it is one plus one plus one, no longer an undifferentiated 'us'. The poem here points, in Bonnie Costello's words, to 'the power of the first-person plural pronoun and alert[s] us, intentionally or not, to its dangers, probing the implications of its use'.[61] It rejects the romanticization of community, but the qualification of the 'we' also seems to suggest that an improbable, momentary, and ephemeral community may emerge in the poem out of a mixture of neighbourly

---

58   Ibid., p. 13.

59   Ibid.

60   For a discussion of the word 'Phthisis' in this poem, see Jannuzzi, 'Mongrel Rose', pp. 414–15.

61   Bonnie Costello, *The Plural of Us: Poetry and Community in Auden and Others* (Princeton, NJ: Princeton University Press, 2017), p. 3.

and familial ties — a community of purpose that may also include the speaking voice and the sick girl. They are 'bunched together' in a moment, forming an improbable new entity, making it possible for the voice to think of Cesira as 'my girl' — 'A wheel in a rut | Jerks back my girl on the padding | And the hedges into the sky'[62] — a possessive that modifies the significance of 'her father' in the first verse, thus instituting a community or even family of choice. This in turn allows the poem to end with an agreement about the 'we' in the penultimate stanza — 'Knowing she has to die | We drive home | To wait | She certainly does in time' — which may even be a worried realization that the ability to speak and act in the first person plural as the subjects of this particular community may still be the result of a complicity with the very cause of Cesira's condition, namely patriarchal culture.

The sequence 'Italian Pictures' begins with 'July in Vallombrosa', a reflection on British expatriates and Italian ladies recovering in a sanatorium in Vallombrosa, outside Florence, where the lyric subject, speaking in the first person singular, maintains a clear distance from its multiple objects and draws its epiphanic moment from a position of externality to the depicted groups, addressed in the second or third person singular. 'The Costa San Giorgio' and 'Costa Magic', on the other hand, perform the creation of communities that are changeable and require constant shifts of perspective, negotiating closeness and distance, communality and property, critique and complicity: they perform what Bonnie Costello sees as one of the fundamental abilities of poetry, namely to 'constantly modulat[e] among various "we's" and check [...] one against the other.'[63] These shifting perspectives are expressed by the poems' creation of different audiences simultaneously, as in Anglo-Mongrels, but also by their refusal to present a solid, stable, collective entity.

The vacillation in the 'Italian Pictures' between the singular and plural first persons, and the uncertainties about the stability of a community based on national identity or national language, certainly reflects a number of questions pertaining to the local debates that Loy experienced in Florence: Loy's engagement with the Futurist group

---

62   Loy, 'Costa Magic', p. 14.
63   Costello, Plural of Us, p. 15.

dynamics, the language of their manifestos, and Marinetti's program-
matic call to 'destroy the I in literature', which Gottfried Benn still iden-
tified in 1951 as one of the main features of modernist literature, and
of modernist poetry in particular;[64] the public debates about the inter-
section between local, regional, and national identity in Tuscany and
Italy; and the precarious or reluctant experience of belonging which
characterized the Anglo-American expatriate community in Florence.
However, it is also a marker of Loy's style more broadly.

Thus, performing the fundamental nature of lyric in its iterability
through their shifting pronouns, multilingual prosody, and emphasis
on the materiality of poetic language, Loy's poems open themselves
up to multiple addressees. Although these addressees are entangled
with one another and with the speakers through words rather than
physically, to borrow Reuben Brower's 1951 formulation,[65] these en-
tanglements hardly yield stable collectives or communities of readers.
Instead, they are interrupted, they remain mobile and ephemeral, per-
haps as the expression of an unfulfillable desire or as a resistance to
the increasingly dogmatic communities of the twentieth century. Re-
phrasing Sean Pryor's assessment of the modernist debates about the
efficacy of poetry in a 'modern fallen world' and its complicity with
the political status quo, one could say that, considering the kind of
communities emerging in Loy's poetry, 'the problem was not to de-
cide whether poetry only imagines a beauty which can never exist,
or instead makes a beauty which has not yet existed'[66] — but rather
whether it created the spaces for voicing unofficial, ephemeral com-
munities that already existed, thus turning a seemingly artificial and
excessively aesthetic style relying on the materiality of poetry into a
potentially political tool.

---

64   Gottfried Benn, *Probleme der Lyrik* (Wiesbaden: Limes Verlag, 1951), pp. 15–16. The
     formulation, which Benn quotes in French, is the beginning of point 11 of Marinetti's
     Manifesto tecnico della letteratura futurista (11 May 1912), which was printed in Italian
     and French as a broadsheet of the Direzione del Movimento Futurista, then published
     in the same year in *La Gazzetta di Biella* in Italian and in *Der Sturm* in German.
     Filippo Tommaso Marinetti, *Manifesto tecnico della letteratura futurista*, in *Manifesti
     del Futurismo*, ed. by Viviana Birolli (Milan: Abscondita, 2008), pp. 58–64 (p. 61;
     publication details on p. 205).

65   Reuben Brower, 'The Speaking Voice', in *The Lyric Theory Reader: A Critical Anthology*,
     ed. by Virginia Jackson and Yopie Prins (Baltimore, MD: Johns Hopkins University
     Press, 2014), pp. 211–18 (p. 212).

66   Pryor, *Poetry*, p. 6.

Lyric Poetry and Community Good
Kaaps and the Cape Flats
DEREK ATTRIDGE

> If there is one thing I learned from growing up in Bishop Lavis it's this: there is nothing more unimportant than the lives of poor people. When poor people die they leave nothing after them, no trace that they existed. For me my writing is history told by the losers.
>
> (As daa een ding is wat ek gelee et van opgroei in Bishop Lavis issit dié: daa is niks meer unimportant as die liewens van arm mense nie. As arm mense doodgan los hulle niks agte nie, niks trace dat hulle exist et ie. Vi my is my writing history as told by the losers.)[1]

Nathan Trantraal, interview with Ronelda Kamfer

1

The area of Cape Town known as the Cape Flats (or Kaapse Vlakte in Afrikaans) is an extensive, low-lying sandy plain bordered by mountains and sea which, not surprisingly in view of its unsuitability for

---

*   I would like to extend my thanks to the following for their help during the writing of this essay: Nathan Trantraal, Theo Kemp, Hein Willemse, David Attwell, and Claire Chambers.

1   '"Poetry oo die liewe annie anne kant" — Ronelda Kamfer gesels met Nathan Trantraal oor *Chokers en survivors*' <https://www.litnet.co.za/poetry-oo-die-liewe-annie-anne-kant-ronelda-kamfer-gesels-met-nathan-trantaal-oor-chokers/> [accessed 31 October 2023]. All translations in this essay are my own unless otherwise indicated.

settlement, saw little habitation until after 1948. The Nationalist gov-
ernment that took power in South Africa in that year set about, in
obedience to apartheid dogma, the displacement of 'non-white' South
Africans from urban areas to new townships in less desirable areas, and
thus the 1950s and 1960s saw the forced removal to the Cape Flats of
large numbers of Cape Town residents who did not qualify as 'white'.
Their new accommodation was in subeconomic housing lacking many
basic amenities, on small plots along dusty streets that boasted few fa-
cilities. A significant proportion of them were Capetonians whom the
apartheid policymakers classified as 'Coloured', a label given to those
with a mixed heritage, including the original Dutch settlers, slaves from
South and South East Asia and East Africa, the indigenous KhoeKhoe
and San peoples, and Bantu-speaking Africans from the east and north
of the Cape. The term 'coloured', without the upper case, continues to
be used for the members of a community that should be understood
as based on many shared features other than the spurious notion of
race. Grant Farred, in his account of being coloured in South Africa,
observes that

> South African colouredness is, arguably, best understood as a
> quasi-ethnic identity: a racially indistinct — including in its
> ranks several different physical 'types' — community bound
> together by cultural practices, mores, values, and traditions, all
> of which have evolved in the face of racist white hostility.[2]

As Farred implies, the policy of apartheid was one factor in producing
a strong sense of community among those whose daily existence was
affected by its exclusions and injuries, including individuals and fam-
ilies forced to start new lives together in difficult circumstances. The
recently released results of the 2022 census reveal a total figure for
Cape Town approaching five million inhabitants,[3] many of whom —
perhaps a million — live in the various neighbourhoods of the Cape
Flats. Among these neighbourhoods are Manenberg (the title of a well-
known song by the coloured jazz musician Abdullah Ibrahim, formerly

---

2   Grant Farred, *Midfielder's Moment: Coloured Literature and Culture in Contemporary
     South Africa* (Boulder: Westview Press, 2000), p. 6.

3   See 'Census 2022: Statistical Release' <https://census.statssa.gov.za/assets/
     documents/2022/P03014_Census_2022_Statistical_Release.pdf> [accessed 11
     October 2023].

Dollar Brand), Mitchell's Plain, and Bishop Lavis. (The Flats are also the site of some of the largest and oldest townships created for people classified as 'Black' rather than 'Coloured', such as Langa, Nyanga, Gugulethu, and Khayelitsha.) The legacy of apartheid is evident across these townships in high levels of poverty, unemployment, crime, and drug use, in the lack of educational opportunities, and in widespread health problems.

The sense of community among the coloured population of the Cape Flats springs in part from, and enhances, the use of a common language. The highly distinctive demotic tongue to be heard on the street has a history that goes back to the seventeenth century, when the Dutch of the original settlers began to be modified for communication with slaves and with the indigenous inhabitants of the Cape. As Isobel Hofmeyr observes,

> in confronting the language of the slaves — Malay and Portuguese creole —along with Khoesan speech, this Dutch linguistic cluster had partly creolised. In later years it picked up shards of German, French and Southern Nguni [Xhosa] languages and a goodly layer of English after 1806.[4]

This language was known by a number of terms which, as Hofmeyr points out,

> all pointed to a strong association with poorness and 'colouredness'. Some of these terms included 'hotnotstaal' (Hottentot language), 'griekwataal' (Griqua language), 'kombuistaal' (kitchen language), 'plattaal' (vulgar language) and 'brabbeltaal' (patois/lingo).[5]

The more neutral Dutch term was 'Afrikaansch', which became 'Afrikaans' in the language it named.

In the last quarter of the nineteenth century, a group of Dutch descendants who identified themselves as 'Afrikaners' worked hard to establish the language as the proper tongue of white speakers. This entailed ridding it of its non-Dutch heritage as far as possible, a process

4   Isobel Hofmeyr, 'Building a Nation from Words', in *The South Africa Reader: History, Culture, Politics*, ed. by Clifton Crais and Thomas V. McClendon (Durham, NC: Duke University Press, 2014), pp. 160–68 (p. 160; square brackets in original).

5   Ibid., p. 161.

aided by the compilation of a dictionary and grammar, a translation of the Bible, and the establishment of an academy to oversee and police it. The prestige of this 'suiwer', or 'pure', Afrikaans grew with the emergence of significant poets and novelists. Formal recognition was achieved with the passing of the Official Languages of the Union Act of 1925, according to which Dutch was to be understood as including Afrikaans. Eventually, the 1961 constitution of the newly declared Republic of South Africa demoted Dutch and made Afrikaans one of two official languages, alongside English. Varieties of the language that did not conform to this model were consistently regarded as impure dialects — although coloured speakers make up more than half the number of the roughly six million individuals for whom Afrikaans is a home language.[6] Among these denigrated tongues was 'Kaapse Afrikaans', or Cape Afrikaans, spoken by the coloured inhabitants of the Western Cape, with the greatest density of speakers on the Cape Flats.

Over the past two or three decades, the enterprise of gaining for the Afrikaans of the Flats a status equal to that of the purified form has grown in strength and visibility.[7] Known just as 'Kaaps', or sometimes 'Afrikaaps', this version of Afrikaans has shrugged off its denomination as a dialect, a categorization that was, in any case, a dubious one, since the languages of the world constitute a continuum rather than a group of standard languages surrounded by satellite dialects.[8] Long regarded as an inferior form of Afrikaans, just as its speakers were regarded as in-

---

6   The most common home languages are isiZulu and isiXhosa, and the fourth most common is Sepedi. For a comprehensive account of South Africa's languages, see *Language in South Africa*, ed. by Rajend Mesthrie (Cambridge: Cambridge University Press, 2002). Twelve languages are currently recognized as official in South Africa, all varieties of Afrikaans being considered as a single language.

7   Some of the opposition to this championing of Kaaps comes from speakers of other varieties of non-standard Afrikaans not based in the urban areas around Cape Town. For a comprehensive discussion of poetry in non-standard Afrikaans across diverse regions since 1955, see Bernard Odendaal, 'Omgangsvariëteite van Afrikaans in die digkuns sedert Sestig', *Stilet*, 27.2 (2015), pp. 32–62.

8   I discuss this question in relation to Kaaps in Derek Attridge, 'Untranslatability and the Challenge of World Literature: A South African Example', in *The Work of World Literature*, ed. by Francesco Giusti and Benjamin Lewis Robinson (Berlin: ICI Berlin Press, 2021), pp. 25–55 (pp. 25–30) <https://doi.org/10.37050/ci-19_02>.

ferior citizens (and indeed humans),[9] Kaaps now has many champions
who see it as a key to the struggle to achieve status and rights for the
coloured community. (Some advocates of Kaaps spell the word 'col-
oured' to reflect the way it is pronounced by its speakers, and to escape
the association with apartheid racial classifications: 'kallit', 'kullit', and
'kallid' have all been suggested.)

Pride in Kaaps as a distinct language with capabilities and re-
sources as great as any other grew in tandem with an increasing sense of
the distinctiveness of coloured identity after the democratic elections
of 1994. Among the factors causing this increase was the arrival of
majority rule, which created a concern among the coloured population
that they would suffer in the new dispensation for not being authen-
tically 'Black'. This fear, and the identification with other Afrikaans
speakers, contributed to the electoral success of the Afrikaner nation-
alist party in the Western Cape in 1994 that came as a shock to many
observers.[10]

One striking characteristic of Kaaps is the frequent use of English
vocabulary, a feature which of course had to be eliminated from the
standardized form of the language, 'Anglicisms' being one of the 'im-
purities' that had to be eradicated. This feature is usually described by
linguists in terms of 'code-switching', but I avoid this term for the same
reason that I avoid the term 'mixed-race': it implies the pre-existence of
pure, separate entities — in this case the linguistic systems of Afrikaans
and English — that are then brought into coexistence within speech.
Speakers of Kaaps don't hold in their heads two distinct linguistic
systems from which they choose the words they use; as with many

---

9   Hein Willemse, 'Emergent Black Afrikaans Poets', in *Rendering Things Visible: Essays
     on South African Literary Culture*, ed. by Martin Trump (Johannesburg: Ravan Press,
     1990), pp. 367–401, quotes a 1938 study of what later became known as Kaaps, J.
     H. Rademeyer's *Kleurling-Afrikaans*: 'The coloured language of our country has [...]
     all along served one purpose only: to amuse!' Rademeyer's view of the speakers of
     the language is not untypical: 'Suffice it to say that they are today a wretched and
     degenerate group of human beings, whose laziness, lewdness and tendency to waste
     seem to be innate' (quotations on pp. 396–97).
10   See Zoë Wicomb, 'Shame and Identity: The Case of the Coloured in South Africa', in
     Writing South Africa: Literature, Apartheid, and Democracy, 1970–1995, ed. by Derek
     Attridge and Rosemary Jolly (Cambridge: Cambridge University Press, 1998), pp. 91–
     107.

other creoles, this way of speaking has its own distinctive lexicon and grammar.

In a replay of the struggle to establish Afrikaans in the nineteenth century, activists in the Coloured community are encouraging the use of Kaaps in education, broadcasting, and publishing.[11] The campaign for Kaaps has developed on many fronts: conferences, sessions at book festivals, articles, dissertations, and translations. A trilingual dictionary is in progress, and a number of novels have been published. And — the focus of this essay — several collections of poetry in varieties of Kaaps have appeared, the work of poets who grew up during the period of post-apartheid affirmation of coloured identity.[12]

The positing of a distinct language with its own name is an important weapon in the struggle to acknowledge the speech habits of this section of the population as having equal worth with other recognized languages — which is, of course, also a struggle to gain respect for the culture of this community. For instance, there's a move to acknowledge Kaaps in schools, where, traditionally, only standard Afrikaans was taught. (There are echoes here of the campaign to recognize African-American English, sometimes called Ebonics, in American schools; the promotion of Singlish, in the face of official disapproval, in the Singaporean media; and the project to make the widely spoken Patois of Jamaica — also known as Patwa, Creole, or simply Jamaican — an official language alongside English.) One of the leading writers in Kaaps, Nathan Trantraal — to whom I will return — comments sardonically on the situation in a short text titled 'Skryf 'it soes jy praat' (Write It as You Speak).[13] Asked as a boy in his Afrikaans class to write about 'a day that I will never forget', he is reluctant to give an honest account of the violence and psychological abuse that mark his most vivid memories,

---

11   See e.g. Michael le Cordeur, 'Kaaps: Time for the Language of the Cape Flats to Become Part of Formal Schooling', *Multilingual Margins*, 3.2 (2016), pp. 86–103; Hein Willemse, 'Soppangheid for Kaaps: Power, Creolisation and Kaaps Afrikaans', *Multilingual Margins*, 3.2 (2016), pp. 73–85.

12   A valuable early appreciation of the potential of Kaaps as a medium for poetry was Willemse, 'Emergent Black Afrikaans Poets'; see esp. pp. 377–81.

13   Nathan Trantraal, 'Skryf 'it soes jy praat' <https://www.litnet.co.za/poolshoogte-skryf-i-soes-jy-praat/> [accessed 4 October 2023]. See also Adam Cooper, '"You Can't Write in Kaapse Afrikaans in Your Question Paper. ... The Terms Must Be Right": Race- and Class-Infused Language Ideologies in Educational Places on the Cape Flats', *Educational Research for Social Change*, 7.1 (2018), pp. 30–45.

so he lets his imagination take over to recount a perfect day at the beach. Trantraal explains that if you fail Afrikaans, you fail the entire year, even if you pass all the other subjects,

> wan Afrikaans is jou hystaal, wat of course ironic was, wan Afrikaans wassie ôs se hystaal 'ie. In fact die Afrikaans wat ôs op skool gedoen 'et, het net 'n passing resemblance gehad to die Afrikaans wat ôs byrie hys gepraat 'et.

> (because Afrikaans is your home language, which of course was ironic, because Afrikaans wasn't our home language. In fact the Afrikaans that we did at school had only a passing resemblance to the Afrikaans that we spoke at home.)

When Trantraal much later finds himself *teaching* Afrikaans at his old high school, his class is stunned and baffled when he asks them to write an essay 'as they speak'.

As was the case with 'white' Afrikaans in the early twentieth century, writers of literary works using Kaaps have played, and will continue to play, a crucial role in securing for the language the prestige and stability it requires in order to advance the interests of the community. The most important pioneer in using the language of the coloured community for literary purposes was Adam Small, who died in 2016 at the age of seventy-nine.[14] Another was Peter Snyders, whose debut collection in Kaaps, *'n Ordinary mens*, appeared in 1982. (The story is told of Snyders submitting a poem in Kaaps to a competition in 1976 in some uncertainty about the appropriate category; he ended up choosing 'foreign languages'.) An important cultural endorsement of Kaaps occurred with the growth of Cape Flats hip-hop in the 1980s and 1990s: several hip-hop bands used Kaaps in their lyrics (the best known are Prophets of da City and Brasse van die Kaap), and their writing has been the subject of academic research at the University of the Western Cape (the university designated for coloured students by

---

14 Small played a significant role in promoting the dignity and standing of Kaaps. 'Kaaps is nie 'n grappigheid of snaaksigheid nie, maar 'n taal' (Kaaps is not a joke or a comedy, but a language), he writes in the introduction to *Kitaar my kruis*, 2nd edn (Cape Town: Haum, 1973), p. 9. For an assessment of Small's importance in the development of Kaaps as a literary language, see Nicole Devarenne, 'The Language of Ham and the Language of Cain: "Dialect" and Linguistic Hybridity in the Work of Adam Small', *Journal of Commonwealth Literature*, 45.3 (2010), pp. 389–408.

the apartheid government).[15] Kaaps has featured in television dramas, films, musicals, stand-up comedy, and popular song.

Recent years have seen a burgeoning of writing in Kaaps. Trantraal and his wife Ronelda Kamfer are two of the leading writers: at the time of writing, they have published seven collections of poems between them.[16] Trantraal is also the author of a collection of essays, *White issie 'n colour nie*,[17] and, with his brother André, several graphic novels; and Kamfer is also the author of a novel.[18] Trantraal has translated the American author Jason Reynolds's novel *Long Way Down* into Kaaps.[19] Another writer championing Kaaps by example is Olivia M. Coetzee, who is undertaking a translation of parts of the Bible into Kaaps, and in 2019 published a novel, *Innie shadows*.[20] Coetzee's variety of Kaaps uses relatively few English words; its distinctiveness lies primarily in the choice of vocabulary and the pronunciation of Afrikaans words. A Kaaps novel entitled *Kinnes* ('kinders', 'children') by Chase Rhys appeared in 2018; the endorsement on the cover reads: ''n character study van kinnes innie warzone vannie Cape Flats. Maa ook veel meer. Baie, baie funny en intensely moving.' Not surprisingly, perhaps, the endorsement is by Nathan Trantraal. Recent additions to the growing body of poetry in versions of Kaaps are Ashwin Arendse's *Swatland* (in which Arendse uses the Arabic letter *ghayn* to represent the characteristic *r* sound of the Malmesbury area) and Ryan Pedro's *Pienk ceramic-hondjies*. A more recent addition to the growing body of

15   See Hein Willemse, 'Black Afrikaans Writers: Continuities and Discontinuities into the Early 21st Century — a Commentary', *Stilet*, 31.1–2 (2019), pp. 260–75.

16   Nathan Trantraal, *Chokers en survivors* (Cape Town: Kwela Books, 2013), *Alles sal niet kom wôd* (Cape Town: Kwela Books, 2017), *Oolog* (Cape Town, Kwela Books, 2020); Ronelda Kamfer, *Noudat slapende honde* (Cape Town: Kwela Books, 2008), *grond/Santekraam* (Cape Town: Kwela Books, 2011), *Hammie* (Cape Town: Kwela Books, 2016), *Chinatown* (Cape Town: Kwela Books, 2019). For a very full dossier of material on Trantraal in Afrikaans, see Erika Terblanche, 'Nathan Trantraal (1983–)' <https://www.litnet.co.za/nathan-trantraal-1983/> [accessed 10 October 2023].

17   Nathan Trantraal, *White issie 'n colour nie* (Cape Town: Kwela Books, 2018).

18   Ronelda Kamfer, *Kompoun* (Cape Town: Kwela Books, 2021).

19   Jason Reynolds, *Lang pad onnetoe*, trans. by Nathan Trantraal (Pretoria: Lapa, 2018).

20   Olivia M. Coetzee, 'Bybel in Kaaps' <https://www.litnet.co.za/category/nuwe-skryfwerk-new-writing/bybelinkaaps/> [accessed 5 October 2023], *Innie shadows* (Cape Town: Modjaji Books, 2020).

poetry in Kaaps is Veronique Jephtas's *Soe rond ommie bos*.[21] Trantraal no doubt speaks for all these authors when he writes:

> My Afrikaans lyk soesie mense wat it praat. Die geskiedenis van Coloured mense is heeltemaal locked up innie Afrikaans wat hulle praat. Is Engels, Dutch, Malay, Indonesian Arabic, Khoe. Dis 'n version van Afrikaans wat unedited is, sône gatekeepers en sône affectations.
>
> (My Afrikaans looks like the people who speak it. The history of coloured people is completely locked up in the Afrikaans they speak. It is English, Dutch, Malay, Indonesian Arabic, Khoe. It's a version of Afrikaans that is unedited, without gate-keepers and without affectations.)[22]

The question I want to raise in considering verse production in Kaaps is: can this poetry contribute to the advancement of the community it arises from and depicts? And this implies other questions, such as: Who is it addressed to? Who actually reads it? How does its content relate to its potential role in, and on behalf of, the community?

The choice of Kaaps as the language in which to write and publish poems is not without its problems. The use in poetry of what is thought of as dialect is often a choice made for comic purposes, a practice encouraged by the social and economic disparity frequently to be found between speakers of the 'standard' or 'received' version of a language and those versions spoken by lower classes and in regions distant from the capital. Adam Small, quoted above, insisted that Kaaps was not a comic language (see note 14); nevertheless, Trantraal accused him and Snyders of using it as a 'joke-language',[23] an accusation — though it was only an offhand remark in an interview — that was met with much displeasure among the other supporters of the language. Contemporary poets writing in Kaaps certainly draw on its comic potential from time to time, but it is usually comedy laced with irony, self-mockery, or satire, and does not spring from anything inherent in the language.

---

21   Veronique Jephtas, *Soe rond ommie bos* (Cape Town: Protea Boekhuis, 2021).

22   Quoted and trans. by Anastasia de Vries, 'The Use of Kaaps in Newspapers', *Multilingual Margins*, 3.2 (2016), pp. 127–39 (p. 134).

23   Danie Marais, 'Middagtee met Nathan Trantraal: Kaaps is nie 'n joke-taal nie', *Die Burger*, 2 August 2013, pp. 2–3.

One way in which the use of Kaaps in published works of litera-
ture may advance the interests of the community is through giving its
members a sense of pride in the language. Those in the community
who are aware that their way of speaking is denigrated by speakers
of the standard form of Afrikaans — an awareness heightened by the
educational practices already mentioned — are able to point to literary
works published by well-thought-of presses. This impact of publica-
tion on the Flats should not be exaggerated, however; owing to the
economic and educational deprivation of the area, most members of
the community would not be likely to come across the few novels
and plays written in Kaaps, and even less likely to read poetry in this
(or any) language. On the other hand, poems in Kaaps undoubtedly
mean a great deal to those coloured readers who do encounter them;
Trantraal observes: 'There are Coloured people who are not what you
would consider readers but will read Kaaps books because they see
their lives reflected for the first time in literature.'[24] A small number of
coloured students have been able to pursue degrees involving Kaaps
literature, and many of them have gone on to publish works in the
language. Kaaps is also to be heard occasionally in performance (along
with poetry in other languages) at several venues, both on the Flats
and in the Western Cape more widely: there is an annual Cape Flats
Book Festival in Mitchell's Plain, and annual events are organized in
Cape Town (e.g. the Open Book Festival and the Suidooster Festival),
Stellenbosch (the Woordfees), and the small town of McGregor (Mc-
Gregor Poetry Festival).

However, there is no escaping the fact that the greater part of
the readership of Kaaps poetry is, inevitably, white, middle-class, and
standard-Afrikaans-speaking. Trantraal is fully aware of this: 'If we
are talking about a market, access, reading culture, etc. then yes, I
would say white middle-class Afrikaners are definitely our biggest
audience.'[25] Trantraal is also known to this readership through his col-
umn in Kaaps in *Rapport*, a widely read Afrikaans Sunday newspaper.
English-speaking South Africans who (like myself) studied Afrikaans
as an obligatory school subject, even if they have had little use in their

---

24   Nathan Trantraal, email to the author, 31 July 2023.
25   Ibid.

daily lives for the language, also find Kaaps readable, as do many speakers of one of the Bantu languages who know Afrikaans as a second, third, or even fourth language. Attendance at cultural festivals is bound to be largely middle class, and it is middle-class readers, too, who are more likely to respond to the many high-cultural references in poetry like that of Kamfer and Trantraal — the former, for instance, refers to, among others, Dostoevsky, Simone Weil, Sylvia Plath, and Ted Hughes, while the latter (one of whose collections features a drawing of Bernini's *St Theresa* on the cover) assumes a knowledge of Donatello, Kafka, Picasso, Borges, and many more. Both make mention of poets in the elite Afrikaans canon, such as N. P. van Wyk Louw, Elisabeth Eybers, and Ingrid Jonker. (There are also, it should be added, an even greater number of references to figures and works from popular culture.) The prestige associated with the lyric is what's important here: a way of speaking associated with poverty and lack of education is granted the status of the genre more usually associated with poets like Spenser and Milton, Wordsworth and Dickinson.

To be read largely by middle-class white Afrikaners does not harm the project of gaining for Kaaps, and the community that speaks it, increased respect, therefore; on the contrary, it offers an invitation to these readers to see themselves as part of a much larger Afrikaans-speaking population and to value the cultural productions of places such as the Cape Flats. Alongside the making of a dictionary, the translation of the Bible, the availability of songs, films, plays, novels, and journalism, poetry in Kaaps — and poetry of a high quality — makes a statement that is hard to ignore.

What, then, of the content of this poetry? Writers of Kaaps naturally deal with their own experience, reflecting the challenges of living in a community still feeling the effects of centuries of discrimination as well as the more recent material impoverishment caused by the policies of apartheid and by the failures of the post-apartheid government. Much of the work of these writers reflects the hardscrabble conditions of the community to which they belong. We hear of the effects of dagga (marijuana) and tik (crystal meth), the prevalence of crime, gang activities, illness, joblessness, gambling, prostitution, police, and prisons. Trantraal writes of a diet of jam-and-peanut-butter sandwiches with weak tea, Kamfer of a paedophile uncle. Colourful township characters

— lost souls, small-time gangsters, scroungers, petty entrepreneurs on the make — are described with the generosity born from life in a close community. Evangelical Christian sects proliferate. Family ties are strong, though familial conflict is widespread.

Such poetry receives different responses in the two types of readership I have identified. Fellow coloureds living in the kinds of environment which the poetry describes may be dismayed at having the harshness of their daily existence exposed in this way, though perhaps the gratification at seeing their travails recorded in poems in their own language counters this feeling. The darkness of the content is often alleviated by the warmth with which the characters, however shady, and events, however unpleasant, are described. And those coloured readers who have, at least to some extent, escaped this environment are more likely to applaud the exposure of its conditions as a form of protest.

Middle-class white readers, on the other hand, have to tread carefully. We too register many of these poems as a form of protest, in the long tradition of literary works that expose harsh conditions and struggling existences. And when qualities of generosity, endurance, and courage shine through the poetry, full acknowledgement of what is depicted can be a humbling experience for those whose lives are safer and more comfortable. At the same time, there is a danger that readers whose lives are totally different may take a dubious pleasure in these portrayals of poverty and resistance, especially given the tendency already mentioned to find the use of Kaaps a source of comedy. An examination of a selection of poems by Kamfer and Trantraal will begin to suggest some of the ways in which their work operates in these diverse ways, as a celebration of community, as a protest, and as an invitation to understand and appreciate lives lived in a different environment.

2

The only Kaaps poet included in the 2014 anthology *In a Burning Sea: Contemporary Afrikaans Poetry in Translation* is Ronelda Kamfer. The following short work exhibits the qualities of many Kaaps poems; its wry humour does not detract from the protest it makes against the conditions prevalent in the Cape Flats:

> *Goeie meisies*
>
> Goeie meisies join nie gangs nie
> hulle raakie pregnant op dertien nie
> hulle dra nie tjappies nie
> hulle roekie weed nie
> hulle tik nie
> hulle jol nie saam met taxi drivers nie
> hulle werk nie vir Shoprite nie
> hulle is nie die cleaners nie
> goeie meisies bly nie oppie Cape flats nie[26]

The published translation is by Charl J. F. Cilliers:

> *Good girls*
>
> Good girls do not join gangs
> they do not get pregnant at thirteen
> they do not wear chappie tattoos
> they don't smoke weed
> they do not use tik
> they do not jol with taxi drivers
> they do not work for Shoprite
> they are not cleaners
> good girls do not live on the Cape Flats[27]

(A note explains that 'jol' means 'to have a good time'; a better translation for this example might be 'flirt'. Shoprite is a chain of South African supermarkets that emphasize economy.)

Characteristic of Kaaps is the use of English vocabulary — 'pregnant', 'weed', 'taxi drivers', 'cleaners', 'Cape flats' — and the elision of verbs followed by 'nie' to create a negative — 'raakie' for 'raak nie' (don't become), 'roekie' for 'rook nie' (don't smoke — Kaaps also evinces a typical loss of a diphthong here). There is a similar elision of 'die' in 'oppie' for 'op die' (on the). The spelling of 'djol' rather than the more usual 'jol' reflects a Kaaps preference for what we might think of as the English pronunciation of *j*.

---

26 *In a Burning Sea: Contemporary Afrikaans Poetry in Translation*, ed. by Marlise Joubert (Pretoria: Protea Book House, 2014), p. 150. The poem was first published in Kamfer, *Noudat slapende honde*.

27 *In a Burning Sea*, ed. by Joubert, p. 151.

What the translation loses, of course, is the sense of a distinctive voice identifying the speaker with the place named in the poem: this is not, as the language of the translated version suggests, an outsider's view of the Cape Flats. (The use of the formal 'do not' in every line but one contributes to this sense.)[28] The inescapability of early pregnancy, drug use, inappropriate sexual liaisons, and unemployment is not observed from a distance but from within, with both anger and humour.

Many Kaaps poems celebrate family ties in the midst of adversity. The figure of the mother emerges from Trantraal's poetry as a formidable individual. The following is an excerpt from 'Hammie' (a Kaaps word meaning 'mother' or 'mummy'),[29] a poem which occurs in the section of *Chokers en survivors* entitled 'Mitchell's Plain' (where Trantraal spend his childhood):

> It is by haa wat ek gelee et
> hoe om te hustle.
> Nie dai gangsta-hustle ie,
> ma dai vrou-allien-sôg-vi-ses-kinnes hustle,
> dai righteous hustle.
>
> My ma het my gelee
> ommie sentimental te wiesie.
> Die eeste ding wat sy gepawn et
> was haa trouringe.
>
> My ma groet gangsters en kêkmense dieselle
> wan sytie kêkmense geken
> voo hulle gangsters geraak et
> ennie gangsters voo hulle
> hulle harte virrie Here gegie et.
> My ma respek nieman te veel of te min nie.[30]

Translated into regular English, with all the losses that this entails, we get:

---

28   See Attridge, 'Untranslatability', for a discussion of the challenge of translating Kaaps into either standard Afrikaans or English. This translation also misses the point of line 8, which follows on from the previous line: the reference is not to cleaners in general but to 'the cleaners', i.e. those who work for Shoprite. Not only do the girls in question not work at the checkouts or on the shop floor, they are not even the cleaners.

29   When Kamfer published a collection that includes many poems dealing with her relationship with her mother, she chose to call it *Hammie*.

30   Trantraal, *Chokers en survivors*, p. 31.

It is from her that I learned
how to hustle.
Not that gangster-hustle,
but that woman-alone-caring-for-six-children hustle,
that righteous hustle.

My mother taught me
not to be sentimental.
The first thing that she pawned
was her wedding rings.

My mother greets gangsters and churchgoers the same
because she knew the churchgoers
before they became gangsters
and the gangsters before they
gave their hearts to the Lord.
My mother respects no one too much or too little.

In this example, the humour is in the service of warm admiration, although as so often the background — the easy transition between churchgoers and gangsters — is a dark one. Trantraal has put a great deal of effort into achieving a consistent orthography for the distinctive pronunciation of Kaaps, many examples of which occur in these lines, including the use of a circumflex for the distinctive vowel sounds in 'kêk' (for 'kerk', 'church') and 'sôg' (for 'sorg', 'care for'). English words are drawn into Afrikaans conjugations: thus the usual indicator of past tense, 'ge-', is used with an English word in 'gepawn'.[31]

---

31 There is as yet no standard orthography for Kaaps; every writer has developed a system to reflect their pronunciation. There are also regional variations, even within the Cape Flats. For a comparison of three Kaaps writers who use slightly different versions of the language and different spelling conventions, see de Vries, 'Use of Kaaps in Newspapers'. Trantraal observes that the biggest challenge in writing in Kaaps is 'that there are no dictionaries in Kaaps. And there is no autocorrect in Word for Kaaps words. It is hard to stay consistent in terms of spelling and grammar, etc. And you consume much energy in the whole process of reading everything a hundred times to see if you have spelled one word the same everywhere. That is energy that belongs to the creative process. Sometimes I feel I am a language engineer more than a writer' ('dat daa nie woordeboeke in Kaaps issie. En daa is niks autocorrect in Word vi Kaapse woorde nie. It is swaa om consistent te bly in terms van spelling en grammar, etc. En jy gie baie energy weg annie hele process van alles 'n honned kee te lies om te sien of jy een woord dieselfde spel orals. Dai is energy wat annie creative process behoot, soms voel ek soese taal engineer meer asse writer'; quoted in Carolyn Meads, 'PEN Afrikaans: Om boeke in Kaaps te publiseer' <https://www.litnet.co.za/pen-afrikaans-om-boeke-in-kaaps-te-publiseer/> [accessed 11 October 2023]).

Occasionally, Trantraal and Kamfer write poems which deal directly with the issue of the relation between the coloured, Kaaps-speaking poet from an impoverished background and the largely white and middle-class poetry-reading public. One instance is Trantraal's poem 'Cash for Gold'. The use of an English title — reflecting the sign on a shopfront typical of a poorer area — indicates that this is not in any simple sense an Afrikaans poem.

> Cash for Gold
>
> *Something's in the water*
> *And if I gotta brown-nose for some gold*
> *I'd rather be a bum than a motherfuckin' baller*
> — 'King Kunta', Kendrick Lamar
>
> Ek wonne of ekkie ienagste
> prize-winning poet is
> wat copper wire
> vi kosgeld moet strip
> Ek is possibly die ienagste een
> wattie 'n lift kan kry of afford ie
> en Lavis toe loep, hystoe
> loep, vanaf Cape Town
> International Airport af
> narie literary festival in Potch veby is
> Ek issie een wat in Amsterdam bly
> writer-in-residence
> en as ek hystoe kom
> die goue kettangs moet gan pan
> wat my vrou by Annemarie
> as presents gekry et
>
> My naam lê innie monne van
> Cash for Gold se mense
> ennit lê oppie koffietafels
> van ryk mense in Oranjezicht
> My naam is innie koerant
> en oppie receipts van Cash Crusaders
>
> Ek kry respect en awards
> wat vi genoeg mense baie beteken
> en dan oppe Woensdag
> wat niks beteken ie
> staan ek innie voorhys en wieg
> ie award in my hand
> en vra my ma: 'Wat dink Mammie,
> is dié bronze of copper?'

> Assit copper is issit 'n paa dae se kos
> assit bronze is beteken it niks vi my nie[32]

Once again, a translation into standard English loses the strongly col-
loquial colouring of the original and its creative employment of both
Afrikaans and English vocabularies:

> I wonder if I am the only
> prize-winning poet
> who has to strip copper wire
> for food money
> I am possibly the only one
> who can't get or afford a lift
> and so walks to Lavis, walks home,
> from Cape Town
> International Airport
> after the literary festival in Potch is over
> I am the only one who stays in Amsterdam as
> writer-in-residence
> and when I get home
> has to pawn the gold chains
> that my wife received from Annemarie
> as presents.
>
> My name lies in the mouths of
> Cash for Gold's people
> and it lies on the coffee-tables
> of rich people in Oranjezicht
> My name is in the newspaper
> and on the receipts from Cash Crusaders
>
> I get respect and awards
> that for enough people mean a lot
> and then on a Wednesday
> that means nothing
> I stand in the lounge and weigh
> the award in my hand
> and ask my mum: 'What does Mammie think,
> is this bronze or copper?'
> If it's copper it's a couple of days' food
> if it's bronze it means nothing to me

(Lavis is the Cape Flats township of Bishop Lavis, about an hour's
walk from Cape Town Airport. Potch is Potchefstroom, a university

---

32   Trantraal, *Alles het niet kom wôd*, pp. 42–43.

town in the north of the country. Annemarie is probably Annemarie van Niekerk, an Afrikaans writer and editor living in the Netherlands. Oranjezicht is an upmarket, arty suburb of Cape Town on the slopes of Table Mountain. Cash Crusaders is a chain of South African pawn and second-hand shops.)

Trantraal's language is, again, redolent of the spoken language of the Flats. In standard Afrikaans, the opening might read:

> Ek wonder of ek die enigste
> bekroonde digter is
> wat koperdraad
> vir geld moet stroop om kos te koop

The original is more immediate, catching the Kaaps enunciation in its Afrikaans and using English phrases almost as quotations — one can imagine the phrase 'prize-winning poet' in a laudatory news article, and 'copper wire' in a crime report. My English version is no better, losing the colloquial force of the Kaaps. One translator, Alice Inggs, has valiantly attempted to capture the original's colloquial qualities in English, but the result seems to me to illustrate the problems of such an undertaking:

> I wunner if I'ma only
> prize-winning poet
> that must strip
> copper wire
> fo food money
> I am possibly the only one
> that can't get or afford a lift
> and walks to Lavis, walks
> homeward, from Cape Town
> International Airport
> aftera literary festival in Potch is over
> I ama one that stays in Amsterdam
> writer-in-residence
> and if I come home
> must go pawn the gold chains
> that my wife got from Annemarie
> as presents
>
> My name lies inna mouths of
> Cash for Gold's people
> annit lies onna coffee tables

of rich people in Oranjezicht
My name is inna newspaper
and onna receipts of Cash Crusaders

I get respect and awards
that means a lot fo enough people
and then onna Wednesday
that means nothing
I stand inna frontroom and weigh
a award in my hand
and ask my ma: 'What does Mammie think,
is this bronze or copper?'
Iffits copper it's a coupla days' food
iffits bronze it means nothing to me[33]

It's not clear what this version of English is meant to represent; sometimes the spelling does not appear to indicate anything different about the pronunciation ('onna Wednesday', 'Iffits copper'); at other times it replaces the Kaaps elision of 'die' with an elision of 'the' that doesn't work in the same way ('I'ma only', 'aftera literary festival', 'inna mouths', 'a award').

In Trantraal's poem the contrast between being feted at a literary festival in the Afrikaner heartland and having to leg it home after disembarking at the airport is conveyed without self-pity, as is that between a residency in Amsterdam and the pawning of the gift given to his wife there. The irony running through the poem, of course, is that, as we have seen, it is the owners of coffee tables with strategically placed books of poetry who are the most likely readers of this poem. Is Trantraal biting the hands that feed him?

The ending of the poem, moving as it does from more public scenes to a private one, provides a personal vignette that contains a slight touch of self-mockery. Our poet is now a son at a loose end on a particular day — it happens to be a Wednesday — playing with his award. The poem comes full circle as we return to the possibility of copper providing funds for food (there's no chance that it's a matter of cash for gold), but the equal possibility that the prizes the poet receives will not contribute to the family's daily needs.

---

33 'Three Poems by Nathan Trantraal', trans. by Alice Inggs <https://www.europenowjournal.org/2018/02/28/three-poems-by-nathan-trantraal/> [accessed 5 October 2023].

Ronelda Kamfer's poem 'Volkspele' also bears on the topic of the coloured writer taken up by the white bourgeoisie. Kamfer is less linguistically catholic than her husband; most of the Afrikaans she uses is the standard form, and English vocabulary occurs with somewhat less frequency. In this poem the moneyed white people — the ones who are more likely to read her poems than members of her own community — are treated with contempt.

> *Volkspele*
>
> ek is by 'n party vol depressed
> wit mense
> almal luister Marianne Faithfull
> en lees Bitterkomix
> ek weet nie wat de fok
> ek hier maak nie
> ek sit en luister
> na hulle pyn en hul apathy
> hulle wil weet vir wie ek hier ken
>
> hulle koop mekaar se boeke
> en paintings en het almal
> 'n storie oor hul jare in Europe
>
> ek wens ek was
> iewers anders
> iewers waar mense
> nie almal mekaar haat nie[34]

An English translation loses a good deal of the emotional forcefulness of the original:

> *Folkdances*
>
> I am at a party full of depressed
> white people
> everyone is listening to Marianne Faithfull
> and reading Bitterkomix
> I don't know what the fuck
> I'm doing here
> I sit and listen
> to their pain and their apathy
> they want to know who I know here

---

34   Kamfer, *Hammie*, p. 68.

they buy each other's books
and paintings and all have
a story about their years in Europe

I wish I was
somewhere else
somewhere where people
don't all hate each other

(*Bitterkomix* was a deliberately offensive Afrikaans comic, a badge of middle-class unshockability.)

This, too, is a poem about the gap between the poet and her readers or potential readers; but here the implication is that Kamfer speaks from and for a genuine community, albeit one that — as many poems in Kaaps reveal — is constituted not by unity and similarity but by rupture, mutual exposure, and shared mortality (a community, perhaps, as defined by Blanchot and Nancy).[35] By contrast, the bourgeois white world is one of hypocrisy, misery, one-upmanship, and a community feeling that is only pretended. The paradox remains: by capturing the contrast between these groups in lyric poetry, Kamfer makes a bid to enhance the standing of her community in the eyes of those who read such work, even while denigrating their way of life.

Trantraal also writes of his discomfort in middle-class white company, in a poem titled 'Grahamstown', the seat of the historically white Rhodes University, where Trantraal currently teaches creative writing. (The post-apartheid name of the town is Makhanda; the change involved replacing the name of a British general responsible for the slaughter of Xhosa warriors with the name of a famous Xhosa figure.)

Grahamstown

Oh, don't try and take his suffering away from him — he'd be lost without it.
— John Osborne, Look Back in Anger

Die wit mense kyk my met groot oë an
as ek sê my katte slap byte

---

35 Maurice Blanchot, *The Unavowable Community*, trans. by Pierre Joris (Barrytown: Station Hill Press, 1988); Jean-Luc Nancy, *The Inoperative Community*, trans. by Peter Connor and others (Minneapolis: University of Minnesota Press, 1991). Although Blanchot's and Nancy's interpretations of community are by no means identical, they both resist the idea that it signifies homogeneity and transcendence.

En hulle skrik virrie foreign kosse wat ôs maak
En hulle wietie of hulle mag lag virrie jokes ie
En hulle vra altyd wat hulle moet saambring narie braai toe
Ek kennie ees die wit mense se name wat langs ôs bly
an altwie kante nie

En ek vestaan isse anne land waa ôs nou is
'n Anne culture hie in wit Syd-Afrika
Maa it maak net dat ek my homeland mis
En ek mis my vriende, die worst goeie mense
wat jy ooit sal ken, ek ken nieman bieter

En ek kan nooit wee hystoe gannie
wan is child soldiers en warlords
wat Bishop Lavis regeer
Daa is oolog annie gang waa ek vandaan kom
nou sit ek in self-exile en dink
annie mense wat nog daa is

En ek lee maa ommie vleis nog bloed vannie
kole af te hal en rosyntjies innie slaai te gooi
En ek vetel rondom groot glase wit wyn
stories vannie old country[36]

In standard English:

The white people look at me with big eyes
when I say that my cats sleep outside
And they start at the foreign foods that we make
And they don't know if they should laugh at the jokes
And they always ask what they must bring with them to the barbecue
I don't even know the names of the white people who live next to us
on both sides

And I understand that it's another country where we now are
Another culture here in South Africa
But it just makes me miss my homeland
And I miss my friends, the worst good people
that you will ever know, I know no one better

And I can never go home again
because it's child soldiers and warlords
that rule Bishop Lavis
There is war in the gang where I come from
now I sit in self-exile and think
of the people that are still there

---

36   Trantraal, *Oolog*, p. 44.

And I learn to remove the meat still full of blood
from the coals and to throw raisins into the slaw
And round great glasses of white wine I tell
stories of the old country

Translation into standard English fails to capture the tonal complexity of the poem, signalled initially by the epigraph from Osborne: the complaining outsider knows that he thrives on complaints, and that he cuts a somewhat comic figure in this white middle-class community. As so often with these poets, a serious point — this unfamiliar and somewhat repellent lifestyle is preferable to the violence and danger at home (both situations are described in exaggerated terms) — is made with humour and self-mockery. The poem ends with an image that implies, finally, full assimilation into this society, yet the cliché works against this to sustain the mockery to the end. In the original, the use of English for 'old country' — hardly an expected term for the Cape Flats — heightens the comedy.

The poems of Trantraal and Kamfer invite readers, whether members of their community or outsiders, to empathize with those who suffer from the deprivation of the Flats but at the same time to enjoy the wry humour that gleams through accounts of that suffering. Kaaps may not be a joke-language, but it is a superb medium for this combination of protest, pain, and laughter. These poets exploit its many dimensions in highly skilled writing, adding a dimension of readerly pleasure to the most painful of depictions. While poetry alone is not going to improve conditions in this disadvantaged part of South Africa, such a powerful demonstration of creative subtlety and sophistication may help to counter in some small degree the prejudice that still colours many responses to it. Poetry in Kaaps demonstrates the potential of the language as an expressive resource, and in so doing not only exposes the harm done by centuries of exclusion and denigration — of a people as well as of their language — but makes a powerful claim for the vitality, closeness, and self-awareness of the community.

Casting Dispersions
Revising Lyric Privacy in Simone White's *Of Being Dispersed*
WENDY LOTTERMAN

> Romanticism is nothing
> but liberalism in literature.[1]
> Victor Hugo, *Hernani*

> [Lyric's] general cogency depends
> on the intensity of its individuation.[2]
> Theodor Adorno, *Notes to Literature*

> We are cast about or away and must use
> a sense of qualities as belonging to our-
> selves and others to make an assay.[3]
> Simone White, *Dear Angel of Death*

LYRIC AND LIBERAL SUBJECTS

Simone White's 2016 book *Of Being Dispersed* replaces the constitu-tive privacy of the traditional lyric speaker with a public in which the

---

1   Victor Hugo, *Hernani* (Paris: Larousse, 1971), p. 30.
2   Theodor W. Adorno, *Notes to Literature*, trans. by Shierry Weber Nicholsen (New York: Columbia University Press, 2019), p. 60.
3   Simone White, *Dear Angel of Death* (Brooklyn: Ugly Duckling Presse, 2018), p. 71.

subject is dispersed. The poetry's ambivalent orientation toward lyric — within yet against the form — enjoins the reader to consider the genre's risk of complicity with liberalism through its naturalization of personhood and privacy. I will begin by outlining the influence of classical liberal principles on definitions of personhood and property in US case law, and then read White's poetry for scenes of refusal. Such a refusal of privacy and individuation, I argue, exposes how the lyric subject's conventional exclusion of a public effectively forces race to be read as a property of the individual — i.e. as an identity — rather than as the effect of a social process called 'racialization'. In their constitutive secession from the public, both lyric and liberal subjects receive recognition on the condition of individuation. In White's poems, the post-Romantic lyric is first chosen for its structural homology and historical imbrication with classical liberal subjectivity; it is then exposed as a limit to theorizing the social life of race. My readings of White will focus on her 2016 book *Of Being Dispersed* and compare it with George Oppen's 1968 'Of Being Numerous'.

The Canadian sociologist C. B. MacPherson described the civic ideal of personhood elaborated by John Locke as 'possessive-individualism' — a model that not only protects individual freedom and property rights above 'the common good' but established a dialectical relationship between personhood and property.[4] Property, according to Locke, exists only insofar as it is owned by an individual proprietor or person; likewise, personhood is defined as a 'Forensick [*sic*] Term appropriating Actions and their Merits', denoting a proprietary relation to one's own actions or labor. This definition would eventually determine the outcome of a landmark US case concerning the law's ability to recognize a right to land outside the logic of property. In *Johnson v. M'Intosh* (1823) it is precisely the Piankeshaw Indians' 'common occupancy' of the land to which they seek title that invalidates their right to ownership. Because their ownership was not private, it was not strictly property. What begins as an epistemological difference thus becomes a cause for material dispossession. Not only does the case nullify the Piankeshaws' title;

---

4   C. B. MacPherson, *The Political Theory of Possessive Individualism: Hobbes to Locke* (Oxford: Oxford University Press, 2011).

it also places them outside of a legal framework in which recognition is conferred on individual persons and not groups. The case, which set a lasting precedent, repeatedly makes recourse to Locke's *Second Treatise on Government*, containing his famous essay 'Of Property'. And yet, rather than citing any author with the specific concept of property mobilized by the court's opinion, the court dissimulates the provenance, stating that 'the measure of property acquired by occupancy is determined according to the law of nature'.[5] US property law is thus built upon a classical liberal ideal of ownership that is speciously credited as the 'law of nature'.

MacPherson diagnoses in Locke's vision of an unlimited right to property an attempt to universalize in non-class terms a right that necessarily possessed class content. In this sense, personhood — as a form of property — failed to become the equalizing, natural right that Locke imagined, and was instead differentially distributed across classes. But individuation and legal personhood are not only operative in property cases. In what has now become the most widely cited statute in US decisions concerning social difference, the Civil Rights Act of 1964, the right to recognition and redress is explicitly predicated upon the individuation of the claimant. Discrimination, like property, is private. The law, as many of its administrators have affirmed, is not designed to recognize groups. It recognizes, rather, the individual, defined as 'a particular being as distinguished from a class'.[6] Privacy, then, is a precondition of recognition. I argue that the subject of White's poems, in refusing this precondition, demands a form of recognition that is denied by the law: recognition of the racialized subject and its dispersion within a public.

Lyric privacy was consolidated by the Romantic redefinition of the genre, which historically and regionally coincides with the circulation of classical liberal political values.[7] John Stuart Mill is widely considered a key architect of classical liberal philosophy and wrote

---

5   *Johnson* v. *M'Intosh* (21 US (8 Wheat.) 543 (1823)).

6   See *Bostock* v. *Clayton Cty.* (140 S. Ct. 1731 (2020)).

7   Both Hegel's definition of lyric poetry in his *Lectures on Aesthetics* and Locke's definition of the Western liberal constitutional state in his *Second Treatise of Government* take for granted the existence of an individual whose separation from the group is formally reflected in poetry and law.

enthusiastically of William Wordsworth's *Lyrical Ballads* of 1798. In his 1833 essay 'What is Poetry', Mill famously answered that it is an 'utterance of feeling' that 'supposes [no] audience'.[8] The former premise establishes the poem as an emission from the poet's interiority.[9] The latter qualification contains the implicit dismissal of a public, who may only incidentally enter the sphere of lyric. Where Ancient Greek lyrics were performed chorally and for the enjoyment of an audience, post-Romantic lyrics are not only all monodic, but private. Northrop Frye went so far as to say that the lyric is characterized by 'the individual communing with himself'.[10] The modernist attention to impossible speech further consecrates the ontology of the individual by imagining a coherent subject that precedes its alienation by industrial capitalist social relations. But individuation is not prior to or independent from those relations; rather, it is a by-product of proprietary notions of personhood on which liberal political subjectivity relies.[11] Lyric privacy inherits liberal values and synthesizes their premise; the speaker in post-Romantic lyric poetry has *turned away* from the public.[12]White's poetry refuses to reproduce the generic conventions of personhood, moving instead toward a scene that is (*a*) primarily social and (*b*) ineligible as property. Where the reader might expect to find a person, they instead encounter a public. In other words, the subject of White's poems is inextricable from the scene of socialization. White's poetry thus recovers an unruly mass that precedes its compulsory translation into the idiom of liberalism.[13] This chapter looks specifically at White's

---

8 John Stuart Mill, 'Thoughts on Poetry and Its Varieties', in *The Collected Works of John Stuart Mill*, ed. by John M. Robson and Jack Stillenger (Toronto: University of Toronto Press; London: Routledge & Keegan Paul, 1963–91), 1: *Autobiography and Literary Essays* (1981), pp. 343–65 (p. 348).

9 I am interested in evoking Denise Ferreira da Silva's writing on 'interiority' as a racialized unit of apperception whose excluded remainder is rendered into objects rather than subjects of knowledge. See e.g. her *Toward a Global Idea of Race* (Minneapolis: University of Minnesota Press, 2007), chaps 1–4.

10 Northrop Frye, *Anatomy of Criticism* (Princeton, NJ: Princeton University Press, 1957), p. 32.

11 See MacPherson, *Possessive Individualism*.

12 Frye wrote in *Anatomy of Criticism*, pp. 249–50, that the lyric poet 'turns his back on his listeners', drawing upon the etymology of what some claim to be lyric's minimum condition: apostrophe, or 'turning away' in Greek.

13 Here I have in mind Hortense J. Spillers, 'Mama's Baby, Papa's Maybe: An American Grammar Book', *Diacritics*, 17.2 (1987), pp. 64–81, at the end of which she argues

2016 book *Of Being Dispersed* and compares it with George Oppen's 1968 'Of Being Numerous'.[14] I argue that the structural viability of the 'many' presupposes the ontology of the 'one'. Oppen's elective ambition — immersion in the social — is White's inescapable condition. In this sense, intimacy is not only the negation of privacy but also the refusal to capitulate to a Romantic ideal of community that presupposes the integrity of an original individuation.

White's first-person speaker not only complicates its claim to speech but invites others into the event of language. A poem called 'Metaphor for the Changing Season' from the title section reads:

> All I was thinking or would ever think was happening in a closet. I could never be joined there by anyone but you. You and you and I were all there was. The enfolding thing, to pulsate. Parts broke off and spun away. We were capsular or corpuscular in terms both of destiny and lack of destination. Parts broke off and I looked to you to see if thoughts had been had by anybody.[15]

This poem presents an uncanny combination of traditional lyric apostrophe. White writes 'I looked to you', but the exclusivity of that look is undercut by the ambient quality of thoughts, which are given ambiguous attribution. In the first instance, the speaker's thinking is a temporally unbounded event that is happening within a closet. In the second, thoughts are had by 'anybody', after 'parts broke off'. Dispersal, which is reinforced by the repetition of 'parts broke off', compels the subject to survey the space. Rather than looking to see if 'anybody had any thoughts', the subject 'looked [...] to see if thoughts had been had by anybody', complicating the Cartesian yield of an ego from the act of cogitation.

---

that it is time to make a place for a 'different social subject' (p. 80). While Spillers is speaking specifically about the Black maternal figure, whose position stands outside the symbolic order of both white capitalist patriarchy and psychoanalysis, the essay is also labouring to make room for a subject, like the Black maternal, who is primarily social, i.e. not individuated.

14   Simone White, *Of Being Dispersed* (New York: Futurepoem, 2016); George Oppen, 'Of Being Numerous', in *New Collected Poems* (New York: New Directions, 2008), pp. 163–89.

15   White, *Being Dispersed*, p. 17.

Perhaps the most interesting moment is the failed attempt to posit privacy and exclusivity. 'I could never be joined there by anyone but you' is then immediately undermined by the duplication of 'you' in the following sentence. The speaker's thoughts happen within a closet, one that cannot welcome visitors, except for 'you'. 'You', an already overdetermined pronoun, then doubles.[16] There are, at minimum, three in the closet, a space already associated with disclosure.[17] More than just a metaphor for the changing seasons, this poem models an immanent poetics of intimacy without privacy. Where privacy relies on the exclusivity of material forms, intimacy is immune to its negation by the plural. The first page of White's collection reads:

> […] Los Angeles was on my face;
>
> it was hot and harmless.
> Before I burned up and rolled away,
> black-ass tumbleweed, as had happened so many times
> in dreams that year, it was important that I get there
> or get some information my papa was trying to get across[18]

The subject of this stanza is neither withheld nor fully in focus. She is there, but not localized. The city appears as a projection across her face, highlighting the exteriority of the speaker, who is then reduced to a feature of the landscape, itinerant, at the mercy of the wind, striving for conveyance, to and fro, in speech and in movement.[19] Place not only grammatically precedes person but is prepositionally reversed. The subject is not *in* Los Angeles; rather, Los Angeles is *on* the subject. The reciprocity of subject and context is more explicitly named in the title section, where White writes:

> waters roll off me
> they ride me or I ride them   it is a complexity
> whether one is being
> done for or doing in your element[20]

---

16 By overdetermination, I mean the use of 'you' for both singular and plural forms, following the loss of a T–V distinction in English during the sixteenth century.

17 Cf. 'coming out of the closet'.

18 White, *Being Dispersed*, p. 3.

19 Silva, *Race*, p. 29, calls this 'affectability' — the opposite of self-determination, a mode of being belong to exteriority rather than interiority.

20 White, *Being Dispersed*, p. 14.

The closing stanza of the section's first poem is agnostic on the possibility of individual will, disinterested in triumph over the environment, and dispossessed of control over the conditions that give or withhold agency. 'Done for' not only signifies a reduction to the status of direct object but also something more sinister — doom, finality, death. The most significant detail of the last two lines is the apparent coextension of 'done for' and 'doing', itself a feature of someone *else*'s element. Existing in this space, which does not properly belong to the subject, brings with it the ambiguity of causality. Subject formation and subjectivation are not meaningfully distinct, and nor is decision a reliable mark of individual will. Rather than appear as a locus of being within a coherent chain of causality and action, the subject is instead dispersed, appearing as an inconstant strobe whose existence is always reciprocal: ridden and riding.

In the following sections, I argue that White exposes the genealogical and formal proximity of lyric and liberalism to interrupt the reproduction of a legibly individuated subject, writing against (*a*) recognition and representation as effective modes of redress for racial dispossession; (*b*) the specifically white, masculine aspiration to numerousness that romanticizes the multitude as a rescue for singularity; and (*c*) the movement away from subjectivity by institutionally and materially secure conceptual poets whose representation of lyric as a nostalgic and retrograde form inconspicuously sidelines the negotiation of racial difference within poetry.

REVISING NUMEROUSNESS

White's collection is in direct conversation with Objectivist poet George Oppen's 1968 collection *Of Being Numerous*. The simple substitution in White's title shifts attention to the difference between numerousness and dispersal, the latter evoking not only the massive distribution of Afrodiasporic populations but the thwarted individuation of the Black subject.

George Oppen was a communist, cabinetmaker, and, briefly, a publisher of friends, including William Carlos Williams and Ezra Pound. Oppen's first book, *Discrete Series*, was published with an introduction by Pound in 1934 by the Objectivist Press, which he co-founded with his wife Mary Oppen and Louis Zukofsky, William Carlos Williams, and Charles Reznikoff. The Great Depression reorganized the Oppens' commitments and pushed them further to the political left. The two eventually moved to Mexico, where they escaped the growing attention of the House of Representatives Un-American Activities Committee. During this period, Oppen wrote little. His second book, *The Materials*, was published by New Directions upon his return to the US, followed by *This in Which* (1965). His fourth book, *Of Being Numerous*, is firmly rooted in and inflected by the densely populated metropolis of New York City and arguably in dialogue with Whitman. It is also a work of 1968 — a poem for the era of collective action, solidarity, and civil unrest.

Like Oppen's, White's book is of a moment, nearly fifty years later, when mass social movements were gaining traction in response to a spate of racially motivated police violence.[21] Not only direct actions attracting new actors but also contemporary poetry were beginning to locate their engagement with a reinvigorated attention to antiblackness. Claudia Rankine published *Citizen: An American Lyric* in 2014 to enormous success; the book used apostrophic instability to invite both startling revelations of complicity and identification with the subject of violence. White's book addresses itself not to the guilty or damaged reader but to the epistemological premises that conspire to produce a world in which racial violence finds its stage. White, who received a J.D. from Harvard before getting an M.F.A. in poetry and a Ph.D. in literature, published *Of Being Dispersed* in 2016, the same year as she finished her dissertation. White's unpublished dissertation critiqued not only the ostensibly reparative possibility of law but the epistemic limitations of its critique by lawyers, i.e. critical legal studies. *Of Being Dispersed* is White's second full-length collection after her debut, *House Envy of All the World* (2010), a volume whose title evokes recurring inflection points of desire, property, and the social. *Of Being Dispersed* responds not only to the American legacy of antiblackness and Oppen's book, but also to the centrality of the individual in Amer-

---

21   Black Lives Matter protests began in 2013, after the murder of Trayvon Martin by George Zimmerman, and picked up in 2014 after the murder of Michael Brown by Darren Wilson. Both victims were unarmed Black men, and both murderers were white policemen. Zimmerman was acquitted, and Wilson was never charged.

ican discourse, including political and poetic critiques of antiblackness
that locate the restoration of personhood as the horizon of repair.

Where Oppen replaces the individual with the multitude, White
swaps both the individual and the multitude for the dispersed. As
demonstrated in her poetry, the dispersed subject does not electively
move from singularity to numerousness but is massively distributed,
implacably amongst, and devoid of volition as rescue. The first stanza
of Oppen's 'Of Being Numerous' reads:[22]

> There are things
> We live among 'and to see them
> Is to know ourselves'. (1)

Oppen's poem appears to be invested in levelling the subject with its
environment — living *amongst* — and yet the scene of coextension
is immediately interrupted by the recovery of the subject, lifted out
by the rescue line of self-knowledge. While the poem appears to com-
pel the subject's immersion within the numerousness of the city, the
separation between self and context is always marked, whether by the
reflexivity of a single consciousness or by the will of an individual
who elects to disavow an already given singularity. Singularity is thus
negotiated as an original condition of the subject — a condition that
the poem finds dubious, potentially disastrous:

> Obsessed, bewildered
>
> By the shipwreck
> Of the singular
>
> We have chosen the meaning
> Of being numerous. (7)

For Oppen, numerousness is an elective state — a mode of rescue from
the 'shipwreck | Of the singular'.

The poem continues to negotiate its relation to singularity — both
a disaster and a 'bright light' (9). In section 10, he writes: 'The isolated
man is dead, his world around him exhausted || And he fails! He
fails, that meditative man!' Referencing the 'rescue' of Crusoe, Oppen
positions numerousness as a salve for the 'shipwreck of the singular'. In

---

22   References to 'Of Being Numerous' are given as section numbers in parentheses in the
      text.

other words, he turns singularity into a precondition of assembly. The stanza

> We say was
> 'Rescued'.
> So we have chosen. (6)

indicates a moral evaluation of isolation as plight. We have chosen that a return to civilization is favourable to singularity, we have chosen the group. But Oppen's poem has also made a choice. While the poem appears to reject a lapsarian logic by disavowing the 'tale of our wickedness' which 'is not our wickedness' (1), Oppen replaces original sin with original singularity. There may be no garden of Eden, but there is a Crusoean island where the singular stands alone after shipwreck. The unconditioned position of the subject is one of non-relation. The meditative man may have found relief in the numerousness of the group, but the structural viability of the 'many' presupposes the ontology of the 'one'. This is the crux of White's intervention.

The original 'of' in Oppen's title is itself aspirational. The preposition does not so much name a poetics of immersion and perceptual integration as it does a direction toward which the alienated subject ambles, labouring to transform the often-abstract nouns and concepts into a localized experience of place. Relying minimally on the bold-faced details of Oppen's life, one can read the recessed portrait of New York as a scene of return, from Mexico to New York, and from communist organizing to poetry. Although Oppen is not a Romantic poet — he explicitly dissociated himself from Whitman and lived as a committed Marxist — the notion of 'being' in his tile is not in the first place conditioned by numerousness. Being begins as a condition of the individual, while numerousness is an ambition toward which the subject wilfully moves. As such, numerousness remains a grail that is not internally complex because it is not primarily perceptual.[23]

Oppen moves toward numerousness as rescue and urban absorption as exalted communion. As destinations, these positions remain positively coded, the antithesis to capitalist social relations, or

---

23 Despite the differences between my own approach and Perloff's, she makes a crucial distinction between the conceptual and perceptual in *Of Being Numerous* in Marjorie Perloff, 'The Rescue of the Singular', *Contemporary Literature*, 43.3 (2002), pp. 560–69.

'talk[ing] | Distantly of "The People"' (14). Oppen evokes the omitted first person plural of the constitutional clause — 'we' — as a rejoinder to the recurrence of 'they' in the previous section:

> [...] They are shoppers,
> Choosers, judges; ... And here the brutal
> is without issue, a dead end.
>   They develop
> Argument in order to speak, they become
> unreal, unreal, life loses
> solidity, loses extent, baseball's their game
> because baseball is not a game
> but an argument [...]
> [...]. They are ghosts that endanger
>
> One's soul. [...] (13)

Section 14 balances this feint of derision:

> I cannot even now
> Altogether disengage myself
> From those men.

Where Oppen moves from the original condition of the singular toward an ambivalent but committed communion, White's poem begins from the position of denied singularity and a non-elective — non-Romantic — immersion in the city. Oppen's elective ambition is White's inescapable condition. Where Oppen writes:

> We are pressed, pressed on each other,
> We will be told at once
> Of anything that happens (6)

White's subject is

> pushed out the turnstile by a white man today
> being touched in so hostile a manner is better
>
> as against another demonstration of disgust funny
> eight thousand times since the age of eleven
>
> when you first got followed down the street
> by a stranger trying to grab your boob
>
> you have calculated the nearness
> of whosoever is not repelled by your 'hostility'[24]

---

24   White, *Being Dispersed*, p. 41.

Proximity and distance are dually coded as conditions of racial aggres-
sion. Both violations of touch and social avoidance operate according
to an immanent premise of antiblackness that structures the experi-
ence of the street. These are not scenes of social life into which the
previously singular, individuated subject electively enters, but scenes
within which the racialized subject is dispersed, strewn without choice,
touched without consent. White's collection performs a double refusal
within the lyric: a refusal of both the liberal solution of individual rec-
ognition and the ostensibly leftist aspiration to numerousness, which
is conditioned upon exclusive access to an original singularity. White's
poetry both cites and disaffiliates with late-twentieth-century revisions
of lyric that move the genre out of its obsession with 'the shipwreck of
the singular', toward forms of collective action that, though often rad-
ical and anti-capitalist, fail to account for subjects that are not originally
individuals.

THE SUBJECT OF CONCEPTUALISM

If the poetic reproduction of personhood has funnelled liberal prin-
ciples into modern lyric subjectivity, those principles are not elimin-
ated with the disappearance of a subject. In 2010 the poets Kenneth
Goldsmith and Craig Dworkin co-edited an anthology of conceptual
writing under the title *Against Expression*. The dense tome exhaustively
documents what critic and dedicatee Marjorie Perloff calls 'uncrea-
tive writing' and is positioned, as the title suggests, against legacies of
confessionalism, expression, and lyric subjectivity. Goldsmith, whose
poetic career intersects with the more culturally and financially solvent
art world, explains the historical importance of conceptual poetry vis-
à-vis visual art, issuing the almost perversely Adornian warning that
after the Internet, poetry will never be the same. Goldsmith rehearses
the crisis of photography for realist painting, which had no choice
but to go blurry once the camera went sharp, and proposes that the
Internet will be a similar breed of dark horse for poetry. His introduc-
tion seeks to inaugurate a shift toward mechanical forms of linguistic

production that beat the machine at its own game, making the person behind the poem irrelevant.[25]

Goldsmith's formal account of conceptual poetry ignores the material and political implications of the lyric subject and its disappearance. Just as the ostensible universalism of the Western citizen-subject strategically silences coefficients of whiteness, property, and sex, the elimination of a lyric subject presupposes its universal availability. While a full account of this parallel cannot be provided here, I believe the disappearance of lyric in the late twentieth century is more accurately historicized as a reaction to discursive shifts within the arts and humanities that sought to incorporate 'other voices'. Denise Ferreira da Silva describes this historical turning point in the academy:

> We had something to do with the crisis of science; we, the others of man, were upsetting history: our words and deeds unleashed the predicament of the 'modern order'. In seeking to comprehend this Global event, however, writers of postmodernity and globalization could only announce the death of the subject. Not surprisingly, social analysts described these circumstances as the onset of a new site of political struggle — the politics of representation, that is, the struggle for the recognition of cultural difference — that registered the demise of the metanarratives of reason and history that compose modern representation.[26]

By setting up an incompatibility between the subject of reason and the recognition of ostensibly indissoluble cultural difference, these 'social analysts' — including literary critics — designed a paradigm wherein the representation of difference occasioned the death of the very figure that could manifest difference or the particular, i.e. the subject.[27] In short, the rising visibility of the racial particular resulted in its discursive annexation. I propose that a similar shift in humanistic discourse resulted in the split between person-focused lyric and

---

25 Kenneth Goldsmith, 'Why Conceptual Writing? Why Now?', in *Against Expression: An Anthology of Conceptual Writing*, ed. by Craig Dworkin and Kenneth Goldsmith (Evanston, IL: Northwestern University Press, 2011), pp. xvii–xxii.

26 Silva, *Race*, p. xxi.

27 For another account of this history, see Roderick Ferguson, *The Reorder of Things: The University and its Pedagogies of Minority Difference* (Minneapolis: University of Minnesota Press, 2012).

conceptual poetry. In the introduction to *Before Modernism*, Virginia Jackson corrects prevailing accounts of the American lyric tradition by bringing Black poets like Phyllis Wheatley and Laurence Dunbar out of the periphery.[28] Jackson writes:

> Accounts of American lyric as an ethno-nationalist, triumph-ally modernist project that began with the Puritans and cul-minated in the achievement of T. S. Eliot, or as Emerson's twin Transcendental brainchildren Walt Whitman and Emily Dickinson, or as a transatlantic anglocentric rainbow bridge stretching from Shelley to Stevens, or as the self-involvement of Romantic and modern poets that gave way to a post-lyric avant-garde, or as a return to lyric in reaction to that avant-garde, can all be understood as the fictions of racial continuity they always were.[29]

The fiction of racial continuity seeks to naturalize itself through the distribution of genre such that the universality of whiteness survives through its strategic flight to new forms. An account of lyric that fails to understand its investment in whiteness — and maleness — contributes to the fiction of racial continuity that reproduces Black poetry as an ethnically distinct addendum.

Goldsmith's anxiety around the emergence of diversity and its im-plications for his career can be inferred from the writing of his peers. In a 2012 essay for the *Boston Review* titled 'Poetry on the Brink: Reinvent-ing the Lyric', Marjorie Perloff laments the institution of 'poeticity' propagated by creative writing departments and the stultifying effect of their diversity initiatives. According to Perloff, anyone can write the kinds of poems anthologized in an increasingly inclusive era of representation whose diversity initiatives override standards of liter-ary quality. After enumerating a list of easily mimicked tropes, Perloff reads a poem by Black poet and twice former US poet laureate Natasha Trethewey to illustrate her point. The poem, titled 'Hot Combs', de-scribes a scene of hair-straightening activated by sense memory. Perloff

---

28   This includes Jackson's own definition of 'lyric' in the 2012 edition of *The Princeton Encyclopedia of Poetry and Poetics*. As she puts it in *Before Modernism: Inventing American Lyric* (Princeton, NJ: Princeton University Press, 2023): 'My definition also inherited a racist idea of lyric from the nineteenth-century American poetics that definition said nothing about' (p. 18).

29   Jackson, *Before Modernism*, p. 2.

derisively catalogues the poem's facile attempt at poetic imagery, writing:

> This is an all-but-classic reenactment of the paradigm I described at the beginning of this essay: 1) the present-time stimulus (the fortuitous find of old hot combs in a junk shop), 2) the memory of the painful hair straightening ritual the poet's African American mother evidently felt obliged to perform, and finally 3) the epiphany that her mother's face was 'made strangely beautiful | as only suffering can do'.[30]

Perloff goes on to qualify what she calls the poem's 'emotional crescendo' as 'dubious in its easy conclusion that beauty is born of suffering'. What is striking about Perloff's dismissal is the contradiction of its fair-weather attention to race. Perloff's attention to Tretheway's poem is, in the first place, based upon its undeserved spot in Rita Dove's 2011 *Penguin Anthology of Twentieth-Century American Poetry*, which, Perloff argues, panders to racial inclusivity at the expense of quality. And yet, her charge against the poem's easy conclusion seems to wilfully ignore race difference in order to defang her dismissal of its aesthetic merit.

Perhaps the most dubious move that Perloff makes is to introduce the poem as a foil. Immediately after discussing the Tretheway poem, Perloff argues that if so-called 'creative writing' has become this formulaic, it is time to turn to 'uncreative writing'. She elaborates:

> Tongue-in-cheek as that term is, increasingly poets of the digital age have chosen to avoid those slender wrists and wisps of hair, the light that is always 'blinding' and the hands that are 'fidgety' and 'damp', those 'fingers interlocked under my cheekbones' or 'my huge breasts oozing mucus', by turning to a practice adopted in the visual arts and in music as long ago as the 1960s — appropriation.

Apart from any question of quality, the poems that Perloff calls 'formulaic' are overwhelmingly marked by the specificity of a racialized subject position. Those whom she produces as evidence not only occupy and write through positions of racial difference; Perloff further

---

30   Marjorie Perloff, 'Poetry on the Brink: Reinventing the Lyric', *Boston Review*, 18 May 2012 <https://www.bostonreview.net/forum/poetry-brink/> [accessed 19 November 2023].

reads them with an attention bias for their failure to transcend the facile representation of an ethnographic particular or complicate the structure of subjectivity.

Perloff closes her argument by citing the breakdown of Language poetry as a cautionary tale. The Language poets, she explains, provided a serious and necessary challenge to the preciousness of lyric and self-expression, favouring intellectual-political engagement and aligning themselves with French post-structuralism and the Frankfurt School. The death knell rang, however 'by the late '90s, when Language poetry felt compelled to be more inclusive with respect to gender, race, and ethnic diversity', since, she argues, 'it became difficult to tell what was or was not a "Language poem"'. Not only does Perloff assign 'tepid tolerance' to all editorial decisions that operate on a principle of inclusivity and eschew the accessibility of the genre, but she pronounces dead a movement whose refusal of self-expression is sullied by the appearance of race.[31] In other words, Perloff falls for the trap set by liberalism in which difference is disingenuously read under the rubric of identity, which forces its expression to be articulated as a property of the individual rather than as a product of the social. The former formulation can only be authored by the singular first person; the latter can be signed by both the collective and the dispersed.[32]

Many have argued that the total disappearance of the subject by practices of automation and repetition in art is undermined by the signature of the artist. Even if there is no subject, there is still the matter of intellectual property. Dworkin's and Goldsmith's introductions to *Against Expression* ignore this banal but irreducible remainder, skirting neatly around questions of recognition and capital. It is not surprising that the patron saints of conceptual poetry — including Goldsmith (University of Pennsylvania) and Marjorie Perloff (Stanford) — might

---

31 Ibid.

32 See Wendy Brown and Jannet Halley, 'Introduction', in *Left Legalism/Left Critique*, ed. by Wendy Brown and Jannet Halley (Durham, NC: Duke University Press, 2002), pp. 1–37: 'Whereas "liberals" treat identities as mechanisms for voicing injustice that the state must be made to recognize and repair, from this left perspective, identities are double-edged: they can be crucial sites of cultural belonging and political mobilization, but they can also be important vehicles of domination through regulation. Indeed, to the extent that liberalism bribes the left to frame its justice projects in terms of identity, cultural belonging and political mobilization become problematically regulatory' (p. 7).

want to dissimulate the particulars of their subject positions through a critique of poetry that follows from such situated knowledges, which Dworkin calls 'narcissistic'. Referring to the poetry collected in the online archive *UbuWeb*, he describes how

> the anthology privileged modes of writing in which the substitutions of metaphor and symbol were replaced by the recording of metonymic facts, or by the direct presentation of language itself, and where the self-regard of narcissistic confession was rejected in favor of laying bare the potential for linguistic self-reflexiveness. Instead of the rhetoric of natural expression, individual style, or voice, the anthology sought impersonal procedure. [...]
>
> The present volume continues to explore the potential of writing that tries to be 'rid of lyrical interference of the individual ego' (as Charles Olson famously put it).[33]

Dworkin goes on to distinguish the anthologized material as 'work that does not seek to express unique, coherent, or consistent individual psychologies' and that 'refuses familiar strategies of authorial control in favor of automatism'.[34] Not only does Dworkin set up a false equivalence between the human and the post-Enlightenment subject, but he proposes automation as the privileged horizon of the latter's elimination. Such a rejoinder is ironically given within the Olson essay from which Dworkin quotes. In 'Projective Verse', Olson writes:

> Objectism is the getting rid of the lyrical interference of the individual as ego, of the 'subject' and his soul, that peculiar presumption by which western man has interposed himself between what he is as a creature of nature (with certain instructions to carry out) and those other creations of nature which we may, with no derogation, call objects. For a man is himself an object, whatever he may take to be his advantages, the more likely to recognize himself as such the greater his advantages, particularly at that moment that he achieves an humilitas sufficient to make him of use.[35]

---

33   Craig Dworkin, 'The Fate of Echo', in *Against Expression*, ed. by Dworkin and Goldsmith, pp. xxiii–liv (p. xliii).

34   Ibid.

35   Charles Olson, 'Projective Verse', in *Toward the Open Field: Poets on the Art of Poetry, 1800–1950*, ed. by Melissa Kwasny (Middletown, CT: Wesleyan University Press, 2004), pp. 344–54 (p. 353).

The neologism that Olson introduces may indeed be a departure from subjectivism, but only insofar as the subject of such a movement is elevated above scenes of lesser life from which his own animation is exaggerated by contrast. Unlike Dworkin and Goldsmith, Olson is careful not to elide the subject and subjectivism in the service of a straw-man argument that would underwrite the dissolution of social difference. Perhaps the most important qualification in Olson's essay, which is conspicuously ignored in Dworkin's quotation, is 'western man'. It is specifically *western* man whose individual ego has historically run interference in the lyric.

In this way, Olson's misgiving is much closer to Denise Ferreira da Silva's work on the transparent 'I' of post-Enlightenment epistemology and Sylvia Wynter's writing on the overrepresentation of 'Man'. In her essay 'Unsettling the Coloniality of Being/Power/Truth/Freedom: Towards the Human, after Man, its Overrepresentation — an Argument', Wynter proposes that 'Man', the hegemonic ethnoclass of Western epistemology, has been elided with the 'human'. The over-representation this specifically white, male, propertied subject as the universal subject of world history condemns those populations it remainders — poor, Black, femme, differently abled, and other decentred 'genres of being human' — to be ethnographic objects of knowledge.[36] Epistemic and representational exclusion has, Wynter argues, licensed the expropriation of land inhabited by 'savages' and slavery. She tracks how, in the absence of Judaeo-Christian justifications, the New World forced the West to invent a secular category of 'Other' to rationalize its claim to sovereignty over foreign land. She writes that the West could therefore only see the new peoples it encountered in Africa and the New World as the 'lack of its own narrative ideal'.[37] Such a recognition was a direct consequence of the West's new narrative ideal of 'Man' as a political subject of the state and therefore of its own self-conception as supra-ethnic and rational; the apparently lawless indigenous peoples of colonial encounter thus provided a requisite foil for this newly secular self-understanding. Wynter writes:

---

36   Sylvia Wynter, 'Unsettling the Coloniality of Being/Power/Truth/Freedom: Towards the Human, after Man, Its Overrepresentation — An Argument', *CR: The New Centennial Review*, 3.3 (2003), pp. 257–337 (pp. 271–72).

37   Ibid., pp. 291–92.

This 'slandering' both of Indians and of Negroes can be seen in its precise role and function. That is, as a lawlike part of the systemic representational shift being made out of the order of discourse that had been elaborated on the basis of the Judeo-Christian Spirit/Flesh organizing principle (one in whose logic the premise of nonhomogeneity, articulating its master code of symbolic life and death, had been mapped onto the physical cosmos) to the new rational/irrational organizing principle and master code.[38]

The West's master code and its principle of nonhomogeneity produce the Janus-face of modernity for which the recto of rational 'Man' is racial difference. This racialized remainder thus functions as the 'lack of the West's ontologically absolute self-description.'[39] What Olson identifies, but Dworkin misses, is that the 'individual ego' interfering with lyric poetry was that of 'western man'. The Conceptualists' supersession of the subject renders invisible the West's productive distinction between representations of universality and difference.

CASTING DISPERSIONS

White closes the first section of her poem 'Preliminary Notes on Street Attacks', which details the experience of dissimulating Blackness for safety in predominately white publics, with the line 'on sight I am a unified person'. The second section of the same poem reads:

> You thought a poem like this would have a chorus and require its listeners to hold hands or touch each other in the face, gently. You thought you'd go for dyspeptic undoing of l'esprit de l'escalier with classical movement, undo the poem altogether,
>
> but you don't want to be liked for cleverness. [...]
>
> [...] You believe yourself to be above murder, you don't spit on people. Probably, you think you can learn anything and explain.
>
> Publicly and for money, you are in service to explanation. One possible metaphor for microaggression is aphorism. You cannot come back from explanation to explain the poetry of the poetry.[40]

---

38   Ibid., p. 300.
39   Ibid., p. 282.
40   White, *Being Dispersed*, p. 45.

White turns apostrophe around, turning toward rather than away from the public. Here, 'you' is the scene of encounter between the subject and the social. Crucially, 'you' does not refer to a coherent or stable subject. 'You' are the reader, then 'you' appear to be the poet, unsuccessfully attempting to undo the poem from within. Then 'you' are the complacent, complicit agent of ordinary racial violence, then you are presumably the poet, again, unable to abstract or explain the poetry of the poem. This carousel of subjects complicates traditional models of apostrophe, which are no less evoked. White's subject inhabits the lyric mode in order to expand its sphere of reference and recognition. While the poem may not be able to undo itself, or explain itself, it acts against the lyric genre's consolidation of the subject, which belies the racialized experience of dispersion, of being 'cast about or away', forced to 'use a sense of qualities as belonging to ourselves and others to make an assay'. White's poem is the assay. Its roving second-person pronoun casts about for qualities belonging to the self — or selves — and others to adequately examine the friction between liberal individuation and racial dispersion.

The line break between 'l'esprit' and 'de l'escalier' signals both the impossibility of undoing the Hegelian locus of phenomenological experience — 'l'esprit' — and the struggle to enunciate oneself in the scene of relation, always thinking too late of the right thing to say — the so-called 'wit of the staircase'. But the condition of belatedness is also structural. Gayatri Spivak's so-called first right of refusal — to refuse what one was originally refused — is a disavowal of liberal redress in the form of inclusion. In the third section, White writes:

> The line to you grows longer, scaled down
> by an English witness. You're upset. At a loss
> for nettles that never undid the primary illness,
> the sensuous thing is unstudied. Not Blake,
> nobody.[41]

The line, the lifeline, extended down from the Romantics through Blake and into the present does not pull White's subject up but grows longer, creating slack, leaving her upset, at a loss, unstudied. The line break indicates that neither Blake nor anybody after has offered a

---

41   Ibid., p. 46.

model of lyric subjectivity that could access the experience of Black dispersal, at the same time as it offers 'Nobody' as an alternative to Blake.

White does not write herself into the legacy of lyric inheritance that would place her downstream from Blake, but nor does she depart from the trappings of lyric altogether.[42] While the subject is often rendered in the second person or conspicuously omitted before verbs in the passive voice, the fifth section of the book, titled 'Lotion', is a prose account of her skin and hair routines with a stable and untroubled 'I'. White's simultaneous refusal to reproduce an inherited mode of subjective expression is not the same as conceptualism's disdain for all things tainted by lyricism. On the contrary, her inconsistent and intentional deployment of the 'I' offers the reader an occasion to think about the context in which the first person singular offers or withholds a lifeline from the specifically Black and dispersed subject of White's poetry.

The move from numerousness to dispersal is not a revision of the utopian imaginary that orients Oppen's multitude but a revision of the premise that licenses inclusivity and multiplicity as a logical response to social difference. To disambiguate these two operative terms, I rely on the work of Hentyle Yapp, who frames performances of racialized anger as an ungovernable remainder of liberalism. Using Ai Weiwei as a case study, Yapp examines how the Marxist topos of the 'multitude', popularized by Michael Hardt and Antonio Negri's 2004 eponymous volume, fails to cognize affect or what Yapp called 'racialized anger'. This unruly corollary resurfaces in *Fairytale*, Ai's 2007 contribution to *documenta* in which 1001 Chinese tourists are brought to Kassel amongst a range of agglomerated non-Western objects. Not only does

---

42 This posture of disinheritance and critique can be observed in some of White's own assessments: 'When I am waiting for a poem to get started, I am waiting for an arrangement *on behalf of all of us* based upon my happening to be here, among all these practices today. No poet of the past can provide me access to this makeshift will, unless it were as a personal obsession with descending along a particular vector, as William Carlos Williams describes, with which I am fascinated and also positively want to be involved in criticizing' ('New American Poets: Simone White', sel. by Anna Moschovakis <https://poetrysociety.org/poems-essays/new-american-poets/simone-white-selected-by-anna-moschovakis> [accessed 3 November 2023]; emphasis in original).

Yapp position Ai's insistence on mass repetition as a refusal of liberal humanism's dubiously reparative instinct to recognize individuality; he also reworks the left political imaginary of writers like Jean-Luc Nancy, Roberto Esposito, Antonio Negri, and Michael Hardt, whose accounts of plurality, community, and multiplicity do not account for the original massification of the racialized other. For Yapp,

> racialization arrests being as always (plural) before singularity can be granted to such subjects, reworking Nancy's being singular plural. […] Ai revises the multitude and relational through two entangled notions: racial anger and the types of subjects imagined to produce relationality.[43]

Yapp goes on to specify that the subject of relationality — massively distributed, comradely, rhizomatic, impersonal — is neutralized through the subordination of individual identity to social bonds. And yet, such a relational *turn* requires that there is an original individuality from which to turn *away*. What these frameworks miss is thus the affective condition of being originally subsumed by a racialized mass, thus making both the liberal solution of individual recognition *and* the leftist turn toward the relational insufficient and impossible. If racial anger is 'a structural affect, not an individual singular feeling', then what might its subject look like within the lyric form?[44]

White's oscillation between localization and dispersal is demonstrative of the inability to inherit Oppen's modernism. Neither does the poetry turn toward the liberal ethos of individual recognition through the representation of a coherent subject position, nor does it counter this tradition by accepting Oppen's Marxism, which presents a romanticized vision of the communal as a turn away from 'the shipwreck of the singular'. Oppen's solution — or rescue — is itself revealed to depend upon a specifically white, occidental origin story.

'Dispersal' may name any number of operations by which a mass is redistributed. But White's use of the term is distinctly Foucauldian, as her 2016 dissertation at the CUNY Graduate Center, 'Descent: American Individualism, American Blackness and the Trouble with In-

---

43　Hentyle Yapp, *Minor China* (Durham, NC: Duke University Press, 2020), p. 94.
44　Ibid.

vention', suggests.[45] White, a former lawyer, examines the conditions under which the law enables and makes impossible its own critique. Looking specifically at the field now formalized as critical legal studies, White adapts Michel Foucault's approach to madness and medicine in *The Archaeology of Knowledge*, wherein the premise of discursive unity is revealed to be logically invalid and 'systems of dispersion' are introduced as a hermeneutic frame that attends to the 'rules of formation' by which any object appears, including its 'coexistence, maintenance, modification, and disappearance'.[46] In other words, rather than develop a narrative logic to license a particular grouping, dispersion recognizes that the discursive event is contingent, massively distributed, and impermanent. The logic of dispersion is ultimately anti-Oedipal, which is to say that it refuses the stability of origin and tradition, and thus asks us to read *Of Being Dispersed* not as an heir to 'Of Being Numerous' but as an act of disinheritance. This is not to say that the distinction between Oppen and White can be reduced to Marx and Foucault; neither work is so orthodoxically attached or ekphrastic. And yet, White's rejoinder is not only addressed to Oppen but to any social theory whose material conditions of existence trace back to a specifically white or European origin story.

POSTSCRIPT: TOWARD A LYRIC PUBLIC

In 1988, literary critic Paul Breslin identified a rift in contemporary poetry. There were those, he argued, who seamlessly inherited an early American transcendental vision of an already-given unity that could lift us beyond divisions of difference, such as Wendell Berry, and those who were sceptical of this ahistorical ideal and laboured, through poetry, to present ways of communing. Breslin's assessment of the field came by way of survey: his article 'The Simple, Separate Person and the Word En-Masse' reviewed four then-new titles for *Poetry*, the monthly magazine of the Poetry Foundation. Breslin's review begins by taking up Berry's 1975 essay 'The Specialization of Poetry', which laments

---

45 Simone White, 'Descent: American Individualism, American Blackness and the Trouble with Invention' (unpublished doctoral dissertation, City University of New York, 2016).

46 Michel Foucault, *The Archaeology of Knowledge*, trans. by A.M. Sheridan Smith (New York: Pantheon, 1972), p. 38.

the oversaturation of self-talk in post-1945 American poetry. Berry diagnoses an overinvestment in poetics of the self — a radically particular self whose singularity is antithetical to communal experience. As evidence, he looks to the eventual US poet laureate Mark Strand, whose nostalgic, highly lyrical poetry endorses his own conclusive and decontextualized take that 'the self, in a sense, is all we have left'.[47]

While Breslin co-signs Berry's lamentation, he presents Berry himself as an outdated counterpoint whose desire to recover shared experience under the auspices of universal subjectivity presents more problems than it solves. He observes:

> When contemporary poets seek a way out of specialization, they usually involve a version of community that comes out of Walt Whitman, in which the self is, by an act of its own consciousness (rather than by shared social effort) gathered into a non-coercive, perfectly democratic national unity.[48]

And yet, according to Breslin, the emotional stirrings prompted by Whitman's lyrical promise of a perfect democratic harmony between self and mass do not lead us any closer to the realization of that ideal. He concludes that the true common desire is to 'have something in common, while retaining full individualist privileges — which of course would be impossible if the collective identity were more than a shimmering abstraction'.[49] Breslin ends his essay with a kind of open call for an imagined poetry that, in 1988, was scarcely available.

> The best American poetry, it seems to me, is increasingly distinguished by its distrust of Whitmanian wholeness, its resignation to more provisional kinds of unity. [...] But the poets who have come closest to a cure have done so by accepting the problem of *dispersal* as a challenge, by regarding common ground as something to be cleared by work, not as the Promised Land of some already-given totality such as 'nature' or 'tradition'.[50]

---

47   Mark Strand, quoted in Wendell Berry, 'The Specialization of Poetry', *Hudson Review*, 28.1 (1975), pp. 11–27 (p. 15).

48   Paul Breslin, 'The Simple, Separate Person and the Word En-Masse', *Poetry*, 153.1 (October 1988), pp. 30–47 (p. 31).

49   Ibid.

50   Ibid., p. 32; my emphasis.

According to Breslin, the best lyric poetry accepts the problem of dispersal and remains dubious of any community that emerges from an individual consciousness. If community, or the version that he imagines for lyric, were the result of a collective social effort, then its constituents would not be each of them whole. If Whitman's democratic harmony relies on preserving personhood and its attendant privileges, then Breslin's lyric community is marked by a dispossession of liberal individualism. I would argue that Simone White's poetry takes this one step further: not only does it refuse the privileges of a classically liberal individualism, but it is positioned on the fore side of individuation. The result is a kind of lyric mesh that lets the outside in. Where privacy is meant to reinforce the division between inside and out, property and public domain, intimacy is an absence of the division between interiority and socialization that structures both classical liberalism and the post-Romantic lyric.

'So Clear That One Can See the Breaks'
Colonialism, Materiality, and the Lyric in Jen Bervin's *The Desert*

TOBY ALTMAN

INTRODUCTION

'All poetry is of the nature of soliloquy', John Stuart Mill proclaims: 'It may be said that poetry, which is printed on hot-pressed paper, and sold at a bookseller's shop, is a soliloquy in full dress, and upon the stage.'[1] If it is not quite a mixed metaphor, it is a mixed message. Mill's metaphor isolates the poem, dematerializes it. The poem becomes as evanescent as an actor's voice as they step out into the footlights. Yet Mill also acknowledges that poems exist as material objects. In doing so, he restores the social world which his metaphor takes away. The solitary actor vanishes; the communal space of a noisy print shop takes his place. If there is a contradiction here, Mill seems untroubled by it. The materiality of the poem is sandwiched between two versions of the same metaphor: we begin with soliloquy and end 'upon the stage'. The metaphorical solitude of poetic performance seems to disguise the material circumstances of poetic production and circulation. As Virginia Jackson writes,

---

1   John Stuart Mill, 'What Is Poetry?', in *The Broadview Anthology of Victorian Poetry and Poetic Theory*, ed. by Thomas J. Collins and Vivienne J. Rundle (Plymouth, MA: Broadview Press, 1999), pp. 1212–20 (p. 1216).

> the circulation of poetry 'on hot-pressed paper' is exactly what
> the generic conventions of the lyric cannot acknowledge —
> that is, the lyric can no more acknowledge its literal circum-
> stance than can the actor, and is at the same time no less
> dependent than the actor on the generic recognition of the
> audience it must pretend is not there.[2]

The lyric relies on print, and the whole world of historical, political, and economic relations that print implies. But it cannot acknowledge its reliance on that world — otherwise it would cease to be lyric.

Describing the fate of what she calls, circumspectly, 'Dickinson's texts', Jackson warns us, 'we cannot go back to a moment before they became lyrics'.[3] Instead, she suggests, 'we must try to keep both their material and contingent as well as their abstract and transcendent aspects in view at the same time'.[4] There is no way out of lyric reading — but we can work to recognize what the lyric represses. Jackson is addressing scholars, whose concern with the lyric is methodological. What might happen if a poet wrestled with the same question — if a poet tried to restore the material and social world to her own lyric discourse?

In this essay, I turn to Jen Bervin's artist book *The Desert*, reading it as a response to the dematerialization of the lyric.[5] Published in 2008 in an edition of forty copies, *The Desert* is a facsimile of the first seven chapters of John C. Van Dyke's 1901 travelogue and aesthetic treatise *The Desert: Further Studies in Natural Appearances*, printed on large sheets of abaca paper.[6] Working with a team of Seattle seamstresses, Bervin sewed over the reprinted text with blue silk thread, leaving isolated patches of Van Dyke's language unsewn (Figure 1).[7]

---

2   Virginia Jackson, *Dickinson's Misery: A Theory of Lyric Reading* (Princeton, NJ: Prince-
     ton University Press, 2005), p. 56.
3   Ibid, p. 116.
4   Ibid.
5   For a more extensive review of Bervin's career, see Toby Altman, '"What Beauty Was":
     Jen Bervin's Untimely Sonnets', *English Literary History*, 89.2 (2022), pp. 489–522 (pp.
     492–93).
6   John C. Van Dyke, *The Desert*, 2nd edn (Tucson: Arizona Historical Society, 1976).
7   The image in Figure 1 is from Bervin's website, <https://www.jenbervin.com/
     projects/the-desert> [accessed 3 November 2023]. Unless otherwise noted, the
     images of *The Desert* in subsequent figures are of the copy held at the University of
     Iowa. Images appear courtesy of the artist.

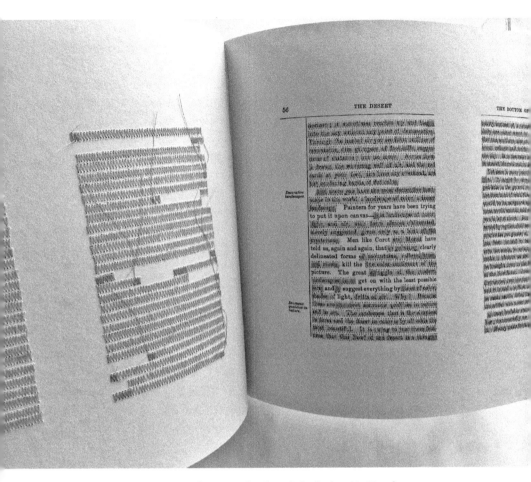

Figure 1. Jan Bervin, *The Desert*, taken from the back of pp. 54–55, and the front of pp. 56–57.

One might read the unsewn language as a poem by Jen Bervin. But Van Dyke's original language remains legible, if veiled, under the thread. It interacts with the language that remains unsewn, creating unsteady composites of voice. *The Desert* is intrinsically dialogic. It refuses the solitude that, for Mill, defines the poetic. Further, the labour of the seamstresses is evident and often meaningful — their mistakes and corrections add to the text's meaning. They are labourers, charged with producing the text, but they are also its authors and first readers. *The Desert* not only foregrounds its materiality; it centres the communal labour that produces it. *The Desert* is an exceptional, unusual object. But it hopes, through its exceptionality, to return us to the humdrum world of communal labour in which poems get made.[8]

In the first section of this essay, I turn to that world, tracing a set of apparently unrelated discourses — early colonial encounters with the American West, John C. Van Dyke's aesthetics, John Stuart Mill's account of the lyric as the product of an 'uncultivated' poetic mind. Each of these discourses relies, differently, on John Locke's theory of improvement, in which working a piece of land for profit turns it into property. Each of these discourses positions its object as the exterior of capitalism and colonialism. The desert and the lyric cannot be improved, cannot become property. Zebulon Pike, Van Dyke, and Mill rely on the lyric or the desert (or both) to reinforce the integrity and identity of the interior of capitalism and colonialism.

This essay thus contributes to a recent turn in scholarship on the lyric. Earlier studies, such as Jackson's *Dickinson's Misery* and Jonathan Culler's *Theory of the Lyric*, focus on the genre itself: when it came to be, how to define it or limit it, whether it is an impingement on the historical plurality of poetic genres.[9] In her recent monograph *Before Modernism: Inventing American Lyric*, Jackson acknowledges and addresses some of the limitations of the debate. Reflecting on the critical anthology she edited with Yopie Prins, *The Lyric Theory Reader*, she admits,

> the truth is we should have seen then what has become much clearer to me [...]: modern lyric theory — and especially modern lyric *reading* — has been racist, and a great deal of the whiteness of lyric theory can be traced to the history of American poetics.[10]

---

8   In attending to the materiality of Bervin's text — and treating it as a critique of Van Dyke — this essay builds on a previous ecocritical reading of *The Desert* by Dale Engass, 'Cropping *The Desert*: Erasure and Reclamation in Jen Bervin and John C. Van Dyke', *ISLE: Interdisciplinary Studies in Literature and Environment*, 28.2 (2021), pp. 563–86.

9   Jonathan Culler, *Theory of the Lyric* (Cambridge, MA: Harvard University Press, 2015).

10   Virginia Jackson, *Before Modernism: Inventing American Lyric* (Princeton, NJ: Princeton University Press, 2023), p. 54; emphasis in original. See also *The Lyric Theory*

Jackson's new work does not abandon her commitment to tracing the history of what she calls 'lyricization'. Instead, it aims to 'retell the history of American poetics as the history of gendered and racialized lyricization'.[11] This essay remains agnostic on the generic questions raised by Jackson and Culler; I do not provide a new theory of the lyric or comment on the genre's historical or cultural expansiveness. Instead, I supplement Jackson's account of the racialized development of American lyric with an account of its colonial development, exploring the way that nineteenth-century lyric and colonial discourses repeat — and, arguably, constitute — each other.[12]

The conjunction of such discourses creates opportunities for poets working in the present. In the final section of this essay, I return to *The Desert*, showing how the material complexity of Bervin's text disrupts both colonialism and the lyric. In *The Desert*, I argue, Bervin does more than restore the repressed materiality of the lyric. She demonstrates how an expanded poetics which incorporates the communal circumstances of its own production can challenge the logics of capitalism and colonialism, indeed of property itself. Before we can join her in this utopian aspiration, however, we must make our own journey into the desert.

1. THREE COLONIAL ENCOUNTERS IN THE AMERICAN WEST

The desert occupies a paradoxical place in the discourses of colonialism and capitalism.[13] It is dismissed as abject emptiness; simultan-

---

Reader, ed. by Virginia Jackson and Yopie Prins (Baltimore, MD: Johns Hopkins University Press, 2014).

11 Jackson, *Before Modernism*, p. 54.

12 This essay's contribution to that project is necessarily limited and gestural, but it aims to contribute to a broader project of thinking the lyric in relation to the legal categories of the capitalist and colonial state. See Birte Christ and Stefanie Mueller, 'Towards a Legal Poetics', *Amerikastudien/American Studies*, 62.2 (2017), pp. 149–68. More particularly, this essay attempts to build on the work of Black scholars who have read literary genre and form through land use in and around plantation economies. See Sonya Posmentier, *Cultivation and Catastrophe: The Lyric Ecology of Modern Black Literature* (Baltimore, MD: Johns Hopkins University Press, 2017), as well as Sylvia Wynter, 'Novel and History, Plot and Plantation', *Savacou*, 5 (1971), pp. 95–102, among others.

13 I alternate between these terms in the discussion that follows. When discussing the American West, it is possible to indulge such slippage. In the landscapes of this essay, capitalism is always colonialism and colonialism always capitalism.

eously, it is imagined as a necessary absence whose negativity secures the continued productivity of colonized spaces. Take, for instance, Zebulon Pike, one of the earliest Anglo-American explorers to enter the desert South-West. Like his better-known peers, Merriweather Lewis and William Clark, Pike was dispatched by President Thomas Jefferson in 1805 to survey vast tracts that were — on paper, at least — the property of the United States, following the Louisiana Purchase. In an 1811 report, he observes, 'the country presents to the eye a barren wild of poor land, scarcely to be improved by culture'.[14] Surveying the region's resources, Pike complains that it 'appears to be only capable of producing sufficient subsistence for those animals which live on succulent plants and herbage'.[15] The land fails to generate more than what is sufficient for subsistence; it does not have the capacity to produce profit. Nevertheless, it is not simply useless. From the desert, Pike continues,

> may arise a great advantage to the United States, viz. the restriction of our population to some certain limits, and thereby a continuation of the union. Our citizens being so prone to rambling, and extending themselves on the frontiers, will, through necessity, be constrained to limit their extent on the west [...] while they leave the prairies, incapable of cultivation to the wandering and uncivilized Aborigines of the country.[16]

The desert forms a natural limit to the 'rambling' of the pioneers. It protects the integrity of the colony against entropic decay, its otherwise ineluctable tendency toward cultural and political dissolution. Pike further imagines that the desert might serve as a zone of exclusion for indigenous peoples.[17] He proposes to make the desert a space of abjection, a zone of otherness whose borders maintain the integrity of his young nation.

---

14   Zebulon Pike, *Exploratory Travels through the Western Territories of North America* (Denver, CO: Lawrence, 1889), p. 728.

15   Ibid.

16   Ibid., pp. 428–29. Pike use of the word 'desert' encompasses the whole arid zone of the continent west of the 100th meridian.

17   Pike's proposal anticipates the official policy of the US government under President Andrew Jackson's administration. See Roxanne Dunbar-Ortiz, *An Indigenous Peoples' History of the United States* (Boston: Beacon Press, 2014), pp. 109–14.

Pike's proposal reflects the logic of colonialism as it has developed since the sixteenth century. Note an apparently innocent word that infiltrates his report, 'improved': the desert is 'scarcely to be *improved* by culture'.[18] Pike uses the word in an obsolete sense: 'to enclose and cultivate wasteland or unoccupied land in order to make it profitable'.[19] The word emerges in the fifteenth century as part of the legal apparatus that justifies the enclosure of common lands.[20] By the seventeenth century, it had worked its way to the centre of English theories of property, providing a justification for the appropriation of land in Ireland and the Americas. In his *Second Treatise of Government*, John Locke admits that 'God [...] hath given the world to men in common'.[21] This primordial communism lasts only as long as the world remains unworked. Land becomes the property of the person who works it. 'Nor is it so strange', Locke insists,

> that the *property of labour* should be able to over-balance the community of land: for it is *labour* indeed that puts *the differ-ence of value* on every thing; and let any one consider what the difference is between an acre of land planted with tobacco or sugar, sown with wheat or barley, and an acre of the same land lying in common, without any husbandry upon it, and he will find, that the improvement of *labour* makes the far greater part of the value.[22]

Improvement transforms land into private property; without improve-ment, there is no property. As Ellen Meiksins Wood notes, 'Locke's whole argument on property turns on the notion of "improvement"'.[23]

Locke regards the refusal to improve land as wasteful. He com-plains in particular about the way indigenous peoples manage their land, noting that 'there cannot be a clearer demonstration' of his theory

---

18   Pike, *Exploratory Travels*, p. 728; my emphasis.

19   *Oxford English Dictionary*, s.v. 'improve' <https://www.oed.com/dictionary/improve_v2?tab=meaning_and_use> [accessed 31 August 2023].

20   The *Oxford English Dictionary* first notes the relevant sense in 1473, where the word appears in a legal settlement for a property dispute in the north of England.

21   John Locke, *Second Treatise of Government*, ed. by C. B. Macpherson (Indianapolis, IN: Hackett, 1980), §26.

22   Ibid., §40; emphasis in original.

23   Ellen Meiksins Wood, *The Origin of Capitalism*, 2nd edn (London: Verso, 2017), p. 110.

than several nations of the *Americans* [...] whom nature having
furnished as liberally as any other people, with the materials of
plenty [...]; yet for *want of improving it by labour,* have not one
hundredth part of the conveniences we enjoy.[24]

Indigenous peoples, Locke suggests, forfeit their rights to their lands
because they fail to improve them. As Wood concludes, 'this redef-
inition of occupancy and waste means that land in America is open
to colonization because an acre of land in "unimproved" America has
not produced exchange value comparable to that of improved land in
England'.[25]

When Pike encounters the desert, he does so through this Lock-
ean frame, asking whether it can be improved. If, as he fears, the desert
can 'scarcely be improved', then it can scarcely become property. It
remains in that primordial communism which capitalism encounters
only as its own abjection. Within the frame of a Lockean encounter,
the desert — its beauty, its ecological richness, its status as a sacred
space for indigenous peoples — is illegible.

It has not been easy for subsequent travellers to break that frame.
Take John C. Van Dyke, who arrived in the West in the winter of 1898.
A professor of art history at Rutgers University, Van Dyke was the
leading American champion of *l'art pour l'art,* and a close friend of
steel magnate Andrew Carnegie. Van Dyke travelled to the desert —
according to his own dubious self-mythology — to seek treatment for
asthma. He took his treatment in the roughest way, heading out into
the desert alone, with a horse and a rifle. After three years wandering
the backcountry, he returned with the manuscript for *The Desert.*

The Desert, Zita Ingham and Peter Wild write, 'marks the first work
to celebrate the country's arid sweeps. [...] For up until Van Dyke's
time the nation all but uniformly considered its deserts as wastelands,
as God's puzzling mistakes in Creation.'[26] Unlike Pike, Van Dyke rec-
ognizes that the desert has value beyond its capacity to generate profit.
He writes rapturously of its beauty: 'the most decorative landscape in

---

24   Locke, *Second Treatise,* §41; emphasis in original.
25   Wood, *Origin of Capitalism,* p. 158.
26   Zita Ingham and Peter Wild, 'The Preface as Illumination: The Curious (If Not Tricky)
      Case of John C. Van Dyke's *The Desert', Rhetoric Review,* 9.2 (1991), pp. 328–39 (p.
      329).

the world, a landscape all colour, a dream landscape'.[27] He expresses
concern about the encroachments of capitalism: 'it might be thought
[...] that its very worthlessness would be its safeguard against civil-
ization [...]. But not even the spot deserted by reptiles shall escape
the industry or the avarice (as you please) of man'.[28] He proposes
permanently protecting the desert from capitalist agriculture — that
is, from improvement:

> You cannot crop all creation with wheat and alfalfa. Some
> sections must lie fallow that other sections may produce. Who
> shall say that the preternatural productiveness of California
> is not due to the warm air of its surrounding deserts? [...]
> The deserts should never be reclaimed. They are the breathing-
> spaces of the west and should be preserved forever.[29]

His argument for protecting the desert repeats Pike's proposal for
abandoning it. Like Pike, Van Dyke imagines the desert as exterior to
capitalism. Like Pike, he imagines that the desert secures the continu-
ance of capital. Pike treats the desert as a space of abjection; Van Dyke
celebrates its beauty. The difference is one of emphasis, not substance.
The Desert translates Pike's colonial framework into the language of
aesthetics.

Likewise, Van Dyke offers an obverse version of Pike's proposal to
treat the desert as a space of containment for indigenous peoples. Van
Dyke assumes that the desert *is* separate, sequestered from European
history — and that it is beautiful because of that separation. In his
'Preface-Dedication', he rhapsodizes about western air:

> When you are in Rome [...] look out and notice how dense is
> the atmosphere between you and St. Peter's dome. That same
> thick air is all over Europe, all around the Mediterranean, even
> over in Mesopotamia and by the banks of the Ganges. It has
> been breathed and burned and battle-smoked for ten thousand
> years. Ride up and over the high table-lands of Montana — one
> can still ride there for days without seeing a trace of humanity
> — and how clear and scentless, how absolutely intangible that
> sky-blown sun-shot atmosphere![30]

---

27   Van Dyke, *Desert*, p. 56.
28   Ibid., p. 57.
29   Ibid., p. 59.
30   Ibid., p. ix.

In Van Dyke's account, the pollution of a European city does not disperse across the globe; it accumulates, intensifies. The air becomes a register of human industry, a writing surface upon which history is inscribed. In the West, Van Dyke suggests, the traveller encounters uninscribed air: air that has not — not yet — been smudged with human history. Although Van Dyke occasionally breaks his reveries to acknowledge indigenous populations in the desert, he evidently regards them as outside of history; nor does he reckon with the genocidal history of the spaces through which he travels.[31] This erasure is not accidental. In his previous book, *Nature for its Own Sake: First Studies in Natural Appearances* (1898), Van Dyke admits: 'In treating of this nature I have not considered it as the classic or romantic background of human story, nor regarded man as an essential factor in it.'[32] Van Dyke's aesthetics requires the wilful removal of human history; he might be said to define the aesthetic against the presence of the human.

At the close of his 'Preface-Dedication' to *The Desert*, Van Dyke comments on his own relationship with the desert. Noting that the beauty of the desert has been ignored, he imagines the landscape calling out for someone to appreciate its beauty: 'The desert has gone a-begging for a word of praise these many years. It never had a sacred poet; it has in me only a lover. [...] Perhaps the poet with his fancies will come hereafter.'[33] In insisting that he is a 'lover', not a 'poet', Van Dyke may be said to clarify the genre of his text. Although his prose is lyrical, he does not understand himself to be writing a poetry of the desert. Rather, he is creating the conditions under which a future poetry of the desert becomes possible.

What kind of poet does Van Dyke imagine arriving 'hereafter'? He imagines a figure much like himself: a solitary traveller, wandering

---

31   He also suppresses the circumstances of his own journey. David Teague notes: 'Van Dyke most likely sat on the front porch of his brother's ranch house [and] rode the train to locations across the countryside.' Further, Teague suggests Van Dyke made his initial trip to the desert not to seek treatment for asthma but to pay off John McLuckie, former mayor of Homestead, Pennsylvania, on Carnegie's behalf. David Teague, 'A Paradoxical Legacy: Some New Contexts for John C. Van Dyke's "The Desert"', *Western American Literature*, 30 (1995), pp. 163–78 (pp. 166, 172).

32   John C. Van Dyke, *Nature for its Own Sake: First Studies in Natural Appearances* (New York: Charles Scriber's Sons, 1898), p. ix.

33   Van Dyke, *Desert*, p. xi.

under no direction but that of his own aesthetic appetites, consciously (or not) erasing the history of the spaces he moves through. The poet Van Dyke imagines is, in other words, a lyric poet — almost a caricature of the lyric poet. Jackson argues that Emily Dickinson's texts become lyric when they are 'taken out of their sociable circumstances' — the communal networks for and in which Dickinson wrote and circulated her work.[34] Van Dyke's poet does not have that luxury: isolated from the first, he has no sociable circumstances from which his poems might be removed. Likewise, Culler argues, 'the fundamental characteristic of lyric [...] is not the description and interpretation of a past event but the performance of an event in the lyric present, a time of enunciation'.[35] Culler's poet has the capacity to choose whether to speak in the present or describe the past. Van Dyke's does not. Occupying a landscape without history, he has no time but the time of enunciation.

Van Dyke is not the only nineteenth-century figure whose account of the lyric emerges from the epistemic framework of colonialism. In 'Two Kinds of Poetry', Mill distinguishes 'the poetry of a poet, and the poetry of a cultivated but not naturally poetic mind'.[36] He offers Shelley as an example of the former and Wordsworth of the latter. Mill principally uses the word 'cultivation' in its figurative sense.[37] But he also invites its literal sense into his essay. After admitting that 'there are poetic *natures*', he concludes:

> There is a mental and physical constitution or temperament peculiarly fitted for poetry. This temperament will not of itself make a poet, no more than the soil will make the fruit; and as a good fruit may be raised by culture from indifferent soils, so may good poetry from naturally unpoetical minds.[38]

The poetry of the uncultivated mind does not require labour. It either bears fruit or not. Before the cultivated mind can bear fruit, however, la-

---

34 Jackson, *Dickinson's Misery*, p. 21.

35 Jonathan Culler, 'Lyric, History, and Genre', *New Literary History*, 40.4 (2009), pp. 879–99 (p. 887).

36 John Stuart Mill, 'Two Kinds of Poetry', in *Broadview Anthology*, ed. by Collins and Rundle, pp. 1220–27 (p. 1221).

37 *Oxford English Dictionary*, s.v. 'cultivation' <https://www.oed.com/dictionary/cultivation_n?tab=meaning_and_use> [accessed 31 August 2023].

38 Mill, 'Two Kinds of Poetry', p. 1221; emphasis in original.

bour is required. Mill reprises the metaphor in his evaluation of Shelley and Wordsworth, noting: 'Culture, that culture by which Wordsworth has reared from his own inward nature the richest harvest ever brought forth by a soil of so little depth, is precisely what was wanting to Shelley.'[39] Wordsworth, the metaphor suggests, has, through the diligence of his husbandry, extracted profit from an unpromising piece of land. He has applied what Locke calls the 'improvement of *labour*' to his own temperament. Before it can produce poetry, the cultivated mind must be improved.

Mill aligns the lyric with the uncultivated temperament: 'Lyric poetry [...] is the poetry most natural to a really poetic temperament, and least capable of being successfully imitated by one not so endowed by nature.'[40] There are limits to what cultivation and improvement can accomplish. A poet like Wordsworth may be able to coax a harvest from an unpromising soil, but he cannot attain to the lyric. The lyric is, like the desert, a country that can 'scarcely be improved by culture'. When a poet like Wordsworth — a poet who lacks a poetic temperament — strays into the country of the lyric, he does so as a tourist, a visitor, or, indeed, as a colonist. There are those, Mill writes,

> in whom poetry is a pervading principle. In all others, poetry
> is something extraneous and superinduced; something out of
> themselves, foreign to the habitual course of their every-day
> lives and characters; a world to which they may make occa-
> sional visits, but where they are sojourners, not dwellers.[41]

The lyric poet, then, *is* a dweller — indigenous to the country of the lyric.

Elsewhere, Mill is disdainful of non-European societies, and he uses poetry as justification for his disdain. Children prefer stories to poems, he notes in 'What Is Poetry?', before asking:

> In what stage of the progress of society, again, is storytelling
> most valued, and the storyteller in greatest request and hon-
> our? In a rude state; like that of the Tartars and Arabs at this
> day, and [...] almost all nations in the earliest ages.[42]

---

39   Ibid., p. 1224.
40   Ibid., pp. 1223–24.
41   Ibid., p. 1221.
42   Mill, 'What Is Poetry?', p. 1213.

In adulthood, both individuals and societies turn to poetry:

> Passing now from childhood, and from the childhood of soci-
> ety, to the grown-up men and women of this most grown-up
> and unchildlike age — the minds and hearts of greatest depth
> and elevation are commonly those which take the greatest de-
> light in poetry.[43]

In Mill's account, the maturity and superiority of European civilization is evident in its love of poetry; the poem consummates the teleological progress from childhood to maturity, personal or civilizational.

The lyric poem is excluded from capitalist production and land management, yet it is also evidence for the superiority of European — capitalist — modernity. It is situated within and against its own culture. Mill's account of the lyric is homologous with Pike's and Van Dyke's account of the desert. We might describe the desert as a lyric space. Or we might say that the lyric is a desert: the unproductive exterior which secures the identity of the culture that produces it.

2. JEN BERVIN'S HEREAFTER

'Perhaps the poet with his fancies will come hereafter', Van Dyke imagines at the close of his 'Preface-Dedication'. There is something reticent about his fantasy. If, as Culler writes, the lyric is as an 'active form of naming, which performatively seeks to create what it names', then this is a profoundly unlyrical moment.[44] Van Dyke longs for a poet to follow him. But he forgoes apostrophe; he resists performa-tivity. He does not raise the poet from the desert sands through the autochthonous power of his rhetoric. He imagines, meekly, that the poet might come in some unspecified 'hereafter'.

In *The Desert*, Jen Bervin reprints the entirety of Van Dyke's 'Preface-Dedication', including the passage quoted above. But she and her team of seamstresses sew over much of its language. When it re-appears, it is both recognizable and transformed (Figure 2). Who, exactly, is speaking here? The words bear Van Dyke's uneffaced sig-nature. But they diverge from his original. Gone is his reticence, his

---

43   Ibid.
44   Culler, 'Lyric, History, and Genre', p. 887.

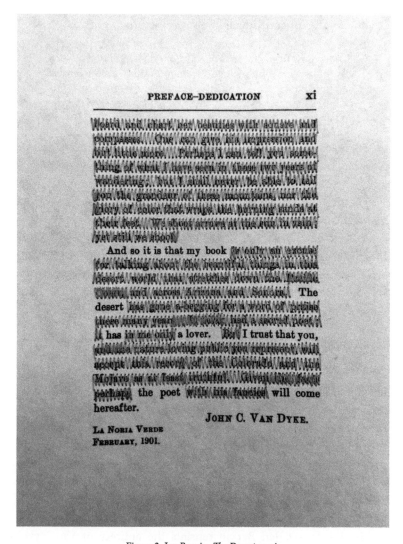

Figure 2. Jan Bervin, *The Desert*, p. xi.

refusal to assume the mantle of the lyric. Bervin's version engages in flagrant acts of apostrophe and performativity, addressing the reader and entreating them — if not ordering them — to become the poet the text imagines: 'I trust that you, | the poet will come | hereafter.' Bervin's sewing transforms Van Dyke into the lyric poet his text otherwise imagines. Because the original remains legible beneath the screen of blue thread, the reader is invited to measure the transformation that has occurred. We witness the moment when Van Dyke goes from describing the lyric to embodying it.

Bervin's version of the 'Preface-Dedication' might be said to issue a caution to its readers. *The Desert* is an ambivalent, composite object. As I will argue shortly, *The Desert* wrestles with — and critiques — Van Dyke's image of the poet. Likewise, it contests the habits of colonial thinking that underlie his engagement with the desert. But it does so by working within, occupying, Van Dyke's voice. Bervin may critique Van Dyke's vision of the lyric. But she also creates Van Dyke as a lyric speaker. She may disrupt his colonial fantasies. But she also reprints and recirculates them. *The Desert*, then, is not unequivocal in its engagement with lyric — or with colonialism. Rather, it is a critique of the lyric that emerges from within the lyric, a critique of capitalism that employs the tools of capitalist industry.

The Desert wears its complexity proudly. Looking at a page of *The Desert*, with scattered unsewn phrases surrounded by ridges of blue thread, the reader is always aware that they are encountering at least two voices at once, that their task as a reader involves negotiating between those voices. *The Desert* and other books like it in Bervin's catalogue are often described as 'erasure' poems.[45] Bervin does not use the word. In a conversation with the book-artist Dianna Frid, she insists: 'I dislike the term. [...] I'm trying to make poems that point to the fact that many voices can be present in a text.'[46] Bervin's poems resist becoming soliloquies. They are polyvocal, the products of communal and historical engagement — rather than, in Mill's terms, 'solitude and mediation'.[47] In this sense, Bervin's poems are not lyric. But they can expand to contain the lyric within them, one of the many voices that resonate within them. When Bervin reconstructs Van Dyke as a lyric speaker in the 'Preface-Dedication' of *The Desert*, she does so

---

45   For a more in-depth survey of the history of erasure poetry — and Bervin's contentious
      relationship with that tradition — see Altman, 'What Beauty Was', pp. 493–94.

46   Jen Bervin, interviewed by Dianna Frid, *Bomb Magazine*, 15 September 2016 <https:
      //bombmagazine.org/articles/jen-bervin-and-dianna-frid/> [accessed 31 August
      2023].

47   Mill, 'What Is Poetry?', p. 1216.

through a dialogic engagement with his voice. The circumstances in which he becomes a lyric speaker violate the terms of the lyric.

If *The Desert* is polyvocal, it is also polymaterial: a printed book and a sewn object, text and textile. Bervin has recently deepened her critique of erasure to incorporate the material complexity of her work. Drawing on Karen Barad's theory of agential realism, in which 'matter [is] a dynamic and shifting entanglement of relations, rather than [...] a property of things',[48] Bervin notes:

> I do think of my activation of this approach in sculptural and textile terms — as additive or subtractive, open work or lace-making ground. Or perhaps in *The Desert*, where the method is more literally textile, I think of it more as a veiling, mirage, or weathering of the text [...]. Instead of erasure, let's definitely call it 'entanglement' — in the quantum and enmeshed senses of the word.[49]

Bervin suggests that her work should be read through the entanglements it produces — of voice and history, of thread and paper. 'Matter and meaning are not separate elements', Barad argues.[50] To read *The Desert* — to attend to the text's full meaningfulness — one must reckon with the specific matter from which it is composed: abaca paper, blue silk thread. One must think the presence of the women who created it, the hands of the many seamstresses who worked the text, creating the entanglement of voices we see in Bervin's version of the 'Preface-Dedication'.

If matter and meaning are not separate elements, neither are matter and genre. The polymaterial of *The Desert* interrupts its assimilation to the genre of erasure; in Bervin's work, material entanglement shapes poetic genre. What happens to the lyric, then, when it encounters the polymateriality of *The Desert*? We have already seen how Bervin's

---

48   Karen Barad, *Meeting the Universe Halfway: Quantum Physics and the Entanglement of Matter and Meaning* (Durham, NC: Duke University Press, 2007), p. 35. Bervin is not alone in recognizing the utility of Barad's framework for describing polymaterial feminist textile-poetry; see also Adele Bardazzi, 'Textile Poetics of Entanglement: The Works of Antonella Anedda and Maria Lai', *Polisemie*, 3 (2022), pp. 81–115.

49   Claudia Rankine and Jen Bervin, '"We Have Always Been in Conversation"', in Jen Bervin, *Shift Rotate Reflect: Selected Works (1997–2020)*, ed. by Kendra Paitz (Normal: Illinois State University, 2022), pp. 56–85 (p. 69).

50   Barad, *Meeting the Universe*, p. 3.

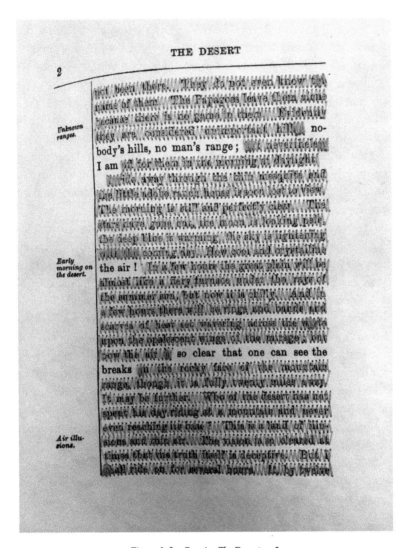

Figure 3. Jan Bervin, *The Desert*, p. 2.

reworking of the 'Preface-Dedication' restages the lyric, breaking its seal of solitude. The isolation of the lyric gives way to the polyvocality of communal life.

In the main body of the text, Bervin engages directly with the history that Van Dyke (and the lyric) represses. In the note that closes the poem, Bervin observes: 'John Van Dyke writes of the American deserts as necessary breathing spaces; my sewn poem is narrated by the air.'[51] For Van Dyke, the air is a surface upon which — some — civilizations write. Bervin proposes to speak as that surface. She takes up a paradoxical position: within the colonial framework of Van Dyke's account, her voice is silence itself. The poem speaks as the exterior of colonialism and its aesthetics, the exterior colonialism creates for itself (Figure 3). As the passage begins, the air declares its independence: 'no- | body's hills, no man's range'. It positions itself as an exterior: an 'unknown range' which, in turn, solidifies the position of the known within property and patriarchy.

If this is a repetition of the kind of colonial thinking we find in Pike, Van Dyke, and Mill, it is a repetition with a — material — difference. In Bervin's version, the desert air has the purity and clarity that Van Dyke ascribes to it. But that purity accentuates its historicity. Its materiality is evident in its brokenness, the damage that it has sustained: 'so clear that one can see the | breaks'. In the austere clarity of desert air, nothing else is visible: 'Have we not seen | The sky slashed to pieces | Have we not seen | the "practical men" | practice | flaying', the poem demands.[52] For Bervin, the desert is not an uninscribed space; rather, it is a space where the conditions of inscription become visible.

What are the breaks *The Desert* asks us to see? It asks us to see the breaks that it produces: the punctures in the page through which thread travels; the long swathes of muted sewing; the columns of Van Dyke's text, which are framed and separated from each by a wide gutter. Bervin's pages are broken, punctured, divided into plots. She links the book's materiality to the history of colonialism in the desert — sometimes explicitly, as in the passage in Figure 4.

The passage enlists Van Dyke's language to describe the physicality of Bervin's text, the 11 × 8.5 inch rectangle of its page: 'I make out | a | great rectangle | There is no doubt about | one corner of it'. It is a telling moment to encounter this kind of metapoetic (or metamaterial) reflexivity. In Van Dyke's text, the passage recounts an encounter with indigenous people — or rather, with their absence. Climbing a desert

51   Jen Bervin, *The Desert* (New York: Granary Books, 2008), unnumbered end pages.
52   Bervin, *Desert*, pp. 60–61.

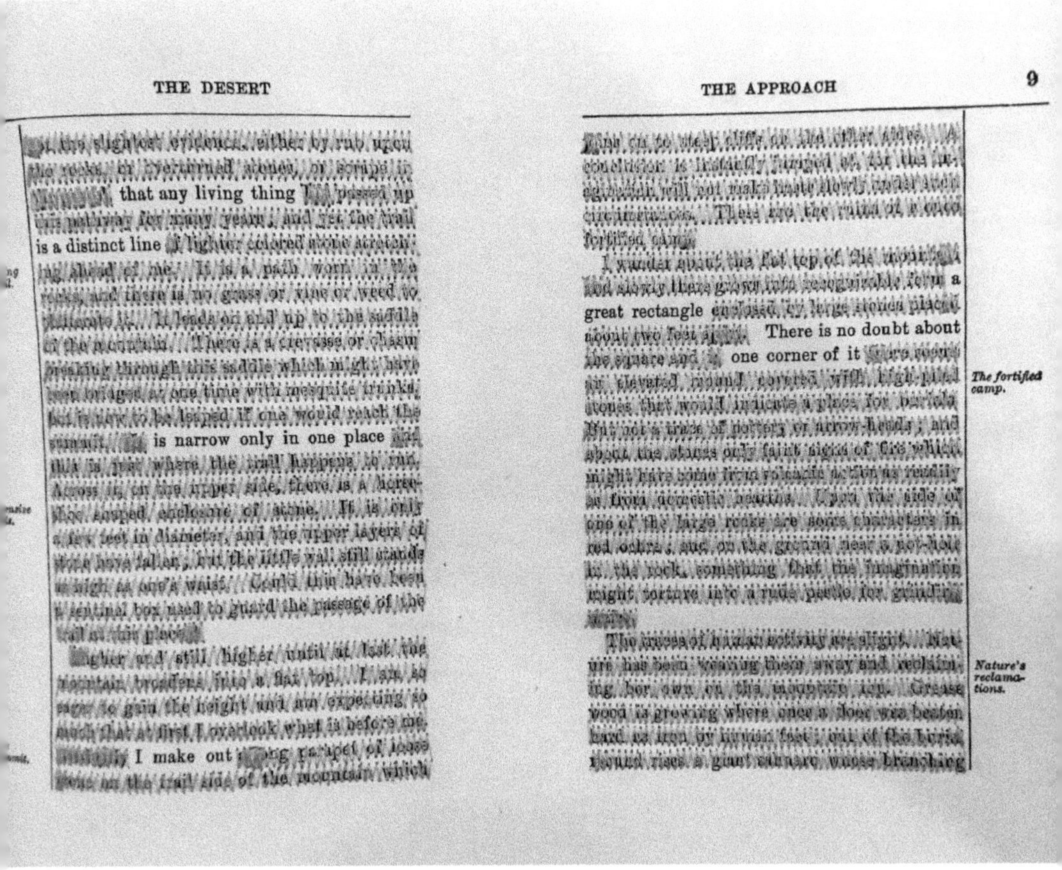

THE DESERT

THE APPROACH 9

that any living thing [...] passed up [...] is a distinct line [...]

[...] is narrow only in one place [...]

[...] I make out [...]

great rectangle enclosed by large stones placed about two feet apart. There is no doubt about the square and [...] one corner of it [...]

The fortified camp.

Nature's reclamations.

Figure 4. Jan Bervin, *The Desert*, pp. 8–9.

mountain range, Van Dyke discovers the remains of an isolated fort at the summit, partially erased through long abandonment: 'these are the ruins of a once fortified camp [...] a great rectangle enclosed by large stones placed about two feet apart.'[53] We are, at this point in Van Dyke's text, ten pages removed from his theory of air, a theory which erases native peoples from history; he has already discovered persisting marks of their history, inscribed into the landscape. Or, he has invented these traces. Given the suspicions that critics like Teague harbour about Van

53   Van Dyke, *Desert*, p. 9.

Figure 5. Jan Bervin, *The Desert*, front cover.

Dyke's trip to the desert, it seems likely that the scene is a fabrication — of his imagination, of the colonial imagination writ large. Bervin's *Desert* locates itself within this imaginary space: the 'rectangle' of the fortification becomes the rectangle of the page she sews upon — the space of her composition, the space of colonial false consciousness and fantasy.

   As she writes on and in this colonial rectangle, Bervin also punctures it: she writes *by* puncturing its surface. It would be tempting to over-read this gesture: to delight in the way that *The Desert* inflicts punishment on the, notably, white substrate of its writing. This would be to imagine a distance between Bervin's text and the colonial landscape in and on which it is written — a distance that *The Desert* does not imagine for itself. Rather, *The Desert* treats the small-scale violence of the sewing machine's needle as indexical: of the larger violence of colonialism, of writing itself. Indeed, Bervin gives title to her text by perforating the heavy stock of the book's cover (Figure 5). Elsewhere in *The Desert*, the punctures of the sewing machine serve to obscure Van Dyke's language. Here, the act of puncturing *produces* language. Writing would seem to be — if not violent itself — metonymic of the larger violences that are requisite to Van Dyke's aestheticized experience of the desert.

In restoring the historical complexity that Van Dyke denies to the American West, *The Desert* insists that the history of colonialism is not history. It persists in and as the present. Yet *The Desert* also suggests that the present can be transformed. 'There is no hour composed of equal parts', the unsewn text announces, a reminder that historical time is plural and — to use a word key to Bervin's poetics — porous.[54] As Engass observes, *The Desert* is itself a porous text: 'the abaca fibre [...] is famous for its twin properties of strength and porousness', and 'the perforations made by sewing machine render the paper literally porous'.[55] If the punctures in *The Desert* are metonymic of the violence of colonialism, they also remind us that poetic making can transform, rework, renew the spaces in which history has etched its wounds.

Let us turn to one such moment of porosity — admittedly a small one, measured against the scale of colonial violence. Yet, in a text that encourages one to 'see the breaks', it's worth attending to such breaks, wherever they emerge. Each copy of *The Desert* differs slightly from the others. For instance, in the copy of *The Desert* held in Special Collections at the University of Iowa, the line quoted above, 'There is no hour composed of equal parts', is itself composed of unequal parts (Figure 6).[56] Evidently, the seamstress has mistakenly sewed over part

---

54   Bervin, *Desert*, p. 33. My formulation here is intended to echo the working note that closes Jen Bervin, *Nets* (New York: Ugly Duckling Presse, 2004): 'I stripped Shakespeare's sonnets bare to the "nets" to make the space of the poems open, porous, possible — a divergent elsewhere. When we write poems, the history of poetry is with us, pre-inscribed in the white of the page; when we read or write poems, we do it with or against this palimpsest' (unnumbered end pages).

55   Engass, 'Cropping *The Desert*', p. 571.

56   The copy of *The Desert* held at the University of Wisconsin does not contain the same error.

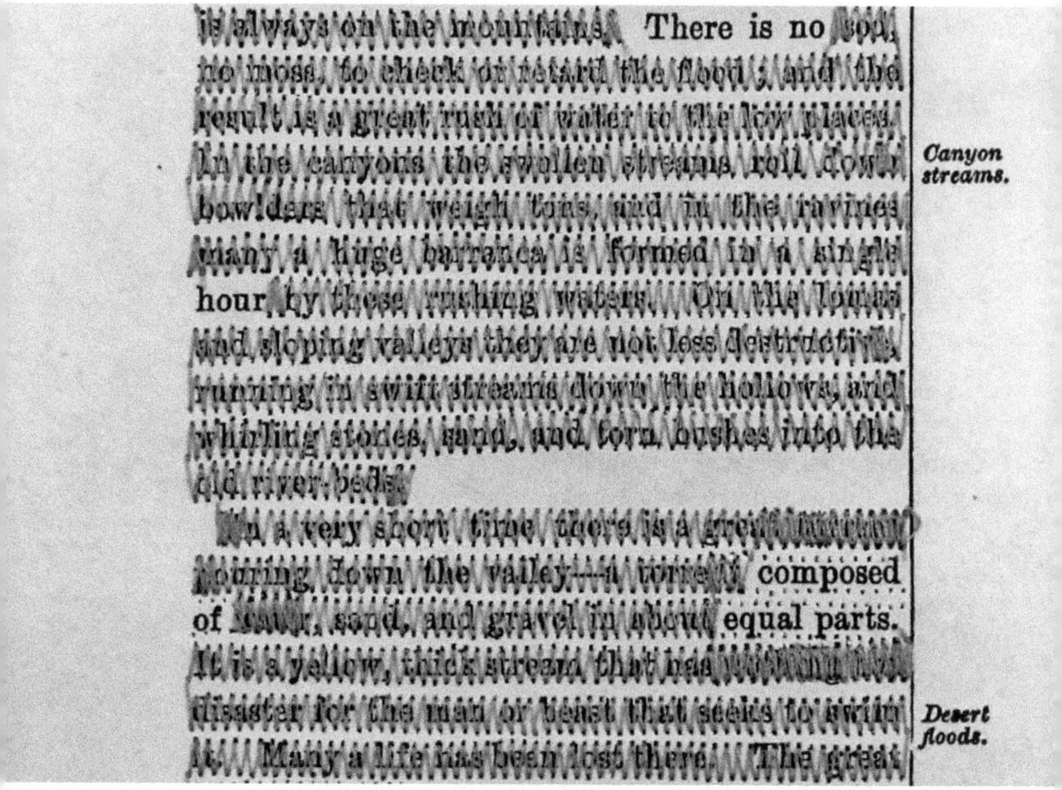

Figure 6: Jan Bervin, *The Desert*, p. 33 (detail).

of the poem. Instead of throwing out the mistake and replacing it with a corrected sheet, someone — perhaps Bervin herself — has pulled out the thread, leaving a series of punctures on the page. The page is inscribed, then uninscribed; unwritten, then written. It is palimpsestic, containing discrete moments — and kinds — of textual and textile labour.

Encountering these moments of error, one is reminded that the seamstresses who produced the book were also its first readers — and necessarily so: to sew the text, they would have to read it carefully, handling the great rectangles of unsewn pages. They would need to read — as Bervin encourages us to do — both *Deserts* side by side, comparing them to produce their difference. They would need to read again, checking their work — the corrections we find in copies of the book are evidence that they have done so. The scene of their reading would not be solitary or meditative, but communal and noisy. They read the poem and they made the poem in a shared space, sewing machines clattering around them, other hands and other eyes reading and working alongside them — including Bervin's (she sewed some copies of the text herself). In some places, the mistakes seem to echo, gloss, or critique the text they accompany. For instance, in the copy held in the Art Library at the University of Wisconsin, the word 'predecessors' is framed with a tell-tale set of holes (Figure 7). The unsewn text affirms its singularity: 'its faults | and breaks are many', but its 'predecessors. | are few'. We might read this as an expression of the aesthetic autonomy Van Dyke champions, a lyric voice separating itself from the social world that produces it. In sewing over, then removing the thread from the word 'predecessors', the seamstress — is it Bervin herself? — reminds us that such solitude emerges from and requires the labour of others.

Paying such close attention to small defects in individual cop-ies of *The Desert* may raise the spectre of what Virginia Jackson calls 'lyric reading' — that is, a reading which transforms its objects into lyric by projecting intentionality, personal voice onto them. Of Susan Howe, for instance, Jackson complains that 'she reads the smallest as-pects of Dickinson's handwriting not just as graphic marks, or even as performances of Dickinson's literary personae but, literally, as "*Emily Dickinson*"'.[57] I would suggest that something different happens when we apply our attention to the smallest aspects of *The Desert*. Examining any given copy of *The Desert*, it is impossible to say who is responsible for what. Did Bervin sew this copy herself? Or did one of her seam-stresses? Did Bervin correct this error, or did a seamstress pull out her own stitching? Because these questions cannot be answered, the text asks its readers to imagine the scene — and the contingency — of its own production, the dispersal of its authorship. Its communal ma-teriality interrupts the progress of lyric reading, resisting the reader's inclination to ascribe lyric intention to the text.

---

57   Jackson, *Dickinson's Misery*, p. 177; emphasis in original.

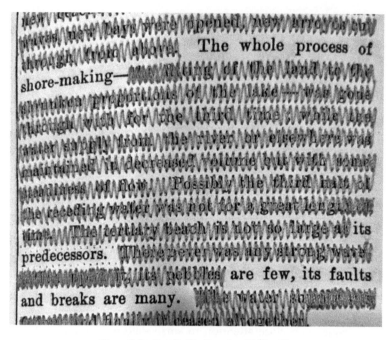

Figure 7. Jan Bervin, *The Desert*, p. 50 (detail).

Attending to these details, the reader experiences a break in the logic of improvement. The more *The Desert* is worked, the less it belongs to Bervin — or anyone who worked on it. It is a text which refuses to become (literary) property. Instead of producing property, *The Desert* proposes that the communal labour of poetic making might restore the world to its original commonality — even if only a 11 × 8.5 inch rectangle of it. The text is not naive or utopian. It locates itself in the symbolic and historical centre of capitalist production — the garment factory, with its exposed, precarious labour force.[58] It also locates itself in the abject exterior of capital, the desert, 'scarcely to be improved by culture'. As it reminds its readers, insistently, of the circumstances of its own material production, it also reminds us of the conjunction of these two extremes: the way that the centre produces

---

58 For a sustained reading of Bervin's relationship with factory work — and capitalist production more broadly — see Kathryn Crim, 'Marx, *Silk Poems*, and the Pretext of Qualities', *Representations*, 151 (2020), pp. 96–126.

its own exterior and vice versa. In the noisy, communal space of the garment loft, Bervin's seamstresses produce the austere silence of the desert — but only because those austere silences precede them, waiting, embedded, in Van Dyke's prose, for a poet with all her fancies to come hereafter.

Lyric, Detachment, and Collectivity
On Carl Phillips's 'Hymn'
HAL COASE

> Nothing, it would seem, is more difficult
> to conceive, to elaborate, and to put into
> practice than 'new relational modes'.[1]
>
> Leo Bersani, 'Sociality and Sexuality'

MODES OF DETACHMENT

Who needs community? In their 1998 essay 'Sex in Public', Lauren Berlant and Michael Warner noted that 'language for community is a problem for gay historiography'.[2] In the midst of the AIDS pandemic, a number of studies had approached the task of mapping the semi-public sites of queer social life, armed with the language of community, solidarity, and resistance. Berlant and Warner's response to the emergence of this communal imaginary was ambivalent. On the one hand, the 'imaginative power of the idealization of local community for queers',[3] as exemplified for them by John D'Emilio's study

---

1 Leo Bersani, 'Sociality and Sexuality', *Critical Inquiry*, 26.4 (2000), pp. 641–56 (p. 641).

2 Lauren Berlant and Michael Warner, 'Sex in Public', *Critical Inquiry*, 24.2 (1998), pp. 547–66 (p. 554).

3 Ibid.

Sexual Politics, Sexual Communities, could hardly be denied: the mere presence of queer hangouts on city sidewalks troubled the zoning of privacy that served as 'the affectional nimbus that heterosexual culture protects and from which it abstracts its model of ethics'.[4] On the other hand, the word 'community' — and the imaginary that nurtured it — was implicated in that model of heteronormative ethics. In 1994, the New York Department of City Planning had recommended the rezoning of downtown areas, effectively closing establishments frequented by queers, after a consultation in which 'community district offices' reported that 'adult entertainment establishments negatively impact the community'.[5] This was community as removed from vibrant underground scenes or the invigoration of AIDS organizing; 'community' here meant nothing other than the lockstep coordination of economic interests in defence of property, its policing, and the family it would house in perpetuity.

In a brief essay titled 'Community', the American poet Carl Phillips riffs on the word's significances. As a writer, Phillips notes, the need for 'community' seems commonsensical: it promises us a space of generosity that can provide a 'system of exchanged support'.[6] Yet it can never quite be freed from a more reductive sense of propertied genteelness and exclusivity:

> But in its origins the word 'community' itself has to do mostly with shared physical space, and a community consists of people who have in common the buildings they've erected, from the Latin *munio,* to build or fortify. This latter idea of fortifying does seem a likely link to thinking of community as a form of support, *for* a group from *within* that group.[7]

---

4   Ibid., p. 555.

5   Department of City Planning, 'Adult Entertainment Study' (New York: Department of City Planning, 1994), p. 52 <https://www.townofnewburgh.org/uppages/NYNYC_1994.PDF> [accessed 10 October 2023].

6   Carl Phillips, *My Trade Is Mystery* (New Haven, CT: Yale University Press, 2022), p. 90.

7   Ibid., p. 84; emphasis in original. Phillips, for the benefit of his argument, chooses in his etymology to evoke the physical enclosure of a space rather than a mutual obligation. The *OED,* however, derives 'community' from *mūnis* ('bound, under obligation'), and Lewis and Short give 'root mu-, to bind' as the derivation of *commūnis. Oxford English Dictionary, s.v.* 'common, adjective and adverb' <https://doi.org/10.1093/OED/8839776486>; Charlton T. Lewis and Charles Short, *A Latin Dictionary* (Oxford: Clar-

Phillips is chafing here against the concept's rigidity, against also the memory of how, during an itinerant childhood on various air force bases, community 'meant a sharing merely of space, and only potentially — not inevitably — of sensibility'.[8] His suspicion that the *wrong* community would be worse than no community at all leads him to the oxymoron of 'the community of one that solitude can be'.[9] Community, it turns out, is no more valuable than the sum of its parts, and it might even threaten those parts wherever it imposes itself too rigidly. It was with a similar guardedness, in the aftermath of the New York City Council's ruling, that Berlant and Warner wrote of their preference for 'world' and 'public' over 'community' and 'group':

> By queer culture we mean a world-making project, where 'world', like 'public', differs from community or group because it necessarily includes more people than can be identified, more spaces than can be mapped beyond a few reference points, modes of feeling that can be learned rather than experienced as a birthright. The queer world is a space of entrances, exits, unsystematized lines of acquaintance, projected horizons, typifying examples, alternate routes, blockages, incommensurate geographies.[10]

This world is apprehended as a messy display of how people might love or fuck were things otherwise. In opposition to the identitarian alignment of a community, it is the sum total of the movements that traverse and enlarge it, rather than the parts it contains. Like Phillips, Berlant and Warner are interested in a mobile and expansive sensibility — 'modes of feeling' — as opposed to the bounds of identity and the community that encloses it. This is, in a word, the world of cruising, a world that Berlant and Warner took to be at risk of an extinction wrought by the dual pressures of repressive lawmaking and sex-negative assimilationist rhetoric, both carried forward under the banner of community. They were envisioning a utopian elsewhere as already expressed in existing practices which they feared might vanish:

---

endon Press, 1879), s.v. 'commūnis' <https://www.perseus.tufts.edu/hopper/text?doc=Perseus:text:1999.04.0059:entry=communis> [accessed 2 November 2023].

8   Phillips, *My Trade*, p. 86.

9   Ibid., p. 92.

10   Berlant and Warner, 'Sex in Public', p. 558.

not only sexual acts but also 'self-cultivation, shared knowledge, and the exchange of inwardness'; loose happenings of drag, performance, music, and dance; queer practices of what they termed 'counterintimacies' which could return to the public sphere those 'forms of affective, erotic, and personal living' that heteronormative culture would prefer to immure in the privacy of the home.[11]

This sketch of queer theory's turn-of-the-century hopes and misgivings, as articulated by Berlant and Warner, provides a backdrop to my close reading of Phillips's 'Hymn' from his 2000 mid-career collection *Pastoral* in the second part of this essay. It is intended, firstly, as nothing more than a historical horizon, building upon what the novelist Garth Greenwell has characterized as the 'cruising devotion' without which it is difficult to parse Phillips's poetics.[12] Many of Phillips's poems are accounts of cruising for community, and their tropes of communion, lust, and loss arise out of the ambivalences inherent in that phrase. Beyond a straightforward contextualization of the poems within homoeroticism, my argument in what follows is that the restrictiveness of the term 'community' can be understood as a problem shared by queer theory and lyric poetry in the twenty-first century.[13] I am interested in passing between these two theoretical 'meanwhiles', and locating Phillips's poetics at the dissolve between them. More than a coincidence, less than a direct equivalence, this homologous trouble with community when tracked across both fields is intended to help us think about the alternative models of intimacy which Phillips's poems present.[14]

---

11   Ibid., pp. 561–62. For the orientation of such practices towards a utopian futurity, see José Esteban Muñoz, *Cruising Utopia* (New York: New York University Press, 2009). It is worth noting that Muñoz also eschews the word 'community', appealing instead to 'queerness as collectivity' (p. 11).

12   Garth Greenwell, 'Cruising Devotion: On Carl Phillips', *Sewanee Review*, 128.1 (2020), pp. 166–86.

13   For an account of how literary criticism and queer theory at the turn of the century both pursued readings 'suspicious of the status of persons and personhood' (p. 34), see Michael D. Snediker, *Queer Optimism and Other Felicitous Persuasions* (Minneapolis: University of Minnesota Press, 2009).

14   An aetiology of this shared 'trouble with community' across both fields is beyond the scope of this essay, although it would pass through deconstructionism's distrust of the word, as when Jacques Derrida, 'Sauf le nom (Post-Scriptum)', trans. by John Leavey, in *On the Name* (Redwood City, CA: Stanford City Press, 1995), pp. 35–88, writes of community's 'connotation of participation, indeed, fusion, identification' and

A problem shared is not always a problem halved. For queer theory, the intractability of the questions that come after the observation that desire is intrinsically disintegrative, unmappable, and hence *counter*communal has, since 1998, contributed to what Gila Ashtor describes as 'the "self-critical" turn in queer studies':

> Whereas the first generation of queer critique could still locate revolutionary potential in the indefinable, open-ended, infinitely mobile horizon of anti-identitarian identity, a new generation of work demands that queerness be problematized, contextualized and deconstructed in an urgent effort to examine what underlying ideological conditions produce a queerness that is surprisingly complicit with existing politico-ethical norms.[15]

This second wave of continuing critique involves asking how the field might get beyond what Lee Edelman valorized as queer negativity: 'its figural status as resistance to the viability of the social'.[16] Frustrated by the limits of such negativity, Robyn Wiegman and Elizabeth Wilson have called for a reassessment of queer theory's 'attachment to a politics of oppositionality',[17] a politics that, despite taking anti-normativity as its watchword and deconstruction as its method, has matured within a historical period marked by the forceful assimilation of certain queer subjects to political norms and the violent expulsion of others. This felt dissonance between what gets said inside the academy and what gets done outside it has contributed to the sense of impasse that Ashtor skilfully unfolds.[18] One way of opening some space around this frustrated position would be to return to Berlant and Warner's earlier

---

describes his desire for 'another being-together than' community, 'another gathering-together of singularities' (p. 46).

15   Gila Ashtor, *Homo Psyche: On Queer Theory and Erotophobia* (New York: Fordham University Press, 2021), p. 3. For queer studies as a 'subjectless' field that 'remains open to a continuing critique of its exclusionary operations', see David L. Eng, Judith Halberstam, and José Esteban Muñoz, 'What's Queer about Queer Studies Now?', *Social Text*, 23.3–4 (2005), pp. 1–17 (p. 3).

16   Lee Edelman, *No Future: Queer Theory and the Death Drive* (Durham, NC: Duke University Press, 2005), p. 3.

17   Robyn Wiegman and Elizabeth A. Wilson, 'Introduction: Antinormativity's Queer Conventions', *differences: A Journal of Feminist Cultural Studies*, 26.1 (2015), pp. 1–25 (p. 11).

18   See esp. Ashtor, *Homo Psyche*, chap. 4.

suspicion of community and attempt to listen to it afresh. Clearly, that which positions itself *against* community rejects integration, but can such rejection provide the basis for alternative modes of relation that are, at least, collective and communicable? Is there, in other words, a shared experience of living at the limit that does not take its cues and co-ordinates from the centre? What comes after refusal and detachment?

'Queer detachment', writes Matthew Burroughs Price, is a 'nar-rative strategy — part refusal, part acquiescence, reaching toward se-creted alcoves that might protect and cultivate it', a structure of feeling that 'abounds' in modernist writing.[19] Burroughs Price builds a geneal-ogy of this posture that has one origin in decadence, specifically in a Paterian subject that is 'neither public nor private, neither embedded in nor distanced from homophobic social landscapes, [...] less asocial than semiwithdrawn, experiencing aesthetic impressions yet shrinking into himself to analyze them'.[20] This idea brings us closer to the prob-lem of community as posed within modern poetics. Throughout the twentieth century, the lyric self was typically understood to be with-drawn from (or bereft of or waiting for) an ideal community.[21] This lyric alienation was given its most well-known formulation by Theodor Adorno, whose 'On Lyric Poetry and Society' begins with a descrip-tion of a 'sphere of expression whose very essence lies in either not acknowledging the power of socialization or overcoming it through the pathos of detachment'.[22] For Adorno, such refusal or detachment was 'the subjective expression of a social antagonism' induced by the ma-terial convulsions of capitalist modernity.[23] As Virginia Jackson's work has made clear, shades of the same argument can be traced backwards

---

19   Matthew Burroughs Price, 'A Genealogy of Queer Detachment', *PMLA*, 130.3 (2015), pp. 648–65 (p. 656).

20   Ibid., p. 651.

21   The variety of approaches that share alienation as a defining feature of the lyric can, perhaps, be contradistinguished with reference to their distinct temporalities: when is this 'ideal community' to be recovered from? A lyric that gestures *towards* a longed-for futurity provides the basis of Muñoz's readings of Frank O'Hara and James Schuyler in *Cruising Utopia*, p. 25.

22   Theodor Adorno, 'On Lyric Poetry and Society', in *Notes to Literature*, 2 vols (New York: Columbia University Press, 1991–92), i (1991), ed. by Rolf Tiedemann, trans. by Shierry Weber Nicholson, pp. 37–54 (p. 37).

23   Ibid., p. 45.

and forwards across the twentieth century.[24] A less well-known example can be found in a letter of 20 August 1941, written from Casarsa by a nineteen-year-old Pier Paolo Pasolini to his friend Luciano Serra in Bologna:

> Pierpaolo poi è addirittura antitetico al 'guidogozzano' il quale ultimo si ritira dentro se stesso, si umilia, si fa anonimo, *cosa tra le cose*, laddove 'Pier Paolo' si distacca, è un grido, *è la certezza di essere differente dagli altri e dall'ambiente.*
>
> (Pierpaolo is then actually antithetical to 'guidogozzano', the latter withdraws within himself, humbles himself, makes himself anonymous, *thing among things*, whereas 'Pier Paolo' is detached, is a cry, *is the certainty of being different from others and from the environment.*)[25]

Pasolini is determined here to distinguish himself from the *crepuscolarismo* of Guido Gozzano, in which a version of the decadent aloofness described by Burroughs Price had been mellowed out with a strong dose of ennui. Pasolini's new poetry will be antithetical to the inactivity of a submissive 'cosa tra le cose' — 'thing among things' — because the figure of the poet '"Pier Paolo"' will be detached, like 'a cry', and as such he will stand for 'the certainty of being different from others and from the environment'. Pasolini's phrasing is helpful thanks to the economy with which it compresses the various postures of lyric alienation. There are the paradigmatic positions as later put by Adorno — the refusal of socialization ('si ritira') versus the pathos of detachment ('si distacca') — as well as an opposition between a thing-like passivity and a combative activity. A further twist is given by the strange manner in which Pasolini's orthography differentiates the gloopy, thing-like substance of 'Pierpaolo' and '"guidogozzano"' (all one word, and left uncapitalized like a common noun) from the detached figure of '"Pier Paolo"'. The use of inverted commas further complicates any clear-cut claim to authenticity (as does the third person when applied to himself): this '"guidogozzano"' would presumably be a persona adopted with the

---

24   See Virginia Jackson, 'Lyric', in *The Princeton Encyclopaedia of Poetry and Poetics*, 4th edn, ed. by Stephen Cushman and others (Princeton, NJ: Princeton University Press, 2012), pp. 826–34.

25   Pier Paolo Pasolini, *Lettere: 1940–1954*, ed. by Nico Naldini (Turin: Einaudi, 1986), p. 82; my translation, emphasis in original.

same ironic detachment as '"Pier Paolo"', even if the latter is intent on extricating himself from his surroundings rather than dissolving into them.[26]

Pasolini's letter reminds us that alienation can cover for any number of distinct poses: disgust or disinterest, resistance or submissiveness. The detachment that engenders alienation is, after all, innately relational (the first question would be 'detachment *from what?*'), and often denotes more a set of provisional strategies or orientations than any single quality of poetic expression. In contemporary scholarship, the trouble with defining lyric has become bound up with attempts to adequately distinguish modes of detachment. Jeremy Page has recently written of a poetics of 'self-detachment' as 'the point at which the self loses its center of gravity, its embodiment and its "mineness", yet remains'.[27] The self, in this reading, is not merely what Daniel C. Dennett called a 'theorists' fiction': an ontologically useful sham, a sham nonetheless.[28] For Page, the self is what remains *after* the centre is gone, after embodiment has dissolved, and after 'mineness' ('"Pier Paolo"') comes undone. Anahid Nersessian has examined how three American poets 'experiment with coolness and detachment as a critical response to capital', finding in their work 'an ethical withdrawal from the impulse to dictate how any other person should encounter themselves'.[29] The poet James Longenbach suggests that the 'impulse to be lyrical is driven by the need to be no longer constrained by oneself', so that what he terms 'lyric knowledge' is the product of the repeated breaking and recomposition of formal constraints, analogous to the self as it is formed out of a perpetual process of estrangement.[30] What

---

26   The letter prefigures the polemics of the 1950s in *Officina* and beyond, in which the limits of lyric expression — and its relation to engaged civic poetry — were central. See Éanna Ó Ceallacháin, 'Polemical Performances: Pasolini, Fortini, Sanguineti, and the Literary-Ideological Debates of the 1950s', *Modern Language Review*, 108.2 (2013), pp. 475–503.

27   Jeremy Page, 'The Detached Self', *Poetics Today*, 43.4 (2022), pp. 663–95 (p. 663).

28   Daniel C. Dennett, *Consciousness Explained* (Boston, MA: Little, Brown and Co., 1991), p. 429.

29   Anahid Nersessian, 'Notes on Tone', *New Left Review*, 142 (2023), pp. 55–73 (pp. 58, 73).

30   James Longenbach, 'Lyric Knowledge', *Poetry*, February 2016 <https://www. poetryfoundation.org/poetrymagazine/articles/70307/lyric-knowledge> [accessed 16 October 2023].

these accounts have in common is a claim on lyric as a privileged site in which to think through detachment as an ethical, political, or epistemological position. Tweaking Adorno's formulation, we might say that they approach lyric as a sphere of expression whose essence lies in acknowledging the pathos of socialization and overcoming it with the power of detachment.

These analyses return us to the question of what comes *after* detachment: what is it that a lyric of detachment calls towards that is beyond present imaginaries of community? And why would the pathos of socialization need to be overcome in the first place? In the lyric of Carl Phillips, we find one response to these questions as channelled through gay male eroticism. To see this more clearly, the remainder of this essay turns to 'Hymn' from *Pastoral*. The choice of text is in part intended as a corrective to readings of Phillips's career which take this collection to signal a turn away from the eroticism of his earlier writing.[31] While the poems in *Pastoral* present sex between men in ways that are deliberately grafted onto a language of spirituality and sacrament, the 'absence of women' does not, as one early reviewer suggested, mean that the poetry is 'abstract'.[32] Such a comment assumes that the poetic representation of sex between men necessitates a trade-off between the 'representation' and the 'poetic', as though the texts must translate their explicit content into indirect forms. What Phillips actually achieves is the marriage of conventional poetic tropes with the direct depiction of non-normative sexual practices.

It is therefore the presence of queer eroticism in Phillips's poetics that I associate with his use of lyric to address a future collectivity that outstrips identity *and* resists the aestheticization of non-relationality. This gesture is inseparable from the lyric tropes of *Pastoral*: nearly every poem nestles its language around an apostrophized 'you', and nearly every poem makes recourse to the lore of religious community — psalms, parables, myth, or mysticism — in order to work through

---

31 In a recent essay, Phillips reflects on comments from readers on his supposed move away from sexual explicitness following his first two collections: "'I liked it when you were still a gay poet", an audience member said to me at a Q and A' (Phillips, *My Trade*, p. 48).

32 Daniel Garrett, review of *Pastoral*, by Carl Phillips, *World Literature Today*, 74.3 (2000), p. 600.

the self's distance from that 'you'. The cruising eye of 'Hymn', which is also its lyric-I, roams with a sense of detachment: it measures its distance from a community that dissolves the moment that this distance is closed. In place of community, at the moment of contact from which the possibility of community recedes, Phillips's poetics crafts a communion in which identity is dispersed through a syntactical extension that almost never gets to the point. That is to say that the lyric-I becomes inseparable from the object which it is posed in search of, and to name this inseparability 'communion' is to emphasize a parallel with devotional poetry that I turn to in the following section. This poetics curbs Leo Bersani's famous anti-relational rendering of sex as a 'self-shattering and solipsistic *jouissance*'.[33] It lingers on the brink of that model of dispossession, obliteration, and ecstasy, and in the last instance it moves towards an imagined collectivity that extends beyond the individual (self-shattered or not) — a move that recalls Bersani's own shift in his later writings towards 'proliferating relational possibilities' as encountered in aesthetic experiences.[34] In doing so, 'Hymn' honours detachment as what it takes to go on wanting, as a plane of possibility where homoeroticism and the lyric are momentarily aligned.

'HYMN'

Pastoral proceeds as a constant deferral of an arrival in community. Its lyric-I, which materializes most often towards the close of the poems, begins in search of an object. The recursive elusiveness of that object — recovered then lost, covert then revealed — is the collection's leading motif. If the erotic undertow of *Pastoral* were limited to this schema, then it would be interpretable within the boilerplate terms of lyric alienation: an Adornian 'pathos of detachment' (or Pasolini's cry of difference) unfolding through the drama of fleeting sexual encounters. What is more unusual in Phillips's writing, and altogether more queer, is the power of detachment to not only constitute the self but pose the self as subject to a process of continual erasure, a process that does not

---

33   Leo Bersani, 'Is the Rectum a Grave?', in *AIDS: Cultural Analysis/Cultural Activism*, ed. by Douglas Crimp (Cambridge, MA: MIT Press, 1988), pp. 197–222 (p. 222).

34   For an account of this move within Bersani's thought away from the anti-relational and towards aesthetic encounters of 'self-extension', see Tim Dean, 'Sex and the Aesthetics of Existence', *PMLA*, 125.2 (2010), p. 387–92 (p. 391).

arrive at a synthesis in which the lyric-I is calibrated by difference and finds form through antagonism, but drifts instead towards a state of idealized anonymity of which the self is one of several collateral effects. To put it in overly schematic terms, Phillips's cruising scenes express not the longing *for* an object but longing *as* an object, longing as a state evacuated of its subject, a searchingness that can't stop circling itself. My aim is to show how this enigmatic mode of detachment is the result of precise poetic and rhetorical mechanisms, as well as suggesting that it can be historically situated among collective practices of gay men after AIDS. How do syntax and line modulate or excite this searchingness? What does cruising — with its codes of anonymized, impersonal intimacies — have to do with tensile sentences that stretch themselves towards breaking? These questions guide one illustration of what a queer poetics attentive to form can look like in practice.

Phillips's first collection, *In the Blood*, was published in 1992. In an interview from 1994, Phillips states that 'the nature of desire itself' had been his subject matter, adding that 'one's experience [of coming out in the time of AIDS] is going to be quite different from those of the gay men who did so in the 1970s and early 1980s':

> I've been interested in how one reconciles the freedom of that earlier time period with the danger that can now attend sex — how to do that, without compromising the very real fact of sexual desire that most of us feel?[35]

His first collection travels through anonymous sexual encounters with men — 'fucking in small, public spaces',[36] as the poem 'Mix' has it — coalescing around what an early review described as 'a voice that is alternately urbane, physically and emotionally abandoned, devotional, teacherly and streetwise'.[37] The erraticism and intensity of the encounters described holds that voice back from cohering into a self. It is the anonymity of the sex, and the eroticism generated by anonymity, that produces a language at once intimate and impersonal, a balance disclosed in the opening lines of *In the Blood* in the poem 'X':

---

35   Quoted in Charles H. Rowell, 'An Interview with Carl Phillips', *Callaloo*, 21.1 (1998), pp. 204–77 (p. 206).

36   Carl Phillips, *In the Blood* (Boston, MA: Northeastern University Press, 1992), p. 8.

37   Erin Belieu, review of *In the Blood*, by Carl Phillips, and *American Prodigal*, by Liam Rector, *Agni*, 41 (1995), pp. 189–94 (p. 189).

> [...] X,
> as in variable,
>
> anyone's body, any set
> of conditions, your
>
> body scaling whatever
> fence of chain-metal Xs
>
> desire throws up [...][38]

This pursuit of the 'variable', and therefore anonymized, potential of desire — marked as 'X', 'anyone's body, any set | of conditions' — is what allows the poems to function paradigmatically as lyric: their reiterative address to a 'you', transferred and transmuted each time that 'desire throws up' another sexual encounter, is inextricable from the restless momentum of cruising which they take as their narrative grounding.

This correspondence reaches its most complete and stylized form in Phillips's fourth collection, *Pastoral*. The opening poem, 'A Kind of Meadow', loiters on a forest edge: a zone of transition between 'shadow | and what inside of it || hides, threatens, calls to' and the clearer light of a field, one that will reoccur as a site of sexual and spiritual regeneration across the collection.[39] The 'assembled' trees are imagined as a 'Chorus', and — not quite entering — the poem hangs about on the threshold of that collectivity:

> [...] expecting perhaps
> the stag to step forward, to make
>
> of its twelve-pointed antlers
> this branching foreground to a backdrop
> all branches[40]

This anticipation of the arrival of something singular, a singularity that would gain definition against the entanglement of the forest branches, is equated at the poem's end with the movement of desire itself:

> [...] *Only until*
> there's nothing more
> *I want* — thinking it, wrongly,

---

38   Phillips, *In the Blood*, p. 3.
39   Carl Phillips, *Pastoral* (Saint Paul, MN: Greywolf Press, 2000), p. 3.
40   Ibid.

a thing attainable, any real end
to wanting, and that it is close, and that
it is likely, how will you not

this time catch hold of it: flashing,
flesh at once

lit and lightness, a way
out, the one dappled way, back —[41]

Anastrophe, the reversal or tousling of standard syntax, is the most consistent feature of Phillips's poetics. 'The formula', as Dan Chiasson puts it, 'is this: the sentence represents the mind, making sense of what the body, in the form of line and stanza breaks, forces upon it.'[42] This could be rephrased without the dualism which Chiasson has in mind: there is the movement of syntax as an arrangement of time (anticipation, excitement, pursuit) and the stanzaic arrangement of space in which that movement occurs. A classicist by training and long-time teacher of Latin and Greek, Phillips is highly attentive to the shaping of his syntax by line and the rhetorical forms embedded in such choices: 'syntax', he has commented, 'is about negotiating power and creating hierarchies.'[43] In the passage quoted, this process of hierarchization involves parsing the statement '*I want*' through a series of postpositional phrases that keep the object of desire — 'it' — front and centre, *even as* we are warned of the wrongness of thinking that it is 'a thing attainable'. The lines, that is to say, set up the pursuit of this object, before dissolving into the visual ephemera of which it is composed.

The poem 'Hymn', from the second section of the collection, picks up where 'A Kind of Meadow' left off. In the earlier poem, the desire for 'a thing attainable' fizzles out into the flashing of dappled light. 'Hymn', as its title's pun suggests, converts that 'it' into a person, an unattainable *him*. The scene is again that zone of transition at the forest's edge. The poem begins as a figure steps forward out of the trees and into light:

---

41   Ibid., p. 4; italics in original.

42   Dan Chiasson, 'End of the Line: New Poems from Carl Phillips', *New Yorker*, 8 April 2013 <https://www.newyorker.com/magazine/2013/04/15/end-of-the-line-6> [accessed 14 October 2023].

43   Garth Greenwell, Richie Hofmann, and Carl Phillips, 'On Art, Sex, and Syntax', *Yale Review*, 110.1 (2022), pp. 119–33 (p. 121).

Less the shadow
than you a stag, sudden, through it.
Less the stag breaking cover than

the antlers, with which
crowned.
Less the antlers as trees leafless,

to either side of the stag's head, than —
between them — the vision that must
mean, surely, rescue.

Less the rescue.
More, always, the ache
towards it.[44]

This play of subtraction, a relaxed antithesis, 'less this, than that', is once again the grasping towards a desired object that recedes into the detail which each line displaces our attention onto, a phenomenophilic give-and-take which enacts the very 'ache | towards' the figure it is describing. Garth Greenwell, reading the poem along similar lines, takes these opening stanzas as a metaphorical transfiguration of the human into the figure of the stag.[45] It is important to note that the second line — 'you a stag' — omits simile, and that the repetition of 'Less' seems to direct us not towards similitude but rather a partition of this figure's qualities, a move that passes metonymically downwards from shadow to stag, stag to antlers, antlers to 'the vision' that is rested between them. The steady anastrophic drift of details and their placement — 'sudden, through it', 'with which | crowned', 'between them' — gives the lines their trajectory of descent, as they trace a gaze that reveals itself to be less concerned with the facticity of what is in front of it — is that a shadow or a person, are those branches or antlers? — than with the hidden meaning of its composition. It is thinking, to misquote Keats, that is only capable of posing facts and reason by reaching irritably after mysteries and doubts.

---

44   Phillips, *Pastoral*, p. 22. Carl Phillips, 'Hymn' and excerpt from 'A Kind of Meadow' from *Pastoral*. Copyright © 2000 by Carl Phillips. Reprinted with the permission of The Permissions Company, LLC on behalf of Graywolf Press, Minneapolis, Minnesota, graywolfpress.org.

45   'Stag' itself, in gay US slang, would refer to sexually available men, and a 'stagline' to a gathering of male prostitutes; see John Rechy, *City of Night* (New York: Grove, 1963): 'Cars still go round the block to choose a paid partner from the stagline' (p. 275).

Where do these mysteries arrive from? 'Hymn', like much of *Pastoral*, borrows its symbolic substance from Christian hagiography. The story here is that of St Eustace, a Roman general who converted to Christianity after a vision of the Crucifixion seen between the antlers of a stag. A celebrated engraving of the scene by Albrecht Dürer (Figure 1) shows the soldier kneeling beside his horse and hunting hounds, his hands raised, his face turned in profile towards the stag that stands between two bare trees. Dürer's depiction departed from more theatrical iconographies of the same scene in which the saint had typically been depicted falling from his horse. Its superabundant detailing is finely drawn and balanced so that, as the art historian Erwin Panofsky writes, it instils 'a sense of quietude', and although it is Dürer's largest engraving, it is — 'almost paradoxically' — his most 'delicate'.[46] Delicacy of detail is also a property of Phillips's opening stanzas, and a glance at Dürer's engraving can help us make sense of what their antithetical refrain of 'Less ...' amounts to. The persistent trimming of detail, the lessening of vision to the minutiae of observable phenomenon, the unremarkable manner in which the icon is reduced to an almost incidental scale and position (the crucifix itself measuring no more than 2 cm in full) — Dürer's composition likens revelation to the mundane activity of paying attention, of *leaning in* to pinpoint, amidst its dense patterning of rhyming shapes, what is singularly different. In an analogous manner, the opening lines of 'Hymn' are less interested in the spectacle of an accomplished metaphor than in performing the eye's sweep across that metaphor's constituent parts. They caress physical detail, and test out the bounds of sight and sensation, so that the two senses of 'vision' — the one mundane, the other transcendent — come to seem indivisible.

The rhetorical stringency of that progressive 'lessening' is therefore in service to a mystical conception of the world, one that doesn't necessitate a step up the metaphysical ladder but puts, instead, the possibility of divine communion firmly on Earth, kicking that ladder away in the process. Writing on the case of the seventeenth-century mystic Benedetta Carlini, Patricia Simons details how 'recourse to mystical

---

46   Erwin Panofsky, 'Dürer's "St. Eustace"', *Record of the Art Museum, Princeton University*, 9.1 (1950), pp. 2–10 (p. 2).

Figure 1. Albrecht Dürer, *St Eustace*, *c*.1501, engraving, 35 × 25.9 cm,
Metropolitan Museum of Art.

fantasy endowed her passion with a structure and a rhetoric. Rather than sublimation through piety, Benedetta's case history indicates an intensifying of acts spiritual *and* sexual'.[47] In 'Hymn', iconographic borrowings from Eustace should likewise be read not as rerouting desire towards an abstraction of divine love but as allowing for its gaze to be guided by a grammar of longing that remains embedded in the observation of worldly phenomenon and baited by sexual anticipation. That this heightened reading of the visual can traffic between the language of mysticism *and* the mechanics of cruising is one achievement of Phillips's poetics.

Cruising, writes Jack Parlett in *The Poetics of Cruising*, is 'a perceptual arena where acts of looking are intensified and eroticized':[48] the sexually assertive gaze is bent on fixing the telling detail, hoping that its gaze will in turn be taken as a sign. The metonymic exactingness with which 'Hymn' translates this practised intensity into its syntax results in the subtraction of the self from the equation: you stare too intensely, you forget altogether that you are staring.[49] It is here that a second noteworthy feature of the syntax of the opening stanzas is important: their elision of a subject. The only complete clause comes in the third stanza: 'the vision that must | mean, surely, rescue', where 'the vision' is, fittingly, itself the phrase's grammatical subject and the presence of an onlooking subjectivity can only be inferred from the suggestive intrusion of 'surely'. The self is nowhere to be seen, absorbed as it is in the strain of seeing. This would support reading the poem within the long tradition of devotional lyricism, in which self-sacrifice, or self-annihilation, is one outcome of the mystical sensibility that Phillips here makes his own. Merrill Cole, in *The Other Orpheus*, describes how to 'figure interpersonal relations in the language of Christian devotion, and thereby to make sacrifice the proof and substance of human love,

---

47   Patricia Simons, '"Bodily Things" and Brides of Christ: The Case of the Early Seventeenth-Century "Lesbian Nun" Benedetta Carlini', in *Sex, Gender and Sexuality in Renaissance Italy*, ed. by Jacqueline Murray and Nicholas Terpstra (New York: Routledge, 2019), pp. 97–124 (p. 104; emphasis in original).

48   Jack Parlett, *The Poetics of Cruising: Queer Visual Culture from Walt Whitman to Grindr* (Minneapolis: University of Minnesota Press, 2022), p. 2.

49   For a discussion of the gaze and its significances in cruising, see George Chauncey, *Gay New York: Gender, Urban Culture, and the Making of the Gay Male World, 1890–1940* (New York: Basic Books, 1994), p. 188.

is the inaugural strategy of Western love poetry'.[50] The self, in this tradition, is given up, abased, or sacrificed, as testimony to its own insignificance when faced with the incomprehensible magnitude of divine love, the idea being that such incomprehensibility can only be negatively marked by the self's vanishing. Cole was interested in the relation between this strategy and 'the sacrificial economy' of male homoeroticism in modernist poetry, as well as the possibility of discovering alternative erotic modes that would not be limited to the language of acquisition and loss, selfhood and sacrifice.[51] The next stanzas of 'Hymn' appear to turn precisely on this question, taking place as they do within a further blurring of distinction between the divine and the mundane, between erotic and sacred:

> When I think of death, the gleam of
> the world darkening, dark, gathering me
> now in, it is lately
>
> as one more of many other nights
> figured with the inevitably
> black car, again the stranger's
>
> strange room entered not for prayer
> but for striking
> prayer's attitude, the body
>
> kneeling, bending, until it finds
> the muscled patterns that
> predictably, given strain and
>
> release, flesh assumes.
> When I think of desire,
> it is in the same way that I do
>
> God: as parable, any steep
> and blue water, things that are always
> there, they only wait
>
> to be sounded.[52]

Without recourse to the trope of devotional self-sacrifice, it is hard to make sense of the fifth stanza's switch from a desirous 'ache towards'

50   Merrill Cole, *The Other Orpheus: A Poetics of Modern Homosexuality* (New York: Routledge, 2002), p. 6.

51   Ibid., p. 143.

52   Phillips, *Pastoral*, pp. 22–23.

an ungraspable object to the contemplation of death. The stanzas then extend this association of devotional imagery and sex, and that association hinges directly on the suggested likeness of death to desire, most vividly illustrated by the 'black car' — both a hearse and a pickup — or the kneeling body — both a sexualized pose and 'prayer's attitude'.

Like Cole, it was on a resemblance between Catholic mysticism's 'pure love' (in which self-annihilation is a necessary condition for divine communion) and the practice of barebacking amongst gay men (in which the receiver risks HIV infection) that Bersani made the case for an 'impersonal intimacy' in which subjectivity is annihilated as it is 'penetrated, even replaced, by an unknowable otherness':

> Of course, both barebacker and the proponent of pure love continue to exist, for other people, as identifiable individuals; but at the ideal limit of their asceses, both their individualities are overwhelmed by the massive anonymous presence to which they have surrendered themselves.[53]

The comparison is also made explicit by Garth Greenwell in his own reading of 'Hymn': 'the limit-experience of sex [...] is similar to the mystic's limit-experience of God in the way that it confounds discursive rationality and courts the bewilderment and even the extinction of the self'.[54] What I note, however, is that the *courting* of bewilderment and extinction marks the expressive limit of this semblance in 'Hymn'. When death is overtly evoked, it is as part of the *reinsertion* of a subjectivity into the poem's syntax: the 'I' that is held in contemplation of death organizes the following five stanzas around one complete sentence. If these stanzas are set against the parataxical fragmentation of vision as traced through the poem's first four stanzas, this subjectivity performs a drawing away from the kind of eroticized self-

---

53   Leo Bersani, 'Shame on You', in Leo Bersani and Adam Phillips, *Intimacies* (Chicago, IL: University of Chicago Press, 2008), pp. 31–57 (p. 54).

54   Greenwell, 'Cruising Devotion', p. 173. Carl Phillips, *The Art of Daring: Risk, Restlessness, Imagination* (Minneapolis, MN: Graywolf Press, 2014), has also reflected on this connection between self-annihilation and gay sexual practices: 'The more I observed men get multiply, randomly, routinely barebacked by total strangers, the more I began to equate promiscuity with virtual suicide. Or with the despair, the nothing-left-to-lose, that I'd associated with suicide. And, as with suicide (commitment as a form of power that counterbalances a sense of powerlessness), I think promiscuity has a great deal to do with power — the feeling of conquest and/or of being conquered' (p. 108).

shattering which Bersani's parallelism leads towards. This is to say that while the move from desire to death (and back again) has something of the Bersaniesque about it, and is inflected with what Cole calls the 'sacrificial' logic of devotional love, what Phillips's lines pursue is the self's *contemplation* of that limit itself, rather than the dissolution of that limit as enacted upon the self.

Remaining at this limit, the poem's subsequent stanzas perform another turn, or a return, back towards desire and the language of devotion. The emphasis falls again on the sensation of anticipation that attends desire: the contemplation of desire, like the contemplation of God, is a state of being present and waiting 'to be sounded'. This amounts to an amplification of the comparison between an affected stance of lyric detachment (the self composed here as a contemplation of itself) and the eroticism (mystical *and* queer) of submitting oneself to a desirous state of expectation. The poem's final stanzas equate this expectation with the passivity, and durability, of a stone:

> And I a stone that, a little bit, perhaps
> should ask pardon.
>
> My fears — when I have fears —
> are of how long I shall be, falling,
> and in my at last resting how
>
> indistinguishable, inasmuch as they
> are countless, sire,
> all the unglittering other dropped stones.[55]

This final image of the 'dropped stones', and of falling as one stone among many, is more than the theological pose of a pacified receptivity to God; it is the last image with which Phillips refigures intimacy as *neither* nihilistic self-dissolution *nor* solipsistic self-contemplation, but an anonymity that rests within a collectivity. Phillips recalled in an interview a practice common on the gay beaches along Cape Cod in the 1990s:

> I saw here and there several men who would be lying alone, except for a small pile of stones — a cairn of sorts — beside them; I later learned that these signified the lover, now dead, with whom each man had been used to coming to this beach in the past.[56]

---

55   Phillips, *Pastoral*, p. 23.
56   Quoted in Rowell, 'Interview', pp. 213–14.

This practice, Phillips goes on to emphasize, was occurring alongside continued cruising for sex: two counterpointed sentiments, one of desire's continuance, and one of mournful recollection, that ground the opening and closing lines of 'Hymn'.

The conceit of the 'I' as a stone is the bridge between these two poles, connecting as it does the passivity of the self in the hyper-receptive gazing of the opening stanzas to the practice of mourning represented by the collection of 'other dropped stones'. Each gesture involves the lyric-I in a relational exchange: the cruising gaze expects 'the rescue' that will resolve 'the ache' of desire; the stone waits for its collection among 'other dropped stones'; both figure a 'wait | to be sounded', a sentiment which, as the work of Cole and Bersani makes plain, can be readily lifted from Christian mysticism and transferred to modern homoeroticism. Phillips's innovative manipulation of this transference lies in pairing its erotic drive with the second practice of collecting stones in memory of those lost to AIDS. In doing so, the anonymity implicit within each exchange — as marked firstly by the absence of a subject in the opening lines and then by the image of the stone resting 'indistinguishable' among 'countless' others — is the product not of detachment but rather the subject's surrender to, or entering into, alterity. That process of surrender does not involve the reification of an already existing community. Rather, Phillips's erotics of waiting orients itself towards a future in which the subject will be collected, gathered up, or 'rescued' by the arrival of the other.

The connections between theories of lyric detachment and queer interrogations of relationality should run both ways. Phillips's 'Hymn' arrives at its resting place of collectivity — one stone, gathered lovingly among others — by excavating the likenesses of the lyric-I and the cruising subject. Through that likeness, the poem shapes, in the language of Berlant and Warner, a counterintimacy: the anonymity of cruising leads onto the anonymity of death, not as a place of self-annihilation or non-relation, but as an expectant state of *belonging to*, or being gathered within, a collectivity. To return in closing to where this chapter began: Berlant and Warner hazard their own image of an intimate exchange, in the final pages of their essay, that exceeds and disrupts received modes of relation. They do so by pausing over a moment in a New York leather bar, where they watch a performance

of 'erotic vomiting'. A boy — 'twentyish, very skateboard' — sits and
tilts his head up for another man to pour milk down his throat:

> A dynamic is established between them in which they carefully
> keep at the threshold of gagging. The bottom struggles to keep
> taking in more than he really can. The top is careful to give him
> just enough to stretch his capacities. From time to time a baby
> bottle is offered as a respite, but soon the rhythm intensifies.
> The boy's stomach is beginning to rise and pulse, almost con-
> vulsively.[57]

Bracketing, for a moment, the poetics of the performance itself, what is
striking is the account's careful recombination of anonymity, roleplay,
and fluid exchange, a vignette that Berlant and Warner compose in
order to contest the idea that queer sexualities need confine themselves
to the assertion of an impervious and fixed identity. The participants
are here, as in Phillips's poems, engaged in a daring choreography
of passivity and activity, performed in public view, in a manner that
surpasses any normative rendering of sexuality as private sex between
two people. In recounting the performance, Berlant and Warner are
keenly attentive to the arrangement of its rhythms and beats, as well
as the lulls and climactic screams among the crowd watching.[58] In
their closing paragraph, they briefly refer to the performance as a *lyric*
moment:

> We are used to thinking about sexuality as a form of intimacy
> and subjectivity, and we have just demonstrated how limited
> that representation is. But the heteronormativity of U.S. cul-
> ture is not something that can be easily rezoned or disavowed
> by individual acts of will, by a subversiveness imagined only
> as personal rather than as the basis of public formation, nor
> even by the lyric moments that interrupt the hostile cultural
> narrative that we have been staging here.[59]

Phillips's lyric provides another example of how a queer poetics might
travel beyond the interruption of present norms. It does so without re-
course to the language of community, preferring instead to explore the

---

57   Berlant and Warner, 'Sex in Public', p. 565.
58   Ibid.
59   Ibid., p. 566.

erotics of waiting for a future collectivity. This is, as I have been arguing, the poetics of cruising itself: as 'anticipated remembrance',[60] a series of gestures that recite a shared memory of what might come. These gestures find their correspondences in the common elements of Phillips's poetics. The restlessness of syntax, the tracking of the gaze, the vanishment and resurfacing of its subject, and the anonymity which it is reduced to when faced with its desire: such strategies contribute to a lyric moment that is defined by its anticipation of a being together that is not here yet.

---

60   Parlett, *Poetics of Cruising*, p. 56.

Being a Perpetual Guest
Lyric, Community, Translation
A CONVERSATION WITH VAHNI ANTHONY EZEKIEL CAPILDEO

Vahni Anthony Ezekiel Capildeo was a guest speaker at both of the 'Rethinking Lyric Communities' workshops, held in Oxford and Berlin in 2022, which lie at the root of this volume. With immense generosity, Capildeo shared with the participants their reflections on lyric, translation, and community, based on their own poetic practice and engagement with the work and words of other poets. This conversation emerges from and expands on those dialogues.

Editors: *Your writing is far from being a soliloquy. Your poems are often dedicated to specific people and seem to presuppose a collective addressee. Do you understand poetry and translation as ways of interacting with an existing literary or social community? Or are poetry and translation for you rather a way of creating a community — of inventing a collective addressee that transcends geographical, chronological, and linguistic boundaries?*

Capildeo: Thank you for beginning the conversation with the chance to consider how poetry and translation 'speak', and with whom. Throughout the conversation, if I may, I shall answer as a poet, rather than an academic — as someone who constantly either makes or, at some level, is in the contemplative phase before or after making; even when wiping the kitchen counter, even when running for an early morning train. It occurred to me that my answers to your questions will be different if I speak from the place of making something, and how that thing is made, rather than speaking about what that thing is, or why it exists. To speak from the midst of process, and/or to spend more time immersed in process, creates a different rhythm of communicability.

Even if one of my poems arises from critical thought, or if critical principles may be derived from it after the fact — research-based practice, practice-based research — the possibility of (thinking about) writing often presents me with an *untranslatable* set of images and 'music'. For example, this question brings to mind breathing during swimming; fluidity, effort, weightlessness, light, direction, an element which permits belonging both above and under a surface. Let me leave that image, and those sensations, there.

It's interesting that you mention soliloquy. That invokes the idea of theatre — where of course the text (if there is one) is intended to be spoken to an audience, not in an empty room. In fact, in my earlier work (up to 2013 or so), lyrical and dramatic impulses frequently coexist. The variety and strangeness of voice and temper in Robert Browning's *Dramatis Personæ* had a huge influence on me, as did Anthony McNeill's more experimental, yet speaking work. I experienced these theatrical poems as lyrics revoicing themselves in my imagination. This saved me from falling into the contemporary trap whereby lyric poetry packages identity or rehearses anecdotes of the poet's life.

In a sense I have written quite a lot of what I might call 'lyric soliloquies' — poems expressing an individual character's voice, with the pressure of a stated or, more usually, unstated emotional situation. These are poems with a single voice, distinct from what I might call the 'noisy' or 'boundless' lyric I also practise. When I first moved to the UK as a student, I wrote a binder full of lyric poems spoken by 'characters' that distilled elements of the weird scene of Oxford in the 1990s. (These have been destroyed.) To shape language speaking as not-myself seemed the best way to integrate such a new way of life and such unfamiliar people with my imagination, while retaining an independent sense of self. 'The Critic in his Natural Habitat' (in *Utter*, 2013) is an example of a satirical lyric/soliloquy, which freed me — and, perhaps, other readers — from internalizing put-downs.

I would trace my sense of the lyric as a form for *replay*, for being heard and spoken by different actors/readers, to these influences and situations; also, to the drama teacher, Sonya Moze, in Trinidad, who made us write monologues (if I recall correctly, this was the occasion for the first of the disturbing poems about trees that I still obsessively produce!), and to my attending Trinidad and Tobago's Music Festival, where you could hear the same song or piece performed over and over again by as many musicians or choirs as had entered, each trying to make it new, each trying to bring out certain essentials. I have no desire to write purely autobiographical, univocal lyric as a primary form. How would I find out anything about the world? Where would the fun be, for the reader?

However, you are right — in other senses, my poetry is far from being a soliloquy. It is always dialogic and always created in the imagination or hope of encounter. The dead, of course, are interlocutors — writers who have gone before; unwriterly people, whose stories are passed down in oral tradition; and the ordinary dead, who lived irrecoverable lives in the same places I now go about — for the last seven years, a coastal village with an unvisited, quietly historic fishermen's cemetery, and a building with a staircase that has older fingermarks worn in to the stone where I lean for balance.

I do not think of *myself* as interacting with a social or literary community, but as *releasing the poems* to do so; as I'm thinking of the seaside, I have the image of green glass bottles with messages in them (an image liberated from cliché by Scottish writers such as Niall Campbell, in his extraordinary collection *Moontide* (2014)). The dedicatees belong to the paratext; mostly, these are poem-gifts rather than citational dedications, pointing to a nourishing 'real-life' environment of which writing is one small part, rather than towards an/other archive, *oeuvre*, or argument. I'm not sure whether the poems' addressee is collective, so much as 'choose your own adventure' — unpredictable, multiple. The more 'complicated' a poem of mine seems, the more I've tried to work 'ways in' from a variety of angles, i.e. the more accessible it is, if only readers will have no fear and be 'a reader', stop trying to be '*the reader*'. It's very hard to think of interacting with an existing literary or social community, one, because communities are in flux — they shift and overlap and understand 'themselves' and their boundaries differently all the time; two, because a series of startling and unspeakable experiences leads me not to trust too much in poets and critics being consistent or ethical. I love your suggestion of the invention or creation of a community through poetry and translation (note: not through *being a poet or translator*). Alongside that, I would place Martin Carter's phrase 'Discovery of Companion'. I would hope that the interaction between text and reader makes all sorts of connexions light up, carried into the world beyond the book and untraceably into other utterances, other writing, other forms of address and encounter. I would hope any collective be understood and loved as unquantifiable. Even at my noisiest, I am against the measurable, and for the still and small.

In your poetry you often focus on origins: birthplaces, homes, etymologies, and other forms of material or immaterial 'provenance'. Our impression is that you understand such origins as something one cannot return to, because they are imagined. In your studies on the theory of translation, you similarly define source texts as 'imagined originals' to which readers may never return. The title of your first book, No Traveller Returns *(2003), refers to travel as a process of translation and points out the impossibility of coming back to the 'sources'. Do you see poetry and translation as attempts at 'impossible returns to the original community', impossible returns both to textual sources and to the sources of geographical-personal identity?*

Continuing the theme of (not quite) soliloquy ...! *No Traveller Returns* is, of course, Hamlet's phrase, as he considers death: 'The undiscovered country from whose bourn | No traveller returns' (Shakespeare, *Hamlet*, III. 1). Writing in *PN Review* (2016), I resituated — or saw one possible origin for — this famous speech, in the Caribbean: 'discovery' bringing death to the 'New World'. I wondered if this resonance was present for others, whether or not it had been for 'Shakespeare'. Readers, too, can create or invent a collective. Turning to French translators for companionship or elucidation, I found Pierre Le Tourneur in the late eighteenth century: 'cette contrée ignorée dont nul voyageur ne revient'. Does the etymology of *contrée* enfold confrontational encounter, a whisper of guilt down the ages? Markowicz presents us with 'Cette terre inconnue dont les frontières | Se referment sur tous les voyageurs'. In the twenty-first century translation, death is a place with closed borders; or rather, a place closing its borders on people. Suddenly I am back in the Caribbean, seeing massacred or trafficked bodies washed away by turquoise water on white sand; simultaneously, I am in Kent, the garden of England, seeing migrant bodies washed up by colder water in a colder land ... In Kamau Brathwaite's terminology, there is a 'tidalectic' movement between history, environment, literary text, translation/translator, and reader/recipient/actor. I write with the sense of an originary tide of inequality between prestigious texts and their global readership. One collective's play relates to another's nightmare ... For me, origins *exercise more strength than they retain reality*; they are not entirely imagined, but not humanly graspable.

I cannot find sharp enough words for contemporary writers who would be horrified to be accused of softening up the culture for fascism lite. Yet that is what I see in the nostalgia industry. Popular non-fiction and poetry writers pen idyllic landscapes empty of anyone but the occasional tow-headed mystic. This is marketed as preferable to delving into the teeming and multicoloured truth of Britain as island nation: Romans from Arabia, Vikings who may have been to Constantinople, Black Tudors, Virginia Woolf's dreamy, dark good looks handed down (as for so many Brits in the nineteenth century) from South Asian ancestors ... You have only to see the attack on the arts and humanities in universities, where archives and analysis provide not only correctives, but colour. I would not care for an attempt at an impossible return, or even a magically possible return, to any kind of source, in the sense of a quest for purity; nonetheless, I do love curiosity and accuracy, the kind of attention to detail that, almost as a side effect, widens the scope of our lens on 'origins'.

Two notes. First, on the idea of nothing, nothingness; being a citizen of nowhere, knowing nothing, being nobody, coming from nothing. What is recognizable as a home, or a birthplace? What can be *distinguished*, in and by poetry, where ancestral languages have been rendered inaccessible or records have not been kept or traditions of arts and crafts are neither perceived nor (should attention be drawn to them) respected? The *impossible assertion of origin and originality as possible* — not a return to textual or personal-geographical sources, but an act of faith in and task of recovery of what *may or will have been* — is something I seek in, and from, poetry and translation.

Currently, I am working on a series of erasure poems that will inter-mix repeated erasures of a line taken from, or resembling, common speech with new lyric lines. The whole effect will be like a lyric, at first glance, but one that includes the idea of replicability, by present-ing a 'sounding surface' that is already rubbed smooth of some of its words, paradoxically roughened to softness, like the traces of a decora-tive border stencilled long ago on an old wall, or a stone worn away in a quick-running, clear stream. There's a sense for me of the lyric being a place where songful or intensified speech can intersect with the historical; even with mumble or crumbling. M. NourbeSe Philip, *Zong!* (2008), may come to mind for some readers. I'm thinking just as much of the pitiful commemorative verses on rural and working-class tombstones, and the bored, tender, awestricken pause as a visitor deciphers a stranger's memorial.

The second, much briefer note, is on humility, gratitude, and ap-propriation. Sometimes a tradition that is not and cannot be 'mine', by language, landscape, or affect, like the stylized dramas of interiority of Tamil lyric poetry, moves and changes me, as a person and in my prac-tice. This will be a real transformation but also at second hand. In this case, the encounter came about through the work of translator-poets such as Shash Trevett and A. K. Ramanujan. Their work has a relation to sources and knowability which is more profound in both kind and quality than my response, however overcome I feel, and however much my own poetry and translation will never be the same — this cannot be, for me, originary.

Translation plays a crucial role in your work, not only at the level of theory, but also as an activity and a process that informs your writing. Could you give us an insight into your relationship with translation?

The Puerto Rican poet, translator, and scholar Loretta Collins Klo-bah, when I interviewed her for *PN Review*, corrected my references to the 'multilingualism' of her lyrical work, where Spanish and English intertwine, to 'plurilingualism'. That prefix, *pluri-*, rang true to me and gave me pause for thought. It's a softer sound and brought to mind James Joyce's Anna Livia Plurabelle; the riverrun of language, beyond and including languages. As a student of translation theory, I was crit-ical of the metaphors for translation that informed, formed, and limited reviewers and readers of literature in translation. Beginning with the overemphasis on the etymological, and the idea of carrying across, which not only suggests a binary, but implies a burden — then the notion of the ancillary, the handmaidenly, which implies a hierarchy between a probably singular, masterful source and an anxious, servile versioning — then the image of palimpsest, or shinethrough, which in some ways I liked best, but was too waxy, too papery — I found an array of sometimes unconscious limitation on how translation *should behave,* as well as what it might *be.*

I am sensitive to plurilingualism in what appears to be single-tongued. For example, it seems obvious to me that V. S. Naipaul's novel *The Mystic Masseur,* partly set in rural Trinidad, records intergenerational linguistic change, though it is seldom read this way. Sometimes the dialogue between characters who normally speak Trinidad dialect becomes strangely formal, but not in a flowery, bookish way. The way it is patterned reflects a switch to Hindustani or Bhojpuri, of the kind that the generation closer to the emigration from India would make when they wanted to be eloquent or concise, speaking from their fully felt internal selves rather than the imperfection and the charge of 'illiteracy' forced on them in the English colonial situation. It is a private, quick, proud, or exasperated switch.

To be sensitive to this is not just to read for sociolinguistic interest, but to *hear* the different rhythms, the rolled r's, the greater range of phonologically contrasted consonants and short or long pure vowels, the occasional fluting, thunder, or nasality of delivery — to hear neither through, nor alongside, but in a kind of sound-universe *with* the suddenly-formal English on the novel's page. This is a poetic dimension to the prose text, which 'lifts off' for me, when I read as a writer, regarding technique and effect that can be 'translated' (in the carrying-over sense) into lyric practice, where a 'single' voice or cry can invoke, evoke, or seem to be stirred by another way of voicing, proper to another language that also belongs to/with that voice; other sounds, other conventions of expressivity.

Should this example be categorized (perhaps dismissed) as belonging to the 'postcolonial'? So could the unworded co-presence of, say, Gaelic in the English-language lyrics of a writer like Iain Crichton Smith. So could, perhaps, the unworded co-presence of Old Norse and Latin in Old English poetry ... How about Dante's *Purgatorio,*

XXVI, where Dante considers lust, or excessive vs moderate desire, and the last words are spoken in Occitan by the courtly love poet Arnaut Daniel? The plurilingual situation not only can arise in many ways, but arguably is an ordinary condition for the hearing (if not always the sounding) of lyric and other voices. When I write plurilingually, I am not attempting to disrupt or interrupt the lyrical, nor am I writing strategically — at the moment of composition, at least, it seems to me that I am merely writing *musically*, people who work with language being perpetual guests in the house of music.

Regarding an insight into my specific relationship with translation, I should say that I am not a translator or interpreter in the strict sense of either word; though there are languages I 'know' more than others, and texts in which I'll immerse myself, and which become part of the 'sounding universe' against which my poetry-composing mind 'checks' the things it wants on the page. Taking up again the theme of choosing the role of guest, rather than host, let's consider attunement and humility (which includes respect for accuracy or specialist knowledge). Rather than feeling challenged or annoyed by hearing or seeing words or a script I don't 'know' or 'understand', and rather than treating it as pleasingly exotic or a form of birdsong, I try to become extra attentive, extra absorbent, extra open. It's hard to explain rationally what this involves, and some kinds of academic writing might reach for an innovative use of prepositions, such as listening *into*. Perhaps it involves self-forgetfulness? If it's a live performance, I *let myself be moved* (translated? carried across?) by the activation of different conventions of *delivery* as well as attentive to the patterning of sound. Is this poetry that issues from a static body, or one in motion? A mask-like face? A stylized ordinariness? Does the voice become songlike? How is the breath placed? I don't know what my 'host' is offering, but I settle for a moment, trusting in their good gifts.

A number of poets and intellectuals originally from the Caribbean have reflected on the palimpsestic and composite nature of Caribbean cultures and identities, arguing that, as a result of the different phases of colonization, this composite and plural identity partakes of different cultures and languages, many of which, however, have their origins in violence and deracination, and feature therefore as phantoms or tragic losses. For many Caribbean authors, this multilingual stratification is a

powerful tool for the affirmation of community but also represents the
ultimate impossibility of affirming a common origin: this is perhaps a way
forward for thinking of community in post-migration societies. You state
that 'language is my home [...]; not one particular language', and your
poetry is nourished by a host of different languages and traditions merging
with one another: is this aspect of your poetics also a way of responding to
and partaking of this particular version of community?

As I reread this question, I am looking through shutters at a stormy
spring day in the east of England. The wind is tossing a cypress tree.
Small birds are hopping through grass to shelter in a hedge. It's hard
to compass what a way forward for post-migration societies might be,
when the new reality including climate change is that we are asked to
be complicit, here in the privileged north, in the death, detention, or
deportation of people arriving on these shores. Migration is picking
up as never before. At the very least, poets need to be able to praise
and lament; to argue, and to fall in love. Yet it seems to me as if we
are being invited, or pushed towards, not survivors' guilt but what I
would term survivors' brazenness; not even silence, but speech styled
as if perpetually ready for inspection, community as partaking of an
official parade, not of mess or mosaic, not of the wonderfully bewil-
dering scope of human emotivity/movement, physical and internal.
This is our very contemporary violence and deracination: the blood-
nourished rootedness of some, at the expense of others who uproot
themselves as a life-affirming or saving move, because their home has
become, in Warsan Shire's phrase, 'the mouth of a shark'. It makes me
resistant to certain strands of soft-seeming or nostalgic nature writing
popular at the moment in the UK, where celebrating and mourning in
terms of lostness and/or simplicity acts a fig leaf to the otherwise naked
formation of a violently rooted collective body.

There is increasing resistance, in colonialism's beneficiaries,
to acknowledging the horrors of colonialism. This includes the
refusal to consider whether the transgenerational trauma passed
down through the oppressed may correspond to transgenerational
complacency passed down through the oppressors. I am not talking
only of individual histories (which would include the complications
of mixed heritage) but the wider structures, blanks, drifts, and riptides
in 'societies', tangibly evidenced partly in who has paved roads vs who

does not, who expects or enforces quiet in public transport versus who shares food or openly prays, whose existence is acknowledged by Internet algorithms, whose poems are on the radio, whose living communities and heritage inform the shape of the future via AI. I can't feel a tone of pastness when considering origins. If anything, Caribbean and diaspora cultures could keep us attuned and open to origins as constantly in the making. What past *shall we have been*, and for whom, as in becoming the future, with any luck we also become the future future's past? In other words, beyond the future that we can currently imagine relative to our past, there exists a further future that is unimaginable at that present point. While plurilingualism as an aspect of creativity 'begins' autobiographically in my Trinidadian childhood, I'd like to see the way that, from book to book, my writing changes *without anguish* in form, outlook, technique, texture, places, and points of reference as partaking of 'Caribbeanness' in some way.

Without anguish. For although your question rightly speaks of phantoms and tragic loss, and Caribbean anglophone literature has a great tradition of hauntedness — Jean Rhys, Edgar Mittelholzer, Pauline Melville, James Aboud, Kevin Jared Hosein, Sharon Millar are just a few names that spring to mind — there also are fierce, freeing, and joyful ways of inhabiting origin, such as the transformations of self and creolized channelling of spiritual and social history through Carnival. Wilson Harris and Peter Minshall would be among the better-known names globally, but the genius 'on the ground' is beyond description. I could never wholeheartedly talk about the *only* x, y, or z to focus on, perhaps especially at the time of hideous atrocities, such as the ongoing genocide of the Palestinians and the underreported occupation of Kashmir. There's something coercive in the popular put-down, 'whataboutery'. It suggests that dominant interests, whether in the mainstream media or social groups, prefer to impose a narrow focus and to prevent the imagination *ranging* and *adding up*. In the Caribbean and for the Caribbean's children, the ability to 'and/both' has become an aspect of art because it has been and continues to be an aspect of survival. Of flourishing.

I'd like to distinguish between the Caribbean and the Antilles, or at least to say that it's important to name the archipelago variously, to avoid anglophone dominance of the imagination of place. I'd also like to distinguish between writers in, or writing from, the region, and those like me, who live abroad, and have an 'exit' even if they make extended visits 'home'. Returning to the bright clouds driven through a cold sky here at Eastertide in the east of England, I'd like to note that humans and 'the environment' are not so separated, or separable, in the Caribbean. The work of the Barbadian poet-philosopher and innovator Kamau Brathwaite (who also was a Poetry Fellow in Cambridge, the city from which I am writing this answer today) shows us how the actual wind and weather, the literal tide as well as the tide of history, must profoundly shape any truthful poetics. When J. R. Carpenter, whose background is in movement through Canada and France as well as the UK, asked me to contribute a poetic afterword to *This is a Picture of Wind* (2020), where Carpenter charts the winds of the south-west of England and calls attention to climate change, 'naturally' I reached for Édouard Glissant, to learn again how to write the wind ...

You are both a poet and a literary scholar, but you have also worked as a lexicographer for the OED — an activity that is based, among other things, on the assessment, study, and representation of the usages, mutations, and circulation of certain linguistic features in communities of users through different epochs and linguistic areas: did you rather concentrate on the practical, or on the theoretical aspects of lexicography? What kind of impact has this work had on your poetry, if any?

Working in-house for the *Oxford English Dictionary* involved time-targeted editing of the 'live dictionary', via XML-based tagging of linguistic features and electronic notes, using special software, and checking the live dictionary against online and physical databases and materials, with consultancy from in-house and external experts as needed. It was intensely practical as well as analytical, and some of the most detailed work I have ever done! The demands on attention and the level of accuracy required meant that we were encouraged to take screen breaks and water breaks, and not to overstay our working hours too far, lest we start making slip-ups.

The good company in the office, and the strict boundaries around time, staved off the melancholy and isolation to which purely poetical or academic researchers can fall prone. Part of the impact that the *Oxford English Dictionary* had on my poetry was that this camaraderie, and structure, allowed my 'free time' on evenings and weekends to be more purely and shamelessly creative. There was not as much carry-over as one finds in other types of work. I recall going home to my flat in East Oxford and feeling well breathed and exercised mentally, able to relax looking at the movement of a buddleia bush against a wooden fence in my tiny back courtyard 'garden'. The silvery leaves and their ever-changing imprint of shadow on the panels helped me find forms for the tree poems in *Dark & Unaccustomed Words*, my third full-length book, which I completed in 2008, although it appeared only in 2012 (and is out of print). I was finally able to address the lingering horror of having learnt in childhood of the nuclear devastation visited upon Hiroshima and Nagasaki, and how the shadows of leaves remained imprinted after the vegetation had been vaporized by the blast.

Utter, my fourth book (2013), continued to be inspired by those years at the *Oxford English Dictionary*, though I had stopped working there by then. It contains words, such as *cringly*, *dusken*, and *rivelled*, which I loved but were marked as no longer being in regular use, or in use at all. I smuggled these into poems 'unmarked', as it were, in contexts where I hoped they would breathe anew. The driving idea of *Utter* arose from chit-chat within the *Oxford English Dictionary* etymology group, a wonderful place for cake and literary musing in between the high-speed, high-focus stints. The dictionary can be mistaken as monolithic. However, being 'inside' the live dictionary was to feel the coruscating variety of linguistic possibility and to swim in delightful unknowability even while naming and naming. In *Utter*, poems consider things that seem 'monolithic', blank, or unvarying — a field, a tower, time on a Sunday — and how they are alive and teeming with lovely detail. Of course, this lexicography-based feeling of the variegated gorgeousness of language influenced *Measures of Expatriation* (2016). Working at the *Oxford English Dictionary* sensitized me even further to 'noise', rather than silence, as the background against and from which lyric sings out.

In our conversation in Berlin, you talked about your creative response to the Odyssey, *which was commissioned by actor Christopher Kent and musician Gamal Khamis for a narrative recital on ideas of diaspora and migration. Poets Yousif M. Qasmiyeh and J. L. Williams were also involved in the project. Your poems were then published in the pamphlet* Odyssey Calling *(2020). You condensed the* Odyssey *into a series of lyrics so that*

Kent and Khamis could rework it yet again. As you said, translating the epic poem into lyrics was not only a way of making it replicable, replayable, and shareable through different media and bodies, but also a way of breaking down something we have received as a long story of a people or peoples. Refusing to speak for a collective and to provide a poem that could be thought of as the story of a people, you narrow 'the focus to one or two personal situations' and keep 'putting individuals into community situations'. Does turning episodes of Odysseus's journey into lyric fragments mean reopening the epic poem to the very possibility of its circulation within a community both practically and poetically? Are lyric poems more shareable both because they can be re-enacted in different contexts and because they make room for readers as individuals, including you as reader and poet?

It was extremely exciting to write for an actor and a musician. As a poet, I have always longed for my work to be understood as shareable, created for reinterpretation and replay. At an early reading in Trinidad, I handed copies of some poems to people in the audience who had had a significant positive influence on my writing, and invited them to become co-readers, performing the texts and thus freeing them from 'my' voice, to belong to a collective body of voiceable and unspoken memory and experience. Now here was the chance to create texts for people I hardly knew at all, and to do so knowing that my words would be re-mixed in several ways. So, even before thinking about the transformations of epic, I was excited to find my voice, as it were, by giving my voice away.

In the current political conditions in India, academics, journalists, and others have been persecuted for their approaches to the epic traditions around 'the' *Ramayana* — 'the' *Ramayana* of course being plural, as A. K. Ramanujan, Vivek Narayanan, and many others have observed. Their scholarly and imaginative approaches apparently run counter to what seems almost a desire to narrow marvellously fertile traditions into a monolithic sacred text of scientific truth. (I have written about this for *Long Poem Magazine*.) So, it is both hard and easy to admit that inheriting something of that epic tradition formed my way into the *Odyssey*. I distance myself explicitly from posing as an heir to ancient tradition parallel to or (more truly) intersecting with the Greek. I simply recall that in my childhood, my parents sometimes would cite scenes, quite naturally, from the *Ramayana* (in the versions they knew) to compare to our everyday lives and look for guidance — rather like what I've learnt to do, since my conversion to Roman Catholicism, with reading the Bible and the adapted monastic techniques of *lectio divina* — but instead of mulling over a text of the *Ramayana*, we contemplated scenes both lyrically and dramatically. In other words, we replayed it.

I really admire Emily Wilson's approach to translating the *Odyssey* and asked her permission to rely on her version when contemplating the text for reworking. I particularly love her attention to register, and her reconsideration of what would have been plain phrasing, and what would have been elaborate. I opened my imagination and set her text humming, attentive to what would resonate or light up in my memory of the past or awareness of the contemporary, and what would relate to the situations of modern-day refugees and migrants, which Christopher Kent and Gamal Khamis wished to honour and highlight.

Zoë Skoulding, in *Poetry & Listening: The Noise of Lyric* (2020), describes 'thinking about the poem in acoustic spaces, seeing the poem itself as an acoustic space and thinking about how we attend to language in the context of other acoustic phenomena'. I tried to think about the *Odyssey* in lived spaces that I knew from 'real life' — I tried to think extratextually, in order to recontextualize the text — and, in the course of this discipline, or experiment, I found certain scenes or meetings or points of tension *replacing/replaying* themselves, say, in a Scottish cemetery, in a Trinidadian park, or even in a Sheffield tram. Most eerily, in an inside-out version of the process, I was transported in imagination to some original past and distant future that vectorized themselves according to the *Odyssey*, and then I created a lyric from that indwelling. The fragments that replayed/replaced themselves gave me confidence that they were willing to live, that they had life in them, that they could or would replay/replace themselves again, yes, for my readers and for Christopher Kent and Gamal Khamis's audiences.

One of the aspects of 'Odyssey Response' in Like a Tree, Walking *(2021) that we found most intriguing was the way in which you rethought and rewrote the notion of hospitality — a concept that has fascinated scholars for centuries. In section 4 of this work, entitled 'Companion', you mention a notion of hospitality of or through the imagination which seems*

to inform most of your work: could you say more about this concept? In
Odyssey Calling you also emphasize that Odysseus may be a king on his
island, but throughout his journey he is a guest, and he has to convince
people that he is worthy of being hosted. Both positions, that of the guest
and that of the host, can be difficult to occupy, and for everyone these roles
can change in different places and at different times in life. You mentioned
that you refused to become a host in order to remain that perpetual guest
of being a poet. To conclude our conversation, would you like to expand on
this idea of the poet as a perpetual guest in different places, among other
people and ghosts, in language itself?

The idea of *belonging* seems fraught. 'I belong to this place', a feeling
of one-ness with an environment, whether contented or gloomy, too
easily flips into 'This place belongs to me'. 'Who else has been here?'
is an obvious question to ask, which leads into 'Who else might be
here?' To inhabit these questions as if part of a history gentle enough
to remain unwritten, rather than part of a past unquiet enough to
become a horror story, is one of the joys of poetry. I'm not talking about
cultural appropriation but lived experience when I say that it's possible
to *fall in love with* a place. Yet to speak lovingly of that place sometimes
brings mockery, disbelief, or embarrassment, if one is perceived as
unbelonging, or rather *unpossessing*; a pretender, a nowherian. I wonder
why. It's rather as if nobody ought to fall in love, or as if birth family
has a prior claim on all love. One of the reasons that I gave up on the
study of Old Norse was the hostility I encountered, as a scholar 'of
colour', with people sometimes laughing in my face when I answered
their small-talk question 'What do you do?'. Yet I had fallen in love,
both with the unclassifiable colours of landscape under Icelandic light,
and a prose literature of eloquent silences ... I desired not to speak *for*,
merely to speak *from* and *with* ... I feel as if I say these things again and
again, in interviews, on replay, like a haunting, like an exile ...

The Guyanese revolutionary poet, Martin Carter, in his 'Suite of 5
Poems' (2000 [1961]), writes:

> I will always be speaking with you. And if I falter,
> and if I stop, I will still be speaking with you, in
> words that are not uttered, are never uttered, never
> made into the green sky, the green earth, the
> green, green love [...]

I believe that here Carter's lyric addressee is the land of many waters, Guyana, itself, as well as any human listener. He speaks from the land and to the land. The hospitality here involves being attentive to the *population* of a land; as the poet-guest listens, and speaks, the poem *becomes populated* by, and hosts, the unspoken/unspeaking/unspeakable. He loves into, and from, the silent or silenced. Arriving as a perpetual guest means one can host the ghosts of others … I wanted to take an epic that trails after a great war, and to recover personal address from the in-between, the silences, the trivial, and the too-big. The poet as perpetual guest loves through the hurt of the desire to give where there is nothing to bring, becoming part of an ecology of continuity *with* and *against* loss. The poet as perpetual guest cries the possibility of a future.

References

Académie Française, 'Les cieux ou Les ciels', in *Dire, Ne pas dire* (11 June 2020) <https://www.academie-francaise.fr/les-cieux-ou-les-ciels> [accessed 12 February 2022]

Adorno, Theodor W., *Notes to Literature*, trans. by Shierry Weber Nicholsen (New York: Columbia University Press, 2019)

—— 'On Lyric Poetry and Society', in *Notes to Literature*, 2 vols (New York: Columbia University Press, 1991–92), I (1991), ed. by Rolf Tiedemann, trans. by Shierry Weber Nicholson, pp. 37–54

Agamben, Giorgio, *The Coming Community*, trans. by Michael Hardt (Minneapolis: University of Minnesota Press, 1993)

—— 'Expropriated Manner', in *The End of the Poem: Studies in Poetics*, trans. by Daniel Heller-Roazen (Stanford, CA: Stanford University Press, 1999), pp. 87–101 <https://doi.org/10.1515/9780804763912-008>

—— 'The Inappropriable', in *Creation and Anarchy: The Work of Art and the Religion of Capitalism*, trans. by Adam Kotsko (Stanford, CA: Stanford University Press, 2019), pp. 29–50 <https://doi.org/10.1515/9781503609273-004>

—— *The Kingdom and the Glory*, trans. by Lorenzo Chiesa with Matteo Mandarini, in *The Omnibus Homo Sacer* (Stanford, CA: Stanford University Press, 2017), pp. 361–641

—— 'Notes on Gesture', in *Means without End: Notes on Politics*, trans. by Vincenzo Binetti and Cesare Casarino (Minneapolis: University of Minnesota Press, 2000), pp. 49–61

—— *The Use of Bodies*, trans. by Adam Kotsko, in *The Omnibus Homo Sacer* (Stanford, CA: Stanford University Press, 2017), pp. 1011–1288

—— *La voce umana* (Macerata: Quodlibet, 2023)

—— 'What Is a Command?', in *Creation and Anarchy: The Work of Art and the Religion of Capitalism*, trans. by Adam Kotsko (Stanford, CA: Stanford University Press, 2019), pp. 51–65 <https://doi.org/10.1515/9781503609273-005>

—— 'What Is the Act of Creation?', in *Creation and Anarchy: The Work of Art and the Religion of Capitalism*, trans. by Adam Kotsko (Stanford, CA: Stanford University Press, 2019), pp. 14–28 <https://doi.org/10.1515/9781503609273-003>

Ahmed, Sara, 'Collective Feelings; or, The Impressions Left by Others', *Theory, Culture & Society*, 21.2 (2004), pp. 25–42

—— 'The Skin of the Community: Affect and Boundary Formation', in *Revolt, Affect, Collectivity: The Unstable Boundaries of Kristeva's Polis*, ed. by Tina

Chanter and Ewa Plonowska Ziarek (New York: SUNY Press, 2005), pp. 95–111

Alpatova, I., L. Talochkin, and N. Tamruchi, eds, 'Drugoe iskusstvo': Moskva 1956–1988 (Moscow: Galart; Gosudarstvennyi tsentr sovremennogo iskusstva, 2005)

Altman, Toby, '"What Beauty Was": Jen Bervin's Untimely Sonnets', English Literary History, 89.2 (2022), pp. 489–522

Anderson, Benedict, Imagined Communities: Reflections on the Origins and Spread of Nationalism, rev. edn (London: Verso, 2006)

Apter, Emily, 'Afterword: Towards a Theory of Reparative Translation', in The Work of World Literature, ed. by Francesco Giusti and Benjamin Lewis Robinson (Berlin: ICI Berlin Press, 2021), pp. 209–28 <https://doi. org/10.37050/ci-19_09>

Aronson, M., and S. Reiser, Literaturnye kruzhki i salony (Leningrad: Priboi, 1929)

Ashbery, John, 'This Room', in Your Name Here (New York: Farrar Straus and Giroux, 2000), p. 3

—— 'Your Name Here', in Your Name Here (New York: Farrar Straus and Giroux, 2000), pp. 126–27

Ashtor, Gila, Homo Psyche: On Queer Theory and Erotophobia (New York: Fordham University Press, 2021) <https://doi.org/10.5422/fordham/ 9780823294169.001.0001>

Attridge, Derek, The Experience of Poetry: From Homer's Listeners to Shake-speare's Readers (Oxford: Oxford University Press, 2019) <https://doi. org/10.1093/oso/9780198833154.001.0001>

—— 'Singularity', in Oxford Research Encyclopedia of Literature (Oxford University Press, 2020) <https://doi.org/10.1093/acrefore/ 9780190201098.013.1092>

—— The Singularity of Literature (London: Routledge, 2004) <https://doi. org/10.4324/9780203420447>

—— 'Untranslatability and the Challenge of World Literature: A South African Example', in The Work of World Literature, ed. by Francesco Giusti and Benjamin Lewis Robinson (Berlin: ICI Berlin Press, 2021), pp. 25–55 <https://doi.org/10.37050/ci-19_02>

—— The Work of Literature (Oxford: Oxford University Press, 2015) <https: //doi.org/10.1093/acprof:oso/9780198733195.001.0001>

Auden, W. H., 'Introduction', in The Poet's Tongue: An Anthology, ed. by John Garrett and W. H. Auden (London: Bell & Sons, 1935), pp. v–xxxiv

—— introduction to The Oxford Book of Light Verse, in The Complete Works of W. H. Auden: Prose, ed. by Edward Mendelson, 6 vols (Princeton, NJ: Princeton University Press, 1997–2015), I: 1926–1938 (1997), pp. 430–37

—— 'September 1, 1939', in The Complete Works of W. H. Auden: Poems, ed. by Edward Mendelson, 2 vols (Princeton, NJ: Princeton University Press, 2022), I: 1927–1939, pp. 375–77

Austin, John L., *How to Do Things with Words* (Cambridge, MA: Harvard University Press, 1975) <https://doi.org/10.1093/acprof:oso/9780198245537.001.0001>

Ayers, David, 'Modernist Poetry in History', in *The Cambridge Companion to Modernist Poetry*, ed. by Alex Davis and Lee M. Jenkins (Cambridge: Cambridge University Press, 2007), pp. 11–27 <https://doi.org/10.1017/CCOL0521853052.002>

Aytekin, E. Attila, 'A "Magic and Poetic" Moment of Dissensus: Aesthetics and Politics in the June 2013 (Gezi Park) Protests in Turkey', *Space and Culture*, 20.2 (2017), pp. 191–208

Azarova, Natal'ya, 'Mnogoyazichie Aigi i yazyki-posredniki', *Russian Literature*, 79–80 (2016), pp. 29–40

Bachmann, Ingeborg, *Kritische Schriften*, ed. by Monika Albrecht and Dirk Göttsche (Munich: Piper, 2005)

—— *Malina*, in *'Todesarten'-Projekt*, ed. by Monika Albrecht and Dirk Göttsche, 4 vols (Munich: Piper, 1995), III.1

Bahun, Sanja, '"Me you — you — me": Mina Loy and the Art of Ethnographic Intimacy', in *Modernist Intimacies*, ed. by Elsa Högberg (Edinburgh: Edinburgh University Press, 2023), pp. 129–43 <https://doi.org/10.3366/edinburgh/9781474441834.003.0008>

Balzac, Honoré de, 'Gobseck', in *La Comédie humaine*, ed. by Pierre-Georges Castex, 12 vols (Paris: Gallimard, 1976–81), II (1976), pp. 961–1013

—— 'Gobseck', trans. by Linda Asher, in *The Human Comedy: Selected Stories*, ed. by Peter Brooks (New York: New York Review Books, 2014), pp. 225–82

Barad, Karen, *Meeting the Universe Halfway: Quantum Physics and the Entanglement of Matter and Meaning* (Durham, NC: Duke University Press, 2007) <https://doi.org/10.2307/j.ctv12101zq>

Bardazzi, Adele, 'Textile Poetics of Entanglement: The Works of Antonella Anedda and Maria Lai', *Polisemie*, 3 (2022), pp. 81–115

Baudelaire, Charles, 'Au lecteur' <https://fleursdumal.org/poem/099> [accessed 24 August 2023]

—— 'L'Invitation au voyage' <https://www.oxfordlieder.co.uk/song/2632> [accessed 24 August 2023]

—— 'L'Invitation au voyage', in *Oeuvres complètes*, ed. by Claude Pichois, 2 vols (Paris: Gallimard, 1976), I, pp. 55–56

—— 'Invitation to a Journey', in *The Flowers of Evil*, trans. by Cyril Scott (London: Elkin Mathews, 1909) <https://www.gutenberg.org/cache/epub/36098/pg36098-images.html#Invitation_to_a_Journey> [accessed 4 January 2024]

—— 'Invitation to Journey', trans. by Richard Stokes <https://www.oxfordlieder.co.uk/song/2632> [accessed 24 August 2023]

—— 'Invitation to the Voyage', in *Flowers of Evil*, trans. by George Dillon and Edna St Vincent Millay (New York: Harper and Brothers, 1936), pp. 74–77

—— 'The Invitation to the Voyage', in Jack Collings Squire, *Poems and Baudelaire, 'Flowers'* (London: New Age Press, 1909), pp. 56–57

—— 'Invitation to the Voyage', trans. by Edna St. Vincent Millay <https: //fleursdumal.org/poem/148> [accessed 24 August 2023] (originally published in *Flowers of Evil*, trans. by George Dillon and Edna St. Vincent Millay (New York: Harper and Brothers, 1936))

—— 'To the Reader', trans. by Roy Campbell <https://fleursdumal.org/ poem/099> [accessed 24 August 2023] (originally published in *Poems of Baudelaire* (New York: Pantheon Books, 1952))

Bel'chikov, N., *Dostoevskii v protsesse Petrashevtsev* (Moscow: Nauka, 1971)

Belieu, Erin, review of *In the Blood*, by Carl Phillips, and *American Prodigal*, by Liam Rector, *Agni*, 41 (1995), pp. 189–94

Benjamin, Walter, 'Commentary on Poems by Brecht', trans. by Edmund Jephcott, in *Selected Writings*, 4 vols (Cambridge, MA: Harvard University Press, 1996–2003), IV: *1938–1940*, ed. by Howard Eiland and Michael W. Jennings (2003), pp. 215–50

—— 'Kleine Geschichte der Photographie', in *Gesammelte Schriften*, ed. by Rolf Tiedemann and Hermann Schweppenhäuser, 7 vols (Frankfurt a.M.: Suhrkamp, 1972–91), II.1 (1977), pp. 368–85

—— 'Notes from Svendborg, Summer 1934', trans. by Rodney Livingstone, in *Selected Writings*, 4 vols (Cambridge, MA: Harvard University Press, 1996–2003), II, part 2: *1931–1934*, ed. by Michael W. Jennings, Howard Eiland, and Gary Smith (2005), pp. 783–91

—— 'What Is Epic Theatre? (II)', trans. by Harry Zohn, in *Selected Writings*, 4 vols (Cambridge, MA: Harvard University Press, 1996–2003), IV: *1938–1940*, ed. by Howard Eiland and Michael W. Jennings (2003), pp. 302–09

Ben-Merre, David, '"There Must Be Great Audiences Too" — *Poetry: A Magazine of Verse*', *Modernist Journal Project* (n.d.) <https://modjourn.org/ there-must-be-great-audiences-too-poetry-a-magazine-of-verse/> [accessed 9 March 2024]

Benn, Gottfried, *Probleme der Lyrik* (Wiesbaden: Limes Verlag, 1951)

Benstock, Shari, *Women of the Left Bank* (Austin: University of Texas Press, 1986)

Bergson, Henri, *Matter and Memory*, trans. by Nancy Margaret Paul and W. Scott Palmer (London: Allen and Unwin; New York: Macmillan, 1911) <https://hdl.handle.net/2027/umn.31951000932511x>

Berlant, Lauren, *Cruel Optimism* (Durham, NC: Duke University Press, 2011) <https://doi.org/10.1515/9780822394716>

Berlant, Lauren, and Michael Warner, 'Sex in Public', *Critical Inquiry*, 24.2 (1998), pp. 547–66

Berman, Antoine, 'La Retraduction comme espace de la traduction', *Palimpsestes*, 13.4 (1990), pp. 1–7

Bernstein, Charles, 'Community and the Individual Talent', *Diacritics*, 26.3/4 (1996), pp. 176–90

Berry, Wendell, 'The Specialization of Poetry', *Hudson Review*, 28.1 (1975), pp. 11–27

Bersani, Leo, 'Is the Rectum a Grave?', in *AIDS: Cultural Analysis/Cultural Activism*, ed. by Douglas Crimp (Cambridge, MA: MIT Press, 1988), pp. 197–222 <https://doi.org/10.2307/3397574>

—— 'Shame on You', in Leo Bersani and Adam Phillips, *Intimacies* (Chicago, IL: University of Chicago Press, 2008), pp. 31–57 <https://doi.org/10.7208/chicago/9780226043562.001.0001>

—— 'Sociality and Sexuality', *Critical Inquiry*, 26.4 (2000), pp. 641–56

Bervin, Jen, *The Desert* (New York: Granary Books, 2008)

—— interviewed by Dianna Frid, *Bomb Magazine*, 15 September 2016 <https://bombmagazine.org/articles/jen-bervin-and-dianna-frid/> [accessed 31 August 2023]

—— *Nets* (New York: Ugly Duckling Presse, 2004)

Blanchot, Maurice, *The Unavowable Community*, trans. by Pierre Joris (Barrytown, NY: Station Hill Press, 1988)

Borovskii, V., 'Otkroite vse okna!', *Sovetskaya muzyka*, 2 (1962), pp. 23–28

Bozhkova, Yasna, *Between Worlds: Mina Loy's Aesthetic Itineraries* (Clemson, SC: Clemson University Press, 2022) <https://doi.org/10.3828/liverpool/9781949979640.001.0001>

Braun, David, 'Indexicals', in *The Stanford Encyclopedia of Philosophy*, ed. by Edward N. Zalta (Summer 2017) <https://plato.stanford.edu/archives/sum2017/entries/indexicals/> [accessed 4 November 2021]

Brecht, Bertolt, *Gedichte*, ed. by Elisabeth Hauptmann, 10 vols (Frankfurt a.M.: Suhrkamp, 1960–76; Berlin: Aufbau-Verlag, 1961–78), III: *1930–1933* (1961)

—— *Werke: Große kommentierte Berliner und Frankfurter Ausgabe*, ed. by Werner Hecht and others, 30 vols (Berlin: Aufbau-Verlag; Frankfurt a.M.: Suhrkamp, 1988–97), XIV: *Gedichte 4* (1993)

Breslin, Paul, 'The Simple, Separate Person and the Word En-Masse', *Poetry*, 153.1 (October 1988), pp. 30–47

Briley, Alexis C., 'De Man's Obstacles', *Diacritics*, 43.3 (2015), pp. 40–65

Brodsky, N. L., ed., *Literaturnye salony i kruzhki: Pervaya polovina XIX veka* (Moscow: Academia, 1930)

Brower, Reuben, 'The Speaking Voice', in *The Lyric Theory Reader: A Critical Anthology*, ed. by Virginia Jackson and Yopie Prins (Baltimore, MD: Johns Hopkins University Press, 2014), pp. 211–18

Brown, Edward J., *Stankevich and his Moscow Circle, 1830–1840* (Stanford, CA: Stanford University Press, 1966)

Brown, Wendy, and Janet Halley, 'Introduction', in *Left Legalism/Left Critique*, ed. by Wendy Brown and Janet Halley (Durham, NC: Duke University Press, 2002), pp. 1–37 <https://doi.org/10.2307/j.ctv11hpn4c.4>

Brugmans, Henri L., '"L'Invitation au voyage" by Baudelaire', *Neophilologus*, 30.1 (1946), pp. 3–15

Bürger, Peter, *Theory of the Avant-Garde*, trans. by Michael Shaw (Minneapolis: University of Minnesota Press, 1984)

Bullock, Philip Ross, 'The Birth of the Soviet Romance from the Spirit of Russian Modernism', *Slavonic and East European Review*, 97.1 (2019), pp. 110–35

—— 'Intimacy and Distance: Valentin Sil'vestrov's *Tikhie pesni*', *Slavonic and East European Review*, 92.3 (2014), pp. 401–29

—— 'The Pushkin Anniversary of 1937 and Russian Art Song in the Soviet Union', *Slavonica*, 13.1 (2007), pp. 39–56

—— 'Song in a Strange Land: The Russian Musical Lyric beyond the Nation', in *Global Russian Cultures*, ed. by Kevin M. F. Platt (Madison: University of Wisconsin Press, 2019), pp. 290–311 <https://doi.org/10.2307/j. ctvfjcxzz.19>

Bullock, Philip Ross, and Laura Tunbridge, eds, *Song beyond the Nation: Translation, Transnationalism, Performance* (Oxford: Oxford University Press, 2021) <https://doi.org/10.5871/bacad/9780197267196. 001.0001>

Burroughs Price, Matthew, 'A Genealogy of Queer Detachment', *PMLA*, 130.3 (2015), pp. 648–65

'Census 2022: Statistical Release' <https://census.statssa.gov.za/assets/ documents/2022/P03014_Census_2022_Statistical_Release.pdf> [accessed 11 October 2023]

Chatterjee, Monish, 'Tagore and Jana Gana Mana', 31 August 2003 <https: //countercurrents.org/comm-chatterjee310803.htm> [accessed 21 March 2023]

Chatterjee, Partha, *Lineages of Political Society: Studies in Postcolonial Democracy* (New York: Columbia University Press, 2011)

Chaudhuri, Amit, 'In a Silent Way/Indian National Anthem', YouTube, 9 January 2023 <https://www.youtube.com/watch?v=xL6uhjEcHIQ> [accessed 21 March 2023]

Chaudhuri, Rosinka, '*Viśvasāhitya*: Rabindranath Tagore's Idea of World Literature', in *The Cambridge History of World Literature*, ed. by Debjani Ganguly (Cambridge: Cambridge University Press, 2021), pp. 261–78 <https://doi.org/10.1017/9781009064446.014>

Chauncey, George, *Gay New York: Gender, Urban Culture, and the Making of the Gay Male World, 1890–1940* (New York: Basic Books, 1994)

Cheah, Pheng, and Jonathan Culler, eds, *Grounds of Comparison: Around the Work of Benedict Anderson* (New York: Routledge, 2003)

Chiasson, Dan, 'End of the Line: New Poems from Carl Phillips', *New Yorker*, 8 April 2013 <https://www.newyorker.com/magazine/2013/04/15/ end-of-the-line-6> [accessed 14 October 2023]

Christ, Birte, and Stefanie Mueller, 'Towards a Legal Poetics', *Amerikastudien/American Studies*, 62.2 (2017), pp. 149–68

Clark, Carol, and Robert Sykes, eds, *Baudelaire in English* (Harmondsworth: Penguin, 1997)

Clemens, Justin, 'The Role of the Shifter and the Problem of Reference in Giorgio Agamben', in *The Work of Giorgio Agamben: Law, Literature, Life*, ed. by Justin Clemens, Nicholas Heron, and Alex Murray (Edinburgh: Edinburgh University Press, 2008), pp. 43–65 <https://doi.org/10.1515/9780748634637-006>

Coetzee, Olivia M., 'Bybel in Kaaps' <https://www.litnet.co.za/category/nuwe-skryfwerk-new-writing/bybelinkaaps/> [accessed 5 October 2023]

—— *Innie shadows* (Cape Town: Modjaji Books, 2020)

Cole, Merrill, *The Other Orpheus: A Poetics of Modern Homosexuality* (New York: Routledge, 2002)

Conover, Roger, 'Introduction', in Mina Loy, *The Last Lunar Baedeker*, ed. by Roger Conover (Highlands, NC: Jargon Society, 1982), pp. xv–lxi

—— 'Notes on the Text', in Mina Loy, *The Lost Lunar Baedeker*, ed. by Roger Conover (New York: Farrar, Straus & Giroux, 1996), pp. 175–218

Cooper, Adam, '"You Can't Write in Kaapse Afrikaans in Your Question Paper. ... The Terms Must Be Right": Race- and Class-Infused Language Ideologies in Educational Places on the Cape Flats', *Educational Research for Social Change*, 7.1 (2018), pp. 30–45

Cortellessa, Andrea, *Andrea Zanzotto: Il canto della terra* (Bari: Laterza, 2021)

Costello, Bonnie, 'John Ashbery and the Idea of the Reader', *Contemporary Literature*, 23.4 (1982), pp. 493–514

—— *The Plural of Us: Poetry and Community in Auden and Others* (Princeton, NJ: Princeton University Press, 2017) <https://doi.org/10.23943/princeton/9780691172811.001.0001>

Crane, Joan St Clair, 'Edna St. Vincent Millay's Afterthoughts on the Translation of Baudelaire', *Studies in Bibliography*, 29 (1976), pp. 382–86

Crangle, Sara, ed., *Stories and Essays of Mina Loy* (Champaign, IL: Dalkey Archive Press, 2011)

Crick, Joyce, 'Power and Powerlessness: Brecht's Poems to Carola Neher', *German Life and Letters*, 53.3 (2000), pp. 314–24

Crim, Kathryn, 'Marx, *Silk Poems*, and the Pretext of Qualities', *Representations*, 151 (2020), pp. 96–126

Culler, Jonathan, 'Apostrophe', in *The Pursuit of Signs: Semiotics, Literature, Deconstruction*, 2nd edn (London: Routledge, 2001), pp. 149–71

—— *The Literary in Theory* (Stanford, CA: Stanford University Press, 2007)

—— 'Lyric, History, and Genre', *New Literary History*, 40.4 (2009), pp. 879–99

—— *Theory of the Lyric* (Cambridge, MA: Harvard University Press, 2015) <https://doi.org/10.4159/9780674425781>

Damrosch, David, *What Is World Literature?* (Princeton, NJ: Princeton University Press, 2003)

de Man, Paul, 'Anthropomorphism and Trope in the Lyric', in *The Rhetoric of Romanticism* (New York: Columbia University Press, 1984), pp. 239–62

—— 'Lyrical Voice in Contemporary Theory', in *Lyric Poetry: Beyond New Criticism*, ed. by Chaviva Hošek and Patricia Parker (Ithaca, NY: Cornell University Press, 1985), pp. 55–72

de Vries, Anastasia, 'The Use of Kaaps in Newspapers', *Multilingual Margins*, 3.2 (2016), pp. 127–39

Dean, Tim, 'Sex and the Aesthetics of Existence', *PMLA*, 125.2 (2010), pp. 387–92

Denisov, Edison, 'Novaya tekhnika — eto ne moda', in *'Drugoe iskusstvo': Moskva 1956–1976*, ed. by I. Alpatova and L. Talochkin, 2 vols (Moscow: Khudozhestvennaya galeriya 'Moskovskaya kollektsiya', 1991), I, pp. 313–15 (repr. in *'Drugoe iskusstvo': Moskva 1956–1988*, ed. by I. Alpatova, L. Talochkin, and N. Tamruchi (Moscow: Galart; Gosudarstvennyi tsentr sovremennogo iskusstva, 2005), pp. 68–70)

—— 'Novaya tekhnika — eto ne moda', in *Svet — dobro — vechnost': Pamyati Edisona Denisova, stat'i, vospominaniya, materialy*, ed. by Valeriya Tsenova (Moscow: Moskovskaya gosudarstvennaya konservatoriya im. P. I. Chaikovskogo, 1999), pp. 33–38

—— 'Le tecniche nuove non sono una moda', *Il contemporaneo/Rinascita*, August 1966, p. 12

Dennett, Daniel C., *Consciousness Explained* (Boston, MA: Little, Brown and Co., 1991)

Department of City Planning, *Adult Entertainment Study* (New York: Department of City Planning, 1994) <https://www.townofnewburgh.org/uppages/NYNYC_1994.PDF> [accessed 10 October 2023]

Derrida, Jacques, 'Sauf le nom (Post-Scriptum)', trans. by John Leavey, in *On the Name* (Redwood City, CA: Stanford City Press, 1995), pp. 35–88 <https://doi.org/10.1515/9781503615823-003>

Devarenne, Nicole, 'The Language of Ham and the Language of Cain: "Dialect" and Linguistic Hybridity in the Work of Adam Small', *Journal of Commonwealth Literature*, 45.3 (2010), pp. 389–408

Dixon, Gavin, *The Routledge Handbook to the Music of Alfred Schnittke* (Abingdon: Routledge, 2022) <https://doi.org/10.4324/9780429274046>

Dunbar-Ortiz, Roxanne, *An Indigenous Peoples' History of the United States* (Boston: Beacon Press, 2014)

Dutta, Krishna, and Andrew Robinson, *Rabindranath Tagore* (London: Bloomsbury, 1995)

Dworkin, Craig, 'The Fate of Echo', in *Against Expression: An Anthology of Conceptual Writing*, ed. by Craig Dworkin and Kenneth Goldsmith (Evanston, IL: Northwestern University Press, 2011), pp. xxiii–liv

—— *Radium of the Word: A Poetics of Materiality* (Chicago: University of Chicago Press, 2020) <https://doi.org/10.7208/chicago/9780226743738.001.0001>

Edelman, Lee, *No Future: Queer Theory and the Death Drive* (Durham, NC: Duke University Press, 2005) <https://doi.org/10.2307/j.ctv11hpkpp>

Eliot, T. S., 'The Three Voices of Poetry', in *The Lyric Theory Reader: A Critical Anthology*, ed. by Virginia Jackson and Yopie Prins (Baltimore, MD: Johns Hopkins University Press, 2014), pp. 192–200

Eng, David L., Judith Halberstam, and José Esteban Muñoz, 'What's Queer about Queer Studies Now?', *Social Text*, 23.3–4 (2005), pp. 1–17

Engass, Dale, 'Cropping *The Desert*: Erasure and Reclamation in Jen Bervin and John C. Van Dyke', *ISLE: Interdisciplinary Studies in Literature and Environment*, 28.2 (2021), pp. 563–86

Esposito, Roberto, *Communitas: The Origin and Destiny of Community*, trans. by Timothy Campbell (Stanford, CA: Stanford University Press, 2010) <https://doi.org/10.1515/9781503620520>

Evans, John L., *The Petraševskij Circle, 1845–1849* (The Hague: Mouton, 1974) <https://doi.org/10.1515/9783111398440>

Farred, Grant, *Midfielder's Moment: Coloured Literature and Culture in Contemporary South Africa* (Boulder: Westview Press, 2000)

Fel'dman, D. M., *Salon-predpriyatie: Pisatel'skoe ob"edinenie i kooperativnoe izdatel'stvo 'Nikinskie subbotniki' v kontekste literaturnogo protsessa 1920–1930-x godov* (Moscow: Rossiiskii gosudarstvennyi gumanitarnyi universitet, 2018)

Ferguson, Roderick, *The Reorder of Things: The University and its Pedagogies of Minority Difference* (Minneapolis: University of Minnesota Press, 2012) <https://doi.org/10.5749/minnesota/9780816672783.001.0001>

Forster, Leonard, *The Icy Fire: Five Studies in European Petrarchism* (Cambridge: Cambridge University Press, 1969)

Fortin, Jacey, 'Why Do English Soccer Fans Sing "Sweet Caroline"?', *New York Times*, 11 July 2001 <https://www.nytimes.com/2021/07/11/sports/soccer/why-england-sweet-caroline-euro-2020.html> [accessed 24 August 2023]

Foucault, Michel, *The Archaeology of Knowledge*, trans. by A.M. Sheridan Smith (New York: Pantheon, 1972)

France, Peter, 'Introduction', in Gennady Aygi, *Selected Poems, 1954–94*, ed. and trans. by Peter France (London: Angel Books, 1997), pp. 17–27

freddiejg, 'Oz and Pitt Crew Singing Sweet Caroline', YouTube, 30 September 2012 <https://www.youtube.com/watch?v=bdPb8rUZYiI> [accessed 24 August 2023]

Frolova-Walker, Marina, *Stalin's Music Prize: Soviet Culture and Politics* (London: Yale University Press, 2016) <https://doi.org/10.12987/yale/9780300208849.001.0001>

Frost, Elisabeth A., *The Feminist Avant-Garde in American Poetry* (Iowa City: University of Iowa Press, 2003)

Frye, Northrop, *Anatomy of Criticism* (Princeton, NJ: Princeton University Press, 1957)

Gardini, Nicola, 'Zanzotto petrarchista barbaro: saggio sull'"Ipersonetto"', *Studi Novecenteschi*, 19.43/44 (1992), pp. 223–34

Garret, Daniel, review of *Pastoral*, by Carl Phillips, *World Literature Today*, 74.3 (2000), p. 600

Gilburd, Eleonory, *To See Paris and Die: The Soviet Lives of Western Culture* (Cambridge, MA: Belknap Press of Harvard University Press, 2018) <https://doi.org/10.4159/9780674989771>

Giusti, Francesco, 'Mourning Over her Image: The Re-enactment of Lyric Gestures in Giorgio Caproni's "Versi livornesi"', in *A Gaping Wound: Mourning in Italian Poetry*, ed. by Adele Bardazzi, Francesco Giusti, and Emanuela Tandello (Cambridge: Legenda, 2022), pp. 47–70 <https://doi.org/10.2307/j.ctv33b9pwp.7>

—— 'Transcontextual Gestures: A Lyric Approach to the World of Literature', in *The Work of World Literature*, ed. by Francesco Giusti and Benjamin Lewis Robinson (Berlin: ICI Berlin Press, 2021), pp. 75–103 <https://doi.org/10.37050/ci-19_04>

Gleadle, Kathryn, 'The Imagined Communities of Women's History: Current Debates and Emerging Themes; A Rhizomatic Approach', *Women's History Review*, 22.4 (2013), pp. 524–40

Gölz, Sabine I., 'Apostrophe's Double', *Konturen*, 10 (2019) <https://doi.org/10.5399/uo/konturen.10.0.4509>

—— 'Günderrode Mines Novalis', in *The Spirit of Poesy*, ed. by Peter Fenves and Richard Block (Evanston, IL: Northwestern University Press, 2000), pp. 89–130

—— 'Millay Repairs Baudelaire' (unpublished paper)

—— 'One Must Go Quickly from One Light into Another: Between Ingeborg Bachmann and Jacques Derrida', in *Borderwork: Feminist Engagements with Comparative Literature*, ed. by Margaret Higonnet (Ithaca, NY: Cornell University Press, 1994), pp. 207–23

Goldman, Leah, 'Art of Intransigence: Soviet Composers and Art Music Censorship' (unpublished doctoral thesis, University of Chicago, 2015)

Goldsmith, Kenneth, 'Why Conceptual Writing? Why Now?', in *Against Expression: An Anthology of Conceptual Writing*, ed. by Craig Dworkin and Kenneth Goldsmith (Evanston, IL: Northwestern University Press, 2011), pp. xvii–xxii

Greenwell, Garth, 'Cruising Devotion: On Carl Phillips', *Sewanee Review*, 128.1 (2020), pp. 166–86

Greenwell, Garth, Richie Hofmann, and Carl Phillips, 'On Art, Sex, and Syntax', *Yale Review*, 110.1 (2022), pp. 119–33

Grossman, Allen, *The Sighted Singer* (Baltimore, MD: Johns Hopkins University Press, 1992)

Gumbrecht, Hans Ulrich, *Production of Presence: What Meaning Cannot Convey* (Stanford: Stanford University Press, 2004) <https://doi.org/10.1515/9780804767149>

Habermas, Jürgen, *The Structural Transformation of the Public Sphere*, trans. by Thomas Burger and Frederick Lawrence (Cambridge, MA: MIT Press, 1989)

Haines, Christian, 'A Lyric Intensity of Thought: On the Potentiality and Limits of Giorgio Agamben's "Homo Sacer" Project', *Boundary2*, 29 August 2016 <https://www.boundary2.org/2016/08/christian-haines-a-lyric-intensity-of-thought-on-the-potentiality-and-limits-of-giorgio-agambens-homo-sacer-project/> [accessed 11 February 2024]

Hart, Matthew, *Nations of Nothing but Poetry: Modernism, Transnationalism, and Synthetic Vernacular Language* (Oxford: Oxford University Press, 2010)

Hejinian, Lyn, 'Who Is Speaking?', in *The Language of Inquiry* (Berkeley: University of California Press, 2000), pp. 30–39

Hermans, Theo, *The Conference of the Tongues* (London: Routledge, 2007)

—— ed., *The Manipulation of Literature: Studies in Literary Translation* (London: Routledge, 1985)

Hiddleston, Jane, *Reinventing Community: Identity and Difference in Late Twentieth-Century Philosophy and Literature in French* (London: Legenda, 2005)

Hofmeyr, Isobel, 'Building a Nation from Words', in *The South Africa Reader: History, Culture, Politics*, ed. by Clifton Crais and Thomas V. McClendon (Durham, NC: Duke University Press, 2014), pp. 160–68 <https://doi.org/10.1215/9780822377450-034>

Hugo, Victor, *Hernani* (Paris: Larousse, 1971)

—— *Poésie*, 3 vols (Paris: Seuil, 1972)

Hunter, Walt, *Forms of a World: Contemporary Poetry and the Making of Globalization* (New York: Fordham University Press, 2019) <https://doi.org/10.5422/fordham/9780823282227.001.0001>

Ingham, Zita, and Peter Wild, 'The Preface as Illumination: The Curious (If Not Tricky) Case of John C. Van Dyke's *The Desert*', *Rhetoric Review*, 9.2 (1991), pp. 328–39

Itenberg, B. S., *Dvizhenie revolyutsionnogo narodnichestva: Narodnicheskie kruzhki i 'khozhdenie v narod' v 70-kh godakh XIX v.* (Moscow: Nauka, 1965)

Jackson, Virginia, *Before Modernism: Inventing American Lyric* (Princeton, NJ: Princeton University Press, 2023) <https://doi.org/10.23943/princeton/9780691232805.001.0001>

—— *Dickinson's Misery: A Theory of Lyric Reading* (Princeton, NJ: Princeton University Press, 2005)

—— 'Lyric', in *The Princeton Encyclopaedia of Poetry and Poetics*, 4th edn, ed. by Stephen Cushman and others (Princeton, NJ: Princeton University Press, 2012), pp. 826–34

Jackson, Virginia, and Yopie Prins, eds, *The Lyric Theory Reader* (Baltimore, MD: Johns Hopkins University Press, 2014)

Jakelski, Lisa, *Making New Music in Cold War Poland: The Warsaw Autumn Festival, 1956–1968* (Berkeley: University of California Press, 2017) <https://doi.org/10.1525/california/9780520292543.001.0001>

Jameson, Fredric, *Brecht and Method* (London: Verso, 1999)

Jannuzzi, Marisa, 'Mongrel Rose: The "Unerring Esperanto" of Loy's Poetry',
    in *Mina Loy: Woman and Poet*, ed. by Maeera Shreiber and Keith Tuma
    (Orono, ME: National Poetry Foundation, 1998), pp. 404–41
Javitch, Daniel, *Poetry and Courtliness in Renaissance England* (Princeton, NJ:
    Princeton University Press, 1978)
Jephtas, Veronique, *Soe rond ommie bos* (Cape Town: Protea Boekhuis, 2021)
Johnson, Barbara, 'Apostrophe, Animation, and Abortion', *Diacritics*, 16.1
    (1986), pp. 28–47 <https://doi.org/10.2307/464649>
—— 'Poetry and its Double: Two "Invitations au voyage"', in *The Critical
    Difference: Essays in the Contemporary Rhetoric of Reading* (Baltimore,
    MD: Johns Hopkins University Press, 1980), pp. 23–52
—— *The Wake of Deconstruction* (Oxford: Blackwell, 1994)
Johnson, W. R., *The Idea of Lyric: Lyric Modes in Ancient and Modern Poetry*
    (Berkeley: University of California Press, 1982)
Joubert, Marlise, ed., *In a Burning Sea: Contemporary Afrikaans Poetry in
    Translation* (Pretoria: Protea Book House, 2014)
Joyce, James, *Finnegans Wake* (London: Faber, 1975)
Kamfer, Ronelda, *Chinatown* (Cape Town: Kwela Books, 2019)
—— *grond/Santekraam* (Cape Town: Kwela Books, 2011)
—— *Hammie* (Cape Town: Kwela Books, 2016)
—— *Kompoun* (Cape Town: Kwela Books, 2021)
—— *Noudat slapende honde* (Cape Town: Kwela Books, 2008).
Kappal, Bhanuj, '"My Music Is Based on Convergences": Amit Chaud-
    huri on his New Compositions', *The Hindu*, 19 January 2023 <https:
    //www.thehindu.com/entertainment/music/amit-chaudhuri-writer-
    singer-music-single-album-in-a-silent-way-jana-gana-mana-75-india-
    independence/article66395879.ece> [accessed 21 March 2023]
Karnes, Kevin C., *Sounds Beyond: Arvo Pärt and the 1970s Soviet Under-
    ground* (Chicago: University of Chicago Press, 2021) <https://doi.org/
    10.7208/chicago/9780226815404.001.0001>
Katonov, S., 'Dva tsikla — dva resheniya', *Sovetskaya muzyka*, 2 (1965), pp.
    10–13
Keats, John, *Poetical Works*, ed. by H. W. Garrod (Oxford: Oxford University
    Press, 1970)
Kennedy, William, *The Site of Petrarchism: Early Modern National Sentiment
    in Italy, France, and England* (Baltimore, MD: Johns Hopkins University
    Press, 2003)
Keylin, Vadim, *Participatory Sound Art: Technologies, Aesthetics, Politics*
    (Singapore: Palgrave Macmillan Singapore, 2023) <https://doi.org/
    10.1007/978-981-99-6357-7>
Khitrova, Daria, *Lyric Complicity: Poetry and Readers in the Golden Age of Rus-
    sian Literature* (Madison: University of Wisconsin Press, 2019) <https:
    //doi.org/10.2307/j.ctvjghx7r>
Kinnahan, Linda A., 'Costa Magic', in *Mina Loy: Navigating the Avant-
    Garde*, ed. by Suzanne W. Churchill, Linda A. Kinnahan, and Susan

Rosenbaum <https://mina-loy.com/split-texts/gender-power-in-the-street/> [accessed 9 January 2024]

—— 'Mapping Florence: First Tour, Loy at Home', in *Mina Loy: Navigating the Avant-Garde*, ed. by Suzanne W. Churchill, Linda A. Kinnahan, and Susan Rosenbaum <https://mina-loy.com/chapters/italy-italian-baedeker/02-oltrarno-costa/> [accessed 9 January 2024]

Kopytova, Galina, 'Shostakovich's Music for *Salute, Spain!* Discoveries and Perspectives', *Journal of War & Culture Studies*, 14.4 (2021), pp. 479–92

Kurtz, Michael, *Sofia Gubaidulina: A Biography*, trans. by Christoph K. Lohmann, ed. by Malcolm Hamrick Brown (Bloomington: Indiana University Press, 2007)

Larroutis, M., 'Une source de "L'Invitation au voyage"', *Revue d'histoire littéraire de la France*, 57.4 (1957), pp. 585–86

le Cordeur, Michael, 'Kaaps: Time for the Language of the Cape Flats to Become Part of Formal Schooling', *Multilingual Margins*, 3.2 (2016), pp. 86–103

Lemelin, Christopher W., 'To Name or Not to Name: The Question of Shostakovich's Interpretation of Tsvetaeva', *Musical Quarterly*, 93.2 (2010), pp. 234–36

Lewis, C. S., *English Literature in the Sixteenth Century* (Oxford: Oxford University Press, 1954)

Lewis, Charlton T., and Charles Short, *A Latin Dictionary* (Oxford: Clarendon Press, 1879) <https://www.perseus.tufts.edu/hopper/text?doc=Perseus:text:1999.04.0059> [accessed 2 November 2023]

Locke, John, *Second Treatise of Government*, ed. by C. B. Macpherson (Indianapolis, IN: Hackett, 1980)

Longenbach, James, 'Lyric Knowledge', *Poetry*, February 2016 <https://www.poetryfoundation.org/poetrymagazine/articles/70307/lyric-knowledge> [accessed 16 October 2023]

Lorenzini, Niva, *Dire il silenzio: La poesia di Andrea Zanzotto* (Rome: Carocci, 2014)

Loy, Mina, *Anglo-Mongrels and the Rose*, in *The Last Lunar Baedeker*, ed. by Roger Conover (Highlands, NC: Jargon Society, 1982), pp. 109–75

—— 'Costa Magic', in *The Lost Lunar Baedeker*, ed. by Roger Conover (New York: Farrar, Straus & Giroux, 1996), pp. 12–14

—— 'The Costa San Giorgio', in *The Lost Lunar Baedeker*, ed. by Roger Conover (New York: Farrar, Straus & Giroux, 1996), pp. 10–12

—— 'Gertrude Stein', in *Stories and Essays of Mina Loy*, ed. by Sara Crangle (Champaign, IL: Dalkey Archive Press, 2011), pp. 232–34

—— 'International Psycho-Democracy', in *The Last Lunar Baedeker*, ed. by Roger Conover (Highlands, NC: Jargon Society, 1982), pp. 276–82

—— *The Lost Lunar Baedeker*, ed. by Roger Conover (New York: Farrar, Straus & Giroux, 1996)

—— 'Modern Poetry', in *The Lost Lunar Baedeker*, ed. by Roger Conover (New York: Farrar, Straus & Giroux, 1996), pp. 157–61

Lübecker, Nikolaj, *Community, Myth and Recognition in Twentieth-Century French Literature and Thought* (London: Continuum, 2009)

Lyon, Janet, *Manifestoes: Provocations of the Modern* (Ithaca, NY: Cornell University Press, 1999) <https://doi.org/10.7591/9781501728358>

—— 'Sociability in the Metropole: Modernism's Bohemian Salons', *ELH*, 76.3 (2009), pp. 687–711

MacPherson, C. B., *The Political Theory of Possessive Individualism: Hobbes to Locke* (Oxford: Oxford University Press, 2011)

Magro, Fabio, and Arnaldo Soldani, *Il sonetto italiano: Dalle origini a oggi* (Rome: Carocci, 2017)

Manica, Raffaele, 'Petrarca e Zanzotto', in *Qualcosa del passato: Saggi di lettura del Ventesimo Secolo* (Rome: Gaffi, 2008), pp. 383–98

Manne, Kate, *Down Girl: The Logic of Misogyny* (Oxford: Oxford University Press, 2019)

Marais, Danie, 'Middagtee met Nathan Trantraal: Kaaps is nie 'n joke-taal nie', *Die Burger*, 2 August 2013, pp. 2–3

Marinetti, Filippo Tommaso, *Manifesto tecnico della letteratura futurista*, in *Manifesti del Futurismo*, ed. by Viviana Birolli (Milan: Abscondita, 2008), pp. 58–64

Marx, Karl, *Capital: A Critique of Political Economy*, trans. by Ben Fowkes (New York: Vintage Books, 1977)

Massey, Doreen, 'Space-Time, "Science" and the Relationship between Physical Geography and Human Geography', *Transactions of the Institute of British Geographers*, 24.3 (1999), pp. 261–76

McDonald, Peter D., *Artefacts of Writing: Ideas of the State and Communities of Letters from Matthew Arnold to Xu Bing* (Oxford: Oxford University Press, 2017) <https://doi.org/10.1093/oso/9780198725152.001.0001>; supplementary website: <https://artefactsofwriting.com/> [accessed 25 July 2023]

—— 'Seeing through the *Concept* of World Literature', *Journal of World Literature*, 4 (2019), pp. 13–34

Meads, Carolyn, 'PEN Afrikaans: Om boeke in Kaaps te publiseer' <https://www.litnet.co.za/pen-afrikaans-om-boeke-in-kaaps-te-publiseer/> [accessed 11 October 2023]

Meschonnic, Henri, *Ethics and Politics of Translating*, trans. by Pier-Pascale Boulanger (Amsterdam: Benjamins, 2011) <https://doi.org/10.1075/btl.91>

Mesthrie, Rajend, ed., *Language in South Africa* (Cambridge: Cambridge University Press, 2002) <https://doi.org/10.1017/CBO9780511486692>

Mill, John Stuart, 'Thoughts on Poetry and its Varieties', in *The Collected Works of John Stuart Mill*, ed. by John M. Robson and Jack Stillenger (Toronto: University of Toronto Press; London: Routledge & Keegan Paul, 1963–91), I: *Autobiography and Literary Essays* (1981), pp. 343–65

—— 'Two Kinds of Poetry', in *The Broadview Anthology of Victorian Poetry and Poetic Theory*, ed. by Thomas J. Collins and Vivienne J. Rundle (Plymouth, MA: Broadview Press, 1999), pp. 1220–27

—— 'What Is Poetry?', in *The Broadview Anthology of Victorian Poetry and Poetic Theory*, ed. by Thomas J. Collins and Vivienne J. Rundle (Plymouth, MA: Broadview Press, 1999), pp. 1212–20

Millay, Edna St Vincent, preface to Charles Baudelaire, *Flowers of Evil*, trans. by George Dillon and Edna St Vincent Millay (New York: Harper and Brothers, 1936), pp. v–xxxiv

Muñoz, José Esteban, *Cruising Utopia* (New York: New York University Press, 2009)

Nagy, Gregory, *Pindar's Homer: The Lyric Possession of an Ancient Poet* (Baltimore, MD: Johns Hopkins University Press, 1990)

Nancy, Jean-Luc, *The Disavowed Community*, trans. by Philip Armstrong (New York: Fordham University Press, 2016) <https://doi.org/10.5422/fordham/9780823273843.001.0001>

—— *The Inoperative Community*, trans. by Peter Connor and others (Minneapolis: University of Minnesota Press, 1991)

Nandy, Ashish, *Illegitimacy of Nationalism* (Delhi: Oxford University Press, 1994)

Nelson, Amy, *Music for the Revolution: Musicians and Power in Early Soviet Russia* (University Park: Pennsylvania State University Press, 2004)

Nersessian, Anahid, 'Notes on Tone', *New Left Review*, 142 (2023), pp. 55–73

Nicholls, Peter, 'The Poetics of Modernism', in *The Cambridge Companion to Modernist Poetry*, ed. by Alex Davis and Lee M. Jenkins (Cambridge: Cambridge University Press, 2007), pp. 51–67 <https://doi.org/10.1017/CCOL0521853052.004>

Noland, Carrie, *Agency and Embodiment: Performing Gestures/Producing Culture* (Cambridge, MA: Harvard University Press, 2009) <https://doi.org/10.4159/9780674054387>

Noland, Carrie, and Sally Ann Ness, eds, *Migrations of Gesture* (Minneapolis: University of Minnesota Press, 2008)

Ó Ceallacháin, Éanna, 'Polemical Performances: Pasolini, Fortini, Sanguineti, and the Literary-Ideological Debates of the 1950s', *Modern Language Review*, 108.2 (2013), pp. 475–503

Odendaal, Bernard, 'Omgangsvariëteite van Afrikaans in die digkuns sedert Sestig', *Stilet*, 27.2 (2015), pp. 32–62

Oliver, Sophie, 'Mina Loy, Bessie Breuer, *Charm* Magazine and Fashion as Modernist Historiography', *Journal of Modern Periodical Studies*, 11.2 (2020), pp. 248–69

Olson, Charles, 'Projective Verse', in *Toward the Open Field: Poets on the Art of Poetry, 1800–1950*, ed. by Melissa Kwasny (Middletown, CT: Wesleyan University Press, 2004), pp. 344–54

Oppen, George, 'Of Being Numerous', in *New Collected Poems* (New York: New Directions, 2008), pp. 163–89

Orenstein, Gloria Feman, 'The Salon of Natalie Clifford Barney: An Interview with Berthe Cleyrergue', *Signs*, 4.3 (1979), pp. 484–96

Oswald, Alice, 'The Life and Death of Poetry', University of Oxford Podcasts, 2 June 2022 <https://podcasts.ox.ac.uk/life-and-death-poetry> [accessed 8 January 2024]

Packard, Grant, and Jonah Berger, 'Thinking of You: How Second-Person Pronouns Shape Cultural Success', *Psychological Science*, 31.4 (2020), pp. 397–407 <https://doi.org/10.1177/0956797620902380>

Page, Jeremy, 'The Detached Self', *Poetics Today*, 43.4 (2022), pp. 663–95

Panofsky, Erwin, 'Dürer's "St. Eustace"', *Record of the Art Museum, Princeton University*, 9.1 (1950), pp. 2–10 <https://doi-org.proxy.library.carleton.ca/10.2307/3774207>

Parlett, Jack, *The Poetics of Cruising: Queer Visual Culture from Walt Whitman to Grindr* (Minneapolis: University of Minnesota Press, 2022)

Pasolini, Pier Paolo, *Lettere: 1940–1954*, ed. by Nico Naldini (Turin: Einaudi, 1986)

Patty, James S., 'Light of Holland: Some Possible Sources of Baudelaire's "L'Invitation au voyage"', *Études baudelairiennes*, 3 (1973), pp. 147–57

Perloff, Marjorie, 'English as a Second Language: Mina Loy's "Anglo-Mongrels and the Rose"', in *Mina Loy: Woman and Poet*, ed. by Maeera Shreiber and Keith Tuma (Orono, ME: National Poetry Foundation, 1998), pp. 131–48

—— 'Poetry on the Brink: Reinventing the Lyric', *Boston Review*, 18 May 2012 <https://www.bostonreview.net/forum/poetry-brink/> [accessed 19 November 2023]

—— 'The Rescue of the Singular', *Contemporary Literature*, 43.3 (2002), pp. 560–69

Petrarca, Francesco, *Canzoniere*, ed. by Marco Santagata (Milan: Mondadori, 1996)

—— *The Canzoniere; or, Rerum vulgarium fragmenta*, trans. by Mark Musa (Bloomington: Indiana University Press, 1999)

Phillips, Carl, *The Art of Daring: Risk, Restlessness, Imagination* (Minneapolis, MN: Graywolf Press, 2014)

—— *In the Blood* (Boston, MA: Northeastern University Press, 1992)

—— *My Trade Is Mystery* (New Haven, CT: Yale University Press, 2022)

—— *Pastoral* (Saint Paul, MN: Greywolf Press, 2000)

—— *The Tether* (New York: Farrar, Straus and Giroux, 2001)

Pike, Zebulon, *Exploratory Travels through the Western Territories of North America* (Denver, CO: Lawrence, 1889)

Poe, Edgar Allen, 'The Domain of Arnheim', in *The Collected Works of Edgar Allan Poe*, ed. by T. O. Mabbott, 3 vols (Cambridge, MA: Belknap Press of Harvard University Press, 1969–78), III: *Tales and Sketches* (1978), pp. 1266–85

Poetry, Community, Translation, staged reading and discussion with Vahni Anthony Capildeo, Christian Hawkey, and Daniel Tiffany, moderated by Irene Fantappiè, organized by Irene Fantappiè, Francesco Giusti, and Laura Scuriatti, 5 July 2022, ICI Berlin Repository <https://doi.org/10.25620/e220705-1>

'"Poetry oo die liewe annie anne kant" — Ronelda Kamfer gesels met Nathan Trantraal oor *Chokers en survivors*' <https://www.litnet.co.za/poetry-oo-die-liewe-annie-anne-kant-ronelda-kamfer-gesels-met-nathan-trantaal-oor-chokers/> [accessed 31 October 2023]

Posmentier, Sonya, *Cultivation and Catastrophe: The Lyric Ecology of Modern Black Literature* (Baltimore, MD: Johns Hopkins University Press, 2017)

Poulin, A., 'The Experience of Experience: A Conversation with John Ashbery', *Michigan Quarterly Review*, 20.3 (1981), pp. 242–55

Pound, Ezra, and Harriet Monroe, 'The Audience', *Poetry*, 5.1 (October 1914), pp. 29–32

Prescott, Tara, *Poetic Salvage: Reading Mina Loy* (Lewisburg, PA: Bucknell University Press, 2016)

Prokopova, T. F., ed., *Moskovskii Parnas: Kruzhki, salony, zhurfiksy Serebryanogo veka, 1890–1922* (Moscow: Interlak, 2006)

Pryor, Sean, *Poetry, Modernism and an Imperfect World* (Cambridge: Cambridge University Press, 2017) <https://doi.org/10.1017/9781316876909>

Puchner, Martin, *Poetry of the Revolution: Marx, Manifestos, and the Avant-Garde* (Princeton, NJ: Princeton University Press, 2006) <https://doi.org/10.1515/9781400844128>

Ramazani, Jahan, *Poetry and its Others: News, Prayer, Song, and the Dialogue of Genres* (Chicago, IL: University of Chicago Press, 2014) <https://doi.org/10.7208/chicago/9780226083421.001.0001>

—— *Poetry in a Global Age* (Chicago, IL: University of Chicago Press, 2020) <https://doi.org/10.7208/chicago/9780226730288.001.0001>

—— *A Transnational Poetics* (Chicago, IL: University of Chicago Press, 2009) <https://doi.org/10.7208/chicago/9780226703374.001.0001>

Rancière, Jacques, *Dissensus: On Politics and Aesthetics*, trans. by Steven Corcoran (London: Continuum, 2010)

—— *The Flesh of Words: The Politics of Writing*, trans. by Charlotte Mandell (Stanford, CA: Stanford University Press, 2004)

—— *The Politics of Aesthetics: The Distribution of the Sensible*, trans. by Gabriel Rockhill (London: Continuum, 2004)

—— *Politics of Literature*, trans. by Julie Rose (Cambridge: Polity, 2011)

Rankine, Claudia, and Jen Bervin, '"We Have Always Been in Conversation"', in Jen Bervin, *Shift Rotate Reflect: Selected Works (1997–2020)*, ed. by Kendra Paitz (Normal: Illinois State University, 2022), pp. 56–85

Ray, Chelsea, 'Natalie Barney (1876–1972): Writer, Salon Hostess, and Eternal Friend; Interview with Jean Chalon', *Women in French Studies*, 30 (2022), pp. 154–69

Rechy, John, *City of Night* (New York: Grove, 1963)

Restagno, Enzo, 'Un'autobiografia dell'autore raccontata da Enzo Restagno', in *Gubajdulina*, ed. by Enzo Restagno (Turin: EDT, 1991), pp. 3–91

Reynolds, Jason, *Lang pad onnetoe*, trans. by Nathan Trantraal (Pretoria: Lapa, 2018)

Rilke, Rainer Maria, Marina Zwetajewa, and Boris Pasternak, *Briefwechsel*, ed. by Jewgenij Pasternak, Jelena Pasternak, and Konstantin M. Asadowskij (Frankfurt a.M.: Insel Verlag, 1983)

Roberts, Andrew Michael, 'Rhythm, Self and Jazz in Mina Loy's Poetry', in *The Salt Companion to Mina Loy*, ed. by Rachel Potter and Suzanne Hobson (Cambridge: Salt Publishing, 2010), pp. 99–128

Rowell, Charles H., 'An Interview with Carl Phillips', *Callaloo*, 21.1 (1998), pp. 204–77

Rozenfel'd, Boris, ed., *Anna Akhmatova, Marina Tsvetaeva, Osip Mandel'shtam i Boris Pasternak v muzyke: Notografiya* (Stanford, CA: Department of Slavic Languages and Literatures, Stanford University, 2003)

Rubinstein, Antoine, 'Die Componisten Rußland's', *Blätter für Musik, Theater und Kunst*, 8 June 1855, pp. 145–46

Saha, Poulomi, 'Singing Bengal into a Nation: Tagore the Colonial Cosmopolitan?', *Journal of Modern Literature*, 36.2 (2013), pp. 1–12

Scarpa, Raffaella, *Forme del sonetto: La tradizione italiana e il Novecento* (Rome: Carocci, 2012)

Schmelz, Peter J., 'Selling Schnittke: Late Soviet Censorship and the Cold War Marketplace', in *The Oxford Handbook of Music Censorship*, ed. by Patricia Hall (New York: Oxford University Press, 2015), pp. 413–52

—— *Sonic Overload: Alfred Schnittke, Valentin Silvestrov, and Polystylism in the Late USSR* (New York: Oxford University Press, 2021) <https://doi. org/10.1093/oso/9780197541258.001.0001>

—— *Such Freedom, If Only Musical: Unofficial Soviet Music during the Thaw* (Oxford: Oxford University Press, 2009)

Schnittke, Alfred, *A Schnittke Reader*, ed. by Alexander Ivashkin, trans. by John Goodliffe (Bloomington: Indiana University Press, 2002)

Schuhmann, Klaus, *Der Lyriker Bertolt Brecht 1913–1933* (Munich: dtv, 1971)

Scuriatti, Laura, 'Together, on her Own: A Survey of Mina Loy's Textual Communities', in *Groups, Coteries, Circles and Guilds: Modernist Aesthetics and the Utopian Lure of Community*, ed. by Laura Scuriatti (Oxford: Lang, 2019), pp. 71–96 <https://doi.org/10.3726/b11511>

Sedgwick, Eve Kosofsky, *Between Men: English Literature and Male Homosocial Desire* (New York: Columbia University Press, 1985) <https:// doi.org/10.7312/sedg90478>

Shemaroo, 'Jana Gana Mana', YouTube, 7 August 2014 <https://www. youtube.com/watch?v=HtMF973tXIY> [accessed 21 March 2023]

Shpiller, Natal'ya, 'Vokal'nye vechera', *Sovetskaya muzyka*, 6 (1965), pp. 95–96

Silva, Denise Ferreira da, *Toward a Global Idea of Race* (Minneapolis: University of Minnesota Press, 2007)

Simmel, Georg, 'The Sociology of Sociability', trans. by Everett C. Hughes, *American Journal of Sociology*, 55.3 (1949), pp. 254–61

Simons, Patricia, '"Bodily Things" and Brides of Christ: The Case of the Early Seventeenth-Century "Lesbian Nun" Benedetta Carlini', in *Sex, Gender and Sexuality in Renaissance Italy*, ed. by Jacqueline Murray and Nicholas Terpstra (New York: Routledge, 2019), pp. 97–124 <https://doi.org/10.4324/9781351008723-6>

Small, Adam, *Kitaar my kruis*, 2nd edn (Cape Town: Haum, 1973)

sn0wfall, 'Awesome You'll Never Walk Alone Liverpool vs Chelsea 27.04.2014', YouTube, 27 April 2014 <https://www.youtube.com/watch?v=N51jWNsW3F8> [accessed 24 August 2023]

Snediker, Michael D., *Queer Optimism: Lyric Personhood and Other Felicitous Persuasions* (Minneapolis: University of Minnesota Press, 2009)

Spillers, Hortense J., 'Mama's Baby, Papa's Maybe: An American Grammar Book', *Diacritics*, 17.2 (1987), pp. 64–81

Sukhov, A. D., *Literaturno-filosofskie kruzhki v istorii russkoi filosofii (20–50e gody XIX veka)* (Moscow: IF RAN, 2009)

Tagore, Rabindranath, 'The Bengali of Maktabs and Madrasas', trans. by Tista Bagchi, in *Selected Writings on Literature and Language*, ed. by Sisir Kumar Das and Sukanta Chaudhuri (New Delhi: Oxford University Press, 2001), pp. 358–60

—— *I Won't Let You Go: Selected Poems*, trans. by Ketaki Kushari Dyson (Tarset: Bloodaxe Books, 2010)

—— 'An Indian Folk Religion', in *Creative Unity* (London: Macmillan, 1922), pp. 67–90

—— 'Literature', in *Selected Writings on Literature and Language*, ed. by Sisir Kumar Das and Sukanta Chaudhuri (New Delhi: Oxford University Press, 2001), pp. 49–50

—— 'The Morning Song of India' <https://en.wikisource.org/wiki/The_Morning_Song_of_India> [accessed 25 July 2023]

—— 'My Golden Bengal', trans. by Anjan Ganguly <https://www.geetabitan.com/lyrics/rs-a2/aamar-sonaar-bangla-ami-english-translation.html> [accessed 21 March 2023]

—— 'Nationalism in India', in *Indian Philosophy in English*, ed. by Nalini Bhushan and Jay L. Garfield (New York: Oxford University Press, 2011), pp. 21–36

—— 'Nationalism in the West', in *The English Writings of Rabindranath Tagore*, ed. by Sisir Kumar Das (Delhi: Sahitya Akademi, 1994–96), ii (1994), pp. 418–22

—— *The Religion of Man* (New York: Macmillan, 1931)

—— 'Satyer Ahaban' (The Call of Truth), in *Rabindra Rachanabali*, 18 vols (Kolkata: Visva-Bharati, 1991), xii, p. 585

Tassoni, Luigi, *Caosmos: La poesia di Andrea Zanzotto* (Rome: Carocci, 2002)

Teague, David, 'A Paradoxical Legacy: Some New Contexts for John C. Van Dyke's "The Desert"', *Western American Literature*, 30 (1995), pp. 163–78

Terblanche, Erika, 'Nathan Trantraal (1983–)' <https://www.litnet.co.za/nathan-trantraal-1983/> [accessed 10 October 2023]

Tiffany, Daniel, 'Lyric Poetry and Poetics', in *Oxford Research Encyclopedia of Literature* (Oxford University Press, 2020) <https://doi.org/10.1093/acrefore/9780190201098.013.1111>

—— *My Silver Planet: A Secret History of Poetry and Kitsch* (Baltimore, MD: Johns Hopkins University Press, 2014) <https://doi.org/10.1353/book.28577>

Tomoff, Kiril, *Creative Union: The Professional Organization of Soviet Composers, 1939–1953* (Ithaca, NY: Cornell University Press, 2006) <https://doi.org/10.7591/cornell/9780801444111.001.0001>

Trantraal, Nathan, *Alles sal niet kom wôd* (Cape Town: Kwela Books, 2017)

—— *Chokers en survivors* (Cape Town: Kwela Books, 2013)

—— *Oolog* (Cape Town, Kwela Books, 2020)

—— 'Skryf 'it soes jy praat' <https://www.litnet.co.za/poolshoogte-skryf-i-soes-jy-praat/> [accessed 4 October 2023]

—— 'Three Poems by Nathan Trantraal', trans. by Alice Inggs <https://www.europenowjournal.org/2018/02/28/three-poems-by-nathan-trantraal/> [accessed 5 October 2023]

—— *White issie 'n colour nie* (Cape Town: Kwela Books, 2018)

Trantraal, Nathan, email to the author, 31 July 2023.

Tsvetaeva, Marina, 'Poema kontsa', in *Sobranie sochinenii*, 7 vols (Moscow: Ellis Lak, 1994–95), III (1994), pp. 31–50

Tucker, Herbert, 'Dramatic Monologue and the Overhearing of Lyric', in *Lyric Poetry: Beyond New Criticism*, ed. by Chaviva Hošek and Patricia Parker (Ithaca, NY: Cornell University Press, 1985), pp. 226–46

Usher, Stephen, 'Apostrophe in Greek Oratory', *Rhetorica* 28.4 (2010), pp. 351–62

Vaisbord, M., 'Garsia Lorka — muzykant', *Sovetskaya muzyka*, 9 (1961), pp. 128–30

Valentine, Sarah, *Witness and Transformation: The Poetics of Gennady Aygi* (Brighton, MA: Academic Studies Press, 2015)

Van Dyke, John C., *The Desert*, 2nd edn (Tucson: Arizona Historical Society, 1976)

—— *Nature for its Own Sake: First Studies in Natural Appearances* (New York: Charles Scriber's Sons, 1898) <https://doi.org/10.5962/bhl.title.28563>

Vasina-Grossman, Vera, *Mastera sovetskogo romansa*, 2nd edn (Moscow: Muzyka, 1980)

—— *Russkii klassicheskii romans XIX veka* (Moscow: Izdatel'stvo Akademii nauk SSSR, 1956)

Vendler, Helen, *Poems, Poets, Poetry: An Introduction and Anthology* (Boston, MA: Bedford/St. Martin's, 1997)

Villalta, Gian Mario, *La costanza del vocativo. Lettura della 'trilogia' di Andrea Zanzotto: 'Il Galateo in Bosco', 'Fosfeni', 'Idioma'* (Milan: Guerini, 1992)

Vincent, John, *John Ashbery and You* (Athens: University of Georgia Press, 2007)

VocalNationalAnthems, 'Amar Shona Bangla', 9 May 2010 <https://www.youtube.com/watch?v=zVjbVPFeo2o> [accessed 21 March 2023]

Voyce, Stephen, '"Make the World your Salon": Poetry and Community at the Arensberg Apartment', *Modernism/Modernity*, 15.4 (2008), pp. 627–46

Wagner, Ulrike, 'The Utopia of Purposelessness', in *Groups, Coteries, Circles and Guilds: Modernist Aesthetics and the Utopian Lure of Community*, ed. by Laura Scuriatti (Oxford: Lang, 2019), pp. 17–41

Walker, Barbara, *Maximilian Voloshin and the Russian Literary Circle: Culture and Survival in Revolutionary Times* (Bloomington: Indiana University Press, 2005)

Waters, William, *Poetry's Touch: On Lyric Address* (Ithaca, NY: Cornell University Press, 2003) <https://doi.org/10.7591/9781501717062>

Weber, Samuel, *Benjamin's -abilities* (Cambridge, MA: Harvard University Press, 2008) <https://doi.org/10.4159/9780674033955>

Weiss, Penny A., and Marilyn Friedman, eds, *Feminism and Community* (Philadelphia, PA: Temple University Press, 1995)

Welle, John P., '*Il Galateo in bosco* and the Petrarchism of Andrea Zanzotto', *Italica*, 62.1 (1985), pp. 41–53

White, Simone, *Dear Angel of Death* (Brooklyn: Ugly Duckling Presse, 2018)

—— 'Descent: American Individualism, American Blackness and the Trouble with Invention' (unpublished doctoral dissertation, City University of New York, 2016)

—— 'New American Poets: Simone White', sel. by Anna Moschovakis <https://poetrysociety.org/poems-essays/new-american-poets/simone-white-selected-by-anna-moschovakis> [accessed 3 November 2023]

—— *Of Being Dispersed* (New York: Futurepoem, 2016)

Whitman, Walt, 'So Long', in *Leaves of Grass: The Complete 1855 and 1891–92 Editions* (New York: Library of America, 1992), pp. 609–12

—— 'Song of Myself', in *Leaves of Grass: The Complete 1855 and 1891–92 Editions* (New York: Library of America, 1992), pp. 188–247

—— 'To You', in *Leaves of Grass: The Complete 1855 and 1891–92 Editions* (New York: Library of America, 1992), pp. 375–77

Wickes, George, 'Comment on Orenstein's "The Salon of Natalie Clifford Barney: An Interview with Berthe Cleyrergue"', *Signs*, 5.3 (1980), pp. 547–50

Wicomb, Zoë, 'Shame and Identity: The Case of the Coloured in South Africa', in *Writing South Africa: Literature, Apartheid, and Democracy, 1970-1995*, ed. by Derek Attridge and Rosemary Jolly (Cambridge:

Cambridge University Press, 1998), pp. 91–107 <https://doi.org/10.1017/CBO9780511586286.009>

Wiegman, Robyn, and Elizabeth A. Wilson, 'Introduction: Antinormativity's Queer Conventions', *differences: A Journal of Feminist Cultural Studies*, 26.1 (2015), pp. 1–25

Willemse, Hein, 'Black Afrikaans Writers: Continuities and Discontinuities into the Early 21st Century — a Commentary', *Stilet*, 31.1–2 (2019), pp. 260–75

—— 'Emergent Black Afrikaans Poets', in *Rendering Things Visible: Essays on South African Literary Culture*, ed. by Martin Trump (Johannesburg: Ravan Press, 1990), pp. 367–401

—— 'Soppangheid for Kaaps: Power, Creolisation and Kaaps Afrikaans', *Multilingual Margins*, 3.2 (2016) pp. 73–85

Willimott, Andy, *Living the Revolution: Urban Communes & Soviet Socialism, 1917–1932* (Oxford: Oxford University Press, 2017) <https://doi.org/10.1093/acprof:oso/9780198725824.001.0001>

Wood, Ellen Meiksins, *The Origin of Capitalism*, 2nd edn (London: Verso, 2017)

Wynter, Sylvia, 'Novel and History, Plot and Plantation', *Savacou*, 5 (1971), pp. 95–102

—— 'Unsettling the Coloniality of Being/Power/Truth/Freedom: Towards the Human, after Man, Its Overrepresentation — an Argument', *CR: The New Centennial Review*, 3.3 (2003), pp. 257–337

Yapp, Hentyle, *Minor China* (Durham, NC: Duke University Press, 2020)

Yurchak, Alexei, *Everything Was Forever, Until It Was No More: The Last Soviet Generation* (Princeton, NJ: Princeton University Press, 2006)

Zanzotto, Andrea, *Ipersonetto: Guida alla lettura*, ed. by Luigi Tassoni (Rome: Carocci, 2021)

—— *Le poesie e prose scelte*, ed. by Stefano Dal Bianco and Gian Mario Villalta (Milan: Mondadori, 1999)

—— *Tutte le poesie*, ed. by Stefano Dal Bianco (Milan: Mondadori, 2011)

Zitzewitz, Josephine von, *Poetry and the Leningrad Religious-Philosophical Seminar 1974–1980: Music for a Deaf Age* (Cambridge: Legenda, 2016)

Notes on the Contributors

Toby Altman is the author of *Jewel Box* (Essay Press, 2025), *Discipline Park* (Wendy's Subway, 2023), and *Arcadia, Indiana* (Plays Inverse, 2017). He has held fellowships from the Graham Foundation for Advanced Study in the Fine Arts, MacDowell, and the National Endowment for the Arts, where he was a 2021 Poetry Fellow. He currently teaches at Michigan State University, where he is Assistant Professor in the Residential College in the Arts and Humanities (RCAH) and Director of the RCAH Center for Poetry.

Derek Attridge is Emeritus Professor in the Department of English and Related Literature at the University of York, UK. He is the author of books and articles on the history and forms of European poetry, literary theory, and Irish and South African literature. His publications include *Moving Words: Forms of English Poetry* (Oxford, 2013), *The Craft of Poetry: Dialogues on Minimal Interpretation* (with Henry Staten) (Routledge, 2015), and *The Experience of Poetry: From Homer's Listeners to Shakespeare's Readers* (Oxford, 2019).

Philip Ross Bullock is Professor of Russian Literature and Music at the University of Oxford, Fellow and Tutor in Russian at Wadham College, and a former director of The Oxford Research Centre in the Humanities. He is the author of *Pyotr Tchaikovksy* (London, 2016) and editor of *Rachmaninoff and his World* (Chicago, 2022). His research has been supported by awards from the British Academy, Leverhulme Trust, Institute for Advanced Study, Princeton, and Institute for Advanced Study, Paris.

Vahni Anthony Ezekiel Capildeo, Trinidadian Scottish poet and writer of non-fiction, is Writer in Residence at the University of York. Capildeo's interests include traditional masquerade, silence, plurilingualism, and the poetics of place. Their numerous books and pamphlets include *No Traveller Returns* (2003), *Undraining Sea* (2009), *Dark and Unaccustomed Words* (2012), *Utter* (2013), *Measures of Expatriation* (2016), which won the 2016 Forward Prize, *Venus as a Bear* (2018), *Like a Tree, Walking* (2021), which was a Poetry Book Society choice, and *Polkadot Wounds* (2024), which took shape thanks to the Charles Causley Trust. Capildeo is a contributing editor at *PN Review* and a contributing adviser for *Blackbox Manifold*.

Hal Coase is a PhD candidate in co-tutela La Sapienza University of Rome and University of Silesia, with a research project on the poetry of Barbara

Guest and the afterlives of modernism in New York. His criticism has been published in *PN Review*, and academic work in *Text Matters*, *RIAS*, *Revue française d'études américaines*, and *Status Quaestionis*. His poetry has appeared in *The White Review*, and anthologized by Carcanet Press (2020) and Prototype Press (2023). He has written for the theatre in the UK, and his plays, published by Oberon Press, have been performed in the USA and Canada.

Jonathan Culler is Class of 1916 Professor of English and Comparative Literature, Emeritus, at Cornell University. He is the author of *Flaubert: The Uses of Uncertainty* (1974) and numerous books on contemporary critical theory, French and English, including *Structuralist Poetics* (1975) and *On Deconstruction* (1983). His *Literary Theory: A Very Short Introduction* (augmented edition, 2011) has been translated into 26 languages. His latest book is *Theory of the Lyric* (2015).

Irene Fantappiè is Assistant Professor (Tenure-Track) of Comparative Literature at the University of Cassino. After completing her PhD at the University of Bologna, she was Humboldt Fellow and researcher at Humboldt-Universität zu Berlin, and later directed a three-year DFG research project at Freie Universität Berlin. Her research interests include translation, intertextuality, and authorship in Italian and German-speaking literature from the Renaissance to the present day. She is the author of *Franco Fortini e la poesia europea. Riscritture di autorialità* (2021), *La letteratura tedesca in Italia. Un'introduzione (1900–1920)* (with A. Baldini et al., 2018), *L'autore esposto. Scrittura e scritture in Karl Kraus* (2016), and *Karl Kraus e Shakespeare. Recitare, citare, tradurre* (2012).

Francesco Giusti is Career Development Fellow and Tutor in Italian at Christ Church, University of Oxford. Previously he held fellowships at the University of York, the Goethe-Universität Frankfurt am Main, and the ICI Berlin Institute for Cultural Inquiry. He has published two books devoted respectively to the ethics of mourning and to creative desire in lyric poetry: *Canzonieri in morte. Per un'etica poetica del lutto* (2015) and *Il desiderio della lirica. Poesia, creazione, conoscenza* (2016). He co-edited, with Christine Ott and Damiano Frasca, the volume *Poesia e nuovi media* (2018); with Benjamin Lewis Robinson, *The Work of World Literature* (2021); and with Adele Bardazzi and Emanuela Tandello, *A Gaping Wound: Mourning in Italian Poetry* (2022).

Sabine I. Gölz is known for her bold, innovative analyses in modern European literature, pioneering a fresh type of theoretical inquiry. Examining the interplay between texts and a self-reflexively present reader, she explores how writing automates readerly perception – and how we can resist. Author of *The Split Scene of Reading: Nietzsche/Derrida/Kafka/Bachmann* (1998) and impactful essays such as 'Reading in the Twilight', 'Günderrode Mines Novalis', and 'Apostrophe's Double', Sabine I. Gölz is Associate Professor Emerita of German and Comparative Literature at the University of Iowa, where she taught literature, theory, translation, and the history of writing. She has produced and edited six documentary films on musical topics.

Wendy Lotterman is a postdoctoral researcher in literature at the University of Oslo, an associate editor of *Parapraxis*, a magazine of psychoanalysis and politics, and the author of *A Reaction to Someone Coming In* (Futurepoem 2023).

Peter D. McDonald is Professor of English and Related Literature and Fellow of St Hugh's College, Oxford. He is the author of, among others, *Artefacts of Writing: Ideas of the State and Communities of Letters from Matthew Arnold to Xu Bing* (Oxford, 2017, see also artefactsofwriting.com), *The Literature Police: Apartheid Censorship and its Cultural Consequences* (Oxford, 2009); and co-author of *PEN: An Illustrated History* (Interlink/Thames & Hudson, 2021).

Laura Scuriatti is Associate Professor of English and Comparative Literature at Bard College Berlin. Her research focuses on modernist literature, with special interest in life-writing, aesthetics and gender. She is the author of *Mina Loy's Critical Modernism* (2019), the editor of *Groups, Coteries, Circles and Guilds: Modernist Aesthetics and the Utopian Lure of Community* (2019) and the co-editor of *Literary Capitals in the Long Nineteenth Century: Spaces Beyond the Centres* (2022) and of *The Exhibit in the Text: the Museological Practices of Literature* (2008). She has also published on H.G. Wells, Mario Praz, and Carl Van Vechten.

Index

Aboud, James 268
Adorno, Theodor W. 2, 183, 194, 240, 241, 243, 244
Agamben, Giorgio 7, 71–96
Ahsan, Syed Ali 99
Ai Weiwei 203
Akhmatova, Anna 126, 129
Alighieri, Dante 80, 265, 266
Anderson, Benedict 4 n. 8, 16 n. 3, 120
Arendse, Ashwin 166
Arnaut Daniel 266
Ashbery, John 6, 23–25, 29
Ashtor, Gila 239
Attridge, Derek 2 n. 4, 90, 91, 92 n. 56, 162 n. 8, 163 n. 10, 172 n. 28
Auden, W. H. 1, 23 n. 16, 25, 26
Austin, John L. 35 n. 13, 88–90
Aygi, Gennady 120, 123, 127, 128, 131
Ayisov, Edison 117–119
Bachmann, Ingeborg 32 n. 3, 40, 44 n. 27, 64 n. 45
Balzac, Honoré de 65–67
Barad, Karen 224
Barnes, Djuna 144
Barney, Natalie 135
Baudelaire, Charles 6, 11, 12, 20, 21, 27, 28, 32–70
Becher, Johannes R. 73, 74, 77
Beckett, Samuel 121
Benjamin, Walter 7, 36, 57 n. 35, 71–73, 75, 76, 79, 87, 91, 92, 94
Benn, Gottfried 158
Berger, Jonah 18
Bergson, Henri 41

Berio, Luciano 119
Berlant, Lauren 10, 82, 83, 235, 237–239, 255, 256
Berman, Antoine 32–34, 51 n. 32
Bernini, Gian Lorenzo 169
Bernstein, Charles 142
Berry, Wendell 205, 206
Bersani, Leo 82, 235, 244, 253–255
Bervin, Jen 10, 11, 210–213, 221–233
Blake, William 202, 203
Blanchot, Maurice 3–5, 95, 179
Borges, Jorge Luis 169
Boulez, Pierre 119, 123, 127, 128
Bozhkova, Yasna 139, 141
Brathwaite, Kamau 263, 269
Brecht, Bertolt 7, 71–79, 83, 87, 92, 94
Breslin, Paul 205–207
Brower, Reuben 158
Browning, Robert 155, 260
Brugmans, Henri L. 36, 61 n. 40
Burich, Vladimir 121
Burroughs Price, Matthew 240, 241
Campbell, Niall 261
Caproni, Giorgio 80
Carlini, Benedetta 249
Carnegie, Andrew 216, 218 n. 31
Carpenter, J. R. 269
Carter, Martin 262, 273, 274
Cavalcanti, Guido 80
Char, René 123, 128
Chatterjee, Partha 105, 106

Chaudhuri, Amit 98, 111, 112
Chiasson, Dan 247
Cilliers, Charl J. F. 171
Clark, William 214
Coetzee, Olivia M. 166
Cole, Merrill 251–255
Collins Klobah, Loretta 264
Conover, Roger 137 n. 3, 139, 144 n. 26, 148
Costello, Bonnie 6, 23–29, 156, 157
Craig, Gordon 154, 199 n. 33
Crick, Joyce 75–78
Crowley, Martin 136
Culler, Jonathan 2, 6, 35 n. 12, n. 13, 37, 38, 71 n. 1, 72, 79, 81 n. 31, 83, 89, 90, 95, 142, 143, 212, 213, 219, 221
Dal Bianco, Stefano 86 n. 40, 87, 87 n. 45
Damrosch, David 12
Davis, Miles 112
Davydova, Lidiya 124
de Man, Paul 35 n. 13, 40 n. 24, 50 n. 31, 81, 83
Dean, Tim 82, 244 n. 34
Denisov, Edison 117–120, 124, 127, 132 n. 54
Dennett, Daniel C. 242
Derrida, Jacques 3 n. 6, 35 n. 13, 63, 64, 91 n. 56, 238 n. 14
Derzhavin, Vladimir 127
Diamond, Neil 19
Dickinson, Emily 169, 196, 210, 219, 231
Donatello 169
Dostoevsky, Fyodor 169
Dunbar, Laurence 196
Dürer, Albrecht 249
Dutta, Krishna 103
Dworkin, Craig 146, 194, 195 n. 25, 198–201

Dyson, Ketaki Kushari 110
Edelman, Lee 239
Eliot, T. S. 9, 139, 196
Esposito, Roberto 4 n. 8, 141, 142 n. 20, 204
Eybers, Elisabeth 169
Farred, Grant 160
Fellegara, Vittorio 119
Fet, Afanasy 126
Foucault, Michel 205
Frost, Elisabeth A. 147
García Lorca, Federico 12, 121, 122
George V 100, 101
Giraud, Albert 123
Glissant, Édouard 269
Goldman, Leah 117
Goldsmith, Kenneth 194–196, 198–200
Gölz, Sabine I. 11, 12, 26–28
Gozzano, Guido 241
Greenwell, Garth 238, 247 n. 43, 248, 253
Grossman, Allen 27, 28 n. 30, 37, 38, 55
Gubaidulina, Sofia 12, 126–132
Gumbrecht, Hans Ulrich 90
Haines, Christian 92–94
Hammerstein, Oscar 17
Hardt, Michael 94 n. 65, 203, 204
Harkara, Gagan 107, 108
Harris, Wilson 268
Hart, Matthew 147
Hauptmann, Elisabeth 78
Hegel, Georg Wilhelm Friedrich 143, 185 n. 7, 202
Hejinian, Lyn 1
Herz, Henriette 140
Hofmeyr, Isobel 161
Hosein, Kevin Jared 268
Howe, Susan 231

Hughes, Ted 169
Hugo, Victor 22 n. 10, 183
Hunter, Walt 25
Ibrahim, Abdullah 160
Inggs, Alice 176, 177 n. 33
Ingham, Zita 216
Ionesco, Eugène 121
Jackson, Virginia 2, 7, 8 n. 15, 9
    n. 18, 83, 158 n. 65, 196,
    209, 210, 212, 213, 219,
    231, 240, 241
Jannuzzi, Marisa 146 n. 33, 153,
    156 n. 60
Jefferson, Thomas 214
Jephtas, Veronique 167
Johnson, Barbara 31 n. 1, 39 n.
    19, 40 n. 21, 45, 52 n. 33,
    63, 64, 81–83
Johnson, W. R. 2
Jonker, Ingrid 169
Joyce, James 112, 264
Kafka, Franz 121, 169
Kamfer, Ronelda 159, 166, 169,
    170, 171 n. 26, 172 n. 29,
    174, 178, 179, 181
Karnes, Kevin C. 116, 117
Keats, John 105, 248
Kent, Christopher 270–272
Khamis, Gamal 270–272
Kinnahan, Linda A. 152, 153,
    155
Larroutis, M. 65, 66
Le Tourneur, Pierre 262
Lenin, Vladimir 74
Lewis, Merriweather 214
Locke, John 184, 185, 212, 215,
    216, 220
Longenbach, James 242
Loy, Mina 7, 9, 13, 135–158
Lyon, Janet 138 n. 9, 140, 141
MacPherson, C. B. 184–186
Magro, Fabio 87, 87 n. 43, 88

Manne, Kate 40
Marinetti, Filippo Tommaso
    158
Markowicz, André 262
Marx, Karl 40 n. 21, n. 22, 74,
    205
McNeill, Anthony 260
Melville, Pauline 268
Meschonnic, Henri 69, 70
Mill, John Stuart 10, 185, 186,
    209, 211, 212, 219–221,
    223, 226
Millar, Sharon 268
Millay, Edna St Vincent 6, 11,
    12, 27, 32–70
Milton, John 33 n. 10, 169
Minshall, Peter 268
Mistral, Gabriela 124
Mittelholzer, Edgar 268
Moze, Sonya 261
Nagy, Gregory 15
Naipaul, V. S. 265
Nancy, Jean-Luc 3, 5, 179, 204
Narayanan, Vivek 271
Negri, Antonio 203, 204
Neher, Carola 73, 75–77
Nelson, Amy 117
Nersessian, Anahid 242
Nicholls, Peter 9, 9 n. 19, 148 n.
    37
Nono, Luigi 119, 128, 129 n. 43
Oliver, Sophie 144 n. 26, 145,
    146
Olson, Charles 199–201
Oppen, George 9, 184, 187,
    189–193, 203–205
Oppen, Georges 26
Oswald, Alice 139, 139 n. 11
Pach, Walter 144
Packard, Grant 18
Panofsky, Erwin 249
Parlett, Jack 251, 257 n. 60

Pasolini, Pier Paolo 241, 242, 244
Pasternak, Boris 127, 129, 130
Pedro, Ryan 166
Pekarsky, Mark 124
Perloff, Marjorie 138 n. 7, 147, 192 n. 23, 194, 196–198
Petrarca, Francesco 2, 6, 15–17, 21, 22 n. 9, 84–89, 91
Philip, M. NourbeSe 264
Phillips, Carl 9, 10, 236–257
Picasso, Pablo 169
Pike, Zebulon 212, 214–217, 221, 226
Plath, Sylvia 169
Potapova, Vera 126
Pound, Ezra 8 n. 17, 189
Prescott, Tara 152, 153
Prins, Yopie 9 n. 18, 158 n. 65, 212, 213 n. 10
Prishvin, Mikhail 126, 127
Pryor, Sean 147 n. 35, 152, 158, 158 n. 66
Puchner, Martin 138
Pugacheva, Alla 129
Pushkin, Aleksandr 126, 130
Qasmiyeh, Yousif M. 270
Rachmaninoff, Sergei 125
Ramanujan, A. K. 264, 271
Ramazani, Jahan 13, 71 n. 1, 81, 82
Rancière, Jacques 2, 5
Rankine, Claudia 190, 224 n. 49
Ray, Man 144
Restagno, Enzo 130
Reynolds, Jason 166
Reznikoff, Charles 190
Rhys, Chase 166
Rhys, Jean 268
Rimbaud, Arthur 73–75, 83
Robinson, Andrew 103
Rogers, Richard 17

Rozhdestvensky, Gennady 124
Rubinstein, Anton 125
Sappho 1
Schleiermacher, Friedrich 140, 143
Schmelz, Peter J. 116–131
Schnittke, Alfred 12, 126, 130–132
Schoenberg, Arnold 118, 121, 123
Serocki, Kazimierz 119
Serra, Luciano 241
Seuphor, Michel 121
Shakespeare, William 33 n. 10, 229 n. 54, 262
Shelley, Percy Bysshe 81, 82, 196, 219, 220
Shire, Warsan 267
Shostakovich, Dmitry 120, 122 n. 23, 129
Silva, Denise Ferreira da 186 n. 9, 188 n. 19, 195, 200
Simmel, Georg 140, 143
Simons, Patricia 249, 251
Skoulding, Zoë 272
Small, Adam 165, 167
Smith, Iain Crichton 265
Snyders, Peter 165, 167
Soldani, Arnaldo 87, 88
Spenser, Edmund 169
Spivak, Gayatri Chakravorty 202
Stein, Gertrude 135–138, 146
Stevens, Wallace 26, 196
Strand, Mark 206
Stravinsky, Igor 124
Suhrkamp, Peter 78
Tagore, Rabindranath 12, 98–112
Tanzer, Francisco 128, 129, 131, 132 n. 54
Tate, Allen 144

Tchaikovsky, Pyotr 125
Tiffany, Daniel 5, 6 n. 11, 13, 71
    n. 1, 88
Tishchenko, Boris 129
Tomoff, Kirill 117
Tönnies, Ferdinand 140, 141
Trantraal, Nathan 159, 164–181
Tretheway, Natasha 196, 197
Trevett, Shash 264
Tsvetaeva, Marina 129, 130
Tucker, Herbert 83
Tyutchev, Fyodor 126, 130
Van Dyke, John C. 10, 210–233
Van Vechten, Carl 152
van Wyk Louw, N. P. 169
Varnhagen, Rahel 140
Vincent, John 24
Volkonsky, Andrey 120–124,
    127, 128
Voyce, Stephen 139–141
Warner, Michael 10, 235,
    237–239, 255, 256
Weber, Samuel 76 n. 12, 79
Webern, Anton 121, 128
Weil, Simone 169
Wheatley, Phyllis 196
White, Simone 9, 183–194,
    201–205, 207
Whitman, Walt 22, 23, 190, 192,
    196, 206, 207
Wiegman, Robyn 239
Wild, Peter 216
Williams, J. L. 270
Williams, William Carlos 145,
    189, 190, 203 n. 42
Wilson, Elizabeth A. 239
Wilson, Emily 272
Wood, Ellen Meiksins 215, 216
Woolf, Virginia 263
Wordsworth, William 169, 186,
    219, 220
Wynter, Sylvia 200, 213 n. 12

Xenakis, Iannis 119
Yapp, Hentyle 203, 204
Yurchak, Alexei 115–117, 133
Zanzotto, Andrea 84–88, 91, 93
Zawinul, Joe 98, 112
Zukofsky, Louis 190

Cultural Inquiry

EDITED BY CHRISTOPH F. E. HOLZHEY
AND MANUELE GRAGNOLATI

VOL. 1 TENSION/SPANNUNG
Edited by Christoph F. E. Holzhey

VOL. 2 METAMORPHOSING DANTE
Appropriations, Manipulations, and Rewritings
in the Twentieth and Twenty-First Centuries
Edited by Manuele Gragnolati, Fabio Camilletti,
and Fabian Lampart

VOL. 3 PHANTASMATA
Techniken des Unheimlichen
Edited by Fabio Camilletti, Martin Doll, and Rupert Gaderer

VOL. 4 Boris Groys / Vittorio Hösle
DIE VERNUNFT AN DIE MACHT
Edited by Luca Di Blasi and Marc Jongen

VOL. 5 Sara Fortuna
WITTGENSTEINS PHILOSOPHIE DES KIPPBILDS
Aspektwechsel, Ethik, Sprache

VOL. 6 THE SCANDAL OF SELF-CONTRADICTION
Pasolini's Multistable Subjectivities, Geographies, Traditions
Edited by Luca Di Blasi, Manuele Gragnolati,
and Christoph F. E. Holzhey

VOL. 7 SITUIERTES WISSEN
UND REGIONALE EPISTEMOLOGIE
Zur Aktualität Georges Canguilhems und Donna J. Haraways
Edited by Astrid Deuber-Mankowsky
and Christoph F. E. Holzhey

VOL. 8 MULTISTABLE FIGURES
On the Critical Potentials of Ir/Reversible Aspect-Seeing
Edited by Christoph F. E. Holzhey

VOL. 9 Wendy Brown / Rainer Forst
THE POWER OF TOLERANCE
Edited by Luca Di Blasi and Christoph F. E. Holzhey

VOL. 10   DENKWEISEN DES SPIELS
          Medienphilosophische Annäherungen
          Edited by Astrid Deuber-Mankowsky and Reinhold Görling

VOL. 11   DE/CONSTITUTING WHOLES
          Towards Partiality Without Parts
          Edited by Manuele Gragnolati and Christoph F. E. Holzhey

VOL. 12   CONATUS UND LEBENSNOT
          Schlüsselbegriffe der Medienanthropologie
          Edited by Astrid Deuber-Mankowsky and Anna Tuschling

VOL. 13   AURA UND EXPERIMENT
          Naturwissenschaft und Technik bei Walter Benjamin
          Edited by Kyung-Ho Cha

VOL. 14   Luca Di Blasi
          DEZENTRIERUNGEN
          Beiträge zur Religion der Philosophie im 20. Jahrhundert

VOL. 15   RE-
          An Errant Glossary
          Edited by Christoph F. E. Holzhey and Arnd Wedemeyer

VOL. 16   Claude Lefort
          DANTE'S MODERNITY
          An Introduction to the Monarchia
          With an Essay by Judith Revel
          Translated from the French by Jennifer Rushworth
          Edited by Christiane Frey, Manuele Gragnolati,
          Christoph F. E. Holzhey, and Arnd Wedemeyer

VOL. 17   WEATHERING
          Ecologies of Exposure
          Edited by Christoph F. E. Holzhey and Arnd Wedemeyer

VOL. 18   Manuele Gragnolati and Francesca Southerden
          POSSIBILITIES OF LYRIC
          Reading Petrarch in Dialogue

VOL. 19   THE WORK OF WORLD LITERATURE
          Edited by Francesco Giusti and Benjamin Lewis Robinson

Vol. 20   MATERIALISM AND POLITICS
           Edited by Bernardo Bianchi, Emilie Filion-Donato,
           Marlon Miguel, and Ayşe Yuva

Vol. 21   OVER AND OVER AND OVER AGAIN
           Reenactment Strategies in Contemporary Arts and Theory
           Edited by Cristina Baldacci, Clio Nicastro,
           and Arianna Sforzini

Vol. 22   QUEERES KINO / QUEERE ÄSTHETIKEN
           ALS DOKUMENTATIONEN DES PREKÄREN
           Edited by Astrid Deuber-Mankowsky
           and Philipp Hanke

Vol. 23   OPENNESS IN MEDIEVAL EUROPE
           Edited by Manuele Gragnolati
           and Almut Suerbaum

Vol. 24   ERRANS
           Going Astray, Being Adrift, Coming to Nothing
           Edited by Christoph F. E. Holzhey
           and Arnd Wedemeyer

Vol. 25   THE CASE FOR REDUCTION
           Edited by Christoph F. E. Holzhey
           and Jakob Schillinger

Vol. 26   UNTYING THE MOTHER TONGUE
           Edited by Antonio Castore
           and Federico Dal Bo

Vol. 27   WAR-TORN ECOLOGIES, AN-ARCHIC FRAGMENTS
           Reflections from the Middle East
           Edited by Umut Yıldırım

Vol. 28   Elena Lombardi
           ULYSSES, DANTE, AND OTHER STORIES

Vol. 29   DISPLACING THEORY THROUGH THE GLOBAL
           SOUTH
           Edited by Iracema Dulley
           and Özgün Eylül İşcen

Vol. 30   RETHINKING LYRIC COMMUNITIES
           Edited by Irene Fantappiè, Francesco Giusti,
           and Laura Scuriatti

Milton Keynes UK
Ingram Content Group UK Ltd.
UKHW040258291024
450401UK00015B/228/J